SUN™ CLUSTER 3 PROGRAMMING

SUN™ CLUSTER 3 PROGRAMMING

Integrating Applications into the SunPlex™ Environment

Joseph Bianco
Peter Lees
Kevin Rabito

Sun Microsystems Press
A Prentice Hall Title

The publisher offers excellent discounts on this book when ordered in quantity for bulk purchases or special sales, which may include electronic versions and/or custom covers and content particular to your business, training goals, marketing focus, and branding interests. For more information, please contact: U. S. Corporate and Government Sales, (800) 382-3419, corpsales@pearsontechgroup.com. For sales outside the U. S., please contact: International Sales, international@pearsoned.com.

Visit us on the Web: www.phptr.com

Library of Congress Cataloging-in-Publication Data is on file at the Library of Congress.

Pearson Education, Inc.
Rights and Contracts Department
One Lake Street
Upper Saddle River, NJ 07458

ISBN 0-13-047975-6

Text printed in the United States on recycled paper at Phoenix in Hagerstown, Maryland.

First printing, November 2004

The authors dedicate this book to the teams
of talented people responsible for the creation
and support of the Sun Cluster product.

CONTENTS

LIST OF FIGURES

LIST OF TABLES

FOREWORD

A voyage of discovery does not begin with new landscapes, but from seeing with new eyes.

M. Proust

When Joe asked me to write the foreword, I had imagined introducing the reader to some foundational elements of clustering, Sun Cluster, or high availability. The delight I've found from this book is that it covers the background fairly thoroughly while still diving deep into the richness of the Sun Cluster platform. The structure of the book is designed to allow both the novice and the expert to efficiently gain the information they need. That merely leaves me with the task of giving you some appreciation for the authors and what we see as the mission of our shared efforts.

Having been in the high-tech industry for over two decades, I've found that the truly interesting and delightful innovations come not from the diverse creations of technology per se, but from building on the works of others. Invention, though realized through physical and virtual gizmos and widgets, is fundamentally a collaborative human endeavor. Using cleverness on top of ingenuity on top of insight, developers leverage innovations to build solutions to an ever-expanding terrain of challenges. I never cease to learn from developers and customers about the variety of challenges they face and the innovations they develop to solve their problems. Indeed, the most interesting conversations are when customers communicate with developers—that is, when the people with the challenge engage the people whose goal is to provide solutions for that challenge.

This is precisely why I am a personal fan of the authors of this book and why you should take some special interest in the material they've compiled on the following pages. The authors of this book have some of the strongest experience in this interface between our products (Sun Cluster and Sun systems) and our customers (hopefully, you).

I first met Peter Lees as a leader of our Asia-Pacific systems engineers. Systems engineers form the technical backbone of the Sun direct sales organization. Peter is one of a set of Cluster aces who, worldwide, represent the best of the best. With this responsibility, Peter has been engaged with clusters architected and implemented from Tokyo to Sydney. I was less than a month into my current responsibility when I joined a conference call he was leading while trying to build a stronger communication link between engineers in Asia-Pacific and the product organization. Beyond his knowledge of clustering technology, he possesses a deep understanding of what people are trying to achieve. The combination has made him a continuing advisor on priorities and directions for the business.

I met Dr. Joseph Bianco as part of a cross–Sun Microsystem, Inc. team focused on improving customer availability. Joe was the top United States support services engineer involved with clusters. In that role, Joe came to this cross–Sun Microsystems group with some of the most extensive personal experience in setting up clusters for customers up and down the Eastern seaboard of the United States for the past decade. What makes Joe special beyond his technical experience is that his passion is infectious for the product and its ability to solve problems for customers. His ability to help customers be successful with clustering has been unparalleled. He has left a trail of happy and extremely profitable customers for Sun. We've launched several Six Sigma (Sun Sigma, internally) projects associated with capturing some of the key things that Joe and people like him have been naturally doing right and have made them standard practice across our company.

Beyond just doing an incredible job, Joe's real-world experience combined with a natural didactic energy has made him a great presenter to customers as well as a trainer of internal technical folks on the details of setting up, diagnosing, and managing clustering environments.

Similarly, Kevin Rabito has more than twenty years of industry experience and has been with Sun for more than ten years working in support services supporting Sun products. A majority of the time, he has been what was known as the area system support engineer for the Northeast, providing senior-level support for Sun's cluster products. His experience with Sun's clustering products goes from the earliest days of HA1.0 and PDB 1.0 to present Sun Cluster 3.1 products. His responsibility gives him broad experiences with other strategic software including support for High- Performance Computing (HPC), Grid Engine, and SunONE middleware products. More recently, Kevin's skill has made him a strategic ace for our automated data center products and services, N1.

In summary, just as APIs, which are the subject of this book, are the interesting strategic interaction point between our Sun Cluster product and the applications that are running on the clustering platform as a way to get ever-greater availability and control over service levels, so too the authors of this book are the interface between the product organizations like mine and the customers of our technology. They have a special knowledge and expertise that go beyond internal technical details of replication and recovery; they also have the practical knowledge of how these capabilities are most effectively applied to real-world problems customers face.

I have learned a great deal from these individuals over the years and I trust you will as well through the pages of this book.

David Nelson-Gal
Vice President, High-Availability Systems
Sun Microsystems, Inc.

PREFACE

About This Book

This book has been developed for users of the Sun Cluster 3.x environment. Out of the box, Sun Cluster is a powerful software environment capable of providing high levels of application availability to almost any application. While the current version of Sun Cluster ships with software modules that allow for increased levels of availability for the majority of enterprise applications (Oracle, Sybase, DB2, iPlant, SAP, and so forth), the only way to get an application that isn't on the list supported is either to pay a software vendor to create an agent for you or to write it yourself. This book gives the reader the know-how to create custom agents for the Sun Cluster environment.

Audience

This book is intended for programmers, system administrators, and technologists with varying skill sets. The book is designed for everyone hoping to take full advantage of the Sun Cluster 3 environment by giving them the tools and knowledge to create custom resource types. Users do not need any programming knowledge to take advantage of this book; likewise, those who are comfortable with C/C++ or K shell programming will find a wealth of knowledge on every Sun Cluster 3 API, including Remote Shared Memory (RSM). The reader should be comfortable around the Solaris Operating Environment (SOE), and some experience with Sun Cluster technology is helpful but not mandatory. This book is designed for users with varying types of technical skills. The beauty of the Sun Cluster framework is that just about everyone can customize the environment for their specific needs, whether they are novice system administrators or seasoned programmers.

There are three main sections to this book. Each section is geared for a specific purpose and user type. Sections can be skipped or used together.

Many of the examples in this book are illustrated as code snippets or pseudo code. Code snippets are designed to help the reader understand the semantics of the topic without fighting through the arcane syntax of a computer language. However, there are code examples using the various APIs in both the C language and UNIX K shell.

Assumptions

Except in certain cases in which it is beneficial for the task at hand, this book does not spend time explaining the C/C++ or Korn shell language or programming topics. There is equal coverage on K shell and C programming. However, the C API is rich in functionality; therefore, the authors feel that the C/C++ language should be used to get the maximum benefit from the cluster framework. For those readers who are not programmers, the Sun Cluster 3 automated agent builder and generic data services are also covered. These tools are designed to allow nonprogrammers to create custom resource types with little or no programming experience.

As a baseline, Chapters 1 and 3 give readers an overview of cluster technology and the Sun Cluster 3 environment. While these chapters provide enough information to get started, they should not be used as the sole basis of information for the topics covered. The authors encourage the reader to refer to the Sun Cluster software manuals and other books on the subject. This book will not teach the reader how to use, install, configure, or administer the Sun Cluster 3 software. However, the cluster topics essential to the effective use of particular API functions are covered.

Chapter 1: Introduction

This chapter outlines the basics on cluster technology. Included is a synopsis of the different types of cluster technologies in use today. Consideration is also given to the concepts of high availability (Hint: It's important if you want to ensure that your applications are available for the right reason).

Chapter 2: Introducing Sun Cluster 3

The workings of the Sun Cluster 3 framework are reviewed and explained. Topics include global filesystems, devices, and networks. Special attention is given to the resource manager and resource types, including the creation and management of resources.

Chapter 3: Getting Started

Building Sun Cluster resources is not a complex process. Using the SunPlex Agent Builder, anyone with no programming experience can create Sun Cluster resource types.

Chapter 4: Planning for Development

Not every application is suitable for cluster platforms. This chapter explains the development process and requirements for agent development within the cluster environment. System requirements are also explored. Read this chapter if you don't want to spend time debugging an application that won't work no matter what you do.

Chapter 5: Developing with the SunPlex Agent Builder

This chapter explains how to use the automated agent builder. Both the Graphical User Interface (GUI) and command-line utilities are discussed. Use this tool to get up to speed faster, stay organized, and create some standards.

Chapter 6: Understanding the RGM

By using APIs you can create sophisticated resource types that will allow applications to take advantage of the Sun Cluster framework. APIs use a series of callback methods to communicate with the application and Resource Group Manager. This chapter covers in detail the 12 callback methods, including the resource type file.

Chapter 7: Programming with the RMAPI

The Resource Manager API can accommodate both C and shell programming. Both function calls and command line-utilities are covered.

Chapter 8: Managing Processes

This chapter discusses process management under Sun Cluster with the Process Monitor Facility (PMF). This is a unique set of utilities that gives developers the tools to help them manage process trees. Both the PMF command utilities and PMF function calls are discussed.

Chapter 9: Using the DSDL

Layered on top of the RMAPI, the Data Service Development Library is a powerful API for creating Sun Cluster 3 resource types. All of the DSDL functions are covered in this unique and powerful library.

Chapter 10: Developing for Existing Applications

Using the concepts in the previous chapters, a resource type for the MySQL database is developed using the RMAPI and K shell programming. The same example is repeated using the C language with the DSDL API. Another resource is created for the CUPS printer utility, again using both the RMAPI and the DSDL APIs.

Chapter 11: Writing Scalable Services

Scalable services are explored. How to make applications scale under the Sun Cluster framework is discussed.

Chapter 12: Using Remote Shared Memory

Remote shared memory offers exciting opportunities for application scalability. This chapter covers the RSM API.

Chapter 13: Developing Cluster-Aware Applications

This chapter covers the new Cluster Reconfiguration Notification Protocol (CRNP) API. This API gives developers a preemptive programming model to create applications that are cluster-aware.

Font Conventions

A `monospace` font is used to illustrate directory structures and commands within the text, for example, `/global/mydata/data`.

The same font, but bold, is used to show key words of a UNIX application command that are to be typed in a shell exactly as shown, for example, **scconf -pvv**.

Special Characters

% UNIX C shell prompt

$ UNIX Bourne or K shell prompt

Bourne shell prompt for UNIX root user

[] Optional arguments for UNIX commands

Programming Tools and Source Code

To aid the reader, all usable source code will be formatted within a code box. For example:

Example 2.1   Simple example

```
int main(){
   printf("Hello World");
return(0);
}
```

Usable source code implies that it can be copied or downloaded, compiled, and executed within the limits of the environment without modification. However, code snippets will not be contained within a code box and will be demonstrated using the following format:

```
printf("hello world");
```

Callback methods for the Cluster API can be written using either the UNIX shell or C/C++. Shell programmers are limited to using the RMAPI and its features, whereas C/C++ programmers can opt to use either the RMAPI C library or the more powerful DSDL API. It should be noted that the preferred way to create resource types is with C/C++. The RMAPI currently ships with Sun Cluster 3.0, 3.1, but it may not ship with later versions. Only the RMAPI supports UNIX shell programming.

The examples in this book were developed and compiled using the Sun Microsystems Forte Development Environment for C/C++; however, the open source GNU compiler also works and is supported.

Software Requirements

1. Sun Cluster 3.x API package (SUNWscdev), available with the Sun Cluster software—it is not installed by default
2. A C/C++ compiler
3. Linker
4. Make tool
5. Access to a Sun Cluster 3.x development or test environment; we don't recommend using a production cluster for development work for the obvious reasons

Open source software used for some of the examples in this book includes:

- MySQL: Relational database management system, http://www.mysql.com
- Common UNIX Print Server (CUPS): A print server for UNIX environments, http://www.samba.org

These applications can be freely downloaded from the Internet at their respective sites. Please read and adhere to their respective license agreements.

Source Code for Examples

The full source code for the examples can be downloaded from the Web site: http://www.phptr.com/title/0130479756.

ACKNOWLEDGMENTS

When writing a book, the work involved in producing the final product is never the sole work of the author(s). Instead it is a collaborative effort among many people. The authors' role is to synthesize current information and embellish it with their own knowledge and experience to produce a body of work the reader can use. With that in mind, we would like to thank the following people for their help and contributions:

Pat Breen, SE from Sydney, Australia

Robert M. Gerber, Sun Microsystems Sun Services CSSE

Kristien Hens, SE from Belgium

Milind Joshi, Sun Microsystems Cluster Engineering

Naveen Kumar, Sun Microsystems Cluster Engineering

Marty Rattner, Sun Microsystems Cluster Engineering

Nick Solter, Sun Microsystems Cluster Engineering

Mike Tan, SE from Perth, Australia

Ashutosh Tripathi, Sun Microsystems Cluster Engineering

Special thanks to Linda Parks, Sun Microsystems, for taking the time to review and provide valuable feedback for every chapter. Thanks to our publishers, Prentice Hall, specifically Greg Dench for his vision, guidance, and patience. Also a special thanks to Patti Guerrieri for her extensive help in preparing the manuscript.

Joseph Bianco

I'd like to personally acknowledge some important people without whose help and support this book would not have been completed. I'd like to personally thank Scott Woods, VP Customer Care Center, for his role in guiding this project and providing the resources necessary to accomplish our goal. Without Scott, this book would not have been written.

To Victoria, the kind of daughter a father hopes for.

To the late professor Carl W. Cuttita: You may be gone but your lessons live in the lives of those you touched.

To my best friend and wife, Linda.

Peter Lees

Many thanks to Amanda for putting up with my typing away all night; Richard and Tracy McDougall, for being so generously hospitable whenever I traveled to California; Brad Kirley for supporting this endeavour; and Shizuka, Kemuri, Robert, and Senbu for so diligently interrupting me at crucial moments.

Kevin Rabito

To my wife, Darlene, and my children, Kevin, Gregory, Nicole, and Matthew. Thank you for your understanding, encouragement, and support during the late nights and weekends. This, plus a few cups of coffee, made this book possible. During my career in computers, I've had the good fortune of working with many good people whose support and friendship have gone a long way. I'd like to personally thank Phil Refano for giving me the support and help needed on this endeavor.

1

INTRODUCTION

Automobiles were predominately purchased by automobile enthusiasts when they first appeared on the market approximately a hundred years ago. These early models lacked many of the practical features we take for granted today, such as safety, automation, a roof to keep out the rain, and reliability. It wasn't until the automobile became a reliable mode of transportation that society began replacing the horse.

A similar scenario occurred in the computing industry. In the past two decades huge advances have been made in the reliability of information technology: application specific integrated circuits (ASIC), redundant arrays of independent disks (RAID), hot swapping, hot sparing, fault-tolerant computing, redundant components, and computer clusters. All of these technologies have increased the overall reliability and availability of information technology. The increase in reliability has played a significant role in the adoption rate of technology into both societies and businesses. Even with all the advances made in hardware reliability—with the exception of better automated test tools and software development methodologies—little has been done to make software more resilient to failures. It is not enough to make computer hardware highly available. All too often, it's a critical application component that hangs, divides by zero, leaks memory, crashes on invalid data types, points to an invalid memory address, or just plain screws up. Sadder still, when a critical application crashes, often the host machine is unable to perform any form of recovery.

In an effort to increase application reliability, many in-house techniques have been designed. These techniques range from 7x24 dedicated staff whose sole function is to stare at consoles looking for failures, to batch jobs that run at predetermined time intervals. All these techniques try to achieve two basic goals: notify system personnel that an application is no longer available and, if possible, restart the offending application. Unfortunately, most of these approaches lack standards, rigor, or just do not work when put into production environments. Having a dedicated staff to monitor applications, although comforting, isn't practical or cost-effective for many environments, nor is there a guarantee that user errors won't occur during a stressful situation.

The primary purpose of this book is to provide programmers and system administrators with a practical and easy-to-understand guide on how to use the Sun Cluster APIs to enable new and existing applications to take advantage of Sun Cluster high-availability features. These advantages include increased application availability and/or scalability. This book is not about software design methodologies or how to develop good software; there are already more books on the subject, good and bad, than all the software ever written. Writing software is either a personal or business endeavor. As a developer, you can follow established guidelines for good programming practices or you can use your own; therefore, we are not going to tell the reader how to write code. Likewise, the authors have seen many situations in which it's considered a good day if an application crashes only once.

It's not possible to know if users of this book are familiar with cluster technology, so we will not make that assumption. However, to take advantage of this powerful software, it helps to get a good understanding of what cluster computing is and is not. Thus, this chapter is intended to provide the uninitiated reader with a fundamental background in cluster technology. It will explain the different types of clusters available and where Sun Cluster fits into the picture. This chapter will also explain some of the basics of high-availability (HA) computing and how it is used within a clustered environment. The material in this chapter is intended as a short primer on these subjects. The reader who may require further information can consult the References section for a list of excellent books on the subject. If this information is already familiar, the reader should skip this chapter and proceed to Chapter 2. Unless the reader is already familiar with Sun Cluster, he or she should not skip Chapter 2, as this chapter is important in understanding the overall framework of the Sun Cluster environment and where and how the API interacts within the cluster framework.

Clusters and High Availability

Many terms are used in the context of cluster computing, such as high availability, fault tolerance, levels of nines, interconnects, single system image, loosely coupled and tightly coupled, just to name a few. Many of these terms apply in various forms to cluster technology and some terms have no correlation at all. In the following sections, we'll explain some of the most important concepts and ideas and try to paint a picture of the overall cluster landscape.

Clusters 101

This section will briefly cover the different areas of cluster technology. Each of these cluster topologies is designed for different types of workloads; they differ also in functionality, features, and capabilities.

Cluster Types

Those readers who are unfamiliar with cluster technology might be surprised to learn that cluster technology is not new. Cluster technology has been around in various forms for several decades. Cluster technologies can be grouped into one of two basic categories: tightly coupled and loosely coupled. Within these two categories, different philosophies are used for data storage, node communication, job execution, and application availability. In some cases, both types of clusters can coexist. For example, a tightly coupled cluster topology can be configured as a resource in a loosely coupled cluster. While it might be possible to tweak a particular cluster topology to work in a setting it wasn't designed for, it is far better to align the application and business needs to an appropriate cluster topology.

Most vendors of cluster technology offer cluster platforms optimized for one specific task such as high-performance computing (HPC), high availability (HA), or compute farms (grids). Sun Microsystems offers cluster platforms in all three categories.

This section will briefly outline the four basic cluster architectures:

- High-Availability Clusters
- Server Farms
- High-Performance Computing Clusters
- Grid Computing

Each of the four different cluster configurations falls into one of two basic topology types: loosely or tightly coupled clusters.

Cluster Architectures

Loosely Coupled Clusters   Clusters that are loosely coupled (see Figure 1.1) do not use a private network or storage medium. Instead, nodes in a loosely coupled cluster act as independent machines. Communication between nodes is done via a local network, WAN, or through the Internet via a distributed computing protocol such as RPC. Storage also is not shared; however, there usually is a master node that provides a network filesystem (NFS) mount point to a common filesystem. This master node might also dispatch jobs to cluster nodes while keeping track of the results. Loosely coupled clusters are typically used in environments in which nodes work together to break down a large problem into manageable portions. Loosely coupled systems are typically used for grid computing and some forms of HPC. Typical uses for loosely coupled clusters are compute grids and high-performance computing. Due to the topology, high levels of availability are not something that loosely coupled clusters can offer. Sun Microsystems offers both types of cluster technology: loosely and tightly coupled. Table 1.1 categorizes where each Sun Microsystems offering lies.

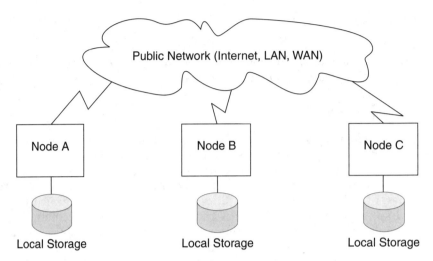

Figure 1.1 Loosely coupled clusters

Table 1.1 Sun Microsystems Tightly and Loosely Coupled Clusters

Cluster Type	Compute	Availability
Loosely coupled	Sun Grid Engine	Netra HA Suite, Sun ONE Application Server
Tightly coupled	HPC	Sun Cluster 3.x

Tightly Coupled Clusters   Tightly coupled clusters are nodes[1] that are connected with a high-speed private network and typically, although not necessarily, share common storage (see Figure 1.2). All nodes in a tightly coupled cluster share a private network on which cluster communications travel. This interconnect is not exposed to public traffic, hence the term *private*. Its sole use is for cluster messages and/or application data. Again, storage is typically shared, but it's not an absolute requirement. For example, node A might have access to a particular storage device to which no other node has access. Typical uses for tightly coupled clusters are high availability, scalability, and some forms of high-performance computing.

Specific Purposes

Compute Clusters   The two primary goals of today's cluster technology are to provide high levels of application availability and scalability. Unfortunately, scalability and availability require different design criteria and philosophies, hence trade-offs will have to be made when both availability and scalability are required.

---

1. Machines in a cluster are commonly referred to as a node.

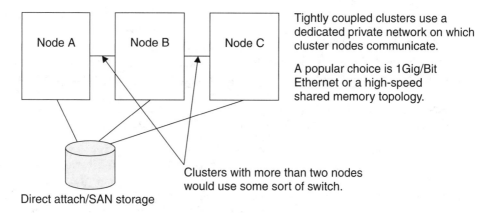

Figure 1.2 Tightly coupled clusters

Cluster computing was initially designed for scalability; therefore, it was primarily used as a high-performance computing environment where availability was not an issue. Clusters designed for scalability are often used for computationally intensive applications such as modeling, simulations, and digital image rendering. In these types of environments, processing speed takes precedence over everything else. It is more cost-effective to string together a handful of low-cost computers and have them work together than to buy a large, expensive, multi-everything machine to do the same job. This "clustering" approach has tremendous benefits, namely cost and flexibility. If more computing power is needed, simply add more low-cost computers to the cluster. If a machine fails, just replace it with a new one.

High-Availability Clusters   The design criterion for an HA cluster is to have a computing environment that offers high levels of uptime. The functions of an HA cluster platform are to detect, isolate, and recover from a system failure, all the while continuing to provide application services, and all this must happen while maintaining the highest levels of data integrity. (By saying *system failure,* the authors are referring to a cluster subsystem such as a cluster node, storage (array/disk), software applications, operating systems, or network access (public or private).)

High levels of uptime are provided by HA clusters through the use of redundant components such as servers, storage, networks, and anything else that can be considered as a single point of failure. In itself HA is a bit of a misnomer; the uptime or availability of a cluster is useful only if we equate it to application uptime. It is of little use to have a highly available computing environment with poor application availability.

It wasn't until the business community began to use cluster computing as a way to scale business applications, namely databases, that availability become a necessary requirement. Today, when cluster technology is used to host business applications, availability is often the primary motive for a cluster implementation, not scalability. Clusters used in mission critical environments are commonly set up in a hot standby configuration. In a hot standby configuration one node is configured as the primary, and it solely runs the application while another node(s) sits idle, monitoring the primary. In the advent of a failure, the standby node is immediately put into service to host the application. The advantage to this configuration is that the standby node is always available with adequate resources to host the applications that were running on the primary node. The disadvantage is the cost of hardware that is not being used unless a failure occurs. It is important to point out that although failures can happen, it's not a common scenario. It is not unusual to have a cluster up and running for over a year with not a single failure.

HA clusters also can be configured in active-active configurations where the environment is not mission critical. In an active-active configuration each node in the cluster is configured as a primary machine for an application, so there are no idle machines. In addition, each node also acts as the standby for other nodes. The advantage to this configuration is that every node in the cluster is configured to do work. The disadvantage is that if a node fails a standby node will have to take on an extra workload. It is a bit tricky to configure nodes in active-active configurations. As you can imagine, putting additional work on a node that is already under a heavy load is going to make it a tad slow. But these issues are design trade-offs to be worked out with those who are involved in designing the environment.

HA clusters offer great flexibility in their use. For example, Sun Cluster is a tightly coupled HA cluster with the added capabilities of supporting parallel databases and application scalability. Myriad server types, storage, filesystems, and applications can be used. Most HA clusters support a range of 4 to 16 servers in a configuration with choices for cluster topology, storage (direct attach, NAS, SAN), and private networks. One popular cluster topology available with Sun Cluster entails several servers running applications with one backup server monitoring the primary servers, referred to as N+1. Figure 1.3 depicts this popular configuration. In an N+1 configuration, nodes A and B both service applications for clients. Applications are typically not limited to databases, Web services, or NFS. In the advent of a failure of either node A or B, node C (the "plus one" in N+1) would host the application(s) of the failed node. Depending on the application, clients might notice little if any downtime.

Like HPC clusters, HA clusters use the private network to pass cluster information and application data. The private network can be gigabit/sec Ethernet or some shared memory architecture. In addition, HA clusters such as Sun Cluster also offer application scalability and support for parallel database systems such as Oracle 9i RAC (Real Application Clusters). Since HA clusters and, in particular, Sun Cluster can be configured to host myriad application types, a node failure will have a different effect on the type of application that is running on the cluster. Table 1.2 outlines the effect on an application in the event of a node failure.

From a development standpoint, a key point to remember is that if a node fails in an HA cluster, the application residing on that node will be temporarily unavailable until a standby node finishes the recovery process. The length of time the recovery takes is a function of application type, amount of storage, filesystem used, client connections, and workload.

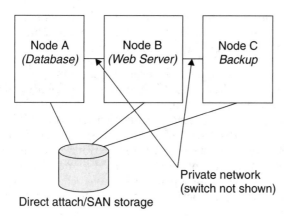

Dedicated interconnect topology consisting of 100/1000 Mbit/Sec Ethernet or shared memory topology

Applications run on nodes A and B; node C acts as a standby.

Depending on the application, some scalability can be performed between nodes A and B.

Clients connect to the cluster via a public network.

Private network (switch not shown)

Direct attach/SAN storage

Figure 1.3 HA clusters

Table 1.2 Application Impact for Node Failures in an HA Cluster

Application Usage	Node Dependency	Typical Usage	Node Failure Impact on Application
Pure parallel processing applications	Every node in cluster	Render farm, simulations, modeling	High, single failure can bring down application
Application bound to single server	Single node	Database, Web server	Temporary loss of service until application is migrated to new cluster node
Parallel databases	Node membership is a function of service configuration	Decision support system (DSS), data warehousing	Temporary loss of service until cluster notifies applications of reduced resources
Scalable Web services	Node membership is a function of service configuration	Scalable Web services	Reduced throughput, no loss of service

Example Cluster Applications

Grid Computing   A grid is a loosely coupled collection of resources used for distributed or high-performance computing. This type of cluster is useful for problems that require a vast amount of computing resources to solve. Grid computing also is quite useful for batch-job-type environments. One famous example of grid computing is the Search for Extra-Terrestrial Intelligence, or SETI. The main function of SETI is to use radio telescopes to scan the heavens in search of communication signals from space that might be coming from other life forms. This is a daunting search because there are billions of stars to search. Such computing problems that have huge amounts of data to process are good candidates for grid computing.

The topological layout of a grid is not much different from other types of clusters; however, there is one fundamental difference. While a high-speed dedicated private interconnect can be used, compute grids do not require them. Grid nodes can use network connections that are local, wide area, and geographic. Figure 1.4 depicts implementations of several grid clusters. The grid master node manages the job queues and job execution. Execution hosts receive instructions from the master to execute jobs. Submit hosts can submit jobs to the grid. The one drawback to this type of cluster is that master and execution hosts must have access to a global data store such as a network filesystem mount point, storage area network (SAN), or network attached storage (NAS).

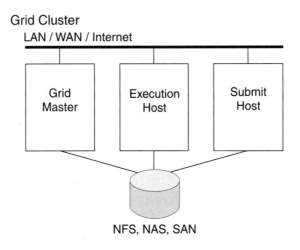

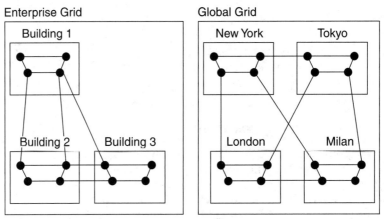

Figure 1.4 Grid clusters

The Sun grid engine allows organizations to implement grids from collections of homogeneous or heterogeneous computers throughout their organization. For example, execution hosts can be Sun Solaris or Linux servers of varying capacities and capabilities, as can submit hosts. Also, there is no limit to the number of execution hosts that can be in a grid. As for availability, an execution host can be configured to act as a shadow master for the grid master. If the grid master fails, the shadow master can recover the queues and become the grid master. It should also be noted that Sun Grid Engine (SGE) works well in a Sun Cluster environment, where SC3 can provide a highly available filesystem via a Global Filesystem for SGE queues as well as hardware monitoring. Grid computing promises to usher in a new era of distributed computing. It's worth noting that Sun Cluster, HA, and HPC clusters can be resources on compute grids.

High-Performance Clusters   Using a tightly coupled framework, HPC clusters are predominately designed for computationally intensive tasks such as simulating the airflow over an airplane wing or rendering characters for animation sequences. The calculation required to compute these types of simulations is mind-boggling. Typically, these types of compute jobs are broken down into manageable pieces. These small pieces are then distributed to nodes in the cluster. Each node works on its pieces of the problem. Once the calculations are completed, they are assembled together for the final output. Taking a large problem and breaking it down into small, manageable tasks allows users to create powerful compute environments using inexpensive servers. The key to performance is the extensive use of a private network. Often the private network is based on a remote shared memory (RSM) technology (see Chapter 12), thus creating a very large single-system image of an application. Here lies a fundamental difference between grids and HPC. HPC clusters use high-speed low-latency interconnect, allowing for large data sets to move quickly between nodes, whereas with compute grids, standard networks and even the Internet form the interconnect fabric. The Message Passing Interface (MPI) is commonly used as the underlying communications framework for HPC clusters. It is also worth mentioning that SGE can use MPI for parallel execution jobs. HPC clusters also can act as a resource within a grid.

High Availability

The term *high availability* or HA is used to express a system's potential for responding to a user's request at any given time. A common misconception is that HA is synonymous with cluster computing; HA and cluster computing are two distinct technologies. The confusion lies in the fact that often clusters are also highly available computing platforms. For example, a single machine that is not part of any cluster can be highly available, such as a Sun Fire 15K server. Conversely, a Sun Fire 280R does not have the high-availability features found in Sun's high-end machines; however, putting a 280R into a cluster will substantially increase the availability of the applications running on it. Also, not all cluster topologies have HA attributes such as compute clusters. The grade of availability is reported as a mea-surement of uptime, as discussed in the following section.

Business Case for HA

Making a business case for an HA solution can be straightforward, but often it is not. This is because many variables can come into the decision making process. First of these is the expense of the environment. When you factor in the cost of software, hardware, training, and any potential customizing, HA solutions are expensive; even low-end HA systems can be expensive.

Therefore, an analysis of the cost of downtime should be performed (see "Causes of Downtime" in this chapter) before any HA system is procured. A quick, albeit sim-ple, question to ask is: Does this HA system protect a revenue stream? If the answer to the question is yes, how much is the total revenue stream worth per some unit of time? Compare that cost with the total cost of the HA solution. For example, if a Web server is recording $10,000 a day in ebusiness, it will cost roughly $416 per hour of downtime. Out of that $416, how much is profit? We can't forget the cost of doing business. Does it pay to have a $100,000 HA solution to protect this revenue stream? The question isn't easy to answer as there are many variables to consider, such as:

1. Do you care if the system goes down for two hours? Perhaps your customer base is so loyal that it will wait until you're ready without going to another vendor.
2. What is the cost of lost labor for the outage?
3. Is it really cheaper to have a Web server farm full of low-cost computers?
4. How reliable is the software? As a general rule, hardware is more reliable than software.
5. At what point does the cost of managing a Web farm of low-cost machines (machines, management, floor space, power, cooling, and so forth) become more expensive than the revenue that is being captured?

Getting experts from finance involved is an excellent idea when looking at the business requirements for HA. They can help you determine some of the true costs of downtime as well as point out some of the hidden costs such as man hours, oppor-tunity costs, and operations. By knowing the true cost of downtime, it is an easy task to determine the return on investment (ROI). As technologists we all dread that famous question from the CEO, *So what did I get for all this money you spent?* Determining the true cost of doing HA for a given application will help determine the ROI for the environment as well as help determine the size and scope of the configuration.

Service Availability

Within the computing industry, levels of availability are commonly expressed as a percentage of yearly uptime for a given component, for example, 99.999%. A system (computer, storage, component) that offers 99.99% availability will be available for

8,765 hours and 50 minutes or 365 days, 5 hours and 50 minutes (recall that there are 365.25 days per year), or the system will be unavailable for 52.6 minutes of unplanned downtime per year. This figure does not include planned downtime. Planned downtime is any time period during which the environment is brought down for maintenance or updates.

Technology managers should pay particular attention to availability numbers. All too often a vendor claims high levels of availability, only to discover that the claims can be made possible only with large periods of planned outages for maintenance. It is not difficult to achieve 99.999% availability if the machine is serviced for 50% of the availability period. This is equivalent to one hour of uptime, two hours of support service—which reminds us of that famous sports car company! Four thousand miles of driving requires a full engine tune-up. As one would expect, as the level of "nines" increases, so does the cost of the environment. Looking at Figure 1.5, it's not a mistake that the boxes overlap. High-end severs built with high levels of redundancy, such as a Sun Microsystems F15k server, can achieve high levels of uptime; likewise, a properly configured cluster can approach application uptimes rivaling that of low-end fault-tolerant systems.

When a computer vendor claims that his or her equipment has an availability of 99.99%, it refers to the availability uptime for the underlying hardware and not the operating system. Why is that? If a vendor has reliable hardware with availability numbers in the range of 99.999% and the operating system is in the 99.9% range, combining the two numbers would yield a lower availability number. Because of the numerous variables involved, rarely are any two identical applications configured, tuned, or used the same way; availability figures rarely if ever include applications.[2]

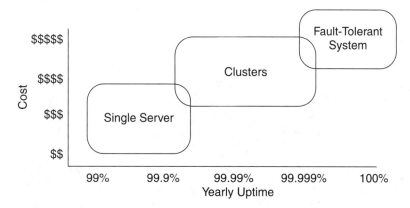

Figure 1.5 System availability versus cost of system or environment

---

2. A vendor can give specifics on the version of application and configuration; however, its limitations and how the application is to be used must be specified.

To illustrate the point, imagine that two different data centers use identical hardware and software. Data center A uses a database for online transaction processing (OLTP) and data center B uses a database for a decision support system (DSS).

Reviewing Table 1.3, it is clear that OLTP and DSS applications have vastly different requirements and workloads; so in a failure scenario, recovery times will be different for each environment even though the computing environments are identical. Typically, database A (OLTP) will have equal amounts of read and write access, thus the transaction logs will likely need recovery in the advent of an outage. However, database B (DSS) will have little if any recovery because most decision support systems have little write activity.[3] Database B would take longer to recover than database A, hence any general availability statements that included an application without qualifying its usage would not be accurate. Refer to the following list of issues affecting application recovery time in an HA environment.

1. The number of application instances running. More instances will increase recovery time.
2. The number of database instances. More instances will increase recovery time.
3. Type of databases (OLAP, OPTP, DSS, or Parallel).
4. External data feeds.
5. Amount and type of connected storage (Fiber Channel, SCSI, SAN).
6. System configuration—CPUs, memory, filesystem.
7. Number and type of user connections.

Application Availability

Whatever the level of nines a particular server uptime offers, it will be of little use if an application stops working in the middle of the day. When Information System (IS) managers evaluate high-availability solutions, they often get bogged down with the "level of nines" that a vendor is offering. Referring to Table 1.4, as the level of nines increases so do uptime and cost.

Table 1.3 Online Transaction Processing versus Decision Support System

OLTP	DSS
Large number of small transactions daily	Small number of large transactions usually weekly or monthly
Response times measured in fractions of a second	Response times measured in minutes to hours
Availability critical	Downtime not as critical

---

3. Updates to DSS are typically done during off-peak hours.

Table 1.4 Availability as a Percentage of Uptime

Uptime %	Downtime per Year	Downtime per Week
99	3.65 days	1 hour, 41 minutes
99.9	8.76 hours	10 minutes, 5 seconds
99.99	52.6 minutes	1 minute
99.999	5.25 minutes	6 seconds
99.9999	32 seconds	0.6 seconds

Naturally all technology managers want the highest levels of availability for their environments. Higher levels of "nines" gives technology managers assurance that the vendor is confident in a system's reliability. However, these two terms are often transposed. Reliability is a measurement of a system's ability to function continuously without interruption. Availability is a measurement of a system's ability to meet a committed application service-level agreement.

When referring to levels of availability, it's important to understand that the level of availability is expressed for a single system.[4] So how is availability affected when two identical machines are clustered together? When calculating the availability of a given system, the simple equation shown in Figure 1.6 is used.[5] In this expression, system availability is expressed as the quotient of the MTBF over the MTBF plus the MTTR. If the availability of a cluster is to be computed, all the MTBF and MTTR components of the cluster (servers, storage, networks, and so forth) would have to be known. It should not be surprising that the availability of a clustered environment is going to be lower than the availability of a single server.

The reader might be wondering: But I thought clustering my servers together is supposed to increase my availability? So why would any technology manager want

$$Availability = \frac{MTBF}{MTBF + MTTR} \cdot 100$$

Where $MTBF$ = Mean Time Before Failure
and $MTTR$ = Mean Time To Repair.

Figure 1.6 Function used to calculate the mean availability of a given system

---

4. This may include attached storage, but usually it does not as each major subsystem will have its own availability number.

5. Calculating availability is a complicated task. For the sake of simplicity, this formula is used. Typically, availability is calculated for a single component; here we are expressing the formula as a sum of all the availabilities calculations of a clustered environment, that is, nodes, storage, and network. Also, it is important to remember that "mean" in this equation refers to averages.

to cluster his most critical applications if the cluster availability is going to be lower than a single system? While it's true that a cluster's availability numbers are lower than a single system, the reverse is true for applications.

Application recovery on a cluster is much faster than on a single system. Let us compare some facts for clustered and non-clustered applications. In a non-clustered environment, if an application goes down or hangs, a system administrator can just restart the application and all might be well. But what if the machine panics, or experiences a hardware failure? At this point someone would call the service vendor to get the server replaced or repaired, both of which take time. The problem is compounded if there is no service contract or spare parts on hand, or worse, the data center is in the middle of a mountain range that requires two days to reach via horseback. In this scenario, all you can do is wait for the arrival of a service person or try bringing up the application on an alternate, albeit different, machine. Either prospect is a time-consuming task, made worse if data recovery is necessary. In this highly probable scenario, application recovery can take many hours if not days, assuming that the system administrator does everything correctly. Under such circumstances few (if any) system administrators can build a fairly complex system without mistakes.

Should the same unfortunate scenario occur on a cluster, recovery would begin immediately upon detecting a failure. Recovery would entail migrating the application to the standby server, thus dramatically reducing application recovery time without user intervention. A point worth reiterating is that availability for systems, clusters, and applications are different measurements. The only measurement that should matter is application availability. Unfortunately, not all applications can work in a clustered environment. Consult Chapter 4 for application requirements.

Cluster Availability

Viewing the availability for a clustered environment should not be any different from viewing the availability of a single server. This is because regardless of configuration, losing a node in an HA cluster will not render the cluster unusable. In a hot standby configuration, the total system availability should be defined within the boundaries of a single stand-alone node in the cluster. In other words, the cluster environment is the computer. Losing a portion of the infrastructure will not render the environment unusable.

A good way to view availability with respect to clusters is to understand the application and its requirements with respect to scalability and availability. The matrix listed in Table 1.5 is useful in determining how cluster availability affects different types of applications. The third column indicates the minimum number of nodes the application will need for normal operation. In the last column, availability refers to the aggregate availability for all components in the cluster, not just a single node.

Causes of Downtime

When looking at cluster availability, does it pay to use nodes with 99.99% ratings (52.6 minutes of downtime per year) as opposed to nodes with 99.999% ratings

Table 1.5 Effects of Cluster Availability on Applications

Application	Scalability or Availability	Number of Nodes an Application Needs	Does lower cluster availability affect application?
Nonparallel database	Availability	1	No, as long as database instances are able to migrate to a similar server. Lower cluster availability number does not affect database.
Parallel database	Both	2 (minimum)	Performance is affected if database relies on all cluster nodes to process workloads, for example, using Oracle 9iRAC in parallel mode.
Web server	Availability	1	No effect.
Web server load balanced	Scalability	2 (minimum)	Performance is affected. Potentially limits logins.

(5.25 minutes of downtime per year)? In order to answer this question, we offer the following theoretical example.

Imagine two clusters configured with nodes that have the same performance and storage capabilities. Nodes in cluster A are rated with 99.99% uptime, while cluster B nodes are rated at 99.999% uptime. In each configuration, node A hosts a database 100 gigabytes in size and node B is a standby node. In order to illustrate the point, we make the following assumptions:

1. The only difference between clusters is their availability numbers.
2. There will be a single failure in a one-year period. The failure constitutes a complete server failure. The primary node hosting the application fails completely.
3. A 100-gigabyte database will recover in 5 minutes and will be ready for user connections.
4. Total system recovery for both clusters is 60 seconds (detect a down server and initiate a failover).

Table 1.6 shows that the system with 99.999% availability is twice the cost of the system with 99.99% availability, but the total downtime and application availability is the same. However, the situation is more interesting if you look at the maximum yearly downtime for each server. For example, with 99.99% availability, the yearly downtime is 52.5 minutes. In our example, we can suffer ten 5-minute outages and still be within the 99.99% availability number; however, with 99.999% uptime, we could only suffer one outage (see Table 1.7).

Table 1.6 Application Downtime for One Failure

Level of Nines	Cost of Servers	Cluster Recovery	Database Recovery	Total Downtime
99.99	1 X	60 seconds	5 minutes	6 minutes
99.999	2 X	60 seconds	5 minutes	6 minutes

Table 1.7 Application Downtime for Maximum Failures Allowed

Level of Nines	Cost of Servers	System Recovery	Database Recovery	Total Downtime
99.99	1 X	60 seconds	5 minutes	1 hour (10 failures)
99.999	2 X	60 seconds	5 minutes	6 minutes

In the case where nodes have 99.99% availability, we could suffer 10 outages with each outage lasting 6 minutes, or any combination of outages not exceeding 60 minutes of downtime per year (with database recovery). Using nodes with 99.999% ratings, only one outage lasting 6 minutes would occur. In and of itself, this example doesn't say much other than using a machine with higher levels of uptime has the potential of failing less often. However, recall that the system availability calculation is application independent, which is also true for cluster nodes. The beauty of clusters is that when a node does fail, a standby node is available to take over the application requirements. Internet service providers (ISPs) have been doing this for years. Instead of buying a handful of very large expensive systems with high levels of availability, ISPs purchase a large number of smaller systems with lower levels of availability. Should a Web server fail, requests going to the failed server are rerouted to another server. According to this example, paying for servers with very high levels of uptime seems wasteful, if not redundant. This is not to say that system availability is not important; on the contrary, it is very important in a 7x24 operation. There exists a fundamental issue when determining how much system availability is needed for the servers. In order to correctly size the availability requirements of a system, a technology manager must calculate the monetary loss per unit of time for an application's lack of availability.

So when does it pay to use nodes in a cluster that offer high levels of uptime, for example, Sun Fire 15K servers? Answering this question is not straightforward. A detailed business operations and application analysis is necessary in order to make an appropriate decision. To appreciate the importance of knowing the cost of an outage, Tables 1.8 and 1.9 depict two hypothetical applications. The objective of the example is to show how the server availability can affect the organization from a revenue perspective. Both applications are compared with clusters where node availability ratings are at 99.99% and 99.999%, respectively.

Table 1.8 Applications Running on Servers with 99.99% Availability Rating

Application	Downtime Cost per Minute	Outage Lasting Entire Unplanned Downtime Period	Yearly Cost of Outages
Application A	$10,000	52 minutes	$520,000
Application B	$ 500	52 minutes	$ 26,000

Table 1.9 Applications Running on Servers with 99.999% Availability Rating

Application	Downtime Cost per Minute	Outage Lasting Entire Unplanned Downtime Period	Yearly Cost of Outages
Application A	$10,000	5 minutes	$50,000
Application B	$ 500	5 minutes	$ 2,500

The following assumptions are made:

1. A single node will be down for as long as the level of nines indicates. For example, 99.99% is equivalent to 52.6 minutes of unplanned downtime per year.
2. The failure is equal to the total yearly outage.
3. Failed nodes are repaired immediately, thus MTTR is zero, so no cluster is ever running with one node.
4. Failures are cumulative for all cluster nodes.

Looking at the tables, it's clear that if application A was being hosted on a cluster with nodes with 99.99% availability and if those nodes suffered outages equaling their total yearly downtime, the cost of the outage would be substantial when compared to using nodes rated at 99.999% availability.

The cost savings would be straightforward only if the cost of servers that offered 99.99% availability were equal to servers that offered 99.999% availability; in reality, it is not. Servers with higher levels of availability cost considerably more than those that offer lower levels of availability. The cost of nodes with higher availability is easy enough to get. The true cost of having an application outage is more difficult. However, once the cost of an outage has been determined, it's an easy task to plug in the number of nodes with higher availability to determine where the break-even point is. The point is, not knowing the cost of application downtime will undoubtedly lead to cluster configurations that are either too expensive to yield a return on investment or worse, configurations that fall short of meeting application uptime requirements.

Even for the developer, it's important to know what the cost of application down-time is. By knowing the cost of downtime, the resource developer can develop agents that suit the application's business needs more effectively. For example, instead of restarting a hung application N number of times where each restart lasts three min-utes, it might be more cost-effective to move the application over to another node via a node switch operation that might take only one minute to perform. That two-minute savings in application recovery could add up to thousands of dollars saved in lost productivity.

Availability Solutions

Fault Tolerance

Although HA means many things to many people, vendors who offer hardware or software that enables HA functionality clearly distinguish themselves from vendors who offer fault-tolerant systems, as HA systems (hardware or software) are not fault-tolerant. This is an important distinction to understand, therefore we will repeat it. High-availability systems are **not** a replacement for fault-tolerant sys-tems. Fault-tolerant computing offers different capabilities from HA.

Typical environments that require fault-tolerant computing are any environ-ments that because of failure can lead to loss of life or great financial losses such as air traffic control systems, nuclear power plants, and stock market exchanges. Fault-tolerant systems are generally composed of a single machine with redundant components for every aspect of the computing system, that is, CPUs, memory, stor-age, server, networks, and so forth. By redundant we mean subsystems that can withstand the loss of a primary component and still continue operating, for example, losing a CPU or I/O connection without a system crash. In the advent of a failure, a redundant component is used with no interruption of service. Because of all the redundancy, fault-tolerant computing systems are expensive to buy and maintain, hence they have a limited audience.

HA Clusters

For those environments that require high levels of uptime, HA computing is a way to get high levels of availability for software without the higher cost associated with fault-tolerant computing. However, unlike fault-tolerant computing, HA clusters do not have fault tolerance at every part of the hardware stack. Typically only storage systems, interconnects, and power supplies are fault-tolerant (losing one of these components will not affect the cluster or cause a service disruption). Also, unlike fault-tolerant computers, HA systems have a recovery window that can last from seconds to hours. In general, when recovery operation is taking place, services that were running on the faulty node will not be available until a full or partial recovery has been completed. Although fault-tolerant computing has some distinct advan-tages over HA computing, HA computing also offers capabilities that are not avail-able in typical fault-tolerant computing, such as application monitoring and migration. Table 1.10 outlines the two technologies.

Table 1.10 Fault-Tolerant versus High-Availability Technologies

Fault-Tolerant	High-Availability
No system downtime. Ensures that computing infrastructure is always available. Application never goes down due to hardware failures.	Applications and/or system will be temporarily unavailable until recovery is completed. Through monitoring, application faults can be detected, applications can be restarted, or can migrate to standby nodes.
Due to redundancy, fault tolerance is expensive.	Off-the-shelf systems can be made highly available. Likewise, larger systems can employ fault-tolerant type functionality at a lower cost.
Necessary for environments where human life loss or large monetary losses are likely in the advent of a hardware failure.	Excellent for environments where a temporary application outage is tolerable.
Not immune to application outages. Fault tolerence does nothing for application outages. Application restarts can be a manual process. If entire environment goes down, application is not available.	Down server does not affect application availability. Applications are migrated to standby nodes.

Summary

In this chapter we briefly discussed the various forms of cluster computing and the basics of high availability. Sun Microsystems offers three cluster products: Sun Grid Engine, Sun HPC, and Sun Cluster. Sun Cluster falls into the tightly coupled cluster category providing users with the unique capabilities of high availability and scalability. High availability is an attribute that can be possessed by clustered and nonclustered systems alike. Also, cluster availability is different from application availability. Being able to differentiate between the two will undoubtedly lead to computing environments that are better aligned with business requirements, while helping to define the software development requirements.

2

INTRODUCING SUN CLUSTER 3

Sun Microsystems Sun Cluster software is an expandable, robust, scalable, and highly available computing environment built around an object-oriented framework. Sun Cluster is designed for mission-critical applications operating in the Internet, intranet, and data center environments. This chapter provides an introduction to the Sun Cluster product and explains some of the key areas that will be of interest to developers. If the reader is already familiar with Sun Cluster this chapter can be skipped; however, if the reader has no familiarity with Sun Cluster, this chapter will provide an introduction to the areas that are most important to resource developers. It's important to note that Sun Cluster is a large, complex piece of software, with books dedicated to the subject; therefore, the reader should not expect this chapter to cover every detail. One notable book is *Designing Enterprise Solutions with Sun Cluster 3.0* (2002). Consult the References for further information.

Feature Set of Sun Cluster

- Continuous availability.
- Closely integrated with the Solaris Operating Environment (SOE).[1]
- Support for x86 Solaris.
- Scalable application support.
- Single management view of resources.

---

1. Check release notes for versions supported.

- Global filesystems, IP services, and device access.
- Support for up to 16 nodes.
- Agents for all leading enterprise applications. A partial list includes Oracle, SAP, Siebel, Sybase, DB2, Informix, SunOne, and Apache Web server.
- A comprehensive set of APIs for application development.
- Support for Remote Shared Memory (RSM) via Sun Fire Link or Scalable Coherent Interface (SCI).
- IP Network Multipathing (IPMP) for public networks.
- Support for enterprise-class storage including Storage Area Networks (SANS).
- Solaris Resource Manager Integration.
- Geographically diverse clusters.

About Sun Cluster

The Sun Cluster software is a general-purpose, tightly coupled, cluster solution. The fundamental design criteria are data integrity and application availability. However, there are some interesting facts about Sun Cluster of which developers need to be aware.

Installation

Sun Cluster is a sophisticated product, rich in both features and capabilities that are primarily used in mission-critical environments. Like any product that this reasonably sophisticated, installation and configuration is time consuming and can get complicated. Installation is best done by experienced, trained personnel. There are two primary ways to be sure that Sun Cluster is installed and configured correctly.

1. Onsite installation done by trained personnel.
2. Factory installation. A system is configured and shipped according to customer requirements from the factory.

While it's always fun to play with sophisticated technology, the authors highly recommend a factory installation or having the installation of both development and production environments done by trained personnel. There is little value in spending a great deal of time and effort in developing a resource type, only to find that it doesn't work when needed because the cluster framework wasn't correctly configured. Having the cluster framework installed by trained personnel will pay dividends in both development and production environments. If time to application deployment is an important option, factory installation is an attractive solution.

Cluster Nodes

Once installed, there is no method to stop the cluster software when running on a node. When a node boots, it looks for a valid cluster to join. If one isn't detected, it will attempt to create one. The only way to get a node not to join a cluster is to boot the node using **boot -x** at the open boot prom (OBP) prompt. Otherwise, nodes are always part of a cluster.

Storage

The Sun Cluster framework provides a unified image of filesystems, global networking, and global device access, ensuring an environment that is scalable and easier to administer. A unique attribute of Sun Cluster is that any storage device attached to a node (that is, disk, array, tape, or CD) can be made into a global device. As a developer this offers some tempting possibilities; however, care should be taken when creating global devices. Just because you can create a global device out of a CD-ROM disk does not mean it's a good practice. This chapter's section, "Global Devices," covers this in detail.

Failures

Although Sun Cluster offers high levels of availability for hardware and applications, equipment failures can and will happen. The cluster framework is not designed to withstand multiple simultaneous failures and still continue to operate, for example, when a node failure occurs in conjunction with an interconnect failure. It should be noted that in the advent of a failure, data integrity has a higher priority than application availability. Also, there is no need for developers to monitor hardware, I/O paths, OS processes, or network connections; Sun Cluster takes care of this.

Applications can use various file locks, shared memory segments, server sockets, and open files as part of their normal operations or as a way to document state. When finished, properly written applications will free memory, close files, and release any resources that were allocated. In a clustered environment, there is no guarantee that an application will get the chance to perform a clean shutdown—likewise for client applications using clustered applications. This topic will be covered in following chapters.

Sun Cluster Framework

While there are many subsystems of the Sun Cluster 3 (SC3) framework, to developers there are four main sections of importance. Understanding these areas will help the developer exploit the benefits of the SC APIs. The main areas of importance to developers are:

1. Global devices
2. Cluster filesystem
3. Global networks
4. Resource group manager

Global Devices

When developing cluster applications data must reside on shared storage. This is to ensure that in a failure scenario, standby nodes will be able to access data. Unlike stand-alone machines, Sun Cluster has the ability to allow the storage devices attached to a node such as disk drives, storage arrays, tape, and CD-ROM drives to be available to another node within the cluster. In Figure 2.1, node A and node C have storage devices attached to them. Using Sun Cluster, node B can be granted access to the device, even though only nodes A and C are physically attached to it.

Storage devices are referenced with a global disk ID (DID) that is supplied to node hardware by means of a DID driver. Should a failure occur, Sun Cluster will automatically redirect device access to another path only applicable for dual- and multi-ported storage devices. Access to devices not directly attached to the node is gained by means of the cluster interconnect. The DID driver automatically probes all nodes within a cluster and builds a list of available devices. Each device is assigned a unique ID that includes major and minor numbers. Global devices are accessed using the DID device number rather than the standard c(x) t(y) d(z) notation. For example, d10s7 translates to device d10 slice 7. Each node maintains its own copy of the global name space located in the `/dev/global` directory. Device files are stored in the `/dev/global/rdsk` directory for blocks, the `/dev/global/dsk` directory for disks, and in the `/dev/global/rmt` directory for tape devices. Assigning a global access naming convention ensures device consistency across the cluster. Knowing that nodes can have access to storage to which they do not have physical access, developers should not use or check for the existence of specific disks within the application. Also, storage need not be bound to or dependent on a resource such as a logical host.

Sun Cluster allows for storage to be an independent resource that can migrate to different nodes (as long as a node has physical access to it). For example, in Figure 2.1, the storage attached to node A can be migrated to node C and vice versa. However, node B can never be the host to storage as it does not have physical

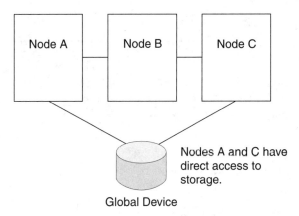

Global Device

Nodes A and C have direct access to storage.

Figure 2.1 Global devices

access. It can, however, have full access to the storage through nodes A or C. Global device access enables the use of dual-ported devices in clusters greater than two nodes. Also global devices enable the creation of a cluster storage environment that is easy to scale and manage.

Global Filesystems

Sun Cluster software introduces new capabilities to existing filesystems. An advantage of a Global Filesystem (GFS) is that each node within a cluster can mount filesystems simultaneously and thus provide a cluster-wide persistent datastore. The Sun Cluster kernel interface enables the export of a valid UNIX filesystem globally to all cluster members. The cluster filesystem semantics are implemented under the virtual filesystem (VFS) within the operating system kernel. This approach acts as a proxy layer between the kernel and storage device (see Figure 2.2).

By applying the identical semantics to the UNIX filesystem, implementation of the cluster filesystem structure is performed under the VFS layer. Therefore, file formats such as UNIX filesystem (UFS), Veritas filesystem (VxFS), and High Sierra filesystem (HSFS) can be created and exported globally. Implementing a cluster filesystem under the vnode layers insulates developers, users, and applications from the underlying workings. Applications do not need to be rewritten to take advantage of GFS because the internal locking mechanism manages both cache coherency and concurrent access. Like traditional UNIX filesystems, cluster filesystems are independent of the underlying volume manager, thereby giving system administrators a choice of using Solaris Volume Manager (SVM) or Veritas Volume Manager (VxVM) software.

A globally mounted filesystem can be manipulated using identical Solaris OE filesystem semantics (mount/unmount) as a non-GFS filesystem, and is transparent to applications and end users. Filesystems designated for global access are mounted using the `mount` command with the `-g` option (`mount -g`). Although every node

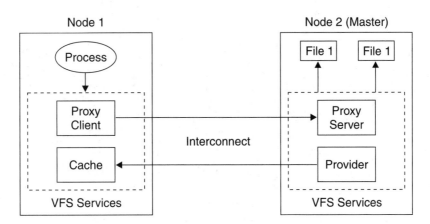

Figure 2.2 GFS proxy layer

could have a GFS entry in its /etc/vfstab file, only one node does the actual mounting of the filesystem, which in turn is mounted on each node, using the same mount point.

Global filesystems use caching extensively on local nodes. Before a read operation is requested, a node checks its local cache. If the requested data is not available in the local cache, the requesting node contacts the filesystem master for the required request. This caching system works the same as a file buffer cache; that is, if two nodes hold data in their caches and one node performs an update, then the other node(s) needing to make an update issues a request—the old page is invalidated and a new page is sent.

When using GFS, all file access is passed via the interconnects. The primary node(s) controls I/O to the filesystem; that is, all read/writes are passed through the primary node. If the primary node becomes unavailable, a secondary node becomes a primary. Implementing a primary and secondary node ensures that global filesystems are always available even if the primary node fails. A powerful attribute of GFS is its capability to transparently retry filesystem transactions: Users or applications will not see an I/O error, only a delay. If there is a path to the storage device, the GFS on that storage device is always available. For example, in Figure 2.3, node A is the primary master for the data-x filesystem and a secondary for the data-y filesystem. Node C conversely is the primary for data-y and the secondary for data-x. Node B is just a user of both filesystems and mounts them globally. Should either node A or C fail, its secondary will become the primary for that filesystem. During normal operation, node A will read and write directly to its filesystem data-x, but if access to filesystem data-y is required, it will be made through the interconnect via node C. Node B, not having direct access to either filesystem, must make requests to either node A or node C. If nodes A and C fail, node B will survive.[2] However, since

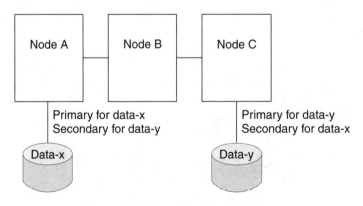

Figure 2.3 GFS with global devices

---

2. This would only be true if there were ample quorum votes.

node B does not have access to a physical storage, it will not be able to master any filesystem. It's important to note that access to a filesystem is transparent to cluster nodes even though access to the filesystem belongs to another node. Put another way, cluster nodes don't communicate with one another about filesystem access. The beauty of GFS is that each node believes it is the owner of the filesystem and the underlying mechanics are transparent to end users, applications, and even nodes.

Global filesystems can also be configured with a primary node but no secondary node. Filesystems configured in this way are not highly available—that is, if the primary node fails, applications accessing the filesystem will generate access errors. While a cluster can be configured in this manner, it should be avoided because there is no good reason to have a GFS without any secondary nodes assigned to it.

Failover File Services

As flexible as global filesystems are, there is a cost associated with their use. Performance is one area that takes a noticeable hit. Applications that create or use numerous small files may not be good candidates for GFS, as the overhead in maintaining GFS caches can be great, thus negating their value. This is also true for applications that generate a large number of writes from nodes that are not the primary. Applications that make heavy use of I/O (such as a large database) might also experience a degradation of performance when using a GFS.

In addition to GFS, Sun Cluster also offers failover file services (FFS). Configuring a filesystem as an FFS allows for the filesystem to fail over with the application as a single unit. In Figure 2.4, node A has an application running on it that accesses /ffs/data1 residing on cluster storage, with node B as the secondary for the application.

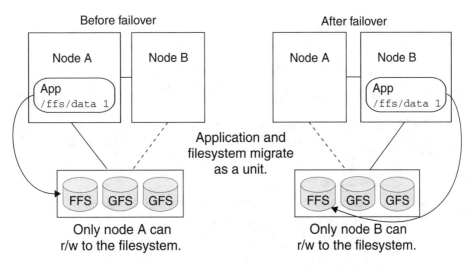

Figure 2.4 Failover file services via HAStoragePlus

In the advent of a failover or switch-over, both the application and filesystem are migrated over to node B. At this point, only node B has access to the application as well as to the filesystem. Failover file services are available through a resource type called HAStoragePlus.[3] To ensure that both the filesystem and the application migrate together, an extension property *AffinityOn* is defined within the HAStoragePlus resource type.

It's also worth mentioning that cluster configurations can have a mixture of GFS and FFS. The caveat of FFS is that, unlike GFS, only one node can access the filesystem at any given time. Using FFS adds another item for developers to be aware of: ensuring that the filesystem is in fact mounted and available before starting an application. Fortunately, there are functions within the APIs to test for the availability of FFS. For those applications that benefit from FFS, Sun Cluster provides that functionality via HAStoragePlus resource type.

Resource Group Manager

The resource group manager (RGM) is a process that resides in user space. The RGM layer provides the software glue that ties applications to the cluster framework. The function of the RGM is to start, stop, and monitor resources. The RGM also is responsible for migrating resources from node to node during planned or unplanned changes to the cluster membership. Applications and developers predominately interact with the RGM layer. A good majority of the Sun Cluster APIs involve extracting information from the RGM layer. Application developers should pay particular attention to this section, because in order to write effective resource types it is important to understand the semantics of how the RGM works. Resources come in two distinctive types: failover and scalable. Although the following sections describe each type of service individually, Sun Cluster can be configured to have a combination of both scalable and failover services running at the same time.

Failover Resources

Failover resources are easy enough to understand. An application runs on a server and when the server malfunctions, the application is migrated over to another machine. If the application stops responding, it can be restarted or, if necessary, migrated over to another machine.

While they can be complicated, for the most part failover resources are easy to configure and manage (see Figure 2.5). The following are the common attributes of a failover resource:

1. Services can only run on one server.
2. Only one instance of the service is active on the cluster.
3. Services can use both global and failover filesystems.
4. Services are temporarily unavailable until failover is complete.

---

3. HAStoragePlus is only available with Sun Cluster 3.0 5/02 and upwards.

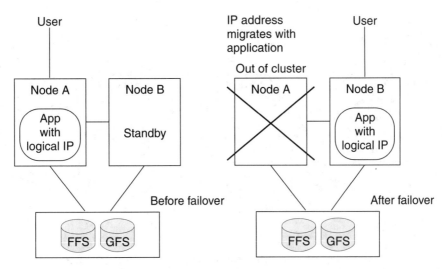

Figure 2.5 Simple failover resource

5. End users connect to a logical IP address to access the service.

6. If necessary, users will have to reconnect to the service.

7. Services can be restarted or migrated to another node.

Scalable Resources

The scalable resource allows for applications to take advantage of the horizontal scale ability of Sun Cluster. Multiple instances of the application can run on the cluster. Applications are configured to work with a global interface (GIF) which has a global IP address assigned to it. Users make requests via the GIF. In Figure 2.6, node A is configured as the GIF node. The GIF node forwards the request on the interconnect to the right node to process the request. That node then responds directly back to the end user. A user-defined load-balancing algorithm is used to spread the workload among the nodes. It also identifies when the GIF should send packets and to which nodes. It's important to understand that scalable services load balance IP-based traffic only.

Scalable resource types have the following attributes:

1. Multiple instances of the application can run on the cluster.

2. End users make requests from a global interface.

3. Global filesystems must be used; all nodes need access to data.

4. GIF node load balances incoming requests and forwards requests to other nodes.

5. Nodes respond back directly to end users.

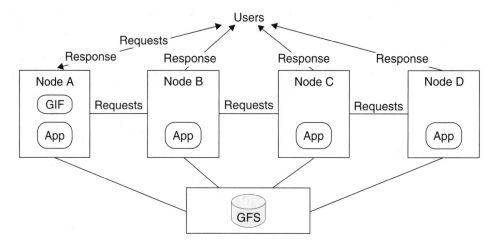

Figure 2.6 Simple scalable resource

Resource Anatomy

Resources in Sun Cluster can be decomposed into three distinct entities: resource types, resources and resource groups. A resource is a list of attributes that describe an application. Resources are created from an underlying template called a resource type and these resource types are skeletons of what a resource can be. Using object oriented terminology, a resource is an instance of a resource type. Explaining it another way, resource types are blank templates used for resource creation. For example, suppose an application X needs to run on the cluster. Before application X can be hosted in a clustered environment, we'll need a template to describe application X, its properties, and what should happen in the advent that either application X stops responding or the cluster experiences a failure of some kind.

Resource Type

A resource type is a template for creating a particular type of resource. Before any resource can be created, it must have its type defined. Resource types can be configured as failover or a network scalable service.

Resources

A resource is an instance or instantiation of a resource type. Resources get their properties defined from the resource type. Resource properties are used to define attributes and behavior of the resource. Resources must be assigned to a group because the RGM does not manage resources directly.

Resource Groups

Resources are grouped together as one logical unit. The RGM manages resource groups. Resource groups can also have dependencies on other resource groups. Also, groups can be constrained to one node (logical host) or operate on multiple nodes (scalable services). Putting it all together, Figure 2.7 outlines graphically the relationship between resources, resource types, and resource groups.

Once a resource type has been defined, it is fairly easy to create and configure resource groups and resources. As stated earlier, Sun Cluster comes with many pre-defined resource types[4] (Oracle, Sybase, Apache, and NFS, to name a few).

Resource Creation

Although the following setups are done using the Sun Cluster command-line tools, the `scinstall` tool can also be used. First, configure the storage you need for the resource, either on GFS or HAStoragePlus (mount points, disks, filesystems, and so forth). Keep in mind the steps below assume many things have already happened, such as a proper cluster installation, storage, and network configuration.

Steps for creating a resource:

1. Register the resource type (this is done only once) for the type of resource you want to create using the `scrgadm` command, where -t is the name of the resource type. `scsetup` can also be used to perform this operation.

   ```
   scrgadm -a -t SUNW.nfs
   ```

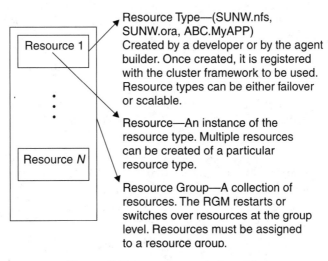

Figure 2.7 Resource relationships

---

4. Most Sun supplied resource types are license-based; however, some are free. Check with your sales representative for an updated list.

2. Now create a group to hold the resource(s), where the -g is the name of the resource group and the -h is the node that can host this group. In this case, both node1 and node2 can host the resource group.

```
scrgadm -a -g mynfs -h node1,node2
```

3. Create a resource where -g is the name of the group, -j is the name of the resource, and -t is the type of resource.

```
scrgadm -a -g mynfs -j mynfs_res -t SUNW.nfs
```

4. Bring the resource group online.

```
scswitch -Z -g mynfs
```

At this point, the resource group is brought online, monitoring begins, and the *mynfs_res* is ready for use. Once the resource type is created, one can see it's a rather easy, straightforward process. This book concentrates on step 1, that is, how to create resource types along with the other mechanisms that make resource types work. However, it's important to know the whole process. In each of the above steps, the resource type can fail and in doing so the RGM will run a callback method on the appropriate action to take.

Sun Cluster Subtopics

While the developer might only be interested in those areas that directly affect him or her, it's worth looking into some of these other important areas. Listed below are short descriptions of the major components of the cluster software.

IPMP

IP Multipathing (IPMP) daemon monitors the public network interfaces for availability. In the advent of a problem, IPMP can bring an interface offline and use another backup interface. For clusters using Sun Cluster v3.1, IPMP is the default; for Sun Cluster v3.0, network adapter failover (NAFO) is used.

CMM

Cluster membership monitor (CMM) is responsible for cluster membership during startup, node addition, deletion, and shutdown.

CCR

The cluster configuration repository (CCR) is a series of ASCII files not intended for user access. All cluster information such as configuration, resource groups, networks, and so forth, is stored in this distributed database.

Quorum Devices

Quorum devices are used to determine cluster membership during cluster formation or in the advent of a cluster state change. Their primary role is to ensure that a valid cluster is formed based on a quorum vote of active members. A distributed computing environment can only work if the majority of the participants are present to determine what is valid configuration—in our case one half of the cluster nodes. For example, in a four-node cluster, at least three nodes must be available to have a valid cluster (3 > 2). But what if you lost two nodes in a bizarre accident? Without quorum devices, this cluster would stop working as the quorum vote would only be two (each node gets a vote). In our four-node scenario, a quorum device can act as a tiebreaker. If two nodes are lost, the quorum device gets a vote, the remaining nodes each get a vote, and the total vote count is three. The cluster would continue to operate even in the unlikely scenario of losing two nodes in a four-node cluster. Disk drives are used as quorum devices in Sun Cluster. The above example is a simplified view of quorum devices. It's important to note that quorum devices play a vital role in the availability of the cluster. As one might guess, quorum devices must be global.

Load Balancing

This is a process that distributes networking requests for scalable services.

Cluster Transport

Nodes use this private network to transmit cluster heartbeats, cluster messages, and in some configurations application data. It must have a minimum of two interfaces with a maximum of six per cluster node.

Volume Manager

A logical volume manager, such as Veritas or Solaris Volume Manager, is used to manage local and global storage.

Application Monitoring

The Sun Cluster environment offers application monitoring through the cluster framework. Even though cluster availability statements don't include application uptime, it's very important to make applications cluster-aware. Once an application and its properties are defined to the cluster, the cluster can begin to monitor an application's status and health. Agents are currently available for the most common application suites such as iPlanet, Oracle, Sap, Informix, Sybase, and others. Unless a specific agent is available for an application, the cluster framework knows nothing about applications outside of their frameworks.

For example, application PrepData downloads data from the mainframe every day at 4:00 A.M. This data gets processed and uploaded into the company database. The database is then queried by the Web server to determine the available inventory for online sales. The database and Web server are registered and monitored by the cluster. But what would happen if the PrepData application were unavailable? How would the lack of the PrepData application affect the entire system?

This is where Sun Cluster technology shows its flexibility. Not only does cluster software add an extra layer of redundancy to the hardware stack, but it also adds a layer of redundancy to the software stack. By putting custom applications, as well as database and Web server software under cluster control, applications can be monitored for a host of conditions specified by the developer. Should a certain condition arise, the cluster software can take a predefined course of action to ensure that critical services are available.

Summary

Sun Cluster offers many features that allow an organization to create computing platforms which offer availability and scalability. Using global devices and global filesystems ensures a cluster environment that is both easy to manage and to expand. Understanding the resource group manager and its role within the cluster framework is essential to developing effective resource types.

3

GETTING STARTED

Up and Running

Often the best way to learn something is to dive right in. In this chapter we'll skip some of the background information about developing resource types to show how to quickly make an application highly available, without doing any programming!

As all hard-working systems administrators and programmers know, the quickest way to create an application is to not actually write any code yourself, but to assemble components that have already been built. Similarly, the quickest way to make an application highly available with Sun Cluster is to use a Resource Type that has already been developed. In the simplest case, this means using a "shrink-wrapped" data service agent provided by Sun or a third-party vendor, such as those available for Sun Cluster resource types (HA NFS, HA DNS), and others. Unfortunately, there are many cases where an off-the-shelf Resource Type is not available for your application, but the Sun Cluster environment does provide a Generic Data Service that can be used to quickly make many applications highly available without requiring any actual programming.

The Generic Data Service, or GDS, is actually a general-purpose resource type: by setting certain *properties* (see Chapter 6) of each resource instance, you configure how the cluster will start, stop, and monitor your application. The handy thing about the GDS is that these properties can be set by a systems administrator during configuration, so it doesn't require programming skills. It is even possible to have several instances of the GDS, each controlling a different application in the cluster.

The best way to explain how the GDS is used to make an application highly available is to use an example to illustrate the required steps. In the rest of this chapter, we will show how to make the Apache Web server into a highly available data service.[1]

Preparing the Cluster

To follow along with the example, you will need to have "root" access to a cluster system. We'll assume that the cluster hardware and software have been correctly installed to a basic level, according to the instructions in the Sun Cluster Installation Guide. In our example, the cluster has two nodes: node1 and node2.

Preparing a Global Filesystem

In order for our Web server to be highly available, the data files must be accessible to both nodes. The easiest way to achieve this is to put the data (HTML files) onto a global filesystem. In fact, in this example we will also put the Web server configuration and log files onto a filesystem globally mounted on /web.

The instructions for creating a new global filesystem are given in the Sun Cluster System Administration Guide,[2] and the exact details of the commands to use will vary according to how your disk storage is attached to the cluster nodes and which volume manager you are using on the cluster (Solstice DiskSuite/Solaris Volume Manager or Veritas Volume Manager). In our example, we will show the commands used to set up a global filesystem using Solaris Volume Manager (SVM), which comes as part of Solaris 9. However, the commands are the same for Solstice DiskSuite 4.2.1 that is used with Solaris 8. We assume that the state databases have already been set up, because this task is only done once for each node. Consult the Solaris Volume Manager Administration Guide if you need assistance.

The first step in setting up a new global filesystem is to work out which disks are going to be used. Since our Apache Web server doesn't require a great deal of data storage space (a few dozen megabytes, perhaps), we will only need to use two disks—one for the data, and one to use as a mirror. To find out what disks are available to both systems, we can use the command /usr/cluster/bin/scdidadm -L, as shown in Example 3.1.

---

1. There is, in fact, a shrink-wrapped HA (and scalable) agent for Apache available for Sun Cluster 3, but the Apache Web server is a useful demonstration application since it ships as part of Solaris and is fairly simple to install and configure.

2. All of the guides referred to in this chapter are available online at http://docs.sun.com.

Example 3.1   Finding shared disks

```
# /usr/cluster/bin/scdidadm -L
1        node1:/dev/rdsk/c0t0d0           /dev/did/rdsk/d1
2        node1:/dev/rdsk/c0t6d0           /dev/did/rdsk/d2
3        node1:/dev/rdsk/c0t8d0           /dev/did/rdsk/d3
4        node1:/dev/rdsk/c0t10d0          /dev/did/rdsk/d4
5        node1:/dev/rdsk/c1t6d0           /dev/did/rdsk/d5
5        node2:/dev/rdsk/c1t6d0           /dev/did/rdsk/d5
6        node1:/dev/rdsk/c2t2d0           /dev/did/rdsk/d6
6        node2:/dev/rdsk/c2t2d0           /dev/did/rdsk/d6
7        node1:/dev/rdsk/c2t6d0           /dev/did/rdsk/d7
7        node2:/dev/rdsk/c2t6d0           /dev/did/rdsk/d7
8        node2:/dev/rdsk/c0t0d0           /dev/did/rdsk/d8
9        node2:/dev/rdsk/c0t6d0           /dev/did/rdsk/d9
10       node2:/dev/rdsk/c0t8d0           /dev/did/rdsk/d10
```

The output from scdidadm(1M) shows us that we have three disks shared by both nodes in this cluster system: items 5, 6, and 7 in the list. The middle column of the output shows how each node refers to the physical device, and the right-hand column shows the *global* device reference. For our example, we will use global disks **d5** and **d7** to hold our new filesystem.

To achieve high availability, we need to create a mirrored volume—all data written to one disk is simultaneously written to the other, so if one disk fails the data is still available on the other. To create this volume, we have to create a named *diskset,* to specify which nodes will potentially access the disks and which disks are in the set. Example 3.2 shows how this is done to create a diskset called webDG.

Example 3.2   Creating a named diskset

```
# metaset -s webDG -a -h node1 node2
# metaset -s webDG -a -m node1
# metaset -s webDG -a -m node2
# metaset -s webDG -t
# metaset -s webDG -a /dev/did/rdsk/d5
# metaset -s webDG -a /dev/did/rdsk/d7
```

You'll notice that we use the *global device names* of the disks—this is important because the global device names always refer to the same physical device, regardless of the node on which you issue the command.

Now that we have created the webDG diskset, we can create the mirrored volume, and then "slice off" 400MB from the volume for a soft partition on which to create the filesystem (see Example 3.3).

Example 3.3   Creating a mirrored volume

```
# metainit -s webDG d1 1 1 /dev/did/rdsk/d5s0
webDG/d1: Concat/Stripe is setup
# metainit -s webDG d2 1 1 /dev/did/rdsk/d7s0
webDG/d2: Concat/Stripe is setup
# metainit -s webDG d3 -m webDG/d1
webDG/d3: Mirror is setup
# metattach -s webDG d3 webDG/d2
webDG/d3: submirror webDG/d2 is attached
# metainit -s webDG d4 -p webDG/d3   400m
webDG/d4: Soft Partition is setup
# newfs /dev/md/webDG/rdsk/d4
newfs: construct a new filesystem /dev/md/webDG/rdsk/d4: (y/n)? y
Warning: 3139 sector(s) in last cylinder unallocated
/dev/md/webDG/rdsk/d4:819200 sectors in 229 cylinders of 27 tracks, 133 sectors
        400.0MB in 15 cyl groups (16 c/g, 28.05MB/g, 13504 i/g)
super-block backups (for fsck -F ufs -o b=#) at:
 32, 57632, 115232, 172832, 230432, 288032, 345632, 403232, 460832, 518432,
 576032, 633632, 691232, 748832, 806432,
```

Now that the filesystem is ready, we can create a mount point and an entry in /etc/vfstab on each node,[3] and then mount the filesystem (see Example 3.4).

Example 3.4   Mounting a filesystem

```
# mkdir -p -m 0755 /web
# rsh node2 'mkdir -p -m 0755 /web'
# echo /dev/md/webDG/rdsk/d4   /web  ufs  1 no global,logging >> /etc/vfstab
# rsh node2 'echo /dev/md/webDG/rdsk/d4  /web  ufs1 no global,logging >>
/etc/vfstab'
# mount /web
```

Now that the filesystem is mounted, we are ready to set up the Apache Web server.

Preparing the Apache Web Server

The first step in preparing the Web server is to check that the software is installed. The Apache Web server is supplied with Solaris 8 or later in the SUNWapchr and SUNWapchu packages. It is, of course, possible to download, compile, and install your own version of Apache, but for this example we will use the Sun-provided packages.

```
# pkginfo SUNWapchr SUNWapchu
system    SUNWapchr    Apache Web Server (root)
system    SUNWapchu    Apache Web Server (usr)
```

---

3. To use the rsh commands used in the example, you will need to configure your ~root/.rhosts file on each node: consult hosts.equiv(4) for more details.

The next step is to decide what configuration parameters we will use for the Web server—in other words, what IP address to use, what TCP port the service will run on, and where to store the data files. We've already established that we will hold the data files under the /web global filesystem, so a good place would be in a directory called /web/htdocs. For our example we'll use a new logical host "webhost" with 10.3.2.1 for the IP address and the standard HTTP server port (80).

We now need to put this information into an Apache configuration file, and put this configuration file onto the global filesystem so that it is accessible to both nodes in our cluster. Example 3.5 shows these steps, and also shows the creation of a very simple index.html file we can use to check our Web server later on.

Example 3.5   Creating the Apache configuration information

```
# echo "10.3.2.1  webhost" >> /etc/hosts
# rsh node2 'echo "10.3.2.1 webhost" >> /etc/hosts'
# mkdir -p -m 0755 /web/htdocs
# echo "Success" > /web/htdocs/index.html
# cp /etc/apache/httpd.conf-example  /web/httpd.conf
```

Next, we need to edit the new /web/httpd.conf file to add the information for the Web server. The easiest way to do this is to add the data in Example 3.6 to the end of the httpd.conf file.

Example 3.6   Data at end of httpd.conf file

```
Listen 10.3.2.1:80
PidFile /var/run/webhost-httpd.pid
BindAddress 10.3.2.1
Servername webhost
DocumentRoot "/web/htdocs"
<Directory "/web/htdocs">
    Options Indexes FollowSymLinks MultiViews
    Order allow,deny
    Allow from all
</Directory>
CustomLog /web/access_log common
ErrorLog  /web/error_log
```

Normally, Apache is started and stopped using /usr/apache/bin/apachectl, but the final step in preparing the Web server is to create a version of this file that will look for our httpd.conf file in /web/httpd.conf rather than in the default /etc/apache/httpd.conf file. To do this, all we need to do is copy /usr/apache/bin/apachectl to /web/apachectl, and then edit that new file:

```
# cp /usr/apache/bin/apachectl /web/apachectl
```

The only line that needs to be changed in `/web/apachectl` is the setting for HTTPD. In the new file the line should read:

```
HTTPD="/usr/apache/bin/httpd -f /web/httpd.conf"
```

With that final change, the configuration of the Web server is complete, and we can begin to make it highly available.

Creating an Agent with the GDS

Using the GDS to create an agent involves a number of steps, shown in Figure 3.1. Not all of the steps are required for every new data service on a cluster—for example, the `SUNWscgds` package only has to be installed once on each node.

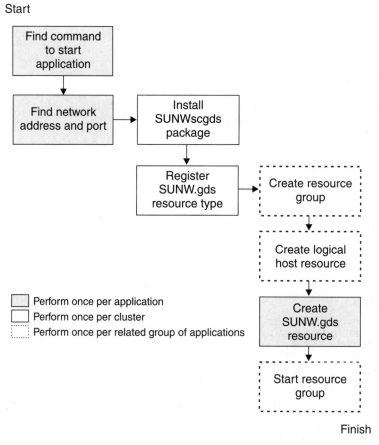

Figure 3.1 Steps to create an agent using GDS

In order to make the application highly available using GDS, we need to know two things:

1. What command is used to start the application
2. What TCP/IP address and port are used by the application

In our example so far, we've established that the start command will be `/web/apachectl start`. The IP address for the Web server must be a logical host configured on the cluster (not an IP of a physical node). We have already ensured that this IP address should be reflected in the Apache configuration file. To recap, the important configuration information for our example is summarized in Table 3.1.

Now we are ready to create the highly available Apache Web server using GDS. First, make sure the GDS software is installed on each node of the cluster—the package SUNWscgds is shipped with the Sun Cluster software but is not installed by default in early releases.

```
# pkginfo SUNWscgds
application SUNWscgds    Sun Cluster Generic Data Service
```

Once the software is installed, the resource type must be registered with the cluster using `scrgadm(1M)`:

```
# /usr/cluster/bin/scrgadm -a -t SUNW.gds
```

This registration only needs to be performed once per cluster, regardless of the number of GDS agents created. Next, we need to create a resource group to hold our Web server application:

```
# /usr/cluster/bin/scrgadm -a -g webserver-rg
```

Once the resource group has been created, we need to put in a logical host resource:

```
# scrgadm -a -L -g webserver-rg -l webhost
```

In most releases of Sun Cluster 3, this command will automatically choose a network interface for the logical host, and set up public network monitoring. In the initial release of Sun Cluster 3.1, however, you will need to manually create an IPMP failover group on each node. This is covered in the System Administration Guide: IP Services, but Example 3.7 shows how this can be achieved. In the example, we use the IP address 10.3.2.10 for the IPMP test address. This step must be repeated on each node with a different test IP address.

Table 3.1 Configuration Summary

Start command:	/web/apachectl start
IP address:	10.3.2.1
Logical hostname:	webhost
TCP/IP port:	80

Example 3.7   Setting up an IPMP group on hme0

```
# ifconfig hme0 addif 10.3.2.10 netmask + broadcast + -failover deprecated up
# ifconfig hme0 group sc_ipmp1
# ifconfig hme0
hme0: flags=1000843<UP,BROADCAST,RUNNING,MULTICAST,IPv4> mtu 1500 index 2
        inet 10.3.2.10 netmask ffffff00 broadcast 10.3.2.255
        groupname sc_ipmp1
        ether 8:0:20:c4:28:10
```

The IPMP group name sc_ipmp1 has no special significance, any name can be used.

Finally, we can create a resource that will control the Web server. In our example, we'll call the resource webserver-res. Example 3.8 shows how to create the resource and then activate it. We can then try to connect to the Web server and retrieve the test file we created earlier.

Example 3.8   Creating and activating the Web server resource

```
# scrgadm -a -j webserver-res -g webserver-rg -t SUNW.gds \
> -y port_list="80/tcp" \
> -x start_command="/web/apachectl start" \
> -y network_resources_used=webhost
# /usr/cluster/bin/scswitch -Z -g webserver-rg
# telnet webhost 80
Trying 10.3.2.1...
Connected to webhost.
Escape character is '^]'.
GET /
Success
Connection to webhost closed by foreign host.
```

There you have it—a highly available Apache Web service has been created without doing any actual programming! The only problem is that a lot of typing was involved. For this reason, the Sun Cluster environment includes a tool to automate much of this work, and to provide extra functionality for those cases where GDS doesn't fit the bill. This tool is called the SunPlex Agent Builder, and is described in Chapter 5.

Operation

When the GDS resource is started by the cluster framework (either when the cluster node starts, a failover occurs, or if the system operator manually starts it), the start command for the application is automatically run, which in turn starts the application. The cluster will then ensure that the application continues to run until the systems administrator instructs it to stop, which means that the application will be automatically restarted if it crashes or will be moved to a new node if the node it is running on fails.

Stopping

In our example, we did not provide any explicit way to stop the application. This would be necessary when the cluster node shuts down or if the service is moved away from the current node. Since we did not provide an explicit program, the cluster framework will simply send a `signal(3HEAD)` to the application—first a SIGTERM signal to try to stop the application gracefully, and then a SIGKILL signal if the application continues to run.

It is possible, however, to specify a command that will stop the application. In our example, the normal way to stop the Apache Web server is the command:

```
/web/apachectl stop
```

We can specify this command when we create the resource:

```
scrgadm -a -j webserver-res -g webserver-rg -t SUNW.gds \
    -y Port_List="80/tcp" \
    -x Start_Command="/web/apachectl start" \
    -x Stop_Command="/web/apachectl stop" \
    -x Network_Resources_Used=webhost
```

With this configuration, when the cluster framework wants to stop the application, the stop command is issued. If the application continues to run after the stop command has been issued, then the cluster will try sending the SIGKILL signal.

Fault Probe

Another feature not explicitly specified in our example is fault probing. That is, while the application is running, the cluster will periodically check that it is operating correctly by running a fault probe. When no fault probe program is explicitly mentioned, the cluster framework will simply attempt to connect to the IP address and port used by the application. If the connection is successful, the framework will try to disconnect, and if that is also successful, the application is assumed to be operating correctly.

Obviously, this method of fault detection can be a little too simplistic, so it is possible to specify a different program for the cluster to use to determine if the application is operating correctly. The fault probe program must return zero if all is well—any other number is interpreted as a fault. A value of 100 causes the application to be restarted, and a value of 201 results in a request to immediately fail over to a different node. Fault probe programs will be discussed in more detail later in the book, but let's assume that we have a program to report on our Apache Web server:

```
/web/apache-check
```

Assuming this program is available as our fault monitor, we can create our resource using the following command (note the new section in bold):

```
# scrgadm -a -j webserver-res -g webserver-rg -t SUNW.gds \
      -y Port_List="80/tcp" \
      -x Start_Command="/web/apachectl start" \
      -x Stop_Command="/web/apachectl stop" \
      -x Probe_Command="/web/apache-check" \
      -y Network_Resources_Used=webhost
```

With this configuration, the cluster will periodically check the status of the application using the probe command and take action if something goes wrong.

Limitations

Up to and including the original release of Sun Cluster 3.1, only network-aware applications (that is, applications that offer a service via an IP connection) can be made highly available using GDS.[4] When you create the resource, you must specify the network ports used by the application, and the default mechanism for checking if the application is running uses a simple connection to the IP address. Of course, if you supply your own Probe_Command, then the cluster will not check that the application is running using the network connection, but you must still provide some network port, as Port_List must be defined for all GDS resources.

Summary

The Generic Data Service provides the means to make an application highly available without developing a specialized Resource Type, and is suitable for proofs-of-concept, or where the application is relatively simple to start, stop, and manage. This chapter demonstrated how to do this for the Apache Web server and the procedure should be adaptable to other applications of similar complexity.

For some applications, as with our Apache Web server example, it may be desirable or necessary to write wrapper programs to act as the start, stop, and probe functions. For others, it may not be feasible to use GDS as the basis for making an application highly available—especially where more complex fault monitoring and fault handling is required. These more complex resource types can be created using the SunPlex Agent Builder tool, described in Chapter 5. Before starting this more complex development, however, it is important to understand more about how the Sun Cluster resource management framework operates, and this is the subject of our next chapter, "Planning for Development."

---

4. Check the release notes of later versions of Sun Cluster to see if this restriction still applies.

4

PLANNING FOR DEVELOPMENT

The Importance of Planning

Now that we've had a quick look at making an application highly available, we should take some time out to say a few words about planning for the development of Sun Cluster agents. As with most development tasks, the success or failure of a project to develop a data service agent is greatly affected by the amount of planning that goes into it, and we have found that a typical medium-complexity agent-development project would normally involve at least three to four days of planning and documenting, especially if the application is not already well understood.

Since ultimately data service agents provide an automated way to start, stop, and monitor applications, it is important for the developer to understand how to achieve these tasks programmatically. For this reason, an understanding of the application is usually more important than any particular experience with the Sun Cluster product. It's also very important to realize that there are certain requirements that applications must fulfill in order to be easily made into highly available services. Consequently, one of the first tasks in any project to develop a Sun Cluster data service agent is to qualify the application.

Qualifying an Application

There are a number of characteristics used to determine whether an application can be made highly available using the Sun Cluster 3 framework. If the application does not possess these attributes, then making it highly available may require modification to the application itself rather than simply creating start and stop methods within the framework.

Here are the key points to consider when making an application highly available.

- Data service access
- Crash tolerance
- Bounded recovery time after crash
- File location independence
- Absence of a tie to the physical identity of the node
- Ability to work on multi-homed hosts
- Ability to work with logical interfaces
- Client recovery

Let's look at each of these in detail to see what's required.

Data Service Access

Generally speaking, the only applications that can be effectively made highly available under the Sun Cluster framework are client-server applications that receive *discrete* queries from an IP-network-based client. Examples of this type of service include databases and Web (HTTP) servers.

Applications requiring a *persistent* network connection are slightly less-suited to the HA model, since continuing the service after a failover requires a reconnection, which usually means you lose any state that was created up to the point of failure. Examples of this type of service include terminal connections, telnet, and FTP.

This does not mean that persistent-connection data services cannot get any advantage from being included in the HA framework. Because the HA failover emulates a very fast reboot of the server, the application becomes available again more quickly than it would on a stand-alone server. It does mean, however, that the client software or end user must be able to cope with this kind of break in the service. For example, an FTP client that automatically retries a download if the connection is broken and continues from where it left off would overcome this problem.

Some applications do not use any kind of network connection for client access, or may not have any kind of client access at all. In these cases, there may be some difficulty in making the application highly available using the Sun Cluster framework, particularly if some sort of fixed line (such as a serial terminal connection) is required. This is because the Sun Cluster framework has built-in mechanisms for migrating IP network addresses between nodes, but does not have a similar facility for other access methods. Fortunately, in modern computing environments, most applications subscribe to the IP client/server model or have limitations that can be worked around quite easily (see "Getting Around Requirements" later in this chapter).

Crash Tolerance

Since the Sun Cluster HA model essentially emulates the fast reboot of a failed system, the application must be able to put itself into a known state when it starts up. Generally, this means that the application state should be committed to persistent storage (on disk) rather than being held in RAM. Depending on the application, it may be necessary for some sort of automatic rollback recovery or consistency check to be performed each time the application starts, to ensure any partially completed transactions are properly taken care of. If an application uses techniques such as a two-phase commit to write data to disk, then it is usually more easily able to recover after a system failure.

Regardless of how they write persistent data, some applications still require manual intervention to start (classic examples include applications utilizing some form of security, and that require a passphrase to be entered at startup). For these applications, it may be possible to achieve a work-around (such as piping responses in from a file). Care must be taken, however, to pay attention to the security and procedural implications of this sort of work-around.

Typically, if an application is automatically started at boot time (with a script in /etc/rc3.d, for example) then it is usually safe to run as a cluster-controlled application without much (or any!) modification.

Bounded Recovery Time

When applications are restarted by the Sun Cluster framework, there needs to be some reasonable (and predictable) limit on how long it will take to recover. Obviously, the amount of time required will depend on what sort of application is involved; for example, a large OLTP database will almost certainly take longer to return to a consistent state than a small Web server due to the relative frequency of data changes.

Some limit is needed because the cluster framework needs to be able to determine when an application is *not* going to restart, which is particularly important if the cluster is attempting to restart the application on the same node. After the limit has expired, the cluster can take appropriate action (such as failing the application over to a different node).

File Location Independence

The location of files and data used by the data service is very important, since this information has to be shared by each node that will potentially run the application. For this reason, application and configuration data locations (or file paths) should not be hard-coded into the application itself.

Applications should store any changeable data, including configuration information, on the shared storage of the cluster—either on a globally mounted filesystem, a failover filesystem, or on globally accessible raw devices. This ensures that the data and behavior of the application are consistent across nodes of the cluster. The upshot of this is that there must be some way of defining to the application where the data and configuration files are stored in the filesystem, such as a command-line argument to the application program binary.

If the paths to data or configuration files are hard-coded into a program, then you can sometimes use symbolic links to overcome the problem. However, be aware that if an application completely removes and recreates a given file that has been redirected using a symbolic link, the behavior may not be as expected. For example, if the directory /var/myapp/data is actually a symbolic link to a globally mounted directory /global/myapp/data, then an application accessing /var/myapp/data/foo will get the correct file (see Figure 4.1). However, if the application unlinks the directory /var/myapp/data and recreates it, the symbolic link may be destroyed. This means that new data will be created in a directory /var/myapp/data that is not accessible to any other nodes in the cluster (see Figure 4.2).

You may also want to consider where to store your application binaries, and there are good arguments each way as to whether application binaries should be installed on shared storage or installed individually on the local storage of each node. With binaries stored locally, it is possible to perform rolling upgrades of the application software by performing the upgrade on the standby node and then manually switching control to that new node as the original node is upgraded. This maintains the availability of the data service to clients, but introduces possible management problems if a failure occurs partway through an upgrade or if the data format is different between application software releases. With binaries installed on shared storage,

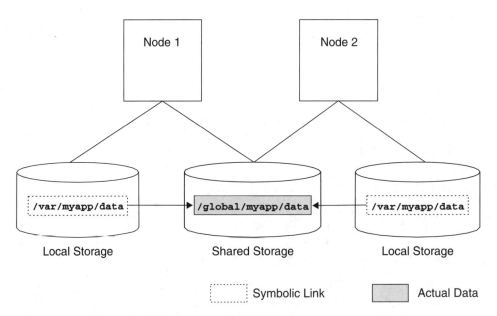

Figure 4.1 Using symbolic links to access global data

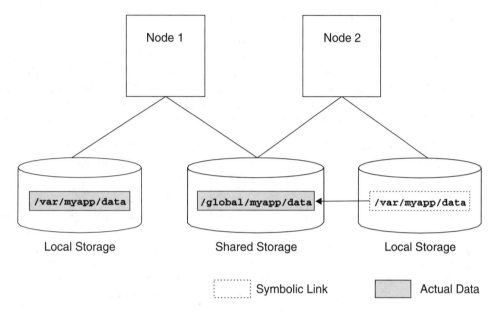

Figure 4.2 Symbolic links after directory recreation

there is only one copy of the software to manage and an upgrade is performed by scheduling downtime for that service as the installation occurs. This consideration comes down to operational preference, rather than any technical reasoning.

Absence of a Tie to Physical Identity of Node

Central to the understanding of Sun Cluster systems is the concept that a highly available IP address (otherwise known as a *logical host*) may operate on one of a number of physical computers at any time, and may in fact move to another computer under certain circumstances. For this reason it is important that applications be able to use the logical hostname rather than the physical name of the host on which it is running. In short, the question to ask yourself is: Can the application provide its service using a hostname that is not the physical hostname of the node?

If an application's configuration is dependent upon the physical hostname, then it almost certainly cannot be made highly available, since failing the application over to a node with a different physical hostname would render it inoperable.

If a program binds its network connection to the special address INADDR_ANY— a wildcard term that means the application will bind to all available IP addresses on the node simultaneously (see in(3HEAD))—then this usually satisfies the requirement.

Ability to Work on Multi-Homed Hosts

A multi-homed host is a host that is connected to more than one public network. Each node may have multiple interfaces, allowing the cluster and its data services to appear on more than one network and also allowing for hardware redundancy. An application should not assume that it must bind itself to the first network interface it can find because this may not be the correct one. In short, the question to ask is: Can the application cope with a host that has more than one network interface?

A data service that binds to a host's IP address must be flexible enough to bind to any and all of the IP addresses specified by its related logical host resource. The simplest way to do this is to have the application bind to INADDR_ANY (most modern network applications do).

In some circumstances, however, this approach is not desirable. Consider the case where two data services provide some service on different IP addresses but on the same IP port. If at some point both services are mastered by the same physical node, having either service bind to *all* IP addresses would mean the other could not bind to that address and the service will fail. In this case, or in the case where binding to INADDR_ANY is not possible, the application must have some configuration option to specify which IP address or port to bind to.

Ability to Work with Logical Interfaces

In some instances, a cluster node may control more logical hosts (and therefore IP addresses) than it has physical network interfaces. To cope with this, the network interfaces are assigned more than one IP address, a technique sometimes called IP aliasing. IP addresses are dynamically added to and removed from physical hosts as they master the logical hosts, by adding *logical interfaces* to the physical network interfaces already on the node. Logical network interfaces are labelled the same as physical interfaces, but with an additional number part, for example:

hme1, qfe3	physical interfaces
hme1:1, qfe3:2	logical interfaces

The data service should be able to deal with a given physical interface having more than one IP address. Again, INADDR_ANY usually makes this an easy task, but occasionally an application will try to manipulate network traffic in particular ways that make it unable to manage more than one IP address per interface. In particular, an application may not recognize the logical portion of an interface (for example, :1), and incorrectly perform operations on the physical interface instead (for example, hme1). In these cases, it may not be possible to make the application highly available. In short, the question to ask is: Can the application cope with more than one IP address on a single network interface?

Client Recovery

As indicated in the previous discussion of the data service access, the most effective HA data services include some capacity in the client to automatically retry a query when the first one is cut off or times out. If an automated retry facility is not feasible, then the end user at least has to be comfortable with the concept of manually retrying a query, such as when an HTTP query from a WWW browser fails.

Requirements for Scalable Services

If you want to make your application into a scalable service (that is, a service that operates on multiple nodes at the same time), you will have to consider a number of additional requirements. We'll leave these until we investigate scalable services in detail in Chapter 11, "Writing Scalable Services."

Getting Around Requirements

For the most part, the requirements for applications to be made highly available are already handled in well-written Solaris applications. Unfortunately, however, there are many applications, especially those ported from other platforms or created by niche developers, that are not well written. They make so many assumptions about the environment in which they will run that they cannot be easily made into highly available data services. This problem is compounded when there is no access to the source code of the application and the creator is unwilling (or unable) to make fixes.

Nevertheless, these applications are frequently a vital piece of an enterprise IT environment, and so must be made highly available somehow. In some instances, it may be possible to circumvent the restrictions and create a Sun Cluster data service, although these work-arounds can often be complicated. Here are some approaches you may need to try to work around problem applications:

- Use the LD_PRELOAD environment variable to cause the runtime linker to insert custom replacements for functions called by application.[1] This is particularly useful for changing the behavior of standard function calls that result in the application getting the wrong information. One good example would be to use LD_PRELOAD to define a different version of gethostname(3c), so that it returns the current *logical* hostname, rather than the *physical* hostname of the node.

- Use symbolic links to redirect file paths for data and/or configuration information, but keep in mind the risks of having the links replaced (see "File Location Independence" earlier in this chapter).

- Redirect startup input data from stored files, but be careful of security implications of storing passwords or similar data.

---

1. This is a relatively advanced subject, and the best place to find out more about LD_PRELOAD is the Solaris *Linker and Libraries Guide* at http://docs.sun.com.

You should also remember that it is not strictly necessary for a data service to operate over an IP network for it to be made highly available, despite the apparent emphasis on this in the preceding rules. An IP network connection is the most common way to access services on a Sun Cluster system, but it is quite possible to make other kinds of applications highly available.

Determining Scope

Once you have determined that your application can be made highly available using Sun Cluster, you should consider the scope of the project you want to attempt. The scope can vary widely depending on the requirements of your particular situation, and it can obviously affect the amount of time it will take to develop the agent and have the data service running successfully in the cluster.

The chief topics to consider when determining scope are:

* Cluster awareness
* Simple failover or scalable
* Fault recovery
* Complex monitoring
* Enterprise architecture considerations

Cluster Awareness

Most applications that are made highly available in a Sun Cluster framework have no internal knowledge of the cluster framework or even if they are running in a cluster. For these applications, the agent consists of wrapper programs used by the cluster to control the starting and stopping of the application. The in-memory state of the application is unlikely to be communicated between cluster nodes or maintained across failovers to different nodes.

This sort of application could be termed *cluster compatible*, since they can run in the cluster environment (having satisfied the qualification requirements discussed earlier in this chapter), but they don't change their internal behavior. They are often reasonably easy to integrate into the Sun Cluster framework.

At the other end of the scale are *cluster-aware* applications. These applications actually communicate directly with the Sun Cluster framework and change their internal behavior based on the cluster state. Furthermore, these applications may run instances simultaneously on multiple nodes of the cluster and communicate among those instances to maintain in-memory state even in the event of a node failure. One example of this sort of application is the Oracle 9i Real Application Clusters (RAC) database server. It should be fairly obvious that this sort of application is usually quite complex and requires more complex handling to integrate it into the Sun Cluster environment.

For most projects, the application will be cluster compatible, but if you decide to make one of your own applications cluster aware, you should allow more time for the development effort. Cluster-aware applications are discussed in more detail in Chapter 13, "Developing Cluster-Aware Applications."

Failover or Scalable

The Sun Cluster 3 environment allows for two types of data service: *failover* and *scalable*. A failover service runs on one node in the cluster at any given time and if that node crashes the application will start on a different node. To clients of the failover service, the restart will appear as if the server rebooted very quickly, but there will still be some delay (however small) between when the service stops on the first node and restarts on the second node.

By contrast, a scalable service takes advantage of the global file service (GFS) and shared IP addresses to run an application on multiple nodes at the same time, providing extra processing power through horizontal scaling and load balancing. A scalable service can also provide much better availability than a normal failover service because even if one node fails the other nodes are still running the service and can often accept new connections immediately.

In general, if you can make your application into a scalable service, you can more fully exploit the capabilities of the Sun Cluster 3 system. However, failover services more easily fit a wider range of applications without resorting to application code changes.

Scalable services are covered in more detail in Chapter 11, "Writing Scalable Services."

Fault Recovery

When planning the scope of your data service project, you should consider the process of fault recovery, particularly when a cluster node fails.

If client applications do not retry connections to a failed service, then downtime can be extended beyond what is required by the cluster because end users will have to manually detect and recover from the failure. This should be identified during the initial phase of agent development, since it may affect the entire scope of the project.

If an application to be made highly available is itself dependent on the availability of some other service (for example, a database), then this must also be taken into account. In some cases, supporting programs must be developed to check for the availability of the service before the application is started. There may also be special requirements on the fault monitoring programs to take action (such as restarting the application) if the required service is itself failed over.

Complex Monitoring

Fault monitoring and the associated application management can be the most complex part of the entire agent design and development process. While there are usually only very few ways to start and stop an application, there are often countless ways to monitor its behavior or remedial action if required. Questions that you should ask when determining the scope of fault monitoring include:

- Should we only check for node failure?
- Should we check if the application has crashed?
- Should we check if the application has hung?
- Should we check if the application provides incorrect data?
- How frequently should we check?
- How many retries should we allow before taking action?
- How do we detect failures outside the cluster environment?

This is where previous knowledge of an application is extremely useful, if not vital. It is also the area where the scope of the project can balloon enormously.

Enterprise Architecture

No cluster system exists in isolation, and external elements in your IT infrastructure may affect service availability, which would render pointless any work to make the application available. Before starting work on a data service agent, you should investigate your IT infrastructure to check that there are as few single points of failure as possible, including network access, power, and so forth. You should also consider software components in your infrastructure: for example, investigating whether using a transaction processing monitor (TP monitor) would assist in speeding client recovery times.

Gathering Application Information

Once you have determined that an application suits the cluster environment, and have determined exactly what the scope of the project will be, the next step is to gather information about the application so that you can start to build the associated resource type. At the most fundamental level, this means you will need to determine exactly how to start, stop, and monitor the application automatically.

Start

Determining how to start the application is the most important part of developing an agent, since it is the only part of the process that the cluster framework cannot handle by itself. You should keep in mind that starting an application doesn't just mean knowing the path to the program, but often includes a number of other components, for example:

- Command-line arguments
- Configuration files
- Environment variables
- User
- Timeout

If there is a chance of multiple instances of an application running on the same cluster, it is particularly important to pay attention to the command-line arguments and configuration files that must be used to differentiate between these instances. These variable items might then be turned into extension properties of the final resource type (see Chapter 6), so that an administrator can control these aspects of the application when configuring the cluster.

In some cases it may be necessary to write a wrapper script to start an application with the correct set of configuration variables, and this is especially true if an application must be started as a particular user other than "root." For Solaris applications that normally start at boot time, there may already be an appropriate script in the /etc/init.d directory that you can use directly or modify slightly to have the required effect. Remember that if you add an application to the cluster that is normally started at boot time, you should remove the original start and stop script(s) from the /etc/rc?.d directories.

The amount of time taken for your application to start is also important. By default, the cluster framework will wait 300 seconds (five minutes) for the application to start up before sending the first probe to check that everything is okay. If your application takes longer than this to start, then you will have to change this delay when creating the agent.

Finally, you should make a note of anything that your application depends upon, including the presence of particular data or filesystems, networks, or other applications. It may be that in order to make one application highly available, others will need to be made highly available as well. If your application depends on another, you can add to the startup code for your agent check for the availability of that service. You should also document this dependency so that administrators can configure the cluster framework appropriately so that applications start in the correct order.

Most applications start after the network has started, but in some cases it may be important to start (or partially start) applications before the network has been configured. As we will see later in the book, the cluster framework allows us to run actions before and after the network has been started, so it is important to make a note of what your application expects to happen and when.

Stop

Stopping your application correctly is important to ensure data integrity when the service is failed over to another node. Not every failover occurs as a result of a system crash, so knowing how to stop gracefully is a vital part of the agent software.

In many cases, it is possible to safely stop an application simply by sending a TERM signal to the running process. In fact if you do not specify a particular program to stop your application, the cluster framework will do this by default. However, if there is a program supplied with your application that can gracefully stop it, then it should be used.

As with starting an application, there are other factors to consider than just the command name, including:

- Arguments, environment, and user
- Timeout
- Effects of kill(1)
- When to stop

The arguments, environment, and user factors are the same as for starting an application (see "Start" earlier in this chapter), and the timeout is similar. As with starting the application, stopping the application is by default given 300 seconds (five minutes) to be successful.

The effects of kill(1) on the application are important because if, when creating an agent using the SunPlex Agent Builder or Generic Data Service (GDS) tools[2] you don't supply a specific command to stop your application, the cluster framework will use kill(1) by default. About 80 percent of the timeout will be used to send the TERM signal, and about 15 percent to send the KILL signal. Even if you do provide a stop command (using one of the tools or not), the timeout value you supply will be used to decide how long the cluster framework will wait for an application to stop before deciding that something has gone wrong. As with the start timeout value, the default stop timeout is 300 seconds.

You should also consider whether the application should be stopped before or after the public network connection is removed. In most cases the application will be stopped before the network connection, but there may be times when you want to be sure that the network has been removed before stopping the application. However, this would normally be the case only when your application doesn't use the network directly.

Monitor

Understanding how an application works is key to integrating it into the cluster environment. Once you have worked out how an application will behave under vari-

---

2. See "Choosing a Tool" later in this chapter.

ous conditions, you can create a monitor program that will check for these conditions and return appropriate values to the cluster framework, which in turn are used to decide what actions if any should be taken by the cluster.

By default, no monitoring is done by the cluster framework. However, if you use one of the provided tools[3] to create a *network-aware* resource type, a simple service probe is automatically provided. This probe just attempts to connect to the service's IP address and port, and if successful assumes that the application is operating correctly. Obviously, most applications require more complex monitoring than this, and Sun Cluster allows you to create very sophisticated monitoring applications to return different fault and failure modes to the cluster framework.

When you create a monitor program, you are in effect creating a type of expert system, in which a piece of software performs the tasks that might otherwise need to be done by a human operator. For this reason, detailed analysis of the application flow and possible failure modes will aid in the development of your resource type.

One way of tracking what your monitor program must do to check that your application is running correctly is to use a flowchart like that shown in Figure 4.3. In this example, we start by having the monitor program request a known piece of information from the application. If the request times out without any response, then the monitor program will check to see if the cluster framework is controlling the application properly, and take appropriate actions. If the request for data is successful, then the monitor program will compare the response from the application to what it expects the response to be: If they are the same, then the monitor will assume that everything is okay, and will go to sleep for a while before starting the whole process again. If the data received from the application is not what the monitor program expected, then it will check to see if *any* data was received and take appropriate action, which may be to send a warning to human operators or to restart or even fail over the application.

As you can see, it is very important to understand how your application behaves before you can write a successful monitoring program. In some cases, the application you are trying to make highly available may already have a program you can use to check the status. In such situations, you simply need to ensure that the program will return zero if the application is okay, and 1 (or nonzero) if there is a problem. In other cases, you may require quite complex programming to assess the state of the application and decide what action to take, particularly if you want to take very specific actions when certain events (such as network failures, for example) occur. The Sun Cluster APIs provide the tools to retrieve a lot of information about the cluster environment itself, but it is your understanding of the application that will determine how successful your monitor program will be.

As with starting and stopping an application, running the monitor program may require specific command-line arguments and environment variables, need a

---

3. Either the SunPlex Agent Builder or the GDS.

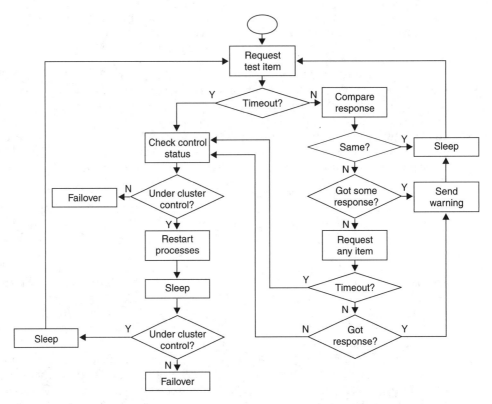

Figure 4.3 Application monitoring flowchart

particular user ID, and require a certain amount of time to run. These factors need to be documented so that you can integrate them into your resource type.

Choosing a Tool

Once you have gathered all of the information you need about the application, and if necessary created the wrapper scripts to start, stop, or monitor the application, you need to decide what tools to use to build the resource type itself. There are essentially three options:

- Generic Data Service
- SunPlex Agent Builder
- Develop source by hand

The one you choose will be dictated by the circumstances and requirements of the application as well as your own abilities and time constraints.

Generic Data Service

The GDS was introduced in Chapter 3, "Getting Started." It is essentially a prebuilt resource type that can be customized at deployment time to suit any network-aware application. In most cases it should only be used for relatively simple applications, since it cannot be heavily customized.

In particular, the monitoring probe command must simply return an integer from zero for success to 100 for complete failure (a special value of 201 will cause a request for immediate failover to another node; see the man page for SUNW.gds(5) for details).

As we saw in Chapter 3, creating an agent using GDS simply involves creating a resource of type SUNW.gds, and assigning values to the properties:

```
START_COMMAND
STOP_COMMAND
PROBE_COMMAND
PORT_LIST
```

Resources and resource properties are discussed in more detail in Chapter 6, "Understanding the RGM."

When choosing a tool, it's worth considering that the GDS also generally has a more streamlined support model from Sun Microsystems because the programs that make up the GDS are part of the supported Sun Cluster packages.

SunPlex Agent Builder

The SunPlex Agent Builder is a tool that can be used either from the command line or with a GUI to generate source code and build a Solaris package with your resource type. Since the tool generates source code, it is possible to use the Agent Builder to provide a template for further customizing. In particular, the builder generates the resource type registration (RTR) file,[4] which can be a complex undertaking by hand.

We'll be looking at the SunPlex Agent Builder in more detail in Chapter 5, "Developing with the SunPlex Agent Builder."

Source from Scratch

If absolutely necessary, it is possible to write the code for your resource type completely from scratch, although this drastic approach is usually only really useful for cluster-aware applications.

---

4. The RTR file is discussed in Chapter 6.

In particular, if you decide to code from scratch, quite a few fairly repetitive functions must be coded, and the RTR file must be constructed by hand. Although this is not impossible, it can be time consuming and the combination of required, optional, defined, and undefined properties can become confusing. For this reason it's usually worthwhile to use the SunPlex Agent Builder to create a basic template, so that all of the required components are in place.

Choosing a Language

The program that makes up a resource type can use any programming language, but two in particular are more usable—C and the Korn shell (ksh).

C

The C programming language is a useful choice for developing resource type programs, since the programs themselves can be compiled and checked for errors before actually running them, which avoids the possibility of syntax errors causing problems on a live cluster.

Furthermore, there is a range of libraries available with the Sun Cluster environment that can be accessed with C, and the Data Service Development Library (DSDL) in particular can only be accessed from C (see Chapter 9, "Using the DSDL").

Additionally, when using a compiled language like C it is possible to distribute a binary-only version of your agent. This may be important if you need to retain the intellectual property or if you want to be sure that the end user of the agent cannot change the code.

When writing an agent using C, it's important to use the correct libraries and header files. The exact paths will vary depending on whether you are using the DSDL or the basic resource management API (RMAPI). The chapters describing these facilities (Chapters 7 and 9) explain how to find and specify the correct paths to libraries and headers.

Korn Shell

Although the Sun Cluster environment provides API-like commands that can be accessed from any shell (including Bourne shell, bash, tcsh, and so forth), the SunPlex Agent Builder provides a way to automatically generate Korn shell (ksh) programs.

Shell programs are useful for prototyping a resource type, since they are easy to edit and modify, even on live cluster systems. In addition, it is not necessary to install a compiler to use shell programs.

On the other hand, agents developed with shell programs must be shipped to end users with readable source code (the scripts themselves), so if retaining intellectual property is a concern, or if you don't want users to be able to change the scripts, you should use C instead.

Others

There's nothing stopping you from using another programming or scripting language to develop the programs used by your agents. In particular, you may want to use C++ instead of C or you may prefer a full-featured scripting language like Perl instead of ksh. If you do choose to use a different language, however, you must find your own way of accessing information about the cluster because there are, for example, no native C++ libraries or Perl modules provided at the time of writing.

Summary

We've seen in this chapter that, as with any development project, you need to do a little planning before creating an agent. In particular, you must understand the capabilities of the application in question, since it may not be possible to make an application highly available if it has particular characteristics. Furthermore, defining the scope of your project—what the agent will and will not do—will help set realistic expectations when the system is put into production.

You should also understand how an application works: how it is started and stopped, and how it can be monitored without manual intervention. It's important to realize that understanding how an application operates is the most crucial part of integrating it into the cluster framework.

In this chapter we also looked briefly at the various tools available to you for developing agents. We'll look more closely at one of them in the next chapter, "Developing with the SunPlex Agent Builder."

5

DEVELOPING WITH THE SUNPLEX AGENT BUILDER

In Chapter 3, "Getting Started," we went through the steps needed to make an application highly available without doing any coding work. All that was required was the cluster system administrator to type a few commands to create an instance of the Generic Data Service (GDS) configured to manage the application in the cluster environment. It became apparent toward the end, however, that there was quite a lot of typing involved in this approach. This may be fine if the application is deployed only once on a single cluster, but it could become cumbersome if deployed in multiple clusters or if you have several applications.

Fortunately, the Sun Cluster software includes a tool called the SunPlex Agent Builder. It can be used either via the command line or through a point-and-click GUI to quickly and easily create resource type packages that can be simply added to a cluster system, reducing the installation and configuration process to a single command.

The Agent Builder is also invaluable for creating more specialized resource types than are possible using the GDS because it can be used to generate programs using C or Korn shell source code. These in turn can be further refined to suit the application.

As with our earlier chapter, we will explore the use of the Agent Builder by following a step-by-step example of creating an agent for the Apache Web server[1]—by first creating an agent made up of GDS driving scripts, and then recreating the agent

---

1. Refer to "Preparing the Cluster" in Chapter 3 to see how to set up Apache to be used in the cluster.

with `ksh` scripts. So, let's begin with the installation of the Agent Builder software itself.

Installing the SunPlex Agent Builder

The packages for the SunPlex Agent Builder are installed by default as part of the normal Sun Cluster 3 installation, but it is often impractical to develop agent software on the actual cluster nodes. For this reason, it is possible to install the required software on a stand-alone SPARC system running Solaris 8 or later. The only package needed is SUNWscdev, which includes both development tools and libraries, but it is a good idea to install the SUNWscman package as well, so that you have easy access to the online manual pages relevant to the Sun Cluster 3.

There is no option in the `scinstall(1m)` utility on the Sun Cluster 3 installation CD to install only these two packages (SUNWscdev and SUNWscman) on a system, so the installation must be done manually, usually as root, using the `pkgadd(1m)` command. The files are installed under the `/usr/cluster` directory; for convenience `/usr/cluster/bin` should be added to your executable search path and `/usr/cluster/man` should be added to your online manual search path. If you use the Bourne shell (`/bin/sh`), Korn shell (`/bin/ksh`), or Bourne-Again Shell (`/usr/bin/bash`) you can achieve this with:

```
$ PATH=/usr/cluster/bin:${PATH} ; export PATH
$ MANPATH=/usr/cluster/man:${MANPATH} ; export MANPATH
```

for the C shell or derivatives, use:

```
% setenv PATH /usr/cluster/bin:$PATH
% setenv MANPATH /usr/cluster/man:$MANPATH
```

You will also need the `make(1)` utility installed, which is found in the SUNWsprot package shipped as part of Solaris. If you plan to use C to develop your agent, you will need to install a C compiler, and add the "cc" program to your executable search path.

Preparing Apache and the Cluster

In the example in this chapter, we will use the same configuration as was described in the section "Preparing the Cluster" in Chapter 3. If you have been following along with the examples, you will need to remove the example agent that you created then. Example 5.1 shows how to do this.

Example 5.1 Removing the previous example agent

```
# scswitch -F -g webserver-rg
# scswitch -n -j webserver-res
# scswitch -n -j webhost
# scrgadm -r -j webserver-res
# scrgadm -r -j webhost
# scrgadm -r -g webserver-rg
```

Review Configuration

The file paths, hosts, and other parameters we will be using in the examples in this chapter will be the same as those used in Chapter 3. The parameters are summarized in Table 5.1.

Using the Agent Builder GUI

The Agent Builder can be used in command-line mode or with a GUI. To start the GUI,[2] open a terminal window and enter the following:

/usr/cluster/bin/scdsbuilder

The GUI is actually a front-end to a suite of resource type development tools, so there are command-line equivalents to the actions you perform using the GUI. We'll discuss the command-line interface (CLI) programs later.

Creating a Resource Type

Building an agent comprises two main steps: creating the resource type and then configuring it. Following this model, the Agent Builder GUI consists of two pages with forms to enter the data. The first page, for creating the resource type, is shown in Figure 5.1.

Table 5.1 Configuration Summary

Start command:	/web/apachectl start
IP address:	10.3.2.1
Logical hostname:	webhost
TCP/IP port:	80

---

2. The Agent Builder GUI is actually a Java program, so your screen color depth must be 8- or 24-bit; 16-bit screens don't work.

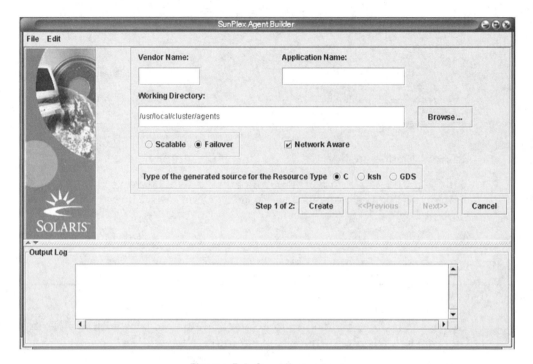

Figure 5.1 Creation page

Vendor and Application Name

Since the Agent Builder creates installable packages, we need to come up with a
package name for our new resource type. Unfortunately, package names are limited
to nine characters,[3] which doesn't give us much to play with. The practice suggested
by Sun for naming packages is to use your company's stock ticker symbol as the
Vendor part of the package name, and then something descriptive for the rest of the
string. In our example we'll use DEMO as the Vendor string and haaws (highly available Apache Web server) for the rest. These two values need to be entered into the
Vendor and Application fields on the first page (Figure 5.2).

Working Directory

The next field on the form is the Working Directory, which should already be filled out
with the directory you were in when you started the Agent Builder. This is the directory where the resource type will be created, and you can change it by typing in the
full path or by simply using the Browse button to choose (or create) a different directory (Figure 5.3).

---

3. Even though Solaris 9 supports 32 characters for package names, the Agent Builder still
only allows nine characters for compatibility with Solaris 8.

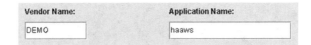

Figure 5.2 Vendor and Application name fields

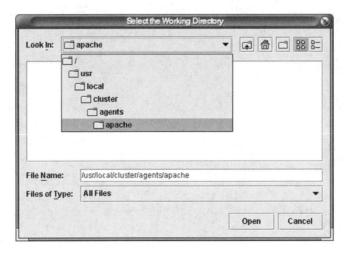

Figure 5.3 Working directory browse dialog

Since the installable package is created under the working directory, it may be convenient to choose someplace that all of the cluster nodes can easily access; for example, a global filesystem or an NFS shared directory (if you are running the Agent Builder on a workstation outside the cluster).

Failover or Scalable

The next step is to choose whether the new resource type will be a scalable resource (for applications that run on multiple nodes simultaneously) or a failover resource (for applications that run on only one node at a time). For this example, we'll only run our Web server on one node at a time, so we'll choose Failover (Figure 5.4).

Network Awareness

We also need the Network Aware checkbox to be on, since the Apache Web server accepts connections from the public network (the LAN) (Figure 5.5). If we were creating a highly available service that did not accept connections via the network (for example, if it accepted connections via UNIX sockets from local applications), then this would be left off. Most Sun Cluster data services, however, are network aware. Checking this box indicates to the Agent Builder that it should use its built-in application probe mechanism if no customer probe program is specified (see "Probe Command" later in this chapter).

Figure 5.4 Scalable or Failover selector

Figure 5.5 Network Aware checkbox

Source Code Language

Next, we must choose which language the resource type code should be written in: the three choices are C, Korn shell (ksh) or the GDS. In this example we are using GDS (Figure 5.6).

The other two options, C and ksh, will be investigated later in this chapter. Note that when we select GDS as the language, the Network Aware option checks on and grays out, since the GDS is predefined to be network aware.

Running the Creation Command

Once all of the fields on the first page have been filled in, we can create the agent by pressing the Create button (Figure 5.7).

Messages will appear in the Output Log window at the bottom of the page, and once the process is complete, an alert box will appear announcing success (Figure 5.8).

The alert box can be cleared by clicking on the OK button, and you should see that the Next>> button on the page has become active (Figure 5.9). Click on this button to proceed to the second page to configure the agent.

Configuring the Resource Type

The second page (Figure 5.10) is where we configure the actual commands used to start, stop, and monitor the application. Only the Start command is actually required—if nothing is entered into the fields for Stop and Probe, the cluster framework will use default mechanisms to achieve these actions. As with the previous page, we can type in the commands directly, or use the Browse button to search for the appropriate commands through the GUI.

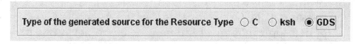

Figure 5.6 Code-generation selector

Figure 5.7 Create button

Figure 5.8 Creation successful message

Figure 5.9 Next>> button active

Start Command

In our example, we will use the apachectl[4] program supplied as part of the Apache Web server to start the application (see Figure 5.11).

Note that as well as the actual program name, we have included the command-line options needed to start the application with the correct parameters.

The Start Timeout field is the amount of time in seconds that the Sun Cluster 3 framework will wait for the application to start after it runs the Start command. If the application does not start in this period, the cluster will assume there is an error, and try to fail the application over to another node. In our example, we'll leave the timeout at the default 300 seconds.

Stop Command

If we don't supply a Stop command for our resource type, the cluster framework will try to stop the application by sending TERM and KILL signals. Since the apachectl program can also stop the Web server, we will use this tool instead (see Figure 5.12).

As with the Start command, there is a timeout value for the Stop command, although it works a little differently. If the application is still running after 80 percent of the Stop Timeout has elapsed, the cluster will assume that this "gentle" stopping has been unsuccessful, and will allocate 15 percent of the time to kill the application by sending KILL signals to the process(es). The remaining 5 percent of

---

4. See "Preparing the Apache Web Server" in Chapter 3 for how to set up this script.

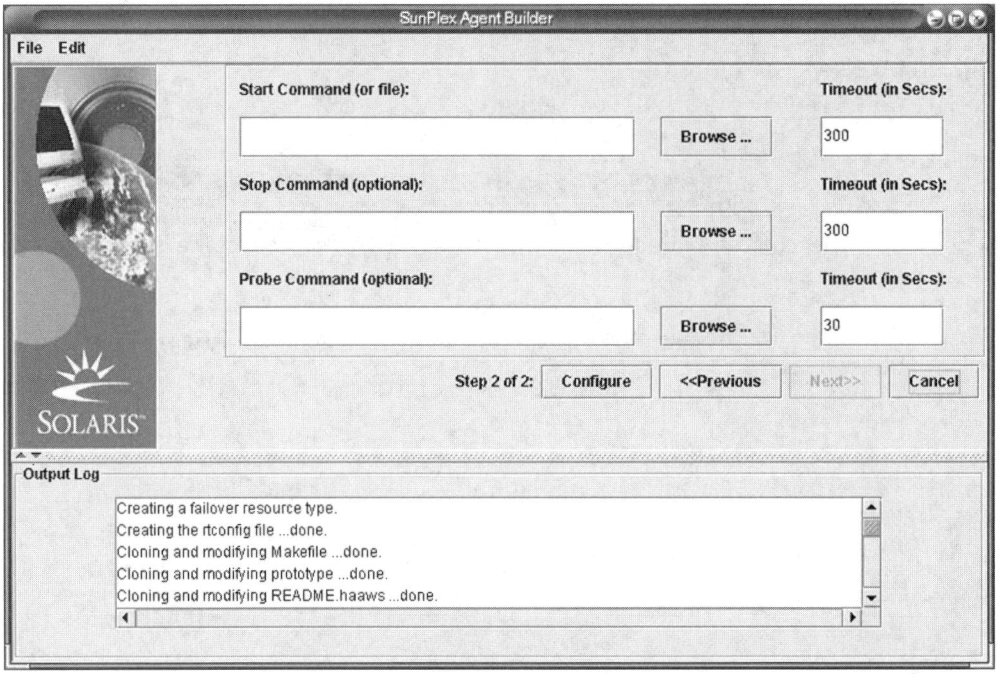

Figure 5.10 Configuration page

Figure 5.11 Start Command field

Figure 5.12 Stop Command field

the timeout is assumed to be overhead. In our example, we will keep the default 300 seconds for the Stop Timeout.

Probe Command

The Probe command is an optional program used to check whether the application is running properly. The command will be automatically run by the cluster framework on a regular basis, and the exit value will be checked. If the program returns a zero, then the cluster framework assumes that the application is running correctly; whereas if the program returns a nonzero value, then the cluster framework will take some action on the application, such as stopping and restarting it, or by failing over to another node.

There is also a Probe Timeout, which is the amount of time the cluster framework will wait after running the probe command before deciding that there will be no response from the application. If a probe times out, then it is treated as a failure, and the cluster framework will reconfigure to try to make the application start again.

In our example we will leave the Probe Command field empty, since there is no program bundled with Apache that can easily return the status of the Web server in the required format (see Figure 5.13). Leaving this empty doesn't mean no probing is done at all—the SunPlex Agent Builder includes a very basic utility called `simple_probe` to check whether TCP network-aware programs are operating.[5] This program connects to the TCP port used by the application (see `port_list` in "Creating and Starting a Resource" later in this chapter) and if it connects successfully, it assumes that everything is okay. Later on, we'll look at a more advanced probe that actually checks if the application is running correctly.

Running the Configuration Command

Once all of the fields have been completed to our satisfaction (remember that Stop and Probe are optional), we can press the Configure button (see Figure 5.14) to configure the resource type and create the installable packages. Again, messages will be sent to the Output Log (you may have to move the scroll bar to see them). Once the configuration is complete, an alert box will appear with a message to that effect (see Figure 5.15).

Figure 5.13 Empty Probe Command field

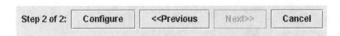

Figure 5.14 Configure button

---

5. UDP network services aren't connection oriented, so they can't respond in the same way as TCP services.

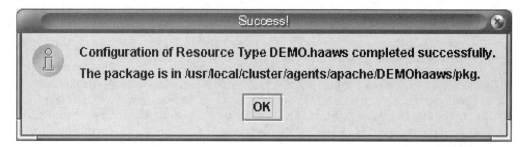

Figure 5.15 Configuration successful dialog

Note that the alert window reports the location of the installable package files. You can then use these files to install the agent onto the cluster.

Installing and Controlling the Agent

Once the SunPlex Agent Builder has been used to create and configure an agent, the package can be installed onto the cluster. Since our example uses the GDS, we need to be sure that this is installed on the cluster nodes before going any further:

```
# pkginfo SUNWscgds
application SUNWscgds        Sun Cluster Generic Data Service
```

If the SUNWscgds package is not already installed, use pkgadd(1m) to install it from your Sun Cluster installation disk.

The agent package is found in the pkg subdirectory of your working directory. This package should be transferred somehow to the cluster, and installed on *each node* that will host the application (use pkgadd(1m) - see ref). See Example 5.2. If the package is not installed on each node, then the verification program will not run properly, and the new resource type cannot be added to the cluster. By default, packages will be installed in /opt.

Example 5.2   Adding the agent package

```
# pkgadd -d DEMOhaaws/pkg/ DEMOhaaws
Processing package instance <DEMOhaaws> from </usr/local/cluster/agents/apache/
DEMOhaaws/pkg>
Sun Cluster resource type for haaws server
(sparc) 3.0.0,REV=
Sun Microsystems, Inc.
Using </opt> as the package base directory.
## Processing package information.
## Processing system information.
## Verifying package dependencies.
## Verifying disk space requirements.
```

```
## Checking for conflicts with packages already installed.
## Checking for setuid/setgid programs.

Installing Sun Cluster resource type for haaws server as <DEMOhaaws>
## Installing part 1 of 1.
/opt/DEMOhaaws/README.haaws
/opt/DEMOhaaws/man/man1m/haaws_config.1m
/opt/DEMOhaaws/man/man1m/removehaaws.1m
/opt/DEMOhaaws/man/man1m/starthaaws.1m
/opt/DEMOhaaws/man/man1m/stophaaws.1m
/opt/DEMOhaaws/util/haaws_config
/opt/DEMOhaaws/util/removehaaws
/opt/DEMOhaaws/util/starthaaws
/opt/DEMOhaaws/util/stophaaws
[ verifying class <none> ]

Installation of <DEMOhaaws> was successful.
```

Creating and Starting a Resource

Once the package has been installed on each node, and the application loaded onto the system as well, the resource type can be quickly and easily added to the cluster, and the data service started, by using the start script (see Example 5.3).

Example 5.3   Starting the resource

```
# /opt/DEMOhaaws/util/starthaaws -h webhost -p 80/tcp
No nafo groups or network adapters specified ... will try to auto-discover the
network adapters and configure them into nafo groups.
Creating a fail over instance ...
Registering resource type <SUNW.gds>...done.
Creating fail over resource group <haaws-harg>...done.
Creating logical host resource <webhost>...done.
Creating resource <haaws-hars> for the resource type <SUNW.gds>...done.
Bringing resource group <haaws-harg> online...done.
```

Once the start script has completed successfully, the highly available service should be running on the primary node (the node that the script was run on).

Note – In Sun Cluster 3.1, starting the resource using the script may fail, as shown below:

```
# /opt/DEMOhaaws/util/starthaaws -h webhost -p 80/tcp
No nafo groups or network adapters specified ... will try to
auto-discover the network adapters and configure them into nafo
groups.
Creating a fail over instance ...
Registering resource type <SUNW.gds>...gds: resource type exists;
cannot create
FAILED: scrgadm -a -t SUNW.gds
```

This error has to do with the resource type versioning framework introduced in Sun Cluster 3.1—the cluster identifies the SUNW.gds resource type as SUNW.gds:3.1, but the script refers to SUNW.gds. This can be quickly fixed by running:

```
# perl -pi -e 's/SUNW.gds$/SUNW.gds:3.1/' \
/opt/DEMOhaaws/util/starthaaws
```

on each node, and then running the starthaaws script again. This problem should be fixed in a Sun Cluster 3.1 update.

Stopping and Removing a Resource

Stopping the data service can be easily achieved by running the related stop script as shown below:

```
# /opt/DEMOhaaws/util/stophaaws -h webhost
Disabling resource <haaws-hars> ...done.
Disabling the network resource <webhost> ...done.
Offlining resource group <haaws-harg> on all nodes ...done.
```

If this script completes successfully, the data service will have stopped running on any node in the cluster.

Finally, if you want to remove the data service completely from the cluster, you can use the supplied remove script, as shown below:

```
# /DEMOhaaws/util/removehaaws -h webhost
Disabling the resource <haaws-hars> ...done.
Removing the resource <haaws-hars> ...done.
Resource type <SUNW.gds> has been un-registered already
Disabling the resource <webhost> ...done.
Removing the resource <webhost> ...done.
Offlining the resource group <haaws-harg> ...done.
Unmanaging the resource group <haaws-harg> ...done.
Removing the resource group <haaws-harg> ...done.
```

Naturally, the normal Sun Cluster administrative commands, as well as the Sun-Plex Manager GUI, can be used to control the behavior of your new agents, just like any prepackaged agents you may already be using. The start, stop, and remove scripts merely combine all of the required commands and arguments into simple scripts for quick deployment.

Generating C or ksh Source with the GUI

Although the GDS provides a quick and easy way to make applications highly available, it does have limitations in terms of flexibility and application control. There may be times when it's preferable to create a completely new resource type using C programs or Korn shell scripts. As we've seen, the SunPlex Agent Builder offers

Figure 5.16 C source option not available

these languages as alternatives to the GDS by a simple mouse click: Merely select the radio button next to ksh or C as the type of generated source for the resource type.

Note that if either ksh or GDS is selected as the source code language, the Network Aware box is automatically checked on and grayed out so that it cannot be changed.

If there is no C compiler "cc" command in your command execution search path, then this option is grayed out and the network-aware option is fixed on. In this case, you can only choose ksh or GDS as the generated source (see Figure 5.16). The exact command "cc" must be matched, so if you are using the GNU C compiler, gcc, you must create a link or symbolic link to the gcc executable with the name "cc," and ensure that it is in your PATH before starting the scdsbuilder program again.

Using the Command-Line Tools

The SunPlex Agent Builder GUI makes creating new resource types quick and easy, as well as providing a user-friendly interface with which to work. Sometimes though, such as when administering remote systems, it is more convenient to use command-line tools rather than a GUI, so that an equivalent command-line interface is available.

The CLI to the SunPlex Agent Builder consists of two commands: scdscreate (1HA) and scdsconfig(1HA). In fact, these are the commands that are used by the Agent Builder GUI to create and configure the resource type—if you look at the output log of the GUI, you will see the same output is produced by the command-line tools.

Creating a Resource Type

The command scdscreate(1HA) establishes the template framework of directories, source code, and configuration files used as the basis of all resource types. The full range of command-line parameters and options is as follows:

```
scdscreate -V Vendor_ID -T resource_type_name [ -a ]
           [ -s ] [ -d install_directory ] [ -k | -g ]
```

The *Vendor_ID* and *resource_type_name* are used to generate the package name for the resource type, and also as the identifier for the resource type in the cluster. For example, specifying `sdscreate -V DEMO -T haaws` would result in a package `DEMO-haaws`, and the resource type would be identified in the cluster as `DEMO.haaws`. *Vendor_ID* corresponds to the Vendor Name field in the GUI, while *resource_type_name* corresponds to the Application Name field (see Figure 5.2). As mentioned previously, no more than nine (9) characters can be used in total for these values, since they are concatenated to create the abbreviated package name and nine is the maximum number of characters for an abbreviated package name in Solaris 8 (see the man page for `pkginfo(4)`).

If you do not specify a directory with the `'-d'` option, the source code and configuration files will be built in a directory named for the resource type package in the current working directory. For example, if your current working directory is `/var/tmp/dsdevelop` and you issue the command:

scdscreate -V DEMO -T thing

then all of the source files will be created under the directory `/var/tmp/dsdevelop/DEMOthing`. In addition, a configuration file `/var/tmp/dsdevelop/rtconfig` will be created containing configuration information for the Agent Builder. You can specify an alternate directory as the top level (called the install directory) by providing a fully qualified path with the `'-d'` option. For example:

scdscreate -V DEMO -T thing -d /var/tmp/mydirectory

will result in the source files being created under the directory `/var/tmp/mydirectory/DEMOthing`—as long as the directory `/var/tmp/mydirectory` already exists. Relative paths such as `../stuff/` don't work with `'-d'`. This option corresponds to the Working Directory field in the GUI.

If you want to create a resource type that is to be a scalable service, the `'-s'` flag should be specified. Without this flag, the resource type will be configured as a failover resource type only. If you want to create a resource type that can be deployed as either scalable or failover, specify the `'-s'` flag, since scalable resources configured into failover resource groups will act as failover. This option corresponds to the Scalable and Failover radio buttons in the GUI.

Resource types for applications that are not network aware—that is, applications not providing a service in the usual client/server model—should specify the `'-a'` flag to disable the networking-related code and remove fault probing from the resource type. This corresponds to the Network Aware checkbox in the GUI. For most applications used in HA cluster environments, this option should not be used. It's also important to note that agents created using Korn shell or the GDS must be network aware—if you want to create an agent that is not network aware, you must use C source.[6]

---

6. This is true for Sun Cluster 3.0 release 5/02 and Sun Cluster 3.1 at the time of writing, but may change in the future. Check the release notes of your version to see if you are able to create network-aware agents without C.

Finally, with no further options the source code generated for the resource type will be C source. If you do not have a C compiler available, or if shell scripting is preferred, `'-k'` should be specified to generate the source code in Korn shell (ksh). If you want to generate a resource type based on the GDS, specify the `'-g'` flag instead. Not surprisingly, this option corresponds to the Type of the generated source for the Resource Type radio buttons in the GUI (see Figure 5.6).

Let's redo our Apache example agent using the command-line tools, this time using ksh as the source code. Since we're creating a new resource type, we will have to choose a new working directory—in our example we'll use /usr/local/cluster/agents/apache-ksh. The complete scdscreate command and its output are shown in Example 5.4.

Example 5.4 Creating the resource type

```
$ scdscreate -V DEMO -T haaws -d /usr/local/cluster/agents/apache-ksh -k
Creating a fail over resource type.
/usr/local/cluster/agents/apache-ksh does not exist.  Creating /usr/local/
cluster/agents/apache-ksh ...done.
Creating the rtconfig file ...done.
Cloning and modifying haaws_mon_check.ksh ...done.
Cloning and modifying haaws_mon_start.ksh ...done.
Cloning and modifying haaws_mon_stop.ksh ...done.
Cloning and modifying haaws_probe.ksh ...done.
Cloning and modifying haaws_svc_start.ksh ...done.
Cloning and modifying haaws_svc_stop.ksh ...done.
Cloning and modifying haaws_update.ksh ...done.
Cloning and modifying haaws_validate.ksh ...done.
Cloning and modifying gethostnames ...done.
Cloning and modifying gettime ...done.
Cloning and modifying hasp_check ...done.
Cloning and modifying Makefile ...done.
Cloning and modifying prototype ...done.
Cloning and modifying README.haaws ...done.
Cloning and modifying simple_probe ...done.
Cloning and modifying DEMO.haaws ...done.
Cloning and modifying depend ...done.
Cloning and modifying pkginfo ...done.
Cloning and modifying postinstall ...done.
Cloning and modifying postremove ...done.
Cloning and modifying preremove ...done.
Cloning and modifying removehaaws ...done.
Cloning and modifying removehaaws.1m ...done.
Cloning and modifying starthaaws ...done.
Cloning and modifying starthaaws.1m ...done.
Cloning and modifying stophaaws ...done.
Cloning and modifying stophaaws.1m ...done.
Cloning and modifying haaws_config ...done.
Cloning and modifying haaws_config.1m ...done.

Creating the utility script starthaaws ...done.
Creating the utility script removehaaws ...done.
Creating the utility script stophaaws ...done.
```

```
Creating the config file haaws_config ...done.
Creating the man page starthaaws.1m ...done.
Creating the man page removehaaws.1m ...done.
Creating the man page stophaaws.1m ...done.
Creating the man page haaws_config.1m ...done.
Creating the package file postremove ...done.
Creating the package file postinstall ...done.
Creating the package file preremove ...done.
Creating the RTR file DEMO.haaws ...done.
```

Running the `scdscreate` command will create and populate the following directories under `install_directory`:

`bin`	placeholder for the binaries
`etc`	RTR file (named *Vendor_ID.resource_type_name*), `pkgmk` files
`man`	placeholder for man pages
`pkg`	placeholder for package
`src`	source files (.c, .h, .ksh) and Makefile
`util`	convenience scripts for adding, starting, stopping, and removing the resource type

Configuring the Resource Type

Once the base source code and configuration files have been generated by using the
`scdscreate`(1HA) command, you can edit and build from the source without any
further configuration. However, to quickly configure the start, stop, and fault-
monitoring commands used by the resource type, the `scdsconfig`(1HA) command
should be used to create the initial configuration and build of the package. The
`scdsconfig` command-line parameters and options are:

```
scdsconfig -s start_command [ -u start_method_timeout ]
           [ -t stop_command ] [ -v stop_method_timeout ]
           [ -m probe_command ] [ -n probe_timeout ]
           [ -d install_directory ]
```

As with the `scdscreate`(1HA) command, unless a fully qualified directory path
is specified using the '`-d`' flag, `scsdconfig` will operate on the current working
directory. In the directory, the `rtconfig` file will be read to determine the package
name (and hence the source directory).

As with the GUI, the only mandatory parameter to `scdsconfig` is the command
used to start the application. This should be a fully qualified pathname to the normal start program or script, along with any parameters that would normally be
typed on the command line. The whole command should be enclosed in single quotes
(' ') if there are any spaces. Examples of valid `scdsconfig` commands with start
parameters are:

```
scdsconfig -s /usr/local/bin/myserver
scdsconfig -s '/usr/local/bin/myserver -c config_file'
scdsconfig -s '/usr/local/bin/myserver \
                -h '/bin/hostname''
```

Note the embedding of a command in the last example. This command (/bin/ hostname) will be executed each time the agent is started, just as if a human operator had typed:

/usr/local/bin/myserver -h '/bin/hostname'

at the command line.

The same pattern is followed for the optional *stop_command* and *probe_command* parameters. The *stop_command* is the program and parameters used to stop the application. If no *stop_command* is specified with scdsconfig, then the application is stopped by sending a terminate signal (SIGTERM) to the processes that were started as a result of starting the application. Since the SunPlex Agent Builder uses the Process Monitor Facility (PMF) to control the application, this is achieved by running pmfadm(1m) with the appropriate arguments. If your application does not stop when it receives a TERM signal, then the appropriate stop command should be supplied.

The *probe_command* is the program and parameters that should be used to check if the application is running correctly. As described in the GUI section, this program should return zero if the application is running correctly, or a nonzero value if the application is not running correctly. If you do not specify a *probe_command*, and if your new resource type is network aware, then the Agent Builder will use the simple_probe program (see "Probe Command" earlier in this chapter), which will attempt to connect to your application's network port. If the probe successfully connects, then it assumes that the application is okay. If your application is not network aware, then there is no default probe program. If you want to monitor such an application, you will have to supply your own probe.

Each of the start, stop, and probe commands also has a related timeout value, as described previously in the GUI section. To recap: The *start_method_timeout* specifies the time in seconds allocated for an application to start. Sufficient time should be allocated to ensure that the application is not falsely failed due to heavy system load or other events. The default value for *start_method_timeout* is 300 seconds. Likewise, the *stop_method_timeout* is the amount of time allocated to stop the application. Eighty percent of the time is allocated to the normal stop method, while 15 percent is allocated to trying to force the application to stop by sending a kill signal (SIGKILL). The remaining 5 percent is deemed to be overhead. The default value for *stop_method_timeout* is 300 seconds. The *probe_method_timeout* is the amount of time the fault probe program will run to determine the status of the application. By default the timeout value is 30 seconds.

Once the scdsconfig command has been run, the assigned or default values for the parameters are appended to the rtconfig file in the install directory. This will be used for future reference if the resource type source is reconfigured. Next, the base configuration and source files are updated with the new information, the binaries are built, and the install package is created.

The full `scdsconfig` command we would use to configure our Apache agent from the command line is shown in Example 5.5.

Example 5.5   Configuring the resource type

```
$ scdsconfig -d /usr/local/cluster/agents/apache-ksh \
> -s '/web/apachectl start'  -t '/web/apachectl stop'
Start method timeout not specified ... using the default value of 300 secs.
Stop method timeout not specified ... using the default value of 300 secs.
Probe command not specified ... will use simple probing.
Probe method timeout not specified ... using the default value of 30 secs.

Configuring the resource type with user supplied data ...
Copying the source files to bin directory ...
/usr/bin/cp haaws_svc_start.ksh ../bin
/usr/bin/cp haaws_svc_stop.ksh ../bin
/usr/bin/cp haaws_validate.ksh ../bin
/usr/bin/cp haaws_update.ksh ../bin
/usr/bin/cp haaws_mon_start.ksh ../bin
/usr/bin/cp haaws_mon_stop.ksh ../bin
/usr/bin/cp haaws_mon_check.ksh ../bin
/usr/bin/cp haaws_probe.ksh ../bin
/usr/bin/cp gettime ../bin
/usr/bin/cp gethostnames ../bin
/usr/bin/cp simple_probe ../bin
/usr/bin/cp hasp_check ../bin
done.

Creating the package for the resource type haaws ...
/usr/bin/cp haaws_svc_start.ksh ../bin
/usr/bin/cp haaws_svc_stop.ksh ../bin
/usr/bin/cp haaws_validate.ksh ../bin
/usr/bin/cp haaws_update.ksh ../bin
/usr/bin/cp haaws_mon_start.ksh ../bin
/usr/bin/cp haaws_mon_stop.ksh ../bin
/usr/bin/cp haaws_mon_check.ksh ../bin
/usr/bin/cp haaws_probe.ksh ../bin
/usr/bin/cp gettime ../bin
/usr/bin/cp gethostnames ../bin
/usr/bin/cp simple_probe ../bin
/usr/bin/cp hasp_check ../bin
/usr/bin/pkgmk -o -d ../pkg -f ../etc/prototype -b /usr/local/cluster/
agents/apache-ksh
## Building pkgmap from package prototype file.
## Processing pkginfo file.
WARNING: parameter <PSTAMP> set to "elveros20030607144424"
## Attempting to volumize 28 entries in pkgmap.
part  1 -- 254 blocks, 36 entries
## Packaging one part.
/usr/local/cluster/agents/apache-ksh/DEMOhaaws/pkg/DEMOhaaws/pkgmap
/usr/local/cluster/agents/apache-ksh/DEMOhaaws/pkg/DEMOhaaws/pkginfo
```

```
/usr/local/cluster/agents/apache-ksh/DEMOhaaws/pkg/DEMOhaaws/reloc/
DEMOhaaws/README.haaws
/usr/local/cluster/agents/apache-ksh/DEMOhaaws/pkg/DEMOhaaws/reloc/
DEMOhaaws/bin/gethostnames
/usr/local/cluster/agents/apache-ksh/DEMOhaaws/pkg/DEMOhaaws/reloc/
DEMOhaaws/bin/gettime
/usr/local/cluster/agents/apache-ksh/DEMOhaaws/pkg/DEMOhaaws/reloc/
DEMOhaaws/bin/haaws_mon_check.ksh
/usr/local/cluster/agents/apache-ksh/DEMOhaaws/pkg/DEMOhaaws/reloc/
DEMOhaaws/bin/haaws_mon_start.ksh
/usr/local/cluster/agents/apache-ksh/DEMOhaaws/pkg/DEMOhaaws/reloc/
DEMOhaaws/bin/haaws_mon_stop.ksh
/usr/local/cluster/agents/apache-ksh/DEMOhaaws/pkg/DEMOhaaws/reloc/
DEMOhaaws/bin/haaws_probe.ksh
/usr/local/cluster/agents/apache-ksh/DEMOhaaws/pkg/DEMOhaaws/reloc/
DEMOhaaws/bin/haaws_svc_start.ksh
/usr/local/cluster/agents/apache-ksh/DEMOhaaws/pkg/DEMOhaaws/reloc/
DEMOhaaws/bin/haaws_svc_stop.ksh
/usr/local/cluster/agents/apache-ksh/DEMOhaaws/pkg/DEMOhaaws/reloc/
DEMOhaaws/bin/haaws_update.ksh
/usr/local/cluster/agents/apache-ksh/DEMOhaaws/pkg/DEMOhaaws/reloc/
DEMOhaaws/bin/haaws_validate.ksh
/usr/local/cluster/agents/apache-ksh/DEMOhaaws/pkg/DEMOhaaws/reloc/
DEMOhaaws/bin/hasp_check
/usr/local/cluster/agents/apache-ksh/DEMOhaaws/pkg/DEMOhaaws/reloc/
DEMOhaaws/bin/simple_probe
/usr/local/cluster/agents/apache-ksh/DEMOhaaws/pkg/DEMOhaaws/reloc/
DEMOhaaws/etc/DEMO.haaws
/usr/local/cluster/agents/apache-ksh/DEMOhaaws/pkg/DEMOhaaws/reloc/
DEMOhaaws/man/man1m/haaws_config.1m
/usr/local/cluster/agents/apache-ksh/DEMOhaaws/pkg/DEMOhaaws/reloc/
DEMOhaaws/man/man1m/removehaaws.1m
/usr/local/cluster/agents/apache-ksh/DEMOhaaws/pkg/DEMOhaaws/reloc/
DEMOhaaws/man/man1m/starthaaws.1m
/usr/local/cluster/agents/apache-ksh/DEMOhaaws/pkg/DEMOhaaws/reloc/
DEMOhaaws/man/man1m/stophaaws.1m
/usr/local/cluster/agents/apache-ksh/DEMOhaaws/pkg/DEMOhaaws/reloc/
DEMOhaaws/util/haaws_config
/usr/local/cluster/agents/apache-ksh/DEMOhaaws/pkg/DEMOhaaws/reloc/
DEMOhaaws/util/removehaaws
/usr/local/cluster/agents/apache-ksh/DEMOhaaws/pkg/DEMOhaaws/reloc/
DEMOhaaws/util/starthaaws
/usr/local/cluster/agents/apache-ksh/DEMOhaaws/pkg/DEMOhaaws/reloc/
DEMOhaaws/util/stophaaws
/usr/local/cluster/agents/apache-ksh/DEMOhaaws/pkg/DEMOhaaws/install/depend
/usr/local/cluster/agents/apache-ksh/DEMOhaaws/pkg/DEMOhaaws/install/postinstall
/usr/local/cluster/agents/apache-ksh/DEMOhaaws/pkg/DEMOhaaws/install/postremove
/usr/local/cluster/agents/apache-ksh/DEMOhaaws/pkg/DEMOhaaws/install/preremove
## Validating control scripts.
## Packaging complete.

***
The package for the haaws service has been created in:
/usr/local/cluster/agents/apache-ksh/DEMOhaaws/pkg
***
```

At this stage, the package is complete and ready to install onto the cluster, in exactly the same way as when we used the GUI (see "Installing and Controlling the Agent" earlier in this chapter) despite the fact that we have created an original resource type rather than using the GDS.

Note that our new package has the same name as the previous one: DEMOhaaws. This means that you must completely remove the previous package before installing this new one, as shown in Example 5.6.

Example 5.6   Removing the old DEMOhaaws package

```
# /opt/DEMOhaaws/util/removehaaws -h webhost
Disabling the resource <haaws-hars> ...done.
Removing the resource <haaws-hars> ...done.
Resource type <SUNW.gds> has been un-registered already⁷
Disabling the resource <webhost> ...done.
Removing the resource <webhost> ...done.
Offlining the resource group <haaws-harg> ...done.
Unmanaging the resource group <haaws-harg> ...done.
Removing the resource group <haaws-harg> ...done.
iron:/web/agent# pkgrm DEMOhaaws

The following package is currently installed:
   DEMOhaaws        Sun Cluster resource type for haaws server
                    (sparc) 3.0.0,REV=

Do you want to remove this package? [y,n,?,q] y

## Removing installed package instance <DEMOhaaws>

This package contains scripts which will be executed with super-user
permission during the process of removing this package.

Do you want to continue with the removal of this package [y,n,?,q] y
## Verifying package dependencies.
## Processing package information.
## Executing preremove script.
Resource <haaws-hars> has been removed already
Resource type <SUNW.gds> has been un-registered already

Network Resource not removed...
You may run removehaaws again with the -h option to remove network resource.
## Removing pathnames in class <none>
/opt/DEMOhaaws/util/stophaaws
/opt/DEMOhaaws/util/starthaaws
/opt/DEMOhaaws/util/removehaaws
/opt/DEMOhaaws/util/haaws_config
/opt/DEMOhaaws/util
/opt/DEMOhaaws/man/man1m/stophaaws.1m
/opt/DEMOhaaws/man/man1m/starthaaws.1m
/opt/DEMOhaaws/man/man1m/removehaaws.1m
```

---

7. This message appears in Sun Cluster 3.1, but in Sun Cluster 3.0 the SUNW.gds agent is removed successfully. This error is related to *Resource Type Versioning*.

```
/opt/DEMOhaaws/man/man1m/haaws_config.1m
/opt/DEMOhaaws/man/man1m
/opt/DEMOhaaws/man
/opt/DEMOhaaws/README.haaws
/opt/DEMOhaaws
## Updating system information.

Removal of <DEMOhaaws> was successful.
```

Remember to remove the packages from all nodes.

If, when you try to run the start script, you see some output that contains the word FAILED, then the script did not complete successfully (see Example 5.7).

Example 5.7 Failed resource installation

```
# /opt/DEMOhaaws/util/starthaaws -h webhost -p 80/tcp
No nafo groups or network adapters specified ... will try to auto-discover the
network adapters and configure them into nafo groups.
Creating a fail over instance ...
Registering resource type <DEMO.haaws>...done.
Creating fail over resource group <haaws-harg>...done.
Creating logical host resource <webhost>...done.
Creating resource <haaws-hars> for the resource type <DEMO.haaws>...Method
haaws_validate.ksh on resource haaws-hars: stat of program file failed.
Validation of resource haaws-hars in resource group haaws-harg on node lead
failed.
FAILED: scrgadm -a -j haaws-hars -g haaws-harg -t DEMO.haaws
-y scalable=false -y Port_list=80/tcp -y Network_resources_used=webhost
```

The configuration is automatically attempted simultaneously on all cluster nodes, and if it fails on only one node then the entire configuration fails. In the above example, on a Sun Cluster 3.1 configuration we can see that validation of the resource failed on node "lead." In Sun Cluster 3.0, the failing node is not reported, so check the contents of /var/adm/messages on *each cluster node* to find the cause of any errors.

Note – One common reason why the start script fails is that the agent package has only been installed on one node.

Advanced Topics

So far in this chapter we've looked at how to get a simple resource type quickly built, packaged, and installed, but there is a great deal more that can (or sometimes must) be done in order to create a sophisticated Sun Cluster agent. Most of the rest of this book will help you with this task, but there are a few advanced topics related to the Agent Builder itself that we should cover before going any further.

The HOSTNAMES variable

Although not used in our example, it is possible to use a special variable *$hostnames* as part of the start, stop, and probe commands for an agent. This variable resolves at run-time to a list of the *logical* hosts on which the resource is running. For example, if you create a failover resource that runs on the logical host `myhost`, then the *$hostnames* variable will be set to `myhost`. A similar effect could be achieved by editing the source code of the resource type to include a function that finds out the value of the `NETWORK_RESOURCES_USED` property of the resource.

The *$hostnames* variable can be used in either the GUI (see Figure 5.17) or on the command line:

```
scdsconfig -s '/usr/local/bin/myserver -h $hostnames'
```

If you use the *$hostnames* variable on the command line, make sure that your shell does not try to evaluate the variable directly. Usually it is sufficient to place the variable inside single quotes (as shown in the example above).

In the future, more variables are planned to be added for use with Agent Builder tools.

Multiple Processes

The discussion so far has assumed that only one program is needed to start an application. In some cases, multiple processes must exist for the program to operate correctly, and as we'll see in later chapters, the cluster Process Monitor Facility has to be told explicitly when it should attempt to restart one process in a group of processes that control an application.

The problem is, since there is only space for a single START command in the Agent Builder interface, how do you tell it that we want to run and monitor separate process trees? If you choose to generate C source for your resource type, you can use a text editor to create a file with a list of the programs you want to run. The file should have permissions set so that it is *not* executable. This file name can then be used as the Start Command for the application as the Agent Builder will automatically detect that (since it is not an executable file) it is a list of programs—each of which should be traced by the cluster framework.

Start Command (or file):

/usr/local/bin/myserver -h $hostnames   Browse ...

Figure 5.17 Using $hostnames

Note – In Sun Cluster 3.1 5/03 release and earlier, the Agent Builder can only handle multiple process trees if you choose to generate C source for your resource type. It will not work automatically for GDS or `ksh` agents (although it is possible to achieve by hand coding). Check the release notes of later releases of Sun Cluster to see if other languages are available.

Changing a Resource Type

You can use the Agent Builder to make changes to a resource type you created earlier. There are two ways of making the Agent Builder GUI use old information instead of creating a new resource type. The first way is to change to the directory containing the old `rtconfig` file and launch the Agent Builder from that directory. The `rtconfig` file will be read and the GUI fields will be filled using the information in that file. The second way to work on old information is to choose Load Resource Type from the File menu, highlight the install directory (the one containing the `rtconfig` file), and press the Load button (see Figure 5.18).

Since both of these methods load an existing resource type skeleton into the Agent Builder GUI, you cannot recreate the agent, you can only change the configuration (start, stop, and probe commands and timeout values).

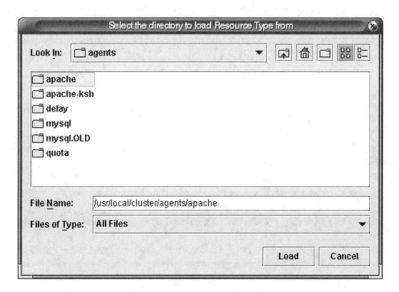

Figure 5.18 Loading an existing resource type

Changing the Source

Once you have created a resource type using the Agent Builder, you may find that you need to make changes to the default start, stop, or probe programs or to refine the way that the resource type behaves. If you chose to generate C or ksh source when creating the resource type, you can edit this source to achieve the changes you want. If you created an agent that uses the GDS, then you cannot make complex changes, so you should probably recreate your resource type using C or ksh.

RTR File

For resource types created using C or ksh, a resource type registration (RTR) file is created by the Agent Builder and placed in the etc directory of the resource type source tree with the name Vendor. Application. If you want to add resource or resource type properties, or change the default values of properties, you can edit this file. RTR files are described in detail in Chapter 6, "Understanding the RGM."

Start/Stop/Probe Source

If you want to change the way that your application is started, stopped, or probed, then you can make changes to the start_application_svc, stop_ application_svc, and probe_application_svc files that are found in the src directory of the resource type source tree. One common reason for making this sort of change is to be able to use resource property values during the start process. For example, you may decide to store the location of the application's configuration file in a resource property so that different instances of your application can be started with different parameters. To access this resource property, you will have to change the start_application_svc source code to read the property and then use its value in the start command. Properties are discussed in detail in Chapter 6, "Understanding the RGM."

Remaking the Package

Once you have made changes to the source code or RTR file, you will have to recreate the installable package. Fortunately, this is easy to do because a make(1) file is automatically created by the Agent Builder. To rebuild the package, simply change to the src directory in the resource type source tree and type **make**. Once the package is rebuilt, it will be available in the pkg directory of the source tree. The command and output are shown below:

```
$ cd /usr/local/cluster/agents/apache/DEMOhaaws/src
$ make pkg
/usr/bin/pkgmk -o -d ../pkg -f ../etc/prototype -b /usr/
local/cluster/agents/apache
## Building pkgmap from package prototype file.
## Processing pkginfo file.
WARNING: parameter <PSTAMP> set to "elveros20030607153756"
## Attempting to volumize 13 entries in pkgmap.
part  1 -- 104 blocks, 19 entries
```

```
## Packaging one part.
/usr/local/cluster/agents/apache/DEMOhaaws/pkg/DEMOhaaws/pkgmap
/usr/local/cluster/agents/apache/DEMOhaaws/pkg/DEMOhaaws/pkginfo
/usr/local/cluster/agents/apache/DEMOhaaws/pkg/DEMOhaaws/
reloc/DEMOhaaws/README.haaws
/usr/local/cluster/agents/apache/DEMOhaaws/pkg/DEMOhaaws/
reloc/DEMOhaaws/man/man1m/haaws_config.1m
/usr/local/cluster/agents/apache/DEMOhaaws/pkg/DEMOhaaws/
reloc/DEMOhaaws/man/man1m/removehaaws.1m
/usr/local/cluster/agents/apache/DEMOhaaws/pkg/DEMOhaaws/
reloc/DEMOhaaws/man/man1m/starthaaws.1m
/usr/local/cluster/agents/apache/DEMOhaaws/pkg/DEMOhaaws/
reloc/DEMOhaaws/man/man1m/stophaaws.1m
/usr/local/cluster/agents/apache/DEMOhaaws/pkg/DEMOhaaws/
reloc/DEMOhaaws/util/haaws_config
/usr/local/cluster/agents/apache/DEMOhaaws/pkg/DEMOhaaws/
reloc/DEMOhaaws/util/removehaaws
/usr/local/cluster/agents/apache/DEMOhaaws/pkg/DEMOhaaws/
reloc/DEMOhaaws/util/starthaaws
/usr/local/cluster/agents/apache/DEMOhaaws/pkg/DEMOhaaws/
reloc/DEMOhaaws/util/stophaaws
/usr/local/cluster/agents/apache/DEMOhaaws/pkg/DEMOhaaws/
install/depend
/usr/local/cluster/agents/apache/DEMOhaaws/pkg/DEMOhaaws/
install/preremove
## Validating control scripts.
## Packaging complete.
```

Adding Items to the Package

Sometimes you may want to add files to the installable package. This can be easily achieved by editing the prototype file in the `etc` directory of the source tree to include the additional files. Consult the online manual pages about the `proto-type(4)` file, and the Solaris developer documentation for details on how to create and modify packages.

Advanced Fault Probing

As we mentioned earlier, the default probe program that is supplied as part of the Agent Builder is very simple—all the program does is attempt to connect to the network port used by your application. If the connection is successful, then the application is deemed to be working correctly. It's fairly obvious that this simplistic approach does not handle the complexity of many applications, so one of the most important changes that you might make to your resource type is to write a more sophisticated probe.

How you write the probe and what actions the probe takes depends entirely on the application you are making highly available. One example of a sophisticated probe program is that used by the HA Oracle agent developed by Sun Microsystems.

The probe in this case actually connects to the database and performs the kinds of actions that a database client would perform—such as creating a temporary table, adding, reading, and deleting entries, and then dropping the table from the database. This sophisticated behavior ensures that the database is acting in the correct fashion and can provide concise exit codes upon failure, thus taking appropriate action for any given situation.

For our example using the Apache Web server, it would be possible to create a program that attempts to connect to the Web server and retrieve a particular known file. The resulting code returned by the Web server could be examined by the program and used to determine what result the probe should return. It would even be possible to compare the file received from the Web server with what the file is supposed to be, in order to detect any possible data corruption.

What should be clear from this is that the key to effectively monitoring an application is understanding how the application works. It is a common misconception that creating a resource type for the Sun Cluster environment requires a cluster expert, but the truth is that an expert in the application to be made highly available is much more important.

Summary

This chapter has been a brief introduction to using the SunPlex Agent Builder to quickly create an agent for an application. This tool can be run using a GUI or command-line interface; it generates an installable package that can be added to the cluster nodes using `pkgadd(1m)`.

We have seen that the Agent Builder can be used to generate agents using Korn shell, C source, or those based on the GDS resource type and that this source can be used as the basis for more complex and sophisticated development.

At this stage, you should be able to create a simple agent for your application and apply it to your cluster. If you find you need to fine-tune the source code of the new resource type, then read on.

6

UNDERSTANDING
THE RGM

In the early chapters of this book we laid out a basic foundation for cluster computing. Chapter 2 introduced you to the technologies of the Sun Cluster product. Chapter 4 outlined application guidelines that should be adhered to in order to make applications cluster capable. Finally, in earlier chapters we learned how to create some simple resource types using the tools bundled with Sun Cluster environment, namely the Agent Builder and the Generic Data Service (GDS). From this chapter forward, we discuss the APIs and requirements needed to create more sophisticated resource types. It is important to understand that the remaining chapters of the book build on the concepts outlined in this chapter and that the book from this point forward is geared toward more experienced system administrators or application developers.

The topics covered in this chapter include callback methods, resource types, and resources. A word about this chapter's title—at first glance it might not appear to reflect the content. Applications under Sun Cluster control predominately interact within confines of the resource group manager (RGM) and the RGM interacts with applications via a software callback model. The act of creating resource types and using and managing them is all within the confines of the RGM.

Note – The API that ships with Sun Cluster 3.x is not compatible with the API used in earlier versions of Sun Cluster. Agents written for earlier versions of Sun Cluster will not run unmodified on a Sun Cluster 3.x cluster.

The Callback Model

The Sun Cluster framework uses a callback model to communicate between the RGM and resources. Callback methods are a way for software modules to execute a function or routine when a particular event happens during the life cycle of the calling program (see Figure 6.1).

The Sun Cluster 3 framework makes use of 12 distinct callback methods. Most of the callback methods have names that describe when and how they are used—for example, START and STOP—while others are not so intuitive, such as INIT and FINI. It is within these methods that we will use API functions to extract cluster state information, and, depending on the situation, instruct the cluster framework to perform some action on behalf of the application. These methods can be implemented in C or C++, UNIX, Korn shell, or any other language.

Note – Callback methods can be written in any language; however, the only interfaces to the cluster framework are through the C programming language or UNIX shell. If another language is to be used, access to the cluster framework will have to be done via shell commands.

Semantic Overview of Sun Cluster Callback Model

The callback semantic model should be straightforward. Figure 6.2 shows the semantics of the Sun Cluster callback model and how the cluster framework interacts with applications under its control.

Referring to Figure 6.2, the flow of resource type creation and its usage for any given application should be straightforward.

1. The resource type registration file (RTR) is created using your favorite editor (discussed later in this chapter). The Agent Builder can also be used to perform

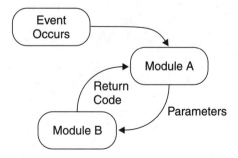

Figure 6.1 Basic callback model

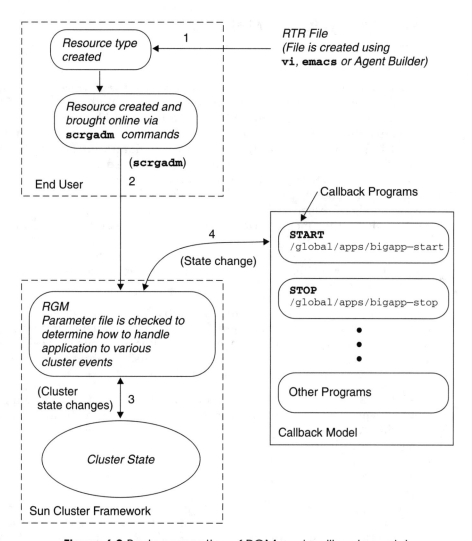

Figure 6.2 Basic semantics of RGM and callback model

this step. One of the callback methods' parameters points the path to the methods as well as other necessary parameters that might be necessary, such as the path to the application startup files. The RTR files is then registered.

2. Using cluster management tools (for example, `scgradm`) the RTR file is used to create resources of that type.

3. The cluster framework notifies the RGM when a change in cluster state occurs (that is, nodes leaving or joining the cluster).

4. Upon event notification, the RGM will execute the appropriate callback method(s) that correspond to the event (that is, to start or stop the application or if necessary to perform some sort of recovery action).

Sun Cluster API Callback Methods

A great benefit of the API framework is that regardless of which method a developer decides to use to create a resource type—the Agent Builder, GDS, RMAPI, or the DSDL—the callback model and callback methods are identical. The differences lie in the flexibility and functionality of each tool and API used. For example, within the DSDL there are functions to use the Process Monitoring Facility (see Chapter 9, "Using the DSDL"), however, these functions do not exist in the RMAPI.[1] Likewise, it doesn't matter whether you are creating failover or scalable resource types, the callback model and methods are identical. Also, it does not matter if the developer uses C or UNIX Korn shell to create callback methods. You'll achieve identical results using either method. However, the DSDL has many powerful convenience functions built into its library set that are not available to shell programming. Hence, using the RMAPI[2] and shell programming might require more code using the DSDL and the C language. At Sun Microsystems, the preferred way to write resource types is to use C with the DSDL.

There are 12 methods that define the callback model; however, it's not necessary to create all of them when developing a resource type. Just as in any programming language, not every function defined within a library needs be used to write a program. However, knowing the full scope of functions in a library will help reduce code redundancy and increase application stability.

Of the 12 callback methods available to developers, two are required for any resource type (START and STOP). The START method is used to start the application while the STOP method is used to stop the application. These two methods also have network equivalences (PRENET_START and POSTNET_STOP) that can be used instead of START and STOP. The PRENET_START starts the application before network interfaces have been brought online. Its counterpart POSTNET_STOP will stop the application only after network interfaces have been brought offline. These methods can be mixed and matched; for example, the START method is used to start the application while the POSTNET_STOP method is used to stop the application. Figure 6.3 shows the basic start and stop sequences of the callback methods; notice the two methods that haven't been discussed yet, (MONITOR_START and MONITOR_STOP).

The PRENET_START method, if defined, would execute before the START method. The network interfaces referred to in the diagram correspond to the logical interfaces defined for HA or scalable services described in Chapter 2.

---

1. Access to the Process Monitoring Facility is done directly through `pmfadm` facility.

2. When using the RMAPI, only shell-based programming is available. Although there are C functions available for the RMAPI, their scope and functionality is limited, thus for complete functionality programmers are best served using the DSDL.

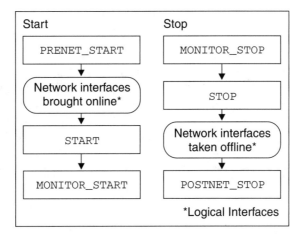

Figure 6.3 Resource start and stop sequences

Note – The required callback methods are (START or PRENET_START) and (STOP or POSTNET_STOP). This allows for quick development of simple resource types. Mix and matching of START, STOP, PRENET_START, and POSTNET_STOP is permissible.

The ability to use only two callback methods is a convenient and powerful advantage, as undoubtedly there will be situations where an application will require nothing more than basic start and stop functionality. Likewise, more sophisticated resource types will require the use of more callback methods called during specific cluster events. It is rare that any resource type will require the use all 12 callback methods.

Callback Definitions

Callback methods can be grouped into three functional types.

- Initialization
- Administrative
- Application monitoring

Initialization Methods

START

START is the most basic method. It is used to start up an application that is to be placed under the cluster control. Care should be given to applications that may require long startup times, such as databases. The return code for the method must return success only if the application has started correctly.

Note – In SC3.0 the DSDL supports a resource restart (RESOURCE_RE-START). If DSDL is to be used to perform resource restarts, both START and STOP methods must be defined even if PRENET_START and POSTNET_STOP are used. On a resource restart, the START and STOP methods are called, if they do not exist, the resource will not be restarted. SC3.1 introduced scha_control (RESOURCE_RESTART) at the RMAPI layer. See Chapter 9, "Using the DSDL."

STOP

It is used to stop the resource started via the START method. Unlike the START method, STOP must be idempotent. Care should be given to applications that require time to stop. This method should return a zero value if the method is successful, even if no work was performed. Depending on settings of other resource parameters, failure of this method can lead to a node dropping out of the cluster and rebooting.

PRENET_START

Similar to the START method, the PRENET_START method differs in that it is invoked before the logical network interfaces are brought online. This method is useful for those applications that require network access, but it is not desirable to have users trying to access the service unless the application is available. For example, a database should be up and available before letting users log in to it. Using this method, a database is started before the logical network interface is brought online. Thus, users will not be able to access the database while it's being brought online. This method can be used in place of or in conjunction with the START method.

POSTNET_STOP

Similar to the STOP method, POSTNET_STOP is used to stop a resource started via the START *or* PRENET_START method. The difference is that this method is invoked first after the network resources have been brought offline. This is useful if you wish to stop the resource after the network resources have been brought offline. This method can be used in conjunction with the STOP method.

INIT

The INIT method is a special method that can be used as a one-time initialization of a resource. This initialization can be a one-time event such as creating required directories or checking file permissions. However, the one-time initialization is a bit of a misnomer. This is because the INIT method is called any time a resource group is switched to a managed state. Also, INIT is also called any time a resource is added to a group that is currently in a managed state.

FINI

The FINI method is another special method that can be a used as one-time initialization event to clean up after a resource is removed from service. Like the INIT method, one-time initialization is a bit of a misnomer. Like INIT, FINI is also called when a resource group is switched to an unmanaged state.

BOOT

The BOOT method is similar to the INIT method in that it can be used to perform required functions when a node joins or rejoins a cluster. Recall from Chapter 2 that nodes boot into cluster mode unless they are specifically instructed not to via the **boot -x** option. This method is only called after a node reboots and later rejoins the cluster. In order for the BOOT method to be invoked, the resource must be in a managed state. Therefore, if the resource is in an unmanaged state when the node rejoins the cluster, the BOOT method will not be invoked. Boot also needs to be indempotent.

Administration Methods

VALIDATE

The VALIDATE method plays an important role in the robustness of a resource during its life cycle. Its basic function is to ensure that all the properties are valid that are passed to the callback method for creation or modification. This method can be thought of as a type checking function for resource types.

Note – When your resource is first created, there are no arguments that are passed to the method, hence the method will fail. A CASE statement can be used to parse the parameters being passed. When using the Agent Builder, the parsing function is provided as part of the resource type creation template; it is also provided by the DSDL.

UPDATE

The UPDATE method is called when a user makes changes to resource property values. Resources need not be static once created. Developers can opt to give end users the ability to make changes to an existing resource's properties. Changes can include application directory, timeout values, nodes to run on, and so forth. The UPDATE method is used to update resources that are currently online and apply any new changes a user wishes to make. Using the UPDATE method gives resource types a dynamic component. Note that the validate method is called before an update of a resource is applied, which in turn, can veto the update. Care should be taken with this method. Although the manuals state that anything can be done within the contents of the UPDATE method, what will happen if an update changes the location of a critical path to data? Will the application be aware of the path change without having to be brought offline? Remember that because you can do anything within the UPDATE method, care should be taken to ensure the consequences for the resource and user connections, as well as the application being monitored.

Application Monitoring Methods

MONITOR_START

This method starts a user-created fault probe. The fault probe should be an endless loop application that can perform a check on the status of the application. Starting the fault probe is best performed via the process monitor facility (PMF) convenience functions described in Chapter 8, "Managing Processes."

MONITOR_STOP

This method is used to stop the user-defined fault probe started with the MONITOR_START method. Stopping the fault probe is best performed via the PMF convenience functions described in Chapter 8, "Managing Processes."

MONITOR_CHECK

If a fault probe makes a request of the RGM to switch over the application, this method can be used to run a program that checks the status of the standby node (that is, it checks to see if the standby node has enough memory to run the application) before a switchover is initiated.

Idempotency

Idempotency is a word you rarely hear unless, of course, you like reading mathematics or computer science books. Idempotency is defined as *Relating to or being a mathematical quantity, which when applied to itself under a given binary operation, equals itself*.[3] Functions that are idempotent will always produce identical results regardless of the number of times a function is invoked, as long as the same input arguments are used. The concept of idempotency plays an important role when developing resource types.

Under normal operations, callback methods are invoked only once during the lifetime of the resource, while some might not get called at all. We define life cycle as *the moment the resource is started to resource termination*. The following is a typical resource life cycle after the resource has been created.

1. RGM calls the START or PRENET_START method and the application starts.
2. Changes are made to the resource. The RGM calls the VALIDATE and UPDATE methods if they exist.
3. The RGM calls the STOP or the POSTNET_STOP method and the application stops.

The above sequence of events is correct when things are working correctly. The RGM guarantees that the START and STOP callback methods are called at least once, but the RGM makes no guarantee that a callback method will be called only once during the resource life cycle. For example, if the START method is invoked but the applica-

---

3. *Merriam-Webster's Collegiate Dictionary.*

tion never gets started, the RGM then invokes the STOP method. If at the same time a system administrator tries to take the resource offline, the STOP method will be invoked twice. If the STOP method produces different results with the same argument list, it could lead to data corruption, hence the need for idempotence. In this case, we want to be sure that regardless of the number of times the STOP method is called, we can expect the same results and error messages are not produced. While it is a good idea to make all callback methods idempotent, only 7 of the 12 are required to be so.

Callback methods that must be idempotent:

1. STOP
2. POSTNET_STOP
3. MONITOR_STOP
4. INIT
5. BOOT
6. UPDATE
7. FINI

Note – Failure to make the STOP, POSTNET_STOP, MONITOR_STOP, INIT, BOOT, UPDATE, and FINI callback methods idempotent can lead to data corruption or the lack of an available resource.

Also, it's imperative that both the STOP and MONITOR_STOP methods return a zero return code even when the method exits correctly regardless of whether the work was done when the method was invoked. Listed in Table 6.1 are brief descriptions of the 12 callback methods previously described.

Callback Exit Codes

The RGM expects callback methods to have the same exit codes.

Success—Zero
Failure—Any other value

Logging callback errors should be done using the syslog(3) facility. Developers should not rely on stdout or stderr for error logging.

Application Monitoring

As discussed in Chapter 1, "Introduction," it's not enough for a cluster to provide hardware monitoring, as this is a basic functionality that all HA type clusters should perform. It is of little use to have a high performance cluster running if no user can access the application because it's unavailable. The ability to perform application monitoring is a powerful and important part of Sun Cluster functionality. Unfortunately, it is also the most complicated part of resource development. Although desirable, application monitoring is not a mandatory requirement for resource development.

Table 6.1 Sun Cluster 3.x Callback Methods Quick Reference

Callback Method	Idempotent	Description
START	NO	Used to start a resource.
STOP	YES	Used to stop a resource.
PRENET_START	NO	Used to bring up a resource after network interfaces have been plumbed up but before the network addresses are available.
POSTNET_STOP	YES	Used to stop a resource after the network resources have been brought down.
VALIDATE	NO	Used to determine that a resource's properties are set to valid values as stipulated in the resource's RTR file. Also called during an update of the resource.
UPDATE	YES	If a resource is active (running on a node) and changes are made to the resource, this method is called to ensure those changes are made consistently across the cluster.
MONITOR_START	NO	Starts the application monitoring agent if one is available.
MONITOR_STOP	YES	Stops the application monitoring agent.
MONITOR_CHECK	NO	Used to check to determine if a standby node is capable of handling the resource before a switch over happens.
INIT	YES	Any one-time initialization steps required by the resource will be performed by this method.
FINI	YES	When a resource is removed from under RGM management, this method is used to perform any necessary cleanup.
BOOT	YES	When a node joins or rejoins a cluster, this method can be used to perform any initialization that a resource might require.

It's important to note that with the exception of process monitoring, the cluster framework itself does not do any application monitoring. Described in Chapter 8, "Managing Processes," the cluster framework does provide a facility to monitor the application process and child processes. However, monitoring application processes is a minimum functionality. All too often an application is "hung" but its process tree is still intact. While the Sun Cluster framework does not provide application-specific monitoring, it does provide a mechanism via callback methods (MONITOR_START, MONITOR_STOP, and MONITOR_CHECK) to start and stop user-created fault probes.

To provide application monitoring, the end user develops an application fault probe. This fault probe should be an endless loop program that continuously checks the state of the application using a routine or function capable of probing the application's status (Figure 6.4).

The example of a fault probe program depicted in Figure 6.4 is not part of the cluster framework. It is up to developers to add application monitoring to their resource types. Example 6.1 is a simplified typical fault probe.

Example 6.1 myfault_probe_start

```
int main(void) {
    do while (x = 0)
     { probe port 2100;
      if (port 2100 is available);
       sleep 10 seconds;
        else
         call scha_control; /*Request restart or fail over*/
        }
}
```

In Example 6.1 the probe is launched via the MONITOR_START method and run continuously until terminated by the MONITOR_STOP method. All the probe does is check to determine if port 2100 is available. If it is, the probe goes to sleep for ten seconds and repeats the action indefinitely. If the probe cannot access the port, it invokes the scha_control function to request either an application restart or resource failover.

If the RGM makes a scha_control call to perform a switch over, how does it know that the standby node is able to run the application? The callback method

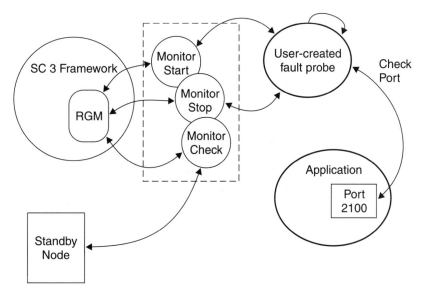

Figure 6.4 Application monitoring

MONITOR_CHECK is used by the RGM to check the status of the standby node. Before the switch over occurs, this method can be used to check the status of the standby node.

This is a simple explanation of the process. Creating fault probes is the most complex part of creating resource types. However, in order to create truly robust cluster-capable applications, fault probes are an important development process. All resource types shipped from Sun Microsystems have application-specific fault probes. For example, Sun Microsystems provides a resource type for Oracle databases. To give you an idea of what can be involved when creating fault probes, we'll explain the basic algorithm used for Oracle databases.

The probe sequence of Sun Microsystems' Oracle resource type is as follows:

1. Log into database via a user-defined login. Check connection ability and stay connected.

2. Wait a few minutes.

3. Query the v$sysstat table, R1.

4. Wait a few minutes.

5. Query the v$sysstat table again, R2. If there is a delta between readings R1 and R2, we know the database is working (you can't have a delta if the database is idle). If there is no delta between R1 and R2, then the probe performs the following transactions:

   • Creates a table

   • Inserts a row

   • Deletes the row

   • Drops the table

   If these transactions are executed without fault, the database is fine and the database is idle, then go to sleep and repeat again. Otherwise, check the error codes and the alert log. A restart or perhaps a full switch over might be necessary.

6. Log into the database again, recheck the connection, and restart the process.

The above sequence is not exact. It was simplified to give you an idea of what is involved. Notice that unless you are familiar with Oracle, you won't have a clue what a v$sysstat is. Here is an important fact: In order to write comprehensive fault probes, it is imperative the developer understand the application that is being monitored. Otherwise, you can instruct the RGM to perform restarts or switch overs when it's unnecessary or worse, not at all.

Life Cycles for Resource Types

For all but the simplest applications, software development typically follows a life cycle. Resource types can also have a development life cycle. The common nomenclature used to describe software is the application name followed by a version number (for example, Solaris 9). Sun Cluster can support multiple versions of a resource type within a cluster environment. Under Sun Cluster 3.0, the use of resource versioning was not required; however, it is mandatory in version 3.1. A good deal of thought has gone into a versioning framework for resource types. This framework will allow developers the ability to create resource types that can have multiple versions of a resource running on the cluster at one time. This allows system administrators the ability to upgrade a given resource to a newer version without removing the old resource type first, thus reducing downtime and ensuring stability.

Creating Resource Types

Resource Type Registration File

The development of resource types begins with the creation of the resource type registration file. The RTR file describes the resource type and its associated properties to the RGM. These properties describe attributes such as the type of resource that will be created (failover or scalable), the callback methods to be used, application directories, timeout values, and any other specific attributes an application might need. Once the contents of the RTR file are verified, they are placed in the cluster configuration repository (CCR). See Chapter 2, "Exploring Sun Cluster Technologies." Once in the CCR, the resource type information is available to create resources, which in turn can be placed into resource groups.

The RTR file is an ASCII file. Creating the RTR file is easy; all that is required is an ASCII editor such as `vi` or `emacs`. The difficult part of creating the RTR file is that the syntax structure can be a bit confusing. However, the Agent Builder can be used to create a template for the resource type (yet another reason to use the Agent Builder). Once the RTR file is created, the `scrgadm` command is used to register the resource type with the cluster framework and the RTR file is no longer used. However, a copy of it is stored in `/usr/cluster/lib/rgm/rtreg/`.

Note – Use the Agent Builder to create a template for your resource type that will include, among other things, an RTR file that can then be further edited, thus saving time and reducing the likelihood of syntax errors.

The format of an RTR file is divided into three sections: *basic*, *system*, and *extension* parameters.

RTR File Sections

Basic—Outlines the fundamental properties of the resource, such as resource name, application directory, and what callback methods will be used.

System—Contains properties that every resource must have, such as timeout values for callback methods. If no values are specified, defaults will be supplied by the RGM.

Extension—Has properties that are unique to the resource, such as a directory for data or any other specific attribute that the application requires.

Building the RTR File

Building an RTR file is not a complicated process. However, there is a basic syntax structure that needs to be followed.

RTR Syntax Rules

1. Put a semicolon at the end of each statement.
2. System and extension properties must be enclosed with matching braces.
3. Comments are preceded with the pound sign.

Example 6.2 shows the three main sections of a simple RTR file. It's worth noting several key points. First, the sample file is purposely short. Typically, RTR files have a good deal of information in them, specifically system properties and they can be long. Notice that the first item defined is RESOURCE_TYPE. The system property RESOURCE_TYPE must be the first item to be defined and failure to do so will lead to registration failure.

Once a resource of this type is created, some resource properties are not update-able, while others can be updated by a system administrator. Also, there is no limit on the number of resources that can be instantiated from a resource type. However, each resource must have a unique name. For example, a resource type for the *mydatabase* application is created and node 1 has two resources in a group named *mydatabase_prod* and *mydatabase_dev*. Both resources *mydatabase_prod* and *mydatabase_dev* are of resource type *mydatabase*, complete with their own property values. It is important to point out there should be one and only one RTR file for a given resource type.

Simple RTR File

Example 6.2   RTR file format

```
######################################################
#Simple RTR File
#All comments are preceded with pound sign
######### Basic Section of RTR ######################
RESOURCE_TYPE = "Simple_Application";
VENDOR_ID = SUNW;
RT_DESCRIPION = "Simple Application";
RT_VERSION = "1.0";
RT_BASE = /usr/local/sampleapp;
FAILOVER=TRUE;
```

```
START = simple_start;
STOP = simple_stop;

############System Property Section################
{
   PROPERTY = Start_timeout;
   MIN=60;
   DEFAULT=300;
}

{
  PROPERTY = Stop_timeout;
  MIN=60;
  DEFAULT=300;
}
##############Extension Property Section#################
{
  PROPERTY = App_Dir;
  EXTENTION;
  STRING;
  TUNABLE = AT_CREATION;
  DESCRIPTION = ""Simple Applications home directory";
}
```

Note – RESOURCE_TYPE must be the first item defined in the RTR file or registration of the resource type will fail.

Table 6.2 shows a list of the resource type system properties that can be used along with their attributes. Again, not every property needs to be used for a given resource type. It's important to note that resource type properties are not update-able using the Sun Cluster administration tools. The only exception is the Installed_nodes property, which ironically cannot be declared in the RTR file as it has to be set by the system administrator.

Resource type properties are grouped into one of four distinct categories:

1. Required—The property must exist in the RTR, so upon creation a value must be defined. Likewise, a null value is not permissible. If the value is left blank, resources cannot be created.
2. Conditional—This property is created only if it exists in the RTR file. If the property is defined with no value, a default will be assigned.
3. Conditional/Explicit—If the property exists in the RTR file, it must have a defined value; otherwise, the property is not created.
4. Optional—If the property is defined in the RTR file, the RGM will use it. If the property is defined without an assigned value, the RGM will create it and assign a default value.

Table 6.2 Resource Type Properties

Property Name	Tunable	Data Type	Default	Usage	Description
API_version	Never	Integer	3	Optional	Version of API used. If not used, the default value for SC3 is 2.
BOOT	Never	String	None	Conditional/ Explicit	Callback method. This should be the actual program name.
Failover	Never	Boolean	FALSE	Optional	Indicates that this resource is a failover resource. If set to TRUE, the resource cannot belong to a resource group that can be online on more than one node.
FINI	Never	String	None	Conditional/ Explicit	Callback method. This should be the actual program name.
INIT	Never	String	None	Conditional/ Explicit	Callback method. This should be the actual program name.
Init_nodes	Never	ENUM	RG_primaries	Optional	Instructs on which nodes the RGM is going to call the INIT, FINI, BOOT, and VALIDATE methods. Values can include RG_primaries or RT_installed_nodes.
Installed_nodes	Never	String Array	All nodes		List of cluster node names that the resource type is allowed to run on. Note this property cannot be declared in the RTR file.
MONITOR_CHECK	Never	String	None	Conditional/ Explicit	Callback method. This should be the actual program name.
MONITOR_START	Never	String	None	Conditional/ Explicit	Callback method. This should be the actual program name.
MONITOR_STOP	Never	String	None	Conditional/ Explicit	Callback method. This should be the actual program name.
Pkglist	Never	String Array	None	Conditional/ Explicit	List of packages that are used with the resource type installation.
POSTNET_STOP	Never	String	None	Conditional/ Explicit	Callback method. This should be the actual program name.
PRENET_START	Never	String	None	Conditional/ Explicit	Callback method. This should be the actual program name.
RT_basedir	Never	String	None	Required	Base directory path for callback methods. Set it to the installation of the path of the callback methods. The path must be absolutely complete with forward slash, that is, /usr/resource/callback. Use if callback methods are not defined with absolute paths.
RT_description	Never	String	Null	Conditional	Resource type description.
Resource_type	Never	String	None	Required	Name of the resource type.
RT_version	Never	String	None	Conditional/ Explicit	Version or resource type.
Single_instance	Never	Boolean	False	Optional	One resource of this type allowed.

Property Name	Tunable	Data Type	Default	Usage	Description
START	Never	String	None	Required	Callback method. This should be the actual program name.
STOP	Never	String	None	Required	Callback method. This should be the actual program name.
UPDATE	Never	String	None	Conditional/Explicit	Callback method. This should be the actual program name.
VALIDATE	Never	String	None	Conditional/Explicit	Callback method. This should be the actual program name.
Vendor_ID	Never	String	None	Conditional	Typically, the stock symbol of the company that created the resource type, that is, SUNW

Tables 6.2 and 6.3 only list the values of valid resource types and resource properties. Most, but not all, resource properties are updateable. When a resource is created, verification is done via the RGM to ensure that required parameters are specified with the correct range of permissible values, such as Port_list.

Table 6.2 lists the properties that can be defined within the RTR, while Table 6.3 lists properties that affect resources of a specified resource type. For example, a resource type can be defined where the Vendor_ID is *ABC*. The property value of Vendor_ID is only valid for resource types, that is all resources created of this type will have an identical Vendor_ID. On the other hand, resource properties are unique to resources. For example, the resource property Port_list can be unique to each instantiated resource (resource A is created with its Port_list set to 90, while resource B has its Port_list set to 8080).

Resource Property Types

The developer has to decide which properties will add additional functionality or usability to a resource type. For example, the property Port_list would be useless for a resource type that doesn't use ports. Conversely, if an application makes use of ports, this property can be used to specify a range of ports to be used by the application. It's best not to assume that the end user will configure an application to use a specific parameter that might be a normal default—say port 80 for Web servers.

Resource properties are grouped into four distinct categories. A resource property can be:

1. Required—The property must exist, therefore upon resource creation a value must be given.
2. Optional—The property exists; however, if no value is given upon resource creation a default value is supplied.
3. Conditional—The property is created only if it exists in the RTR file.
4. Query—The property cannot be set by administration tools, but it can be queried by the RGM.

Table 6.3 Resource Properties

Property Name	Category	Description	Tunable	Comments
Cheap_probe_interval	Conditional	Number of seconds between two quick fault probes.	When disabled	If a default value is specified, this property is optional. If tunable, it is not set in RTR file, then property is only tunable "when disabled."
Load_balancing_policy	Conditional/Optional	String to define which load balancing policy to use	At creation	See Chapter 10
Load_balancing_weights	Conditional/Optional	For scalable resource only	Anytime	See Chapter 10
Extension properties	Conditional	Any additional property that can be defined by an application	Depends on specific property and application	
Failover_mode	Optional	Determines whether the RGM fails over a resource or aborts a node	Anytime	Occurs if a STOP or START method fails
Retry_interval	Conditional	Number of seconds between retry counts	When disabled	Used in conjunction with Retry_count
Retry_count	Conditional	Number of times a monitor will attempt to restart a resource	When disabled	Property is required if default is not specified
Method_timeout	Conditional/Optional	Time (in seconds) before a callback method times out	Anytime	Default is 3,600 seconds
Monitored_switch	Query-only	If disabled, the monitor does not have its START method called until property is enabled again	Never	Only used if resource has a monitor callback method defined
Through_probe_interval	Conditional	Number of seconds between the high-overhead fault probes.	When disabled	
On_off_switch	Query-only	Allows resources to be enabled or disabled	Never	
Network_resources_used	Conditional/Required	List of logical hostnames or shared address network resources	At creation	See Appendix B
Port_list	Conditional/Required	List of ports application is to use	At creation	
R_description	Optional	Description of resource	Anytime	
Resource_dependencies	Optional	List of resources in the same group that must also be online if resource is to be online	Anytime	
Resource_name	Required	Resource name	Never	
Resource_state: on each cluster node	Query-only	Status of resource as reported by the RGM	Never	States are: Online, Offline, Stop_failed, Start_failed, Monitor_failed, Online_not_monitored.

Property Name	Category	Description	Tunable	Comments
Type	Required	Instance resource name	Never	
Status: on each cluster node	Query-only	Set by resource monitor	Never	Values are OK, degraded, faulted, unknown, offline
Status_msg: on each cluster node	Query-only	Set by resource monitor	Never	Tunable per resource per node

Resource properties can also be tuned once running, for example, by changing a specific timeout value when the resource is online. Defining how and when a parameter is tunable is also specified within the RTR file. Parameters that are tunable also have an order when creating resources.

Tunable Property Values

1. None or False—Property can never be tuned
2. True or Anytime—Property can be tuned anytime
3. At_creation—Property can only be changed when a resource is added to the cluster
4. When_disabled—Property can only be tuned when the resource is disabled

Properties unique for resource groups are listed in Table 6.4.

RGM Naming Restrictions

There are some restrictions, not many, to the naming of RGM entities. With the exception of a resource type name determined by RESOURCE_TYPE RGM, names must

- Be ACSII
- Begin with a letter
- Not exceed 241 characters

Names can contain upper- and lowercase characters as well as digits, dashes, and underscores. However, periods cannot be used.

Legal VENDOR_ID = JPK;

Illegal VENDOR_ID = $JPK;

Illegal VENDOR_ID = J.P.K;

If the VENDOR_ID property is used, up-registering the resource type, a period will be inserted between the VENDOR_ID and RESOURCE_TYPE. For example, if VENDOR_ID = ABC and RESOURCE_TYPE = high_tech, on registration the RGM will merge these two properties to form a full name ABC.high_tech; this is the only time that a period is legal in an RGM name.

Table 6.4 Resource Group Properties

Property Name	Category	Description	Tunable	Comments
Desired_primaries	Optional	Desired number of nodes that this group can run on	Anytime	Default is 1. If RG_mode is failover this value can only be 1.
Failback	Optional	Allows the RGM to move a resource back to its original node after a failover	Anytime	
Global_resources_ used	Optional	Indicated if a GFS is being used by this resource group	Anytime	
Implicit_network_ dependencies	Optional	Ensures that the RGM starts or stops network address resources before any other non-networked resources	When disabled	
Maximum_primaries	Optional	Maximum number of nodes where the group might be online at one time	Anytime	
Nodelist	Optional	Comma-separated list of nodes where the group might be online at once	Anytime	
Pathprefix	Optional	Path to directory on the GFS to which resources can write essential files	Anytime	Some resources require this property, that is, NFS
Pingpong_interval	Optional	Time (in seconds) the RGM uses to determine where to bring the group online	Anytime	Used during a reconfiguration or during a forced failover. If the group fails to come up more than once on the node within this time interval, the node is no longer eligible to host the group. The RGM will look for another master.
Resource_List	Query-only	Lists of resources that are contained in the group	Never	RGM updates this property when resources are added or removed
RG_dependencies	Optional	Comma-separated list of resources that the group depends on.	Anytime	Preferred order of bringing groups online and offline (only on the same node)
RG_description	Optional	Description of the resource group	Anytime	

RGM Values

Like naming, the values of any RGM item can have minor restrictions. RGM values are either a numerical value or a description of the property. Both types of properties must follow these rules:

1. Property values must be ASCII.
2. They must not contain nulls, newlines, commas, or semicolons.
3. The maximum length of a value cannot exceed 4,194,303 (4 megabytes -1)

Legal START = simple_start;
Illegal START = simple;start;

Consult Appendix A for a detailed listing of resource types and their attributes.

Resource Property Attributes

Each of the resource types and resource properties must have valid input parameters; for example, "Vendor_ID" is a string and "API_version" is an integer. Table 6.5 lists the resource property attributes.

Table 6.5 Resource Property Attributes

Property Attribute	Description
Property	Resource property name.
Extension	If attribute is used, it indicates that the resource property is an extension property.
Description	A string used to describe a property. This attribute cannot be used on system-defined properties.
Type	Data type. Valid values are string, Boolean, in, enum and stringarray. Enum is a set of string values. Type cannot be used for system-defined properties.
Default	Default value of property.
Tunable	Determines whether the resource property can be modified. Setting this property to NONE or FALSE prevents administrators from modifying the property. A setting of True or Anytime allows for modifications. At_creation can be used to allow administrators to modify properties only at resource creation. When_disabled indicates that modification can only be done when the resource is offline. The default is True.
Enumlist	Permissible set of string values for properties of enum type.
Min	Minimum value for int properties.
Max	Maximum value for int properties.
Minlength	Minimum length for string and stringarray properties.
Maxlength	Maximum length for string and stringarray properties.
Array_minsize	Minimum number of array elements for stringarray properties.
Array_maxsize	Maximum number of array elements for stringarray properties.

Using Callback Methods

An excellent way to see how these callbacks are used is to create a resource type that has all 12 callback methods defined in it and observe how and when they are called. To illustrate this, we will create a resource type that has no special purpose. It will have a simple RTR file and 12 resource types defined but no extension properties. Notice within the RTR file that no additional values have been defined for the callback methods (description, timeout values). Example 6.3 shows the RTR to be used.

Example 6.3   RTR file created

```
#########################################################
# Resource Type Registration File

RESOURCE_TYPE="api_example_1";
RT_BASEDIR=/global/api_example1/;
RT_DESCRIPTION="Simple Resource Type. Used to illustrate how callback methods
are invoked";

#Which methods are going to be used
START = START;
STOP = STOP;
PRENET_START = PRENETSTART;
POSTNET_STOP = POSTNETSTOP;
MONITOR_START = MONITORSTART;
MONITOR_CHECK = MONITORCHECK;
MONITOR_STOP = MONITORSTOP;
VALIDATE = VALIDATE;
UPDATE = UPDATE;
INIT = INIT;
BOOT = BOOT;
FINI = FINI;
```

Now that the RTR file is created, we'll need some callback methods. Example 6.4 is a simple callback method—when called it will put a message in the messages log file stating that it was invoked with if/any arguments. We will use this method as a template for all 12 methods.

Example 6.4   Callback method

```
#!/bin/sh
# START Method for Example 1

SYSLOG_FACILITY='scha_cluster_get -O SYSLOG_FACILITY'

(echo ----------------------------------------------
echo Method: $0
echo Arguments: $*
echo-------------------------------------------------) | logger -p $SYSLOG_FACILITY.err \
-t "SunCluster: api_example_1"
```

To summarize this example in action, we will:

- Copy the script from Example 6.4 into 12 callback method files and label them appropriately. Be sure each file has execute permission.
- Move all the files to a mount point on the GFS.
- Register the resource type via `scrgadm`.
- Create a resource group.
- Create a resource.
- Assign the resource to the group.
- Bring the resource online.
- Move the resource around the cluster.
- Update the resource.
- Delete the resource.

The step-by-step process includes the following:

1. Create and move all files to a mount point on the GFS. Place a copy of the RTR file in the `/usr/cluster/lib/rgm/rtreg` directory.

Note – The `scrgadm` utility expects to find RTR files in the `/usr/cluster/lib/rgm/rtreg` directory. Use the `scrgadm -f` to indicate the RTR file path.

---

2. Register the resource type using

   ```
   scrgadm -a -t api_example_1
   ```

   The `-a` option is to add and `-t` signifies a resource type. This function is performed only once. You can verify that the resource type has been created using `scrgadm -p`. Also, using `scrgadm -pvv` will show property details for each resource type registered within the cluster.

3. Create a resource group using

   ```
   scrgadm -a -g example1 -h clnode0,clnode1
   ```

   The `-a` option is to add, `-g` is for group, and `-h` is for the nodes that will host this resource group, called example1, that can be hosted on either *clnode0* or *clnode1*.

4. Create a resource.

   ```
   scrgadm -a -g example1 -j example_res -t api_example_1
   ```

   After creating the resource type, notice the console or the messages file. The `VALIDATE` method would have fired off and produced the following output (The output was cleaned up a bit to make it easier to read.):

   ```
   clnode0 SunCluster: api_example_1: Method: /global/mis-
   cdg/test01/api_example1//VALIDATE
   ```

```
clnode0 SunCluster: api_example_1: Arguments: -c -R
example_res -T api_example_1
-G example1 -r Resource_dependencies= -r
Resource_dependencies_weak= -r START_TIMEOUT=3600
-r STOP_TIMEOUT=3600 -r VALIDATE_TIMEOUT=3600 -r
UPDATE_TIMEOUT=3600
-r INIT_TIMEOUT=3600 -r FINI_TIMEOUT=3600 -r
BOOT_TIMEOUT=3600
-r MONITOR_START_TIMEOUT=3600 -r MONITOR_STOP_TIMEOUT=3600
-r MONITOR_CHECK_TIMEOUT=3600 -r PRENET_START_TIMEOUT=3600
-r POSTNET_STOP_TIMEOUT=3600 -r Failover_mode=NONE -g
Nodelist=clnode0,clnode1 -g Maximum_primaries=1 -g
Desired_primaries=1 -g Failback=FALSE -g RG_dependencies= -g
Global_resources_used=* -g RG_mode=Failover -g
Implicit_network_dependencies=TRUE -g
Pathprefix= -g RG_description= -g Pingpong_interval=3600 -g
Auto_start_on_new_cluster=TRUE
```

It's interesting to note that the VALIDATE method is the only method that gets invoked at resource creation. Recall from the previous section, VALIDATE is called when a resource is created or when the resource's properties are updated.

5. Bring the resource group online using

```
scswitch -Z -g example1
```

When bringing the resource online, it's easy to see which methods are called by viewing the console or the */var/adm/messages* file. The methods called in order are INIT, PRENET_START, START, and MONITOR_START.

6. Switch the resource to another node using

```
scswitch -z -g example1 -h clnode1
```

Node1 console:

```
clnode0 SunCluster: api_example_1: Method: /global/miscdg/
test01/api_example1//MONITORSTOP
clnode0 SunCluster: api_example_1: Arguments: -R
example_res -T api_example_1 -G example1
clnode0 SunCluster: api_example_1:-------------------------
---------------------------------------------------------
clnode0 SunCluster: api_example_1: Method: /global/miscdg/
test01/api_example1//STOP
clnode0 SunCluster: api_example_1: Arguments: -R
example_res -T api_example_1 -G example1
clnode0 SunCluster: api_example_1:-------------------------
---------------------------------------------------------
clnode0 SunCluster: api_example_1: Method: /global/miscdg/
test01/api_example1//POSTNETSTOP
clnode0 SunCluster: api_example_1: Arguments: -R
example_res -T api_example_1 -G example1
```

Node2 console:

```
clnode1 SunCluster: api_example_1: Method: /global/miscdg/
test01/api_example1//PRENETSTART
clnode1 SunCluster: api_example_1: Arguments: -R
example_res -T api_example_1 -G example1
clnode1 SunCluster: api_example_1:------------------------
-------------------------------------------------------
clnode1 SunCluster: api_example_1: Method: /global/miscdg/
test01/api_example1//START
clnode1 SunCluster: api_example_1: Arguments: -R
example_res -T api_example_1 -G example1
clnode1 SunCluster: api_example_1:------------------------
-------------------------------------------------------
clnode1 SunCluster: api_example_1: Method: /global/miscdg/
test01/api_example1//MONITORSTART
clnode1 SunCluster: api_example_1: Arguments: -R
example_res -T api_example_1 -G example1
```

7. Update a resource property. In this case use the pingpong interval.

```
scrgadm -c -g example1 -y pingpong_interval=1
```

Node1 console:

```
clnode1 SunCluster: api_example_1: Method: /global/miscdg/
test01/api_example1//VALIDATE
clnode1 SunCluster: api_example_1: Arguments: -u -R
example_res -T api_example_1 -G example1 -g
Pingpong_interval=1
clnode1 SunCluster: api_example_1:------------------------
-------------------------------------------------------
clnode1 SunCluster: api_example_1: Method: /global/miscdg/
test01/api_example1//UPDATE
clnode1 SunCluster: api_example_1: Arguments: -R
example_res -T api_example_1 -G example1
```

Node0 console:

```
clnode0 SunCluster: api_example_1: Method: /global/miscdg/
test01/api_example1//VALIDATE
clnode0 SunCluster: api_example_1: Arguments: -u -R
example_res -T api_example_1 -G example1 -g
Pingpong_interval=1
```

Notice that the VALIDATE method is called on both nodes; however, the UPDATE method is only called on the node that has the resource online. Notice the VALIDATE method arguments.

8. Simulate an application restart. Invoke this command on the node on which the resource group is running.

```
scha_control -O restart -G example1 -R example_res
```

In this example, we used an RMAPI convenience function of *scha_control* to invoke a restart. This function would normally be used within a fault probe. Note the sequence of events on the node that has the resource online. The equivalent administration command is `scswitch -R -h target_node -g resouce_group`

```
clnode1 SunCluster: api_example_1: Method: /global/miscdg/
test01/api_example1//MONITORSTOP
clnode1 SunCluster: api_example_1: Arguments: -R
example_res -T api_example_1 -G example1
clnode1 SunCluster: api_example_1:------------------------
-----------------------------------------------------------
clnode1 SunCluster: api_example_1: Method: /global/miscdg/
test01/api_example1//STOP
clnode1 SunCluster: api_example_1: Arguments: -R
example_res -T api_example_1 -G example1
clnode1 SunCluster: api_example_1:------------------------
-----------------------------------------------------------
clnode1 SunCluster: api_example_1: Method: /global/miscdg/
test01/api_example1//POSTNETSTOP
clnode1 SunCluster: api_example_1: Arguments: -R
example_res -T api_example_1 -G example1
clnode1 SunCluster: api_example_1:------------------------
-----------------------------------------------------------
clnode1 SunCluster: api_example_1: Method: /global/miscdg/
test01/api_example1//PRENETSTART
clnode1 SunCluster: api_example_1: Arguments: -R
example_res -T api_example_1 -G example1
clnode1 SunCluster: api_example_1:------------------------
-----------------------------------------------------------
clnode1 SunCluster: api_example_1: Method: /global/miscdg/
test01/api_example1//START
clnode1 SunCluster: api_example_1: Arguments: -R
example_res -T api_example_1 -G example1
clnode1 SunCluster: api_example_1:------------------------
-----------------------------------------------------------
clnode1 SunCluster: api_example_1: Method: /global/miscdg/
test01/api_example1//MONITORSTART
clnode1 SunCluster: api_example_1: Arguments: -R
example_res -T api_example_1 -G example1
```

9. Simulate an application failover

```
scha_control -O giveover -G example1 -R example_res
```

Again, we use an RMAPI convenience function *scha_control* to invoke the failover. The equivalent administration command would be `scswitch -z - g resource_group -h target_node`.

Node1 console (giving up the resource):

```
clnode1 SunCluster: api_example_1: Method: /global/miscdg/
test01/api_example1//MONITORSTOP
clnode1 SunCluster: api_example_1: Arguments: -R
example_res -T api_example_1 -G example1
clnode1 SunCluster: api_example_1:------------------------
-----------------------------------------------------------
clnode1 SunCluster: api_example_1: Method: /global/miscdg/
test01/api_example1//STOP
clnode1 SunCluster: api_example_1: Arguments: -R
example_res -T api_example_1 -G example1
clnode1 SunCluster: api_example_1:------------------------
-----------------------------------------------------------
clnode1 SunCluster: api_example_1: Method: /global/miscdg/
test01/api_example1//POSTNETSTOP
clnode1 SunCluster: api_example_1: Arguments: -R
|example_res -T api_example_1 -G example1
```

Node0 console (receiving the resource):

```
clnode0 SunCluster: api_example_1: Method: /global/miscdg/
test01/api_example1//MONITORCHECK
clnode0 SunCluster: api_example_1: Arguments: -R
example_res -T api_example_1 -G example1
clnode0 SunCluster: api_example_1:------------------------
-----------------------------------------------------------
clnode0 SunCluster: api_example_1: Method: /global/miscdg/
test01/api_example1//PRENETSTART
clnode0 SunCluster: api_example_1: Arguments: -R
example_res -T api_example_1 -G example1
clnode0 SunCluster: api_example_1:------------------------
-----------------------------------------------------------
clnode0 SunCluster: api_example_1: Method: /global/miscdg/
test01/api_example1//START
clnode0 SunCluster: api_example_1: Arguments: -R
example_res -T api_example_1 -G example1
clnode0 SunCluster: api_example_1:------------------------
-----------------------------------------------------------
clnode0 SunCluster: api_example_1: Method: /global/miscdg/
test01/api_example1//MONITORSTART
clnode0 SunCluster: api_example_1: Arguments: -R
example_res -T api_example_1 -G example1
```

At this point we've seen all but three of the methods invoked: BOOT,
MONITOR_CHECK, and FINI. In the next example, node1 will give up the
resource, but we want to have the MONITOR_CHECK method fail. Recall that
the MONITOR_CHECK method checks the health of the standby node to see if it
can host the resource before a switchover is performed. If the exit code of the
method is zero, the RGM will proceed with the failover, otherwise it will not.

Note – Edit the MONITOR_CHECK script to return a nonzero exit code. Be sure to return it to a zero exit code after this test.

---

10. Perform a switchover using

    ```
    scha_control -O giveover -G example1 -R example_res
    ```

    Node0 console

    ```
    clnode0 Cluster.RGM.rgmd: RGM isn't failing resource group
    <example1> off of node <1>, because no current or potential
    master is healthy enough clnode0 Cluster.RGM.rgmd: Resource
    <example_res> of Resource Group <example1> failed monitor
    check on node <clnode1>
    ```

    Node1 console

    ```
    clnode1 Cluster.RGM.rgmd: monitor_check: method <MONITOR_
    CHECK> failed on resource <example_res> in resource group
    <example1> on node <clnode1>, exit code <1>
    ```

11. Perform a reboot on one of the nodes using

    ```
    sync;sync;reboot
    ```

Note – WARNING: Do this test only on a test cluster. Be sure you are not on a production cluster before doing a reboot.

Node1 console

```
clnode1 SunCluster: api_example_1:-------------------------
-------------------------------------------------------------
clnode1 SunCluster: api_example_1: Method: /global/miscdg/
test01/api_example1//BOOT
clnode1 SunCluster: api_example_1: Arguments: -R
example_res -T api_example_1 -G example1
clnode1 SunCluster: api_example_1:-------------------------
-------------------------------------------------------------
```

Notice after the reboot, the BOOT method is invoked only on the node that rejoined the cluster after a reboot.

12. Delete the resource. First disable it using

    ```
    scswitch -n -j example_res
    ```

    Notice the console output. Now delete the resource using:

    ```
    scrgadm -r -j example_res
    ```

Node1 console:

```
clnode0 SunCluster: api_example_1: Method: /global/miscdg/
test01/api_example1//FINI
clnode0 SunCluster: api_example_1: Arguments: -R
example_res -T api_example_1 -G example1
clnode0 SunCluster: api_example_1:------------------------
------------------------------------------------------------
```

Node0 console:

```
clnode1 SunCluster: api_example_1: Method: /global/miscdg/
test01/api_example1//FINI
clnode1 SunCluster: api_example_1: Arguments: -R
example_res -T api_example_1 -G example1
clnode1 SunCluster: api_example_1:------------------------
------------------------------------------------------------
```

Notice how the FINI method is called on both nodes. You can now remove the resource group and type using

```
scrgadm -r -g example1
scrgadm -r -t api_example_1
```

In this example we created a simplified resource type that had all 12 callback methods defined. Through some experimentation, we were able to see when and how each of these methods is invoked. Again, it's important to understand that not every application needs to have all 12 callback methods defined. A variety of callback methods are available to be used for specific events that your application may or may not need. Knowing when and why these methods work is crucial to creating robust resource types.

Summary

While the steps to create a resource type might seem overly complex, in reality it is a straightforward process. An understanding of the RTR file and its parameters is essential in creating resource types that will behave and perform as expected. It is important to remember that not all resources require every property or even resource monitoring; however, every resource does require a definition file (RTR file) and two callback methods: START and STOP.

7

PROGRAMMING WITH THE RMAPI

Introduction

The resource management API (RMAPI) consists of callback methods, C library functions, and command-line utilities to provide an interface to the resource group manager (RGM) and resource types. In this chapter, we will cover the RMAPI's C library functions and command-line utilities. These functions and command-line interfaces (CLIs) can be used to create highly available services and scalable services and can gather information about the cluster. For information regarding the RMAPI callback methods, refer to Chapter 6.

Getting Started

To start, you will need to set up your environment to access the commands or libraries in the RMAPI. If you are developing on a system that is not part of a cluster, you will need to load the SUNWscdev package. You also need to load the SUNWscman package to have access to the Sun Cluster 3.x man pages for reference.

For C development, you will need access to a compiler and to have the following added to your compiler and linker environments:

- Header files: -I /usr/cluster/include
- Static libraries: -L /usr/cluster/lib
- Dynamic libraries: -R /usr/cluster/lib

In your login environment, the *PATH* environment will need `/usr/cluster/bin` added. *MANPATH* will need `/usr/cluster/man` to access the Sun Cluster man pages.

Overview of the RMAPI

When integrating an application, either for high availability or scalability, you will need to write callback methods and possibly some support programs used by those callback methods. An example of a support program would be a monitor program that will be able to tell if your application is available and provides the service users need. The RMAPI provides the access methods to help develop these callback methods and also any support programs that will be needed. As covered in Chapter 6, some callback methods are required while some are not. The RTR file will define what callback methods will need to be developed. The RMAPI's libscha library contains access methods and utility methods made up of C library functions as well as CLIs, giving the developer the choice of writing C code or shell programs.

The RMAPI is a low-level program architecture that is used to interface between the resource group manager and resource types via callback methods and the libscha library, as shown in Figure 7.1.

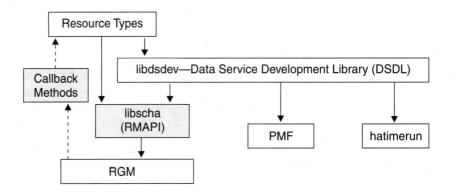

Figure 7.1 Resource management API

Access Methods

In the RMAPI, there are access methods that are considered to be the doorway or interface to the RGM for accessing the cluster. These methods are broken into two groups. The first group, get methods, retrieves information from areas such as:

- Cluster environment
- Resource type
- Resource
- Resource group

The second group, utility methods, provides functionality such as restart or failover control, resource status, and error status. Table 7.1 shows these access methods in their groups.

Table 7.1 RMAPI Access Methods

C Library Call (3HA)	CLI (1HA)
Get Methods	
scha_cluster_open scha_cluster_get scha_cluster_close scha_cluster_getlogfacility scha_cluster_getnodename	scha_cluster_get
scha_resourcetype_open scha_resourcetype_get scha_resourcetype_close	scha_resourcetype_get
scha_resource_open scha_resource_get scha_resource_close	scha_resource_get
scha_resourcegroup_open scha_resourcegroup_get scha_resourcegroup_close	scha_resourcegroup_get
Utility Methods	
scha_control	scha_control
scha_resource_setstatus	scha_resource_setstatus
scha_strerror	None

Get Methods

When programming in C, get methods require a handle to be opened prior to requesting information. Each get method function follows the same accessing flow.

OPEN Handle ◊ **Perform GET** ◊ **CLOSE Handle**

The get method must call the corresponding open function, perform the get function, and then close the handle. The open function is supplied a handle argument that holds the return value from the open call. This handle contains access information that is used by the corresponding get function call and also in the close function call. During the get function call, memory is allocated to hold the information requested by the supplied tag argument. The last argument supplied holds the returned data either as a value or as a data structure. That argument must be of the data type that is required for the specified tag argument. The memory that is allocated during the get method call stays allocated until the corresponding close function is called. At that time, the memory is freed and the handle is invalidated.

In the file `/usr/cluster/include/scha_tags.h`, there is a list of macros defined that can be used as tag arguments. These tag arguments can also be found in the man page for a particular get method. These man pages cover the tag argument and the output argument data type needed. Some tags require additional arguments to be supplied when used, such as a node name. For each get method discussed in the following sections, there is a table of tags that can be used along with a description and the output data type. If additional tag arguments are required, it will be noted in the description column. The `scha_calls` (3HA) man page also covers the output argument data types and the return codes for the access method functions.

The CLI version of the access methods uses *optags* to specify the information that needs to be retrieved. The retrieved information is returned to stdout as formatted strings. The `scha_cmds` (1HA) man page covers these optags and the format of the returned information. The format is based on the optag that is supplied in the command.

In the following sections, the get method along with its functions will be covered. Examples using the get method will follow after each function is described.

Note – C library functions are documented in man page section (3HA). Section (1HA) documents the command-line version.

Cluster Access Methods

The cluster access methods enable the developer to access information about the cluster. Callback methods or any cluster utilities can be developed to obtain information like the cluster name, nodes in the cluster, registered resource types, and resource groups registered within the cluster. Table 7.2 lists the information that can be obtained with the cluster get method.

Table 7.2 Cluster Tag Arguments

Tag Argument	Description	Output
SCHA_NODENAME_LOCAL	Local nodename of the calling program.	char **
SCHA_NODENAME_NODEID[1]	Nodename of the supplied nodeid.	char **
SCHA_ALL_NODENAMES	All nodenames in the cluster.	scha_str_array_t **
SCHA_ALL_NODEIDS	All nodeids in the cluster.	scha_uint_array_t **
SCHA_NODEID_LOCAL	Local nodeid of the calling program.	uint_t *
SCHA_NODEID_NODENAME[1]	Nodeid of the supplied nodename.	uint_t *
SCHA_PRIVATELINK_HOSTNAME_LOCAL	Local privatelink hostname from the calling program.	char **
SCHA_PRIVATELINK_HOSTNAME_NODE[1]	Privatelink hostname of the supplied nodename.	char **
SCHA_ALL_PRIVATELINK_HOSTNAMES	All privatelink hostnames in the cluster.	scha_str_array_t **
SCHA_NODESTATE_LOCAL	State of the local node, either UP or DOWN.	scha_node_state_t*
SCHA_NODESTATE_NODE[1]	State of the supplied node, either UP or DOWN.	scha_node_state_t*
SCHA_SYSLOG_FACILITY	Returns the number of the syslog facility used by the cluster log.	int *
SCHA_ALL_RESOURCEGROUPS	All managed resource groups in the cluster.	scha_str_array_t **
SCHA_ALL_RESOURCETYPES	All registered resource types in the cluster.	scha_str_array_t **
SCHA_CLUSTERNAME	Returns the cluster name.	char **

1. Requires additional char *tag argument

scha_cluster_open()

To access cluster information, the function `scha_err_t scha_cluster_get (scha_cluster_t *handle)` (3HA) is called to initialize a handle prior to accessing the cluster get function. The *scha_cluster_t *handle* is a pointer to address space that will be used by the cluster get function and the cluster close function.

scha_cluster_get()

Once the open function returns successfully, the `scha_err_t scha_cluster_get (scha_cluster_t handle, const char *tag, ...)` (3HA) is used to retrieve the desired cluster information. The first *const char *tag* argument will hold one of the tag arguments, listed in Table 7.2, to retrieve that information about the cluster environment. Upon successful completion of the function, the data will be stored in the last *tag* variable supplied in this function call. This variable must be of the data type described in the output column for the corresponding tag argument as shown in Table 7.2.

Some tag arguments will require additional information to retrieve the specified information. In Table 7.2, tag arguments that retrieve information from a node will require an additional argument for the nodename in the get function call. This additional argument would be between the first argument, which holds the tag argument, and the last argument, which will hold the return value from the get function call. Example 7.1 shows the use of multiple tag arguments.

Example 7.1   Multiple tag arguments

```
scha_err_t        err;
scha_cluster_t    handle;
const char        *phostname;

err = scha_cluster_get(handle,
SCHA_PRIVATELINK_HOSTNAME_NODE, "ClusterA", &phostname);
```

scha_cluster_close()

After retrieving the information with the cluster get function, `scha_err_t scha_cluster_close(scha_cluster_t *handle)` (3HA) must be called to invalidate the handle and free the allocated memory from the cluster get function call. Since the allocated memory stays intact till the cluster close is called, it would be good programming practice to make sure memory is freed when it is no longer needed.

Example 7.2 shows the use of the open, get, and close functions for the cluster get access method. In this example, the registered resource types are retrieved along with the cluster name. The tag, SCHA_ALL_RESOURCETYPES, tells the cluster get function to retrieve all the registered resource types within the cluster framework and store it in the structure *scha_str_array_t regd_rts*. To retrieve the cluster name, the SCHA_CLUSTERNAME tag is used by the cluster get function; this information is stored in *char *str*. The information is then sent to stdout via the printf function.

As always, it's good programming practice to handle error conditions. In this example, error conditions are handled by sending output to stderr and then exiting. Within the Sun Cluster environment, it is preferred to use the Solaris Operating Environment's (SOE) syslog facility to send messages to the console and to log the events in the /var/adm/messages file. This will be covered in the section "scha_cluster_getlogfacility()" in this chapter.

Example 7.2 scha_cluster_get()

```
#include <strings.h>
#include <stdio.h>
#include <stdlib.h>
#include <scha.h>


main()
{
scha_err_t              err;
scha_str_array_t        *regd_rts;
scha_cluster_t          handle;
int                     num;
const char              *str;

err = scha_cluster_open(&handle);
if (err != SCHA_ERR_NOERR) {
        fprintf(stderr, "FAILED: scha_cluster_open()%s\n",
         scha_strerror(err));
        exit(err);
}

err = scha_cluster_get(handle, SCHA_ALL_RESOURCETYPES, &regd_rts);
if (err != SCHA_ERR_NOERR) {
        fprintf(stderr, "FAILED: scha_cluster_get() %s\n",\
         scha_strerror(err));
        err = scha_cluster_close(handle); // Close the handle.
        exit(err);
}

err = scha_cluster_get(handle, SCHA_CLUSTERNAME, &str);
if (err != SCHA_ERR_NOERR) {
        fprintf(stderr, "FAILED: scha_cluster_get()%s\n",\
         scha_strerror(err));
        err = scha_cluster_close(handle); // Close the handle.
        exit(err);
}

printf("Cluster: %s has Registered Resource Types: ",str);

for(num = 0; num < regd_rts-> array_cnt; num++){
        printf("%s ", regd_rts->str_array[num]);
}

printf("\n");
```

```
err = scha_cluster_close(handle); // Close the handle,
if (err != SCHA_ERR_NOERR) {
      fprintf(stderr, "FAILED: scha_cluster_get()%s\n",\
       scha_strerror(err));
      exit(err);
}
}
```

scha_cluster_get - CLI

The scha_cluster_get -O *optag* (1HA) provides the same functionality as the scha_cluster_get() C function except for its use as a single command to get information about the cluster primarily for use in creating shell scripts that need to access cluster information. No handle is required to use this command, thus no open or close is needed.

The optags provided to this command are the same as the ones listed in Table 7.2; the only difference is that the SCHA_ prefix is not used. So the optag SCHA_ALL_RESOURCEGROUPS would drop the SCHA_ and just use ALL_RESOURCE-GROUPS.

The same optags that require additional arguments, as noted in Table 7.2, also apply when using the CLI version. The additional argument is supplied after the -O *optag* argument.

Example 7.3   scha_cluster_get CLI

```
#!/bin/ksh
clustname='scha_cluster_get -O CLUSTERNAME'
echo "Cluster $clustername has the following private hostnames:"
for a in 'scha_cluster_get -O ALL_NODENAMES'
do
 echo "On Node $a: 'scha_cluster_get -O PRIVATELINK_HOSTNAME_NODE
    $a'"
done
```

scha_cluster_getlogfacility()

One important part of developing callback methods is logging. System administrators and operators need to know if some event occurred within the cluster environment. The Sun Cluster environment uses the SOE syslog facility to log event messages to the console and to the /var/adm/messages file. Error messages, warning messages, and state changes can be logged to this syslog facility.

To access the syslog facility, it is necessary to get the log facility number. This can be retrieved with the function call scha_err_t scha_cluster_getlogfacility (int *logfacility) (3HA). This number, stored in *int *logfacility*, is then used by the openlog() (3C) function prior to a call to the syslog() (3C) function. Example 7.4 demonstrates the use of the getlogfacility function and logging to the syslog facility.

Example 7.4 scha_cluster_getlogfacility()

```
#include <strings.h>
#include <stdio.h>
#include <stdlib.h>
#include <scha.h>
#include <syslog.h>

main()
{
scha_err_t      err;
int             lognumber;

err = scha_cluster_getlogfacility(&lognumber);

if (err != SCHA_ERR_NOERR) {
        fprintf(stderr, "FAILED:scha_cluster_getlogfacility()%s\n",\
         scha_strerror(err));
        exit(err);
}

openlog("Log Facility", LOG_CONS, lognumber);

syslog(LOG_ALERT, "Function scha_getlogfacility call suceeded.\n");

closelog();
}
```

scha_cluster_getnodename()

To retrieve the nodename of the local node from a locally run program, the function scha_err_t scha_cluster_getnodename(char **nodename)(3HA) can be used. This function call provides the same functionality as the scha_cluster_get() function call with the SCHA_NODENAME_LOCAL tag argument without the use of an open and close function call. An example of this function is shown in Example 7.5.

Example 7.5 scha_cluster_getnodename()

```
#include <strings.h>
#include <stdio.h>
#include <stdlib.h>
#include <scha.h>
#include <syslog.h>

main()
{
scha_err_t      err;
int             lognumber;
char            *nodename;
```

```
err = scha_cluster_getlogfacility(&lognumber);
if (err != SCHA_ERR_NOERR) {
      fprintf(stderr,"FAILED:scha_cluster_getlogfacility()%s\n",\
       scha_strerror(err));
      exit(err);
}

err = scha_cluster_getnodename(&nodename);
if (err != SCHA_ERR_NOERR) {
      openlog("Sun Cluster", LOG_CONS, lognumber);
      syslog(LOG_ERR, "Function scha_getnodename call failed!\
%s\n", scha_strerror(err));
      closelog();
      exit(err);
}

printf("Nodename: %s\n", nodename);
}
```

Resource Type Access Methods

The resource type get methods provide a mechanism to retrieve information about a particular resource type that is registered within the Sun Cluster environment. When the RGM receives an event, such as enabling a resource, the RGM will call the START callback method. The resource type access method can be used to retrieve information needed by the START callback method. Table 7.3 lists the information that can be retrieved with the resource type get method, the tag argument, and the output data types needed to store the information.

scha_resourcetype_open()

To access resource type information, the function scha_err_t scha_resource-type_open(const char *rtname, scha_resourcetype_t *handle) (3HA) is called to initialize a handle prior to accessing the get function. The *scha_ resourcetype_t *handle* is a pointer to address space that will be used by the resource type get function and the resource type close function. A resource type name, such as *SUNW.nfs* for example, would be supplied to *char *rtname*.

scha_resourcetype_get()

After the open function is successful, the initialized handle is used in the scha_ err_t scha_resourcetype_get(scha_resourcetype_t *handle, const char *tag,...) (3HA) function to access various information about the resource type that was specified in the open function. The information that can be retrieved, shown in Table 7.3, can be accessed by supplying the tag argument to the first *const char *tag*. The last *const char *tag* will hold the return value from this function call. This last argument must be of the type shown in the corresponding output column in Table 7.3.

Table 7.3 Resource Type Tags

Tag Argument	Description	Output
SCHA_RT_DESCRIPTION	Resource type description.	char **
SCHA_RT_BASEDIR	Base directory for this resource type.	char **
SCHA_SINGLE_INSTANCE	If multiple instances (resources) can exist or just one of this resource type.	boolean_t *
SCHA_INIT_NODES	Nodes that can master this resource type.	scha_initnodes_flag_t *
SCHA_INSTALLED_NODES	List of nodes in a cluster that can run this resource type.	scha_str_array_t **
SCHA_FAILOVER	True, if resource of this type cannot be configured in a group that is online on more that one node at a time.	boolean_t *
SCHA_API_VERSION	API version of the resource type.	int *
SCHA_RT_VERSION	Version of this resource type.	char **
SCHA_PKGLIST	Package list for this resource type.	scha_str_array_t **
SCHA_START	Name of start method for this resource type.	char **
SCHA_STOP	Name of stop method for this resource type.	char **
SCHA_VALIDATE	Name of validate method for this resource type.	char **
SCHA_UPDATE	Name of update method for this resource type.	char **
SCHA_INIT	Name of init method for this resource type.	char **
SCHA_FINI	Name of fini method for this resource type.	char **
SCHA_BOOT	Name of boot method for this resource type.	char **
SCHA_MONITOR_START	Name of monitor_start method for this resource type.	char **
SCHA_MONITOR_STOP	Name of monitor_stop method for this resource type.	char **
SCHA_MONITOR_CHECK	Name of monitor_check method for this resource type.	char **
SCHA_PRENET_START	Name of prenet_start method for this resource type.	char **
SCHA_POSTNET_STOP	Name of postnet_stop method for this resource type.	char **
SCHA_IS_LOGICAL_HOSTNAME	True, if resource is a logical hostname.	boolean_t *
SCHA_IS_SHARED_ADDRESS	True, if resource is a shared address.	boolean_t *

scha_resourcetype_close()

Once you have finished with the information from the resource type get function, the `scha_err_t scha_resourcetype_close(scha_resourcetype_t *handle)` (3HA) is called to invalidate the handle and free the allocated memory from the resource type get function call.

In Example 7.6, the resource type get method is used to retrieve the base directory path of the resource type and its START callback method. When the RGM receives an event such as starting a resource, the RGM would need to know the path and the START method for that resource type.

Example 7.6   scha_resourcetype_get()

```
#include <strings.h>
#include <stdio.h>
#include <stdlib.h>
#include <scha.h>


main()
{
scha_err_t                  err;
scha_resourcetype_t         handle;
const char                  *pathstr;
const char                  *startstr;

err = scha_resourcetype_open("foobar",&handle);
if (err != SCHA_ERR_NOERR) {
        fprintf(stderr, "FAILED: scha_resourcetype_open()%s\n",\
         scha_strerror(err));
        exit(err);
}

err = scha_resourcetype_get(handle, SCHA_RT_BASEDIR, &pathstr);

if (err != SCHA_ERR_NOERR) {
        fprintf(stderr, "FAILED: scha_resourcetype_get()%s\n",\
         scha_strerror(err));
        err = scha_resourcetype_close(handle); // Close handle.
        exit(err);
}

err = scha_resourcetype_get(handle, SCHA_START, &startstr);
if (err != SCHA_ERR_NOERR) {
        fprintf(stderr, "FAILED:scha_resourcetype_get()%s\n",\
         scha_strerror(err));
        err = scha_resourcetype_close(handle); // Close handle.
        exit(err);
}

printf("Resource Type START METHOD: %s/%s\n", pathstr,startstr);
```

```
err = scha_resourcetype_close(handle); // Close handle,
if (err != SCHA_ERR_NOERR) {
        fprintf(stderr, "FAILED: scha_resourcetype_get()%s\n",\
         scha_strerror(err));
        exit(err);
}
}
```

scha_resourcetype_get - CLI

This scha_resourcetype_get -O *optag* -T *resourcetype* (1HA) command line (Example 7.7) is useful for getting information about a resource type from the command prompt. Its primary use is for shell scripts that need to access resource type information. Optags are the same as the C function tag arguments listed in Table 7.3, but without the SCHA_ prefix. The resource type is a registered data service like *SUNW.nfs*.

Example 7.7   scha_resourcetype_get CLI

```
#!/bin/ksh
basedir='scha_resourcetype_get -O RT_BASEDIR -T SUNW.nfs'
startup='scha_resourcetype_get -O START -T SUNW.nfs'
printf "Start Method: %s/%s\n" $basedir $startup
```

Resource Access Methods

The resource get methods provide a mechanism to retrieve information about a particular resource that is registered within the Sun Cluster environment. Since each resource is its own instance of a resource type, parameters for each resource may need to be different. For example, the "Super Mega Web Store" database resource may need a different, longer START_TIMEOUT value than what the "My Stock Portfolio" database resource will ever need. Table 7.4 lists the information that can be retrieved with the resource get methods. Also note that the resource type information listed in Table 7.3 can also be retrieved with the resource get method.

scha_resource_open()

Gathering information about a particular resource requires that the open function scha_err_t scha_resource_open(const char *rname, const char *rgname, scha_resource_t *handle) (3HA) is called first to initialize the *scha_resource_t *handle*. In this open function, the resource name, *char *rname* and the resource group name of interest, *char *rgname*, are supplied. A value of NULL can be supplied for the resource group name if it is not known. The function will operate more efficiently, however, if the resource group name is supplied.

scha_resource_get()

Once a valid handle is returned from the open function, resource and resource type information can be retrieved with the scha_err_t scha_resource_get(scha_ `resource_t handle, const char *tag,...) (3HA)` function. Tag arguments from either Table 7.4 (for resource information) or Table 7.3 (for resource type information) are accessed by supplying the tag argument to the first *const char *tag*. Output is returned to the last *char *tag* and must be of the specified type shown in the corresponding output column for that tag argument. If additional arguments are required per the tag argument, this argument is added to the function call as a *char *tag* between the first and last arguments. See Example 7.1 on how additional tag arguments are used.

Table 7.4 Resource Tags

Tag Argument	Description	Output
SCHA_R_DESCRIPTION	Resource description.	char **
SCHA_TYPE	Resource type of this resource.	char **
SCHA_TYPE_VERSION[1]	Resource type version of this resource.	char **
SCHA_RESOURCE_PROJECT_NAME[1]	Solaris project name for this resource, man page `project (1)`. For applying Solaris resource management features.	char **
SCHA_ON_OFF_SWITCH	Disabled or enabled resource. No callbacks are called until enabled.	scha_switch_t*
SCHA_MONITORED_SWITCH	Disabled or enabled the monitor. No Start callback until enabled.	scha_switch_t*
SCHA_RESOURCE_STATE	State of resource on each node, Online, Offline, Stop_failed, Start_failed, Monitor_failed, Online_not_monitored.	scha_rsstate_t*
SCHA_CHEAP_PROBE_INTERVAL	Time (in seconds) between quick fault probe invocations.	int*
SCHA_THOROUGH_PROBE_INTERVAL	Time (in seconds) between high overhead fault probe invocations.	int*
SCHA_RETRY_COUNT	Number of times the monitor will attempt to restart the resource if it fails.	int*
SCHA_RETRY_INTERVAL	Time interval to count the number of attempts to restart a failed resource.	int*
SCHA_NUM_RG_RESTARTS[1]	Number of scha_control RESTART calls made by this resource on this node with n seconds, n = Retry_interval.	int*
SCHA_NUM_RESOURCE_RESTARTS[1]	Number of scha_control RESOURCE_RESTART and/or RESOURCE_IS_RESTARTED calls that have been made on this node with n seconds, n = retry interval.	int*

Tag Argument	Description	Output
SCHA_FAILOVER_MODE	Failover mode, either NONE, SOFT, or HARD	scha_failover_mode_t*
SCHA_RESOURCE_ DEPENDENCIES	List of other resources on which this resource has a strong dependency.	scha_str_array_t **
SCHA_RESOURCE_ DEPENDENCIES_WEAK	List of other resources on which this resource has a weak dependency.	scha_str_array_t **
SCHA_NETWORK_ RESOURCES_USED	List of logical hostnames or shared addresses for scalable services.	scha_str_array_t **
SCHA_SCALABLE	True, if resource is scalable.	boolean_t *
SCHA_PORT_LIST	Network port/protocol used.	scha_str_array_t **
SCHA_LOAD_BALANCING_ POLICY	Load balancing policy in use. LB_WEIGHTED (default), LB_ STICKY, and LB_STICKY_WILD.	char **
SCHA_LOAD_BALANCING_ WEIGHTS	Scalable services load distribution per node. Form of weight@nodeid, weight@nodeid. Default value is empty or even distribution.	scha_str_array_t **
SCHA_AFFINITY_TIMEOUT[1]	Time (in seconds) in which connections from a given client IP address for any service in the resource will be sent to the same node.	int*
SCHA_WEAK_AFFINITY[1]	Enabled, when true, weak client affinity.	boolean_t *
SCHA_UDP_AFFINITY[1]	Enabled, when true, all UDP traffic to the same server node that handles all TCP traffic for that client.	boolean_t *
SCHA_START_TIMEOUT	Start method timeout value.	int*
SCHA_STOP_TIMEOUT	Stop method timeout value.	int*
SCHA_VALIDATE_TIMEOUT	Validate method timeout value.	int*
SCHA_UPDATE_TIMEOUT	Update method timeout value.	int*
SCHA_INIT_TIMEOUT	Init method timeout value.	int*
SCHA_FINI_TIMEOUT	Fini method timeout value.	int*
SCHA_BOOT_TIMEOUT	Boot method timeout value.	int*
SCHA_MONITOR_START_ TIMEOUT	Monitor_Start method timeout value.	int*
SCHA_MONITOR_STOP_ TIMEOUT	Monitor_Stop method timeout value.	int*
SCHA_MONITOR_CHECK_ TIMEOUT	Monitor_Check method timeout value.	int*

continues

Table 7.4 Resource Tags (continued)

Tag Argument	Description	Output
SCHA_PRENET_START_TIMEOUT	Prenet_Start method timeout value.	int*
SCHA_POSTNET_STOP_TIMEOUT	Postnet_Stop method timeout value.	int*
SCHA_STATUS	Status of resource on node on which binary is run.	scha_status_value_t **
SCHA_STATUS_NODE[2]	Status of resource on the supplied nodename.	scha_status_value_t **
SCHA_RESOURCE_STATE_NODE[2]	Returns the state of a resource on a given node.	scha_rsstate_t **
SCHA_EXTENSION[2]	Returns a structure for a given extension property.	scha_extprop_value_t **
SCHA_ALL_EXTENSIONS	Returns the name of all extension properties for the resource.	scha_str_array_t **
SCHA_GROUP	Resource group name where the resource is configured.	char **

1. New as of Sun Cluster 3.1.
2. Requires additional char *tag argument.

scha_resource_close()

After retrieving the information with the resource get function, scha_err_t scha_resource_close(scha_resource_t *handle) is called to invalidate the handle and free the allocated memory from the resource get call.

In Chapter 8, use of the Process Monitor Facility (PMF) and the pmfadm (1HA) command will be discussed. Two parameters supplied to the pmfadm command were the RETRY_COUNT and the RETRY_INTERVAL. Example 7.8 demonstrates how these parameters could be retrieved within a callback method.

Example 7.8   scha_resource_get()

```
#include <strings.h>
#include <stdio.h>
#include <stdlib.h>
#include <scha.h>

main()
{
scha_err_t              err;
scha_resource_t         handle;
const int               *rc;
const int               *ri;

err = scha_resource_open("foobar","foobarrg",&handle);
```

```
if (err != SCHA_ERR_NOERR) {
      fprintf(stderr, "FAILED: scha_resource_open()%s\n",\
       scha_strerror(err));
      exit(err);
}

err = scha_resource_get(handle, SCHA_RETRY_COUNT, &rc);
if (err != SCHA_ERR_NOERR) {
      fprintf(stderr, "FAILED: scha_resource_get()%s\n",\
       scha_strerror(err));
      err = scha_resource_close(handle); // Close the handle.
      exit(err);
}

err = scha_resource_get(handle, SCHA_RETRY_INTERVAL, &ri);
if (err != SCHA_ERR_NOERR) {
      fprintf(stderr, "FAILED: scha_resource_get()%s\n",\
       scha_strerror(err));
      err = scha_resource_close(handle); // Close the handle.
      exit(err);
}

printf("Retry Count= %d, Retry Interval= %d\n", rc,ri);

err = scha_resource_close(handle); // Close the handle,
if (err != SCHA_ERR_NOERR) {
      fprintf(stderr, "FAILED: scha_resource_get()%s\n",\
       scha_strerror(err));
      exit(err);
}
}
```

scha_resource_get - CLI

The `scha_resource_get` `-O` *optag* `-R` *resource* [`-G` *resourcegroup*] (1HA) command is used to access information about the specified resource. The resource group need not be specified because resource names are unique within the cluster. Specifying the resource group will speed response, since searching for the resource when multiple resource groups are configured avoids searching through each resource group. The optag information for the resource, in Table 7.4, and its resource type, in Table 7.3, are used, but without the SCHA_ prefix. See Example 7.9.

Example 7.9   scha_resource_get CLI

```
#!/bin/ksh
rint='scha_resource_get -O RETRY_INTERVAL -R "mysql-r" -G     "db-rg"
rcnt='scha_resource_get -O RETRY_COUNT -R "mysql-r" -G "db-rg"
printf "Retry Count: %d, Retry Interval: %d\n" $rcnt $rint
```

Resource Group Access Methods

The resource group get methods are used to retrieve information about a particular resource group. Information such as dependencies and ping pong interval can be accessed. Table 7.5 lists the information that can be accessed about a resource group using the resource get methods.

scha_resourcegroup_open()

To initialize this handle, the function `scha_err_t scha_resourcegroup_open (const char *rgname, scha_resourcegroup_t *handle)` (3HA) is used. The handle *scha_resourcegroup_t *handle* is a pointer to address space that is used by the resource group get and close functions. The resource group name of interest is supplied to *const char *rgname*.

scha_resourcegroup_get()

Once the open function returns successfully, the initialized handle is used to access various resource group information using the `scha_err_t scha_resource-group_get(scha_resourcegroup_t *handle, const char *tag...)` (3HA) function. The information that can be retrieved, shown in Table 7.5, can be accessed by supplying the tag argument to the first *const char *tag*. The last *char *tag* holds the return value from this function call and must be of the same data type shown in the corresponding output column of Table 7.5.

Again, if the tag requires an additional argument, this is supplied after the tag argument and before the last `char *tag` as shown in Example 7.1.

scha_resourcegroup_close()

After retrieving the information with the resource group get function, `scha_err_t scha_resourcegroup_close(scha_resourcegroup_t *handle)` (3HA) is called to invalidate the handle and free the allocated memory from the resource group get call. Remember, the allocated memory stays intact until the close function is called, so use the close call to ensure that memory is freed when it is no longer needed.

In Example 7.10, the tag argument SCHA_NODELIST is used to retrieve the list of nodes that can become master for the resource group *foobar-rg*. While not much of an issue in a two-node cluster, in clusters greater that two nodes it's possible to partition the resource group so that it may not be mastered on some nodes in the cluster. For example, a three-node cluster may have its resource groups use node B as the failover node. Node A can failover its applications to node B, but not node C. Node C can failover its applications to node B, but not node A. In Example 7.10 the node list is retrieved for resource group *foobar-rg* and is sent to standard out.

Table 7.5 Resource Group Tags

Tag Argument	Description	Output
SCHA_RG_DESCRIPTION	RG description.	char **
SCHA_NODELIST	List of nodes that can be a primary for this resource group.	scha_str_array_t **
SCHA_MAXIMUM_ PRIMARIES	Maximum number of nodes where this resource group can be online at once.	int *
SCHA_DESIRED_ PRIMARIES	Number of nodes desired to be online at once.	int *
SCHA_FAILBACK	Indicates whether to recalculate the set of nodes where the resource group is online when the cluster membership changes.	boolean_t *
SCHA_RESOURCE_LIST	List of resources within the resource group.	scha_str_array_t **
SCHA_RG_STATE	State of the resource group on the local node.	scha_rgstate_value_t *
SCHA_RG_STATE_NODE[1]	State of the resource group on the specified node.	scha_rgstate_value_t *
SCHA_RG_DEPENDENCIES	List of resource groups on which this group depends. List represents order groups are brought online or offline even if not on the same node.	scha_str_array_t **
SCHA_RG_MODE	Indicates if the resource group is a failover group or a scalable group.	scha_rgmode_t *
SCHA_IMPL_NET_DEPEND	Enforce when true. Implicit strong dependencies of nonnetwork address resources on network address resources within the group.	boolean_t *
SCHA_GLOBAL_ RESOURCES_USED	Indicates if the cluster filesystem is used by any resource within the resource group.	scha_str_array_t **
SCHA_PATHPREFIX	Directory where resources within the resource group can write administrative files. Must be a global filesystem.	char **
SCHA_PINGPONG_ INTERVAL	Period in which the resource group cannot be restarted on a node if it failed to come online once before.	int *
SCHA_RG_PROJECT_ NAME[2]	Solaris project name for this resource group, man page project (1). For applying Solaris resource management features.	char **
SCHA_RG_AUTO_START[2]	Automatically, when true, start the resource group when a new cluster is forming. Otherwise manual start of resource group.	boolean_t *

1. Requires additional char *tag argument.
2. New as of Sun Cluster 3.1.

Example 7.10   scha_resourcegroup_get()

```c
#include <strings.h>
#include <stdio.h>
#include <stdlib.h>
#include <scha.h>


main()
{
scha_err_t              err;
scha_resourcegroup_t    handle;
scha_str_array_t        *nodelist;
int                     num;

err = scha_resourcegroup_open("foobar-rg",&handle);
if (err != SCHA_ERR_NOERR) {
        fprintf(stderr, "FAILED: scha_resourcegroup_open()%s\n",\
         scha_strerror(err));
        exit(err);
}

err = scha_resourcegroup_get(handle, SCHA_NODELIST, &nodelist);
if (err != SCHA_ERR_NOERR) {
        fprintf(stderr, "FAILED: scha_resourcegroup_get()%s\n",\
         scha_strerror(err));
        err = scha_resourcegroup_close(handle);
        exit(err);
}

printf("Nodes that can host this resource group:\n");
for(num = 0; num < nodelist-> array_cnt; num++){
        printf("%s ", nodelist->str_array[num]);
}
printf("\n");

err = scha_resourcegroup_close(handle);
if (err != SCHA_ERR_NOERR) {
        fprintf(stderr, "FAILED: scha_resourcegroup_get()%s\n",\
         scha_strerror(err));
        exit(err);
}
}
```

scha_resourcegroup_get - CLI

To access resource group information in either shell scripts or from the command prompt, the scha_resourcegroup_get -O *optag* -G *resourcegroup* (1HA) CLI can be used. Table 7.5 shows the information that can be retrieved about the specified resource group and the optag needed to access that information. When using this command, the SCHA_ prefix is not used in the optag. See Example 7.11.

Example 7.11   scha_resourcegroup_get CLI

```
#!/bin/ksh
nodelist='scha_resourcegroup_get -O NODELIST -G foobar-rg'
printf "Nodes that can host this resource group: %s\n" $nodelist
```

Utility Methods

So far, the methods covered in this chapter are intended to retrieve information about the cluster, resource types, resources, and resource groups. Utility methods provide functionality to set resource status, control resources and resource groups, and to retrieve messages based on the error code provided from the get method or utility method calls.

When developing resource type callback methods, it will be necessary to respond to events that could occur. If, for example, a particular application monitor is having an issue with querying status information on that application, the monitor program will need to determine if the application is slow to respond or not responding at all. At some point, if the application in not responding at all, there will need to be some action. These methods give the ability to take some action—such as sending a message to syslog based on the error code received on an RMAPI function call, restarting or failing over to another node within the cluster, and setting resource status messages.

scha_control()

At some point in time, it will be necessary to request a restart or to move a service to another node. This is where the function scha_err_t scha_control(const char *tag, const char *rgname, const char *rname) (3HA) is used. The resource monitor is responsible for ensuring that the application is available and providing service. If the resource monitor detects that the application is not performing as expected, then the monitor will need to perform some action, such as restarting or moving the application to another node in the cluster. Table 7.6 lists the actions that can be taken with this function. The resource monitor would use this function to perform these tasks if necessary.

When a restart is requested for a resource, the callback methods called in order are:

```
MONITOR_STOP
STOP
START
MONITOR_START
```

Table 7.6 Scha Control Tags

Tag Argument	Description
SCHA_RESTART	Request that the given resource group be brought offline and then online without necessarily moving to another node.
SCHA_RESOURCE_RESTART	Request that the given resource be brought offline and then online without stopping other resources within the group.
SCHA_RESOURCE_IS_RESTARTED	Request that the given resource restart counter be incremented on the local node.
SCHA_GIVEOVER	Request that the given resource group be offlined on the local node and onlined on another node within the cluster.
SCHA_CHECK_RESTART	Performs all validity checks for a given resource group as the SCHA_RESTART does but without restarting the resource group.
SCHA_CHECK_GIVEOVER	Performs all validity checks for a given resource group as the SCHA_GIVEOVER does but without reallocating the resource group.

If the monitor stop and monitor start callback methods are not defined, then just stop and start will be called. If a SCHA_GIVEOVER is requested from a monitor program, the resource group will be relocated to another eligible node within the cluster. Validity checks via the MONITOR_CHECK callback method are performed on the node prior to having the resource group relocated to it. Validity checks are also performed when the SCHA_RESTART tag argument is used.

Tag arguments SCHA_CHECK_GIVEOVER and SCHA_CHECK_RESTART perform the same checks as SCHA_RESTART and SCHA_GIVEOVER but without performing the actual restart or giveover. An application monitor may need to interact directly with the application, instead of having the callback methods stop and start it. The developer will need to perform checks to ensure that the direct start will work.

Resource monitors for an application can be complex. Monitors, depending on the application, will need to have some algorithm to determine when to restart or have the application move to another node. In some cases, the application will not be able to continue running and a fault will need to be set. Example 7.12 is a short example of the use of the scha_control()(3HA) function.

Example 7.12   scha_control

```
#include <strings.h>
#include <stdio.h>
#include <stdlib.h>
#include <scha.h>

 main()
 {
  scha_err_t            err;
  const char            *tag_arg=SCHA_GIVEOVER;
  const char            *rgname="foobar-rg";
  const char            *rname="foo-r";

 err = scha_control(tag_arg, rgname, rname);
 if (err != SCHA_ERR_NOERR) {
       fprintf(stderr,"FAILED:scha_control()%s\n",\
           scha_strerror(err));
       exit(err);
  }
}
```

scha_control - CLI

The scha_control -O *optag* -G *resourcegroup* -R *resource* (1HA) command-line interface provides the same functionality as the C function scha_control() (3HA). It is primarily intended for use in monitoring shell scripts and uses the same optags as in Table 7.6, but without the SCHA_ prefix.

Example 7.13   scha_control CLI

```
#!/bin/ksh
# Restart has failed!
if [[ $? != 0 ]]; then
    scha_control -O GIVEOVER -G foobar-rg -R foo-r
fi
```

If a monitor script tried restarting an application and failed, in this example the scha_control would cause the resource group *foobar-rg* to migrate over to another node in the cluster. In a cluster that is greater than two nodes, the resource group could migrate over to any node that can be a primary for that resource group. There is no option to specify a particular host. This command, if used at the command prompt, would have to be run on the node that is primary to the *foobar-rg* resource group.

scha_resource_setstatus()

The function scha_err_t scha_resource_setstatus(const *rname, const char *rgname, scha_rsstatus_t status, const char *status_msg) (3HA) provides the developer the means to update the status field for a particular resource within a resource group.

State versus Status

The RGM provides state information about resource groups, and both state and status information about a resource. This information can be viewed with the cluster status command scstat (1M). The command by itself will provide information regarding the whole cluster, but for information just about resources and resource groups, the argument -g can be used with this command:

 # scstat -g

```
-- Resource Groups and Resources --

               Group Name              Resources
               ----------              ---------
   Resources:  mysql-rg               nealhost2

-- Resource Groups --

               Group Name              Node Name            State
               ----------              ---------            -----
       Group:  mysql-rg               neaclust1            Offline
       Group:  mysql-rg               neaclust2            Online
       Group:  mysql-rg               neaclust3            Offline

-- Resources --

Resource Name         Node Name      State     Status Message
-------------         ---------      -----     --------------
Resource:nealhost2   neaclust1      Offline    Offline
Resource:nealhost2   neaclust2      Online     Online - Logical-
                                                  Hostname online.
Resource:nealhost2   neaclust3      Offline    Offline
```

The output from this command shows the state of the resource group on each particular node in the cluster. The possible states for resource groups can be: online, offline, pending_online, pending_offline, unmanaged, or error_stop_failed. For resources, on each node, the output shows both the state and the status. The possible states for a resource are: Online, Offline, Start_failed, Stop_failed, Monitor_failed, or Online_not_monitored.

The state of either the resource group or the resource is set by the RGM. A user can change the state of either the resource group or the resource via the scswitch(1M) command. Using this command will trigger an event to which the RGM will respond, such as taking a resource Offline. The RGM will update the state field once the event is completed. The state is based on the enumerated type *scha_rsstate_t* for resources and *scha_rgstate_t* for resource groups. See the section "Data Types" in this chapter regarding these types.

For resources, the RGM provides additional status information. While state information is controlled and updated by the RGM, status information for a resource can be updated by the developer or the system administrator via the API. The status for a resource can be: Online, Offline, Degraded, Faulted, and Unknown. In the scha_resource_setstatus() (3HA) function, there are two arguments that are for the resource status *scha_rsstatus_t*, which is an enumerated type, and the status message *char *status_msg*. The status_msg can be set to NULL if no message is needed.

In Example 7.14, the resource get method is use to retrieve both the status and state of a resource. If the resource status *r_status->status* is Online, then change the status to Offline and set the status_msg. Both the state and status of the resource are printed to stdout before and after the change is made. This also demonstrates that while the RGM controls the state of the resource, the status can be changed independently of the state should you choose to do so.

Example 7.14   scha_resource_setstatus()

```
#include <strings.h>
#include <stdio.h>
#include <stdlib.h>
#include <scha.h>

main()
{
scha_err_t              err;
scha_resource_t         handle;
scha_status_value_t     *r_status;
scha_rsstate_t          *r_state;
char                    *str;
char                    *rgname = "mysql-rg";
char                    *rname = "nealhost2";

err = scha_resource_open(rname, rgname, &handle);
if (err != SCHA_ERR_NOERR) {
        fprintf(stderr, "FAILED: scha_resource_open()%s\n",
         scha_strerror(err));
        exit(err);
}

err = scha_resource_get(handle, SCHA_STATUS, &r_status);
if (err != SCHA_ERR_NOERR) {
        fprintf(stderr, "FAILED: scha_resource_get() %s\n",
         scha_strerror(err));
        err = scha_resource_close(handle); // Close the handle.
        exit(err);
}

printf("SCHA_STATUS: %d\n", r_status -> status);
if(r_status -> status_msg != NULL) printf("Msg: %s\n", r_status -> status_msg);
```

```
err = scha_resource_get(handle, SCHA_RESOURCE_STATE, &r_state);
if (err != SCHA_ERR_NOERR) {
      fprintf(stderr, "FAILED: scha_resource_get() %s\n",
       scha_strerror(err));
      err = scha_resource_close(handle); // Close the handle.
      exit(err);
}

printf("SCHA_RESOURCE_STATE:  %d\n", r_state);

if(r_status -> status == SCHA_RSSTATUS_OK){ // Change status
      printf("Changing status.\n");
      err = scha_resource_setstatus(rname, rgname,
          SCHA_RSSTATUS_OFFLINE, "Out to Lunch");
      if (err != SCHA_ERR_NOERR) { fprintf(stderr, "FAILED:
                  scha_resource_setstatus()%s\n",
                          scha_strerror(err));
            err = scha_resource_close(handle); // Close handle.
            exit(err);
      }
}

err = scha_resource_get(handle, SCHA_RESOURCE_STATE, &r_state);
if (err != SCHA_ERR_NOERR) {
      fprintf(stderr, "FAILED: scha_resource_get() %s\n",
                  scha_strerror(err));
      err = scha_resource_close(handle); // Close the handle.
      exit(err);
}

printf("SCHA_RESOURCE_STATE: %d\n", r_state);

err = scha_resource_get(handle, SCHA_STATUS, &r_status);
if (err != SCHA_ERR_NOERR) {
      fprintf(stderr, "FAILED: scha_resource_get() %s\n",
scha_strerror(err));
      err = scha_resource_close(handle); // Close handle.
      exit(err);
}

printf("SCHA_STATUS: %d\n", r_status -> status);
if(r_status -> status_msg != NULL) printf("Msg: %s\n",
                  r_status -> status_msg);

err = scha_resource_close(handle); // Close the handle,
if (err != SCHA_ERR_NOERR) {
      fprintf(stderr, "FAILED: scha_resource_get()
                  %s\n", scha_strerror(err));
      exit(err);
}
}
```

scha_resource_setstatus - CLI

The command line version, scha_resource_setstatus -R *resource* -G group -s *status* [-m *msg*] (1HA) is intended for use in shell-based resource monitors. It provides the means to update the status field for a resource on a particular node. Status can be updated to one of the following values: Ok, Degraded, Faulted, Unknown, or Offline. The optional *msg* is a text string providing information about the state of that resource such as "Offline due to application upgrades." Refer back to "State versus Status" in this chapter for more information on the status field. See Example 7.15.

Example 7.15   scha_resource_setstatus CLI

```
# scswitch -n -j foobar-r
# scha_resource_setstatus -R foobar-r -G foobar-rg -s OFFLINE -m "Offline for
application updates"
```

scha_strerror()

The function char *scha_strerror(scha_err_t err_code) (3HA) can be used to retrieve an error message based on the supplied *scha_err_t err_code*. The message returned may be terse, but it will be useful in determining what the issue is when dealing with error returns from the RMAPI libscha function calls. This function call is intended to be used with the syslog (3C) function to log messages to the system console and /var/adm/messages file. See Example 7.16.

Note – The scha_strerror() C function does not have a command-line interface available.

Example 7.16   scha_strerror()

```
#include <strings.h>
#include <stdio.h>
#include <stdlib.h>
#include <syslog.h>
#include <scha.h>

main()
{
scha_err_t              err;
scha_resourcegroup_t    handle;
scha_str_array_t        *nodelist;
int                     num;
int                     lognumber;
char                    *str;

err = scha_cluster_getlogfacility(&lognumber);
```

```
if (err != SCHA_ERR_NOERR) {
        fprintf(stderr, "FAILED: scha_cluster_getlogfacility() \
        %s\n",scha_strerror(err));
        exit(err);
}

openlog("Sun Cluster", LOG_CONS, lognumber);

err = scha_resourcegroup_open("foobar-rg",&handle);
if (err != SCHA_ERR_NOERR) {
        syslog(LOG_ERR, "FAILED: scha_resourcegroup_open()      %s\n",
scha_strerror(err));
        exit(err);
}

err = scha_resourcegroup_get(handle, SCHA_NODELIST, &nodelist);
if (err != SCHA_ERR_NOERR) {
        syslog(LOG_ERR, "FAILED: scha_resourcegroup_get() \
         %s\n",scha_strerror(err));
        err = scha_resourcegroup_close(handle);
        exit(err);
}

printf("Nodes that can host this resource group:\n");
for(num = 0; num < nodelist-> array_cnt; num++){
        printf(" %s ", nodelist->str_array[num]);
}
printf("\n");

err = scha_resourcegroup_close(handle);
if (err != SCHA_ERR_NOERR) {
        syslog(LOG_ERR, "FAILED: scha_resourcegroup_get() \
         %s\n",scha_strerror(err));
        exit(err);
}
}
```

Data Types

Both access methods and utility methods use data types that are found within the RMAPI libscha library. These data types are listed in this section as a reference to aid in developing data services using this library. One thing to note is that these types are listed in the file, /usr/cluster/include/scha_types.h.

Enumerated Types

Many of the data types in the libscha library are enumerated types. Since there is no grouping of their usage with either get methods or utility methods, the easiest way to present them is in a table. Table 7.7 shows these enumerated types along with the values and the tag arguments associated with them.

Table 7.7 Libscha Enumerated Types

Type	Values	Tag Argument
scha_switch_t	SCHA_SWITCH_DISABLED=0 SCHA_SWITCH_ENABLED	SCHA_ON_OFF_SWITCH SCHA_MONITORED_SWITCH
scha_rsstatus_t	SCHA_RSSTATUS_OK=0 SCHA_RSSTATUS_OFFLINE SCHA_RSSTATUS_FAULTED SCHA_RSSTATUS_DEGRADED SCHA_RSSTATUS_UNKNOWN	SCHA_STATUS SCHA_STATUS_NODE
scha_rsstate_t	SCHA_RSSTATE_ONLINE=0 SCHA_RSSTATE_OFFLINE SCHA_RSSTATE_START_FAILED SCHA_RSSTATE_STOP_FAILED SCHA_RSSTATE_MONITOR_FAILED SCHA_RSSTATE_ONLINE_NOT_ MONITORED SCHA_RSSTATE_STARTING SCHA_RSSTATE_STOPPING SCHA_RSSTATE_DETACHED[1]	SCHA_RESOURCE_STATE SCHA_RESOURCE_STATE_NODE
scha_rgstate_t	SCHA_RGSTATE_UNMANAGED=0 SCHA_RGSTATE_ONLINE SCHA_RGSTATE_OFFLINE SCHA_RGSTATE_PENDING_ONLINE SCHA_RGSTATE_PENDING_OFFLINE SCHA_RGSTATE_ERROR_STOP_FAILED SCHA_RGSTATE_ONLINE_FAULTED	SCHA_RG_STATE SCHA_RG_STATE_NODE
scha_rgmode_t	RGMODE_NONE=0[2] RGMODE_FAILOVER RGMODE_SCALABLE	SCHA_RG_MODE
scha_failover_ mode_t	SCHA_FOMODE_NONE=0 SCHA_FOMODE_FAILOVER SCHA_FOMODE_SCALABLE	SCHA_FAILOVER_MODE
scha_initnodes_ flag_t	SCHA_INFLAG_RG_PRIMARIES=0 SCHA_INFLAG_RT_INSTALLED_ NODES	SCHA_INIT_NODES
scha_node_ state_t	SCHA_NODE_UP=0 SCHA_NODE_DOWN	SCHA_NODESTATE_NODE SCHA_NODESTATE_LOCAL
scha_prop_ type_t	SCHA_PTYPE_STRING=0 SCHA_PTYPE_INT SCHA_PTYPE_BOOLEAN SCHA_PTYPE_ENUM SCHA_PTYPE_STRINGARRAY SCHA_PTYPE_UINTARRAY, SCHA_PTYPE_UINT	In the structure, scha_extprop_ values, and possible values for the prop_type field.

1. Reserved for possible future use.
2. NOT intended for public use.

Structures

The RMAPI access methods and utility methods need to access data represented in some format such as a list of integers, strings, or arrays of strings. There are a few structures as described here in the libscha library for that purpose.

scha_status_value_t

The *scha_status_value_t* structure, shown in Figure 7.2, is used with the SCHA_ STATUS and SCHA_STATUS_NODE tag arguments. It contains the enumerated type *scha_rsstatus_t status*. See Table 7.7, "Libscha Enumerated Types." A character string status message is referenced by *char *status_msg*.

scha_str_array_t

The *scha_str_array_t* structure, shown in Figure 7.3, is used to store either a string or an array of strings and is used with numerous tag arguments. Refer to Tables 7.2 through 7.5 for tag arguments that use this structure.

Within this structure is *uint_t array_cnt*, which holds the number of arrays. To reference the arrays through the *char **str_array*, an index is needed to refer to a particuliar string. The index max will need to be *array_cnt* - 1.

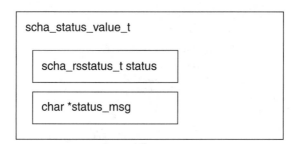

Figure 7.2 scha_status_value_t

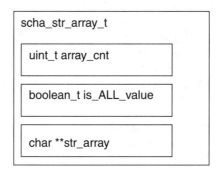

Figure 7.3 scha_str_array_t

```
scha_str_array_t arraystr;
int a;
for(a=0; a < arraystr->array_cnt;a++){
      printf("String: %s\n",arraystr->str_array[a]);
}
```

scha_uint_array_t

The *scha_uint_array_t* structure, shown in Figure 7.4, is used to store an array of integers such as the SCHA_ALL_NODEIDS tag argument. The size of the array is stored in *uint_t array_cnt*, which is basically the number of registered nodes in the cluster. The nodeids are stored in the array referenced by *uint_t *uint_array*.

```
scha_uint_array_t arrayint;
int a;
for(a=0; a < arrayint->array_cnt;a++){
      printf("Nodeid: %d\n",arrayint->uint_array[a]);
}
```

scha_extprop_value_t

The *scha_extprop_value_t* structure is used to access extension properties for a resource. These extension properties are defined in the RTR file for that particular resource type. This structure is used with the scha_resource_get()(3HA) function along with the SCHA_EXTENSION tag argument.

Within this structure, see Figure 7.5, the *scha_prop_type_t prop_type* is an enumerated type that holds the return type of the extension property. Refer to Table 7.7, "Libscha Enumerated Types," for this enumerated type. The value of the returned extension property is within the *val* union. This return value will be stored based on the return type from the *prop_type* value. If *prop_type* is SCHA_PTYPE_STRINGARRAY, then the return value will be in *scha_str_array_t *val_strarray*.

In Example 7.17, the extension property *NetIfList* is retrieved from the logical host resource *foologicalhost*. Within this structure, the *scha_prop_type_t prop_type* is an enumerated type that holds the return type of the extension property. Refer to Table 7.7, "Libscha Enumerated Types," for this enumerated type. The value of the

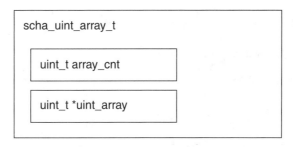

Figure 7.4 scha_uint_array_t

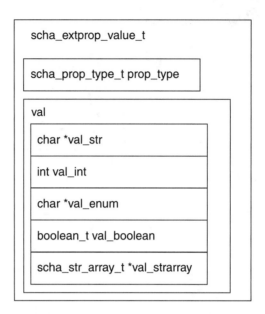

Figure 7.5 scha_extprop_value_t

returned extension property is within the *val* union. This return value will be stored based on the return type from the *prop_type* value. If *prop_type* is SCHA_PTYPE_STRINGARRAY, as *NetIfList* is, then the return value will be in *scha_str_array_t *val_strarray*. Example 7.17 demonstrates how a list of strings would be accessed from the *scha_str_array_t *val_strarray*.

Example 7.17   scha_extprop_value_t

```
#include <strings.h>
#include <stdio.h>
#include <stdlib.h>
#include <scha.h>

main()
{
scha_err_t              err;
scha_resource_t         handle;
scha_extprop_value_t    *fooprop;

err = scha_resource_open("foologicalhost","foobar-rg",&handle);
if (err != SCHA_ERR_NOERR) {
        fprintf(stderr, "FAILED:scha_resource_open()%s\n",\
         scha_strerror(err));
        exit(err);
}

err = scha_resource_get(handle, SCHA_EXTENSION, "NetIfList", &fooprop);
```

```
if (err != SCHA_ERR_NOERR) {
        fprintf(stderr, "FAILED: scha_resource_get()%s\n",\
         scha_strerror(err));
        err = scha_resource_close(handle);
        exit(err);
}

for(cnt=0; cnt < fooprop->val.val_strarray->array_cnt; cnt++){
    printf("Nafo: %s\n", fooprop->val.val_strarray->str_array[cnt]);
}

err = scha_resource_close(handle); // Close the handle,
if (err != SCHA_ERR_NOERR) {
        fprintf(stderr, "FAILED: scha_resource_get()%s\n",\
         scha_strerror(err));
        exit(err);
 }
}
```

scha_err_t

The *scha_err_t* is an integer typedef to hold error return code values. The error return codes for the libscha library are defined in Table 7.8. These codes can also be found on a node in the cluster in the file /usr/cluster/include/scha_err.h.

Table 7.8 scha_err_t Error Return Codes

Error	Value	Description
SCHA_ERR_NOERR	0	No error
SCHA_ERR_NOMEM	1	Not enough swap
SCHA_ERR_HANDLE	2	Invalid resource management handle
SCHA_ERR_INVAL	3	Invalid input argument
SCHA_ERR_TAG	4	Invalid API tag
SCHA_ERR_RECONF	5	Cluster is reconfiguring
SCHA_ERR_ACCESS	6	Permission denied
SCHA_ERR_SEQID	7	Resourcetype, resource, or resourcegroup has been updated since the last access method open call
SCHA_ERR_DEPEND	8	Object dependency error
SCHA_ERR_STATE	9	Object is in the wrong state
SCHA_ERR_METHOD	10	Invalid method
SCHA_ERR_NODE	11	Invalid node
SCHA_ERR_RG	12	Invalid resourcegroup
SCHA_ERR_RT	13	Invalid resourcetype
SCHA_ERR_RSRC	14	Invalid resource
SCHA_ERR_PROP	15	Invalid property
SCHA_ERR_CHECKS	16	Sanity checks failed
SCHA_ERR_RSTATUS	17	Bad resource status
SCHA_ERR_INTERNAL	18	Internal error was encountered

Void Typedefs

There are a few void typedefs used to point to the handles for the cluster, resource type, resource, and resource group open functions calls. They are as follows:

```
typedef void * scha_resource_t;
typedef void * scha_resourcetype_t;
typedef void * scha_resourcegroup_t;
typedef void * scha_cluster_t;
```

Summary

In this chapter, we covered the resource manager API (RMAPI) access methods used to collect information about the cluster, registered resource types, and also configured resources and resource groups. Utility methods give the ability to control failover of a resource group or the restarting of resources within a resource group. They also control setting the status of a resource and retrieving error code messages based on return codes from access method or utility method function calls. This information can be used in developing callback methods for a data service and for any additional programs that may be used by that data service. Utility programs can then be developed that would help system administrators or operational support people in the day-to-day operation of the cluster.

8

MANAGING PROCESSES

At some point in our computer careers, some of us have been paged or received a slew of voice mails from users or a help desk telling us that a particular application is not available. When this happens, if you are in the office, you quickly review any log files to see what the issue might be and then you restart the application manually. It's Murphy's Law that at some point this will occur when you neither have access to the system nor can restart the application. Consequently, users sit idle and unpleasant "management issues" start to occur.

To keep those unpleasant "management issues" from occurring, we need to keep the user community productive by having the application available when it is needed. Fortunately, the Sun Cluster 3.x framework provides the ability to keep applications highly available and provides a set of utilities within the framework to help perform the management of these applications. This chapter will cover some of these command-line utilities.

Introduction

In Chapter 6, the purpose and flow of the callback methods was discussed. Each callback method needs to perform specific tasks and return either success or not. Some callback methods, particularly START, PRENET_START, MONITOR_START, MONITOR_STOP, STOP, and POSTNET_STOP perform specific tasks in order to get the application either online and providing service or offline and not providing service.

The capability to manage these processes is provided within the Sun Cluster environment. These command-line interface (CLI) programs give you the ability to

Table 8.1 Management Facilities

Management Facility	Description
pmfadm(1HA)	Provides a means of monitoring processes including starting, stopping, and restarting if needed.
hatimerun(1HA)	Provides the ability to run a program under timeout conditions.
halockrun(1HA)	Provides the capability of holding a file lock while running a program.

automatically, start, stop, and monitor these processes. For C programmers, C library functions are available within the DSDL-API. These functions will be covered in Chapter 9, "Using the DSDL."

Management facilities within the cluster environment include Process Monitor Facility, a CLI that is accessible via the pmfadm (1HA). Other programs available are hatimerun (1HA) and halockrun (1HA). Table 8.1 shows management facility CLIs within the Sun Cluster environment.

Process Monitor Facility

The Process Monitor Facility, or PMF, provides process management for processes that are under its control. PMF has the ability to automatically start, restart, and monitor processes. It can also get the status and stop these processes. Since the process used will most likely be applications, consideration needs to be given to the characteristics of the application. The PMF is accessible via the pmfadm (1HA) command. In the following sections, we will cover these considerations and demonstrate how to use the PMF.

Process Monitoring Considerations

Before monitoring a process within the PMF, consideration needs to be given to how the process or application will live and behave under PMF control. For the purpose of discussion, we refer to process or processes as an application that will be managed by PMF. One of the benefits of PMF is the ability to restart the application automatically if it stops for any reason.

Applications that are managed by PMF should be able to handle some level of restarting without operator intervention from a previous failure. In other words, the application should be able to handle most cleanup operations by itself after a failure. If an application is unable to handle any restarts without operator intervention, then the application may need either some additional programs to help with cleanup operations or it just may not be a wise candidate for the PMF.

From the perspective of the PMF, the following metrics need to be considered:

- Retry count—Number of times to try to restart a stopped application.
- Time period—Window in which the retry count has to elapse (minutes).
- Child level to monitor—By default PMF monitors all children spawned in an application.
- What actions, if any, to take when an application fails and its retry count within the time period has been exceeded.
- How the application is stopped.

When defining these metrics for the application that will be managed by PMF, the developer needs to consider the following points for the application:

- Will the application be able to restart without user intervention?
- How many retries do I need to determine if something is seriously wrong and other actions need to be taken?
- Are there any support programs that need to be run before restarting the failed application?
- Is it necessary to monitor all levels of children or just a certain level? See "Child Process Monitoring" in this chapter.
- Can the program be stopped by sending it a signal or does the program have its own stop procedure?

When considering the number of times (retry count) to restart an application, the developer needs to know if the application is able to restart by just rerunning the application again or if some action needs to be performed before rerunning.

An application that creates a pid file to prevent running multiple instances of itself may not be able to restart unless the pid file is removed. This is because during normal operation the pid file is removed when the application exits normally. Abnormal termination may not remove the pid file, so having multiple retries within PMF will not succeed in restarting the application. In this case, it would be best to specify no retries to pmfadm and also have it call an action program that will remove the pid file. See "Action Program" in this chapter. Once that action program is successful in removing the pid file, PMF will automatically restart the application. Too many retries also may cause an abnormally long time to fail over the application to another node in the cluster.

Along with the number of times to restart an application, the time period over which the retry count will elapse is also important. Let's look at the following example.

```
#!/bin/sh
pmfadm -c sleep.tag -n 3 -t 1 /bin/sleep 25
```

```
while true
do
    pmfadm -q sleep.tag
    if [$? -ne 0]; then
       echo "Sleep failed"
       exit 1
    fi
sleep 5
done
```

For this example, the sleep command has been put under PMF control. More details regarding pmfadm will follow, but in this example the arguments provided to the pmfadm command are to help understand what is taking place:

- -c —A unique nametag is provided when starting the sleep command under PMF. In this case, sleep.tag is the nametag given to this process monitor. It will be used by the pmfadm command for further use such as to get status and to stop the application.
- -n —specified retry count.
- -t —specified time period for the retry count to elapse.

The process monitor will run the sleep 25 command under a nametag of sleep.tag. If the sleep process stops for any reason, the PMF will restart the application until three retries within one minute is reached. In a while loop, pmfadm is used to query the status of sleep.tag. If the pmfadm query returns an error, it exits out of the loop with a nonzero exit status to indicate that an error has occurred.

As mentioned previously, understanding how an application will operate and behave when managed by PMF is extremely important. In our example, sleep for 25 seconds was put under PMF. So every 25 seconds this application stops. Since the purpose of the PMF is to automatically restart the application, pmfadm restarts sleep 25 again. After 25 seconds it will exit again and repeat this scenario every 25 seconds.

The PMF keeps track of how many times the application is restarted. Remember the metrics given to PMF were three retries within one minute. At the time PMF started managing sleep 25, retries equaled 0. By the time three retries have completed, retries = 0 through retries = 3, 100 seconds would have elapsed. Since we specified three retries in a one-minute period, this script will not fail. The reason is that you will never meet the retry count of three within a one-minute period. This script will continue because any retries that occurred over one minute ago, (i.e., the oldest retries), are ignored. While this might be considered good, the program keeps running. What if something is wrong and the application needs to fail over to another node in the cluster or to be stopped with an error condition set?

Although this is a very simple, nonrealistic example, it illustrates that a thorough knowledge and understanding of the application is needed. In our example a retry count of two would have been a better choice because two retries could have occurred within the time period specified. We've all endured headaches from applications that don't behave well and those that don't behave well within a cluster environment will take your headache to a new level.

Application Monitoring

Chapter 6 covered the 12 callback methods within the RGM. Through the life cycle of some of these methods, it will be necessary to start one or more programs, the application itself, monitor, check status, or perhaps to stop these programs. The PMF gives us the ability to start, monitor, and get status for a given process.

The previous section gave a simple example of PMF with the sleep command. Let's look further at the callback methods. The resource type defines the callback methods used by the RGM as being able to bring the application online and managed or unmanaged and offline. Although the 12 callback methods have specific needs within a defined resource type, a simple flow of a resource type's callback methods would be:

START ◊ MONITOR_START

Application is running and being monitored

MONITOR_STOP ◊ STOP

Using this callback flow and the MySQL database, we'll use the pmfadm command-line interface to walk through these methods. This will give us some "hands on" on how the PMF operates. Using the pmfadm command will give us the ability to see the PMF in action while keeping it simple. There is no need for a compiler at this point. This will also help us to see how the application will "behave" under PMF.

Starting a Process Monitor

Using the resource type's callback methods, the RGM will start the resource with a set of attributes defined within the resource type, the resource, and the resource group. The resource type's START method or MONITOR_START method will need to start some defined process, either the application or the monitor. The PMF via the pmfadm command will need to know the following information:

- A unique nametag
- The program and its arguments
- Retries, time period, and the child monitor level, if necessary
- What action if necessary to take when the retries exceed the number of defined retries within a given time period. (This is optional; other methods can be coded to handle nonsuccessful return codes.)
- Environmental variables, if necessary

This information is used by pmfadm to create a new nametag and start the program. The starting of a new nametag needs to satisfy the startup syntax.

SYNTAX: pmfadm **-c** *nametag* [**-a** *action_prg*] [[**-e**] | [**-E**]] [**-n** *retry_count*] [**-t** *retry_interval*] [**-C**] *program args-to-program*

The resource type registration (RTR) file will have the definitions of methods and parameters for the application. It will be necessary to retrieve these parameters to pass on to the PMF when implementing the resource type's callback methods. Retrieval of these parameters will be discussed in Chapter 10.

```
# pmfadm -c mysql.tag -n 2 -t 5 -C 0
      -a /youractionprogram \
      /usr/local/mysql/bin/mysqld -P 3030 -u mysql \
      -h /usr/local/mysql/data
#
```

With the above example, we start the MySQL database application using the pmfadm (1M) command with the following arguments:

- -c with a unique nametag to start a process managed by PMF. If the nametag is not unique, pmfadm will exit with status 1.
- -n retry count—how many times to restart the process.
- -t retry interval—specified time period in minutes for the retry count to elapse.
- -C child monitoring level—level 0 monitors the parent only.
- -a specified action program is called when the retry count has been exceeded over the retry interval. If this program returns 0, PMF will restart the application and reset the retry counter. Otherwise, pmfadm will exit.
- Application with or without arguments to be started and managed by PMF.

If the application needs environment variables, pmfadm has two arguments available. The -e provides the means to pass an environmental variable to PMF. The -E provides the whole environment to PMF from the environment from which the pmfadm command has been started.

When providing a nametag with the -c argument, that nametag must be unique within the PMF. A good naming convention for the tag would be *RESOURCEGRP_ NAME,RESOURCE_NAME,instance#.type_of_service*.

Child Process Monitoring

As you know by now, if the application that you have managed by the PMF fails, it will be restarted automatically as long as the retry count within the retry interval has not been exceeded. What if that application forks into the child process? Is it necessary to monitor descendant processes of that managed application?

One important requirement mentioned previously is knowing the application and its characteristics. The child monitoring capability of the PMF can be from just the parent application to all levels of children of the parent (Figure 8.1). The default monitoring level is a monitor to all levels. The default monitoring occurs when the -C option is not specified. When the PMF is monitoring children or multiple levels of children, PMF will not restart the parent until all levels of children and the parent have stopped. This may be overkill and it can also hamper the correct operation of the application.

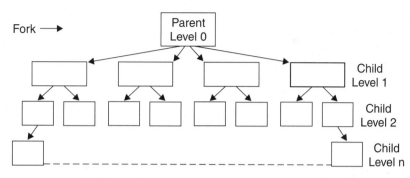

Figure 8.1 Child processes

Consider an application that forks child processes to handle incoming data feeds. The data feed processes live long enough to handle the incoming data, write the data to a database, and then exit. The parent is responsible for handling the incoming request and forking a child process to handle the incoming data.

Not being familiar with the application, you start the application using pmfadm and fail to specify the -C argument. The parent and all children are now being monitored by PMF. After handling 100 requests, the parent dies. Since the children are still processing the incoming data, PMF does not restart the parent. Any new requests will fail because the parent is no longer running. Until all child processes have exited, PMF will not restart the parent. The correct level of monitoring for this type of application would be to monitor the parent only by supplying the -C 0 argument to the pmfadm command. This would allow PMF to restart the parent and keep processing new requests.

A case for monitoring more than just the parent could be made for a program that does some initialization operations such as reading configuration files, rotating log files, forking a child process that is the main application, and then exits. Since the parent process exits after performing initialization and application startup, monitoring the parent process only would cause false restarts under PMF and also possibly contention with the application that is already running. Monitoring child processes would now become the focal point, as the child process now needs to be monitored by PMF. The parent process is no longer active, so when the child process exits abnormally all monitored processes would also exit. The PMF would then perform a restart.

Action Program

The purpose of the action program specified by the -a argument is to provide PMF a program to run that performs any specialized tasks after the retry count has exceeded its specified number within the retry interval. These tasks could include collecting debug information, notifying operators of a problem, or doing some cleanup operations that might be helpful in restarting the application. When the action program completes, a successful return from the action program will cause a reset of the retry count and PMF will continue to restart the application. Failure will cause pmfadm to stop restarting the process and the nametag no longer to exist. For those applications that need some external cleanup operation before starting, using the action program is one way to get this accomplished.

```
# pmfadm -c mysql.tag -n 2 -t 5 -C 0 -a \
      /usr/local/cleanup \
      /usr/local/mysql/bin/mysqld -P 3030 -u mysql \
      -h /usr/local/mysql/data
#
```

For this example, the specified action program of /usr/local/cleanup will be called when the number of retries has elapsed within the five-minute period. This program could be either a custom program designed to perform any application cleanup tasks or an application-provided program that does the same thing. If the program returns 0, pmfadm will continue to restart the application and the retry count is reset to 0. If it does not return 0, pmfadm will exit and the given nametag will no longer exist.

Process Monitor Status

During the development phase and in production, as a developer or system administrator, it will be necessary to check the status of processes running under the PMF. Status of applications that are running under PMF can be checked via the pmfadm command or with the DSDL API calls.

SYNTAX: pmfadm -L | **-l** *nametag* | **-q** *nametag* [**-h** *host*]

Processes running within the PMF are given nametags to further reference and take action upon when necessary. When using the DSDL-API library functions, implicit nametags are given to processes running within PMF. Since these nametags may not be known to the user, the pmfadm command has the ability to query the list of nametags that are within the PMF.

```
# pmfadm -L
   tags: mysql.tag ORASERV_MON_oracle-tpcb-server-r
ORALSNR_MON_oracle-tpcb-listener-r scsymon pnmd
#
```

Once the nametag is known, further information about it can be retrieved.

```
# pmfadm -l mysql.tag
pmfadm -c mysql.tag -n 2 -t 1 /usr/local/mysql/bin/mysqld -P
3030 -u mysql -h /usr/local/mysql/data
        retries: 0
        owner: root
        monitor children: all
        pids: 22632
#
```

This command reports back the command and arguments that were used initially to put the application under PMF control, the number of retries since starting, the owner, the level of monitoring, and the process ID. While this is great for general knowledge, it's a little tough for the developer to use within a callback's shell script.

So for scripting purposes, the developer should be more interested in a return code when checking the status of a particular nametag. The -q argument with the pmfadm command would provide a return code. If the nametag specified is still registered and running, a return code of 0 will be returned. If the nametag is not registered, the return code will be 1.

```
# pmfadm -q mysql.tag
# echo $?
0
#
```

Fault Monitoring

The MySQL database is now under the watchful eye of the PMF. In the flow of the callback methods, the START callback method has completed successfully. The database is running and now the callback method MONITOR_START is next in line. This method starts the program that will monitor the application's health. Since this monitor must be available as long as the application is running, using PMF for the application monitor makes good sense.

In this method, the level of monitoring can be simple or complex depending on the application. The following chapters on the API will discuss the fault monitors in greater detail. For the purpose of the MySQL database example, the application provides a method to ping the database via the mysqladmin command. In the MONITOR_START callback method, a program would be started to ping the MySQL database at some interval and to perform some function if a failure occurred. A simple script will show if the database is available:

```
#!/bin/ksh
#mysqlping.ksh - ping the mysql database
while true
        /usr/local/mysql/bin/mysqladmin -P 3030 \
        -u mysql -silent ping
        # Additional code would be needed to check
        # return code of command. If mysqladmin fails,
        # handle the failure.
        sleep 20
done
```

In previous examples, we provided the pmfadm command with a retry count and a time period for the given process. We'll also need to determine if the monitor should be restarted or not, and if so, how many times the monitor needs to be restarted before we decide to stop retrying and do something else. Whether the monitor is restarted or not, something will need to be done if the monitor fails to continue running. That something else could involve restarting the application, failing over to another node in the cluster, or setting a fault flag, and this can be done by specifying an action program.

```
# pmfadm -c mysqlmonitor.tag -n 2 -t 1 -a /failed_ monitor_prg
mysqlping.ksh
```

If by chance the `mysqlping.ksh` program fails to continue to run after two restarts within a one-minute period, the action program `/failed_monitor_prg` is called to handle the failure of the monitoring program.

In this case, there are no problems, the START and MONITOR_START callback methods have completed. The MySQL database and the `mysqlping.ksh` monitor programs are running and the application is available to the clients.

Stopping the Process Monitor

At some point, the MONITOR_STOP and the STOP callback methods will be called. It will be necessary to stop the monitoring of the application and to stop the application itself. How this is implemented is dependent on the application itself. Since the monitor program `mysqlping.ksh` pings the database, there is no formal shutdown needed to stop the monitoring. Sending this process a kill signal will not harm the application.

The MySQL database provides a method to shut down the database properly. So sending this application a kill signal would not be the preferred way to shut down this database. The `pmfadm(1HA)` command provides two methods of stopping the management of the process. One method, using the `-k` argument, stops both the management of the process and the process via the supplied kill signal. If a signal is not specified, by default the SIGKILL signal will be used. If there are still retries available when the process exits, PMF will restart that process. The second method of shutdown stops the management of the process using the `-s` argument. This process will no longer be restarted if it should exit, even if there are retries still available. If a signal is specified, it will be sent to all processes including any started by the action script. With both methods, a timeout can be given via the `-w` argument, which will wait for the specified seconds for all processes to exit that are associated with the given nametag.

The two nametags for this particular resource we need to be concerned about are *mysql.tag* and *mysqlmonitor.tag*.

```
# pmfadm -l mysql.tag
pmfadm -c mysql.tag -n 2 -t 1 /usr/local/mysql/bin/mysqld -P
3030 -u mysql -h /usr/local/mysql/data
        retries: 0
        owner: root
        monitor children: all
        pids: 22632
```

```
# pmfadm -l mysqlmonitor.tag
pmfadm -c mysqlmonitor.tag -n 2 -t 1 /var/top/mysqlping.ksh
        retries: 0
        owner: root
        monitor children: all
        pids: 22634
```

You can stop these nametags through the PMF and the pmfadm command.

SYNTAX: pmfadm -s *nametag* | **-k** *nametag* [**-w** *timeout*] [*signal*]

To stop the monitoring and the MySQL database, use the following sequence:

1. Stop PMF from managing the monitor and send the default SIGKILL to the monitoring process (mysqlping.ksh).

   ```
   # pmfadm -s mysqlmonitor.tag KILL
   ```

2. Stop PMF from managing the MySQL database.

   ```
   # pmfadm -s mysql.tag
   ```

3. Shut down the MySQL database.

   ```
   # hatimerun -a -e 2 -t 30 \
   /usr/local/mysql/bin/mysqladmin shutdown
   ```

4. Verify that the database is no longer running.

   ```
   # pmfadm -q mysql.tag
   ```

In the above sequence, the monitor program mysqlmonitor.ksh was stopped by telling the PMF with the -s option to stop monitoring the program. Do not restart the process and send the KILL signal. The -s argument prevents PMF from restarting, should there be any retries still available. At this point, the MONITOR_STOP callback method should exit successfully.

Using the same command without the KILL signal, the PMF is told to stop monitoring the MySQL database and not to restart. The command hatimerun (1HA), see "Time-Based Process Management" in this chapter, is used to run the mysqladmin command and shut down the database. Once hatimerun completes successfully, the database has been shut down. To verify that the process is no longer running, the pmfadm command could be run to verify that the mysql.tag no longer exists. Once that is confirmed, the STOP method exits successfully. Before the STOP method exits, the developer will want to ensure that the application is no longer running. Other means of verifying that the application is no longer running may need to be developed in the STOP method.

An application that will not stop by conventional means, due to abnormal conditions, will need to be investigated. The Sun Cluster environment provides the ability to handle error conditions within the APIs and the RGM. Refer to Chapter 6, "Understanding the RGM."

Time-Based Process Management

The hatimerun (1HA) gives the developer the ability to run a supplied program within a specific time period. If the program fails to exit within that time period, the program is sent a SIGKILL signal and hatimerun exits with an error code of 99. This timing ability is convenient for programs that only need to run once within a specified period of time. Since the mysqladmin program does not need to run more than once, and ideally it should stop the database within a specified time, hatimerun is useful in running the mysqladmin command to stop the database program.

SYNTAX: hatimerun [**-va**][**-k** *signalname*] [**-e** *exitcode*] **-t** *timeout*
program *args*

When the time specified by -t expires, hatimerun will stop the specified program by sending it a signal, signal (3HEAD). By default this signal is a SIGKILL. While this is okay for some programs, other programs such as a database may not respond well to this action so specifying a different signal, or perhaps no signal at all, would be the proper action to take.

To specify a signal with the hatimerun command other than the default, the -k argument with the specified signal is used. With this argument, either the signal number or signal name can be supplied.

Note – By default, the SIGKILL is used when there is no -k argument specified.

In general sending kill signals to some applications, such as databases, is not considered to be a good practice. So to avoid having a signal sent when the time expires, the -a argument can be used. When the time does expire, hatimerun exits with an error code of 99 and leaves the specified program running asynchronously.

It is also possible to change that error code by using the -e argument with the code you wish to use. This makes it convenient to use your own exit code conventions. When a program exits within the time specified, the exit code returned will be the exit code of the program given to hatimerun to run. If other problems should occur, hatimerun will exit with a code of 98.

To recap the previous section on stopping the database:

1. Stop PMF from managing the MySQL database.

   ```
   # pmfadm -s mysql.tag
   ```

2. Use hatimerun to run the mysqladmin shutdown.

   ```
   # hatimerun -a -e 2 -t 30 \
   /usr/local/mysql/bin/mysqladmin shutdown
   ```

3. If hatimerun fails, use some other method to stop the database.

Using hatimerun to run the mysqladmin shutdown command ensures that something will happen within a defined period. Either the database does shut down properly or it does not. If mysqladmin fails to complete within the timeout -t of 30 seconds, by default SIGKILL will be sent to the mysqladmin command. Since sending a SIGKILL during a database shutdown can cause problems, this example uses -a to *not* send a SIGKILL and hatimerun exits with an of error code 2, as specified by the -e.

Knowing that this has failed, the agent's STOP callback method needs to do "something else." This might be retrying to stop the application or setting status to indicate that there is a serious problem. Knowledge of the application when a scenario like this occurs will help in determining what needs to be done next.

When using hatimerun, sufficient timeouts need to be used to ensure that ample time is available to complete the task successfully. Various loading conditions can affect the application's response time.

File Locking

The Sun Cluster environment provides the halockrun (1HA) CLI to give shell scripts the means of obtaining a file lock on a file while running a program. By default, an exclusive mode lock is obtained on the file for the duration that the specified program is running. Also by default, halockrun obtains a file lock in blocking mode. To avoid waiting for a lock on a file (nonblocking), the -n argument can be used. If halockrun cannot obtain a lock on a file with the -n argument, it will exit with an exit code of 1. If multiple programs need access to a particular file, halockrun can obtain a file lock in shared mode with the -s argument.

SYNTAX: halockrun [-vsn] [-e *exitcode*] lockfilename program [*args*]

When errors occur while using halockrun, the typical exit status is 99, except when trying to obtain a nonblocking -n lock on a file. To change the exit status if an error occurs, the -e argument can be used to provide an exit status number other than the typical 99 exit status. Under normal operation, halockrun returns the exit status of the program that it ran.

Note – Solaris provides two types of file locking—advisory and mandatory. The halockrun command utilitizes advisory file locking.

Consider an application where only one instance can be run on a node at one time. The application can run on other nodes at the same time, but it cannot fail over to a node that is already running that application. To prevent this from happening, halockrun can be used to run the application and lock a file that is located on a local filesystem.

```
# halockrun -n -e 2 /tmp/one_instance.lock \
/tmp/one_inst_per_node.ksh
```

Using the halockrun command, /tmp/one_inst_per_node.ksh is the program that we want to run only one instance on a node. To ensure that multiple instances on that node cannot be started, the file /tmp/one_instance.lock is specified as the lock file. If this file is already locked, halockrun should not wait (nonblocking) on the file for a lock, it should exit with an error code of 2.

This will allow the program to run on each node in the cluster since the /tmp directory is local to that node. It will prevent more than one instance running on the same node because trying to run the program again under halockrun with the same lock file will fail to lock the file.

Summary

In this chapter, we discussed some of the utilities for managing processes within the Sun Cluster 3.x environment. Applications that run within a clustered environment need to be managed by the cluster framework to provide availability and/or scalability to the users of that application and the Sun Cluster 3.x environment provides these utilities.

9

USING THE DSDL

STOP!!

Before you start reading this chapter, please answer the following multiple-choice quiz:

Question: Do you know how to program in C?

Answer: A   Yes

                    B   Well, I used to, but I'm pretty rusty . . .

                    C   No

                    D   What's C ?

                    E   C is evil. I do my programming with punch cards!

If your answer was C or D, then you should probably skip this chapter—at least until you've had a crash course on the syntax and idioms of the C programming language.[1]

If your answer was A or B, then go ahead and read this chapter—even if you're a little rusty, it should be easy enough to understand and you may be amazed how quickly things come back to you when you see some of the examples.

If your answer was E, then you should probably gently put the book down, walk over to the nearest telephone, and call a good psychiatrist.

Now that we have that out of the way, let's get started.

---

1. One good reference is *The Art and Science of C,* by Eric S. Roberts [1995]. There are many others.

Introduction to the DSDL

In Chapter 7, we looked at the basic resource management API (RMAPI). If you use this API exclusively for a while, it becomes clear that it is quite basic and that it can require you to do repetitive programming such as allocating memory or checking error values, which are not directly connected to your program logic. It's also clear that some of the desirable tools that are available at the command line or in shell scripts, in particular the PMF, are not easily accessible from C programs.

To address these potential difficulties, and in order to make C program development a little easier for the programmer, Sun has provided the data service development library (the DSDL), which is essentially a set of convenience functions for using the RMAPI without all the fiddling about that is needed to use it directly. This convenience comes at the cost of some degree of fine-grained control over how the API is used. But since the DSDL simply encapsulates the functionality of the RMAPI, the basic functions can also be called directly, if necessary. Figure 9.1 shows the relationships among method programs, the RGM, and the various libraries and tools available to the developer.

With a little practice, and depending on the application you are developing, you should be able to mix the use of the direct RMAPI calls and the DSDL to achieve a balance of control and ease of use.

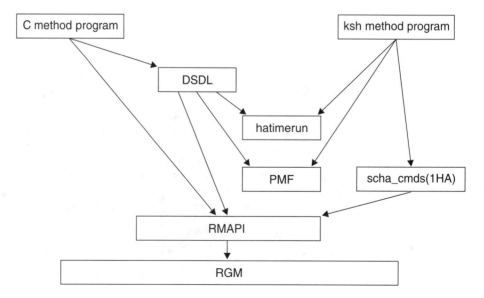

Figure 9.1 Relationships among DSDL, RMAPI, and RGM

In this chapter, we will look at how the DSDL is used in method programs and what the functions in the DSDL actually are and how they are used. We will also look in detail at the more complex data types used in the library.

Using the DSDL

As we hopefully made clear with our attempt at humor at the beginning of this chapter, the DSDL is for use only with the C (or, if you really want, C++)[2] programming language. As of this writing, there is no equivalent library for any of the many other popular languages used today, although there have been requests for ways to use Perl and Java directly. The library was actually originally developed to assist Sun software engineers who were creating the shrink-wrapped resource types such as HA NFS, HA DNS, and HA Apache. Since C was the language of choice for these projects, the DSDL was developed for that language.

Assuming for now that we're happy to use C as our development language, the next question is "Where do I use the DSDL?" The technical answer to this is that the DSDL can be used to write applications that act on resources within the Sun Cluster RGM framework. What this means in practice is that although you can do development work on a stand-alone system, you must have a running Sun Cluster environment to use programs written using the DSDL and that most programs using the library will be the method programs of resource types. The DSDL was tailor-made to be used for these resource type method programs, so if you want to use the library outside that context, you should consider such use experimental.

RTR File Considerations

The DSDL defines and uses some functions that place additional requirements on what goes into your resource type registration (RTR) file. Specifically, you should define four extension properties, shown in Table 9.1, so that the DSDL can operate on your resource type correctly.

Table 9.1 DSDL-Related Extension Properties

Extension Property	Value Type	Related Function
confdir_list	string array	scds_get_ext_confdir_list
monitor_retry_count	int	scds_get_ext_monitor_retry_count
monitor_retry_interval	int	scds_get_ext_monitor_retry_interval
probe_timeout	int	scds_get_ext_probe_timeout

---

2. Using C++ with the DSDL is unlikely to be much different from traditional C development because the library offers no object-oriented interfaces to the cluster environment.

Program Arguments

Programs written using the DSDL have very specific expectations about the way they are called. The general format is:

program [-c|-u] -R *resource-name* -T *type-name* -G *group-name* [-r *system-defined-property=values* . . .] [-x *extension-property=values* . . .] [-g *group-property=values*] .

What this means is that the -R, -T and -G arguments are mandatory, while -c, -u, -r, -x, and -g are optional.[3]

If you think this format looks familiar, you're right: Recall that resource type methods are called by the cluster framework with a well-defined set of arguments:

methodname -R *resource-name* -T *type-name* -G *group-name*

As we'll see later in the chapter, the DSDL automatically performs the command-line-argument parsing for you, so you don't need to do the sometimes laborious argument parsing that can be necessary in method programs written using the RMAPI.

Besides -R, -T, and -G, the other command-line arguments automatically recognized by the DSDL can be used to achieve some results when they are parsed. They are:

-c
Indicates that the resource has just been created. Use this in VALIDATE method programs.

-u
Indicates that the resource has just been updated. This is also useful in VALIDATE programs.

-r *property=values*
Allows a system-defined resource property (not an extension property) to have a new value assigned. The DSDL will use this new value instead of any existing value that may be in the RGM. This flag is used in VALIDATE programs as well, usually to check the validity of proposed changes to the resource.

-x *extension-property=value*
Allows an extension property to have a new value assigned. Again, the DSDL will use this new value instead of any existing value that may be in the RGM. This is also used in VALIDATE programs, for essentially the same reasons as the -r flag.

-g *group-property=value*
Assigns a new value to a *resource group* property associated with this resource. As before, the DSDL will use this new value instead of any existing value that may be in the RGM. It is usually only used in VALIDATE programs, to check the effect of any change to group properties (such as pathprefix) to the resource.

---

3. These options are used by the cluster framework when calling VALIDATE methods.

The $-x$, $-r$, and $-g$ options can be used multiple times to set the values for different resource and extension properties. The $-u$ and $-c$ values are mutually exclusive with each other: A resource can either be "just created" or "just updated," but not both at the same time.

DSDL Functions

The DSDL functions are instantly recognizable, as they all start with the prefix 'scds_' (which stands for Sun Cluster data service) rather than the prefix 'scha_' (standing for Sun Cluster high availability) used by the basic RMAPI. However, even though there is a different library shared object (libdsdev.so) and header file (libdsdev.h) required for development with the DSDL, all of the required files are included in the same package as all of the Sun Cluster 3 development tools: SUNWscdev. The upshot of this is that you don't have to do any special installations to use these facilities and, as with the other development tools, the DSDL library can be installed on a stand-alone (Solaris SPARC) system, so you don't need to use a cluster to do development work.

The DSDL can be thought of as an environment that takes care of much of the error and memory handling that would otherwise be the responsibility of the programmer. Before the environment can be used, it must be instantiated using the scds_initialize(3HA) function. This initialization checks the command-line arguments of the calling program, sets up the logging facility, and then returns a handle that is used as a reference to the new environment in future DSDL function calls.

Once the environment has been initialized, the various DSDL functions can be used as required. Each time a DSDL function is called, the handle created by scds_initialize is passed as one of the arguments. When the environment is no longer needed, scds_close(3HA) should be called to tie up any loose ends. This life cycle is illustrated in Figure 9.2.

Any program using the DSDL must include the rgm/libdsdev.h header file and be linked with the libdsdev.so library. The following incantation should suffice:

```
cc [flags] -I/usr/cluster/include -L/usr/cluster/lib -ldsdev
<source_file>
#include <rgm/libdsdev.h>
```

Note – Some versions of the scds function man pages incorrectly state that the libdsdev.h file is in /usr/cluster/include. It is actually in /usr/cluster/include/rgm.

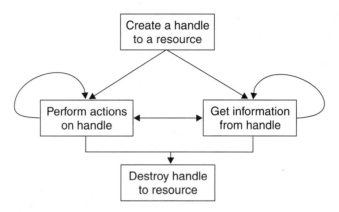

Figure 9.2 DSDL life cycle

In all, there are more than 70 functions within the DSDL, so we'll step through them by category. In general, the functions can be categorized into environment management, resource manipulation, resource group manipulation, resource type manipulation, application control, fault monitoring, memory management, property manipulation, and utilities. The rest of this chapter will describe the functions and provide some notes on usage. Chapter 10, "Developing for Existing Applications," will demonstrate how these functions can be used.

A Note on Man Page Entries

In some early versions of Sun Cluster 3 (before 3.1), the man page entries for the DSDL contain errors in the function signatures. For the most part, these errors relate to whether the function should have a pointer to the scds_handle_t type or just have the type by itself (not a pointer). In each case, the function signature given in this chapter is correct and can be confirmed by inspecting the libdsdev.h header file. Where errors have been made, we've made a note in the function descriptions.

Managing the DSDL Environment

There are really only two functions that directly manage the DSDL environment: one to set up the environment and one to remove it.

scds_initialize

```
scha_err_t scds_initialize(scds_handle_t  *handle, int  argc,char
*argv[]);
```

The intention of this function is to quickly and easily set up everything that will be needed for subsequent function calls to a DSDL environment. It is designed to automatically manage much of the processing that you would otherwise have to do manually for each and every program. It should be called at the beginning of any program using the DSDL, as it prepares the DSDL environment and allocates the *handle* that is used by all of the other function calls. The handle is basically a pointer to the address space used by this instance of the DSDL environment.

The function also processes the command-line arguments supplied to the program by simply passing the values for *argc* and *argv* from the main function of your program to this function—no further processing is required. Example 9.1 shows how this might be used.

Example 9.1 Using scds_initialize()

```
int main(int argc, char *argv[ ])
    {
    scds_handle_t myHandle;

    scds_initialize(&myHandle, argc, argv);
    ...
    }
```

The scds_initialize() function provides an easy way to extract the relevant information from the command line without having to do all the parsing yourself. It also identifies property assignments that may be performed within the command-line arguments and uses any new values supplied in subsequent function calls rather than the old values from the RGM. This function will also check that the fault monitoring information is initialized and valid, and so can be used as a simple VAL-IDATE method program. Finally, the function will prepare the logging environment, using whatever facility is returned by scha_cluster_getlogfacility(3HA).

If scds_initialize() completes successfully, it will return SCHA_ERR_NOERR (in other words, no error). When you have finished using the environment created by this function, you must call scds_close() to clean up. If you do get an error result, it's probably best to exit the program with a suitable (nonzero) return value.

> **Note –** The first argument of this function should be a *pointer* to scds_handle_t, not an *lvalue,* as is given in the scds_initialize (3ha) man page. (See "RTR File Considerations" earlier in this chapter.)

---

scds_close

```
void scds_close(scds_handle_t *handle);
```

The scds_close() function should be called at the end of your program, to release any resources that were allocated when you called scds_initialize(). You only need to call this once for each DSDL environment you created (usually only one per program). The only argument is the handle that was created by scds_initialize().

It's important to note that scds_close() does not clean up all of the memory that might have been used by DSDL function calls. Certain function calls assign and use their own memory, which must be separately freed. The section "Memory Handling" later in this chapter has more details on what you might need to do to clean up before exiting your program.

Functions for Resources

Most of the functions for resources are used to retrieve information from resource properties. Remember that when your program is called, the required arguments include the name of the resource and its group. These arguments are then passed along to scds_initialize(), so the environment that is created is specific to that resource and a lot of the property information is preloaded into buffers. Furthermore, if the program arguments included some property assignments, then those new values are used *instead* of what might already be in the RGM.

The important point to remember is that since your DSDL environment handle already knows what resource you want to look at, you call the resource functions using the handle rather than specifying the resource name, group, and/or type.

scds_get_ext_property

```
scha_err_t scds_get_ext_property(scds_handle_t handle, const
char  *property_name,  scha_prop_type_t  property_type,
scha_extprop_value_t  **property_value);
```

This function is used to get the value of an *extension* property from a resource. When using this function, you must specify the name of the property you are after and its *type*. The type of the property is one of the output argument data types used by the RMAPI (see scha_prop_type_t in Chapter 7, Table 7.7, libscha Enumerated Types), and is the type defined for this property in the RTR file (see "Creating a Resource Type" in Chapter 6).

The value of the extension property is placed in the return argument *property_ value*, which is of type scha_extprop_value_t. See Chapter 7, Figure 7.2, for the format of this data type and examples on how to use it. Once you have finished using this variable, you are responsible for freeing its memory, using the scds_free_ ext_property() function.

Remember, if you assigned a value to this extension property on the command line to your program, then *that* value will be used instead of the value stored in the RGM.

The function will return SCHA_ERR_NOERR if it was successful at finding the property, but you should be aware that it will return this value even if the property you are trying to retrieve has no value assigned, so be sure to check. If the extension property is not defined in the RTR file, then the function will return SCHA_ ERR_INVAL.

Some extension properties are extremely common, and so have their own convenience methods. These are:

- `scds_get_ext_confdir_list`
- `scds_get_ext_monitor_retry_count`
- `scds_get_ext_monitor_retry_interval`
- `scds_get_ext_probe_timeout`

scds_get_ext_confdir_list

```
scha_str_array_t scds_get_ext_confdir_list(scds_handle_t handle)
```

This is a convenience function for accessing the `confdir_list` extension property. Since this extension property is so common, you can use this function instead of the somewhat more cumbersome `scds_get_ext_property()`. Note that this function actually returns the value of the `confdir_list` extension property directly—so you don't have to supply a return parameter. See Chapter 7, Figure 7.3, for information on the `scha_str_array_t` data type and how to use it. Since you don't provide a return argument, you don't have to do anything special to release the memory.

scds_get_ext_monitor_retry_count

```
int scds_get_ext_monitor_retry_count(scds_handle_t handle)
```

This is a convenience function for accessing the `monitor_retry_count` extension property. If you use this function instead of the `scds_get_ext_property()`, you will get the value of `monitor_retry_count` directly, rather than having to supply a return parameter.

scds_get_ext_monitor_retry_interval

```
int scds_get_ext_monitor_retry_interval(scds_handle_t handle)
```

This function is also a convenience method for accessing a commonly used extension property. Using this function allows you to get the value of the `monitor_retry_interval` extension property directly, rather than using the `scds_get_ext_property()` function.

scds_get_ext_probe_timeout

```
int scds_get_ext_probe_timeout(scds_handle_t handle)
```

You can use this function to directly access the `probe_timeout` extension property of your resource without having to use the more cumbersome `scds_get_ext_property()` function.

scds_get_netaddr_list

```
scha_err_t   scds_get_netaddr_list(scds_handle_t handle,
scds_netaddr_list_t **netaddr_list)
```

This function is used to get all of the hostname-port-protocol combinations that are used by your resource. These combinations are determined by combining the network resources (IP addresses) used by the resource with its port list. See scds_ get_rs_hostnames() and scds_get_port_list() in this chapter for how each of these components is determined.

If successful, the function places the results in the *netaddr_list* return parameter, which is a handle to scds_netaddr_list_t. Memory allocation for this parameter is handled automatically, but when you have finished using the data you must free the memory by calling scds_free_netaddr_list().

The scds_netaddr_list_t data type is a structure containing the number of combinations of hostname-port-protocol used by the resource, and then an array of type scds_netaddr_t, which is the actual list of combinations. Each scds_netaddr_ type is a structure containing a string (pointer to char) for the *hostname*, and scds_port_t contains the *port* number and an integer, as defined in netinet/ in.h. Graphically, you could represent this entire data structure as shown in Figure 9.3.

To access this data, you could use a code fragment such as shown in Example 9.2.

Example 9.2   Accessing scds_netaddr_list_t data

```
scds_netaddr_list_t *myNL;
int cnt;

scds_get_netaddr_list(myHandle, &myNL);
for (cnt = 0 ; cnt < myNL->num_netaddrs ; cnt++)
        {
         printf("%d: host = %s, port = %d, protocol = %d\n",
                    (cnt+1),
                    myNL->netaddrs[cnt].hostname,
                    myNL->netaddrs[cnt].port_proto.port,
                    myNL->netaddrs[cnt].port_proto.proto);
        }

scds_free_netaddr_list(myNL);
```

It's worth noting that this is just to demonstrate using the scds_get_netaddr_ list() function. If you actually want to print the net address information to the logfile for debugging, there is a utility function called scds_print_netaddr_ list() that handles this easily.

Note – The first argument of this function is an *lvalue* of scds_handle_t, not a pointer to it, as shown in some versions of the scds_get_ netaddr_list(3ha) man page. See "A Note on Man Page Entries" earlier in this chapter.

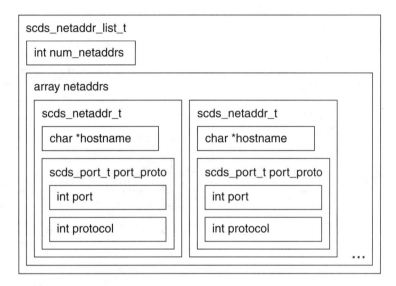

Figure 9.3 scds_netaddr_list_t data structure

scds_get_port_list

```
scha_err_t    scds_get_port_list(scds_handle_t handle,
scds_port_list_t **port_list)
```

This function is used to get the list of port/protocol pairs used by the resource, as stored in the port_list resource property (see "Resource Property Types" in Chapter 6). There's no need to preallocate memory for the *port_list*, but when you have finished using the data, you must release the memory by calling scds_free_port_list().

The scds_port_list_t data type is a structure containing the number of ports, and then an array of the scds_port_t entries. The scds_port_t type is a structure of two elements: the port number as an integer and the protocol as an integer. The protocol number is defined in netinet/in.h. So, for example, TCP is 6 and UDP is 17. Graphically, this can be represented as shown in Figure 9.4.

To access the information about the ports and protocols used by a resource, therefore, you might use a code fragment like the one shown in Example 9.3.

Example 9.3   Accessing port and protocol data

```
scds_port_list_t *myPL;
int cnt;
scds_get_port_list(myHandle, &myPL);
for (cnt = 0 ; cnt < myPL->num_ports ; cnt++)
      {
```

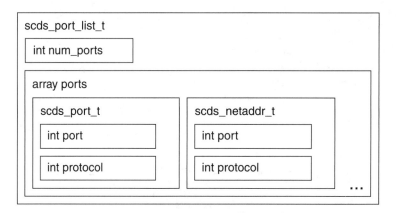

Figure 9.4 scds_port_list_t data structure

```
        printf("%d: port = %d, protocol = %d\n",
                (cnt+1),
                myPL->ports[cnt].port,
                myPL->ports[cnt].proto);
    }
scds_free_port_list(myPL);
```

However, if you want to print the values of the port list to the logfile for debugging, you can use the DSDL utility function, scds_print_port_list(), as described later in this chapter.

Obviously, this function is similar to scds_get_netaddr_list(), as described earlier in this chapter, but it excludes the hostname information. The scds_get_port_list() function should be used when your data service uses multiple ports and/or protocols on the same IP address, whereas scds_get_netaddr_list() should be used when multiple hostnames and/or IP addresses are used as well.

Note – The first argument of this function is an *lvalue* of scds_handle_t, not a pointer to it, as shown in some versions of the scds_get_port_list(3ha) man page. See "A Note on Man Page Entries," earlier in this chapter.

scds_get_resource_name

```
const char *scds_get_resource_name(scds_handle_t handle)
```

This is a fairly simple function that can be used to quickly and easily return the resource name. By using this function, you don't have to keep passing the resource name around the functions in your program—so long as you have the DSDL handle, you have all you need.

> **Note –** The first argument of this function is an *lvalue* of `scds_handle_t`, not a pointer to it, as shown in some versions of the `scds_get_resource_name(3ha)` man page. See "A Note on Man Page Entries."

scds_restart_resource

```
scha_err_t scds_restart_resource(scds_handle_t handle)
```

This function will restart the entire (current) resource; in other words, it calls `STOP` and `START` methods in order (but note that the `PRENET_START` and `POSTNET_STOP` methods are ignored).

You might need to call this function in the `UPDATE` method of a resource type when configuration changes are being made to a resource.

> **Note –** The first argument of this function is an *lvalue* of `scds_handle_t`, not a pointer to it, as shown in some versions of the `scds_restart_resource(3ha)` man page. See "A Note on Man Page Entries."

*scds_get_rs_ **

Most of the functions for retrieving resource property values have a simple format:

value_type `scds_get_rs_`*name_of_property* `(scds_handle_t handle)`

For example, the function you would use to retrieve the `Resource_dependencies` property is `scds_get_rs_resource_dependencies()`.

The main difference between the various functions is the return value, which obviously varies according to the resource property you are retrieving. Table 9.2 is a complete list of the standard resource properties and their corresponding function declarations, including the return value. The data types for the return values are explained in Chapter 7, "Programming with the RMAPI."

> **Note –** Some versions of the `scds_property_functions(3HA)` incorrectly list the function for the `Thorough_Probe_Interval` property as `scds_get_ext_<property-name>`. The information in Table 9.2 is correct.

Table 9.2 Resource Property Functions

Resource Property to Retrieve	Function Declaration
`Cheap_probe_interval`	`int  scds_get_rs_cheap_probe_interval( scds_handle_t handle)`
`Failover_mode`	`scha_failover_mode_t scds_get_rs_failover_mode( scds_handle_t handle)`
`Monitor_stop_timeout`	`int  scds_get_rs_monitor_stop_timeout( scds_handle_t handle)`
`Monitored_switch`	`scha_switch_t scds_get_rs_monitored_switch( scds_handle_t handle)`
`On_off_switch`	`scha_switch_t scds_get_rs_on_off_switch( scds_handle_t handle)`
`Resource_dependencies`	`const scha_str_array_t * scds_get_rs_resource_dependencies( scds_handle_t handle)`
`Resource_dependencies_weak`	`const scha_str_array_t * scds_get_rs_resource_dependencies_weak( scds_handle_t handle)`
`Retry_count`	`int scds_get_rs_retry_count( scds_handle_t handle)`
`Retry_interval`	`int scds_get_rs_retry_interval( scds_handle_t handle)`
`Start_timeout`	`int scds_get_rs_start_timeout( scds_handle_t handle)`
`Stop_timeout`	`int scds_get_rs_stop_timeout( scds_handle_t handle)`
`Scalable`	`boolean scds_get_rs_scalable( scds_handle_t handle)`
`Thorough_probe_interval`	`int scds_get_rs_thorough_probe_ interval(scds_handle_t handle)`

scds_get_rs_hostnames

```
scha_err_t  scds_get_rs_hostnames(scds_handle_t handle,
scds_net_resource_list  **netresource_list)
```

This function is used to retrieve a list of all of the hostnames used by your resource. If the resource has a value for its `network_resources_used` property, then that value is used for the hostnames. If the `network_resources_used` property has not been set, then the list of hostnames is made up of all the host resources (logical and shared address) in the same group as your resource. For example, if your resource group has two logical host resources *web1* and *web2*, and also a shared address resource *web3*, then the list of hostnames returned for your resource *myres* in the same group would be *web1,web2,web3* unless you had specifically set the network_resources_used property on *myres*.

Like `scds_get_port_list()` and `scds_get_netaddr_list()`, this function requires a return value parameter, into which the data is placed. When you have finished with this data, you must free the memory using `scds_free_net_list()`, described later in this chapter.

In this case, the return value *netresource_list* is a handle to `scds_net_resource_list_t` data type, which is a structure containing an integer *num_netresource*, representing the number of network resources, and an array of `scds_net_resource_t` *netresources*. In this context, the network resource is one containing a list of hostnames—in other words, the logical host or shared address used by your application. The `scds_net_resource_t` is a structure containing a string (pointer to char) *name* with name of the resource, an integer *num_hostnames* indicating the number of hostnames in this resource, and an array of strings *hostnames*.

Again, it might be easier to understand this data structure by looking at a diagram—see Figure 9.5. You can access the data structure with something like the code shown in Example 9.4.

Example 9.4 Accessing scds_net_resource_list_t data

```
scds_net_resource_list_t *myNetRes;
int cnt, cnt2;
scds_get_rs_hostnames(myHandle, &myNetRes);
for (cnt = 0 ; cnt < myNetRes->num_netresources ; cnt++)
        {
    printf("%d: resource = %s\n",
                (cnt+1),
                myNetRes->netresources[cnt].name );

    for (cnt2 = 0 ;
                cnt2 < myNetRes->netresources[cnt].num_hostnames;
                cnt2++)
                {
                printf(       "              hostname %d = %s\n",
        (cnt+1),
            myNetRes->netresources[cnt].hostnames[cnt2]) ;
                }
    }

scds_free_net_list(myNetRes);
```

As you've probably guessed by now, if you've been reading this chapter straight through, there is an easier way to print out these network resource hostnames to a

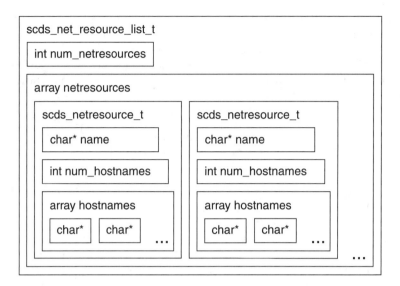

Figure 9.5 scds_net_resource_list_t data structure

logfile for debugging through a utility function called scds_print_net_list().
This function is discussed in more detail later in this chapter.

Note – The first argument of this function is an *lvalue* of scds_handle_t,
not a pointer to it, as shown in some versions of the scds_get_rs_
hostnames(3ha) man page. See "A Note on Man Page Entries."

Functions for Resource Groups

As with the functions for resource, the resource group functions are mostly concerned with retrieving information from the RGM. As with the resource functions,
all of the data about which resource you are referring to is contained within the
resource DSDL handle that was created when you called scds_initialize() at
the beginning of the program.

scds_failover_rg

```
scha_err_t scds_failover_rg(scds_handle_t handle);
```

This function causes the resource group to be "given over" by the controlling node,
thus it is normally used by a monitoring method program when it detects a problem.
It essentially calls scha_control(3HA) with the SCHA_GIVEOVER tag (see Chapter 7, "Utility Methods"), which means that the RGM will automatically decide
which node will restart the data service.

If the function is successful, it never returns, so you should include error checking
after calling this function in case you need to take some other action.

Note – The first argument of this function is an *lvalue* of `scds_handle_t`, not a pointer to it, as shown in some versions of the `scds_failover_rg(3ha)` man page. See "A Note on Man Page Entries."

scds_get_resource_group_name

```
const char *scds_get_resource_group_name(scds_handle_t handle)
```

This function simply returns the current resource group name referred to by the *handle*. Remember not to modify or release the memory pointed to by this function: It belongs to the DSDL environment and thus is cleared when you call `scds_close()`.

Note – The first argument of this function is an *lvalue* of `scds_handle_t`, not a pointer to it, as shown in some versions of the `scds_get_resource_group_name(3ha)` man page. See "A Note on Man Page Entries."

scds_get_rg_hostnames

```
scha_err_t  scds_get_rg_hostnames(char  *resourcegroup_name,
scds_net_resource_list_t **netresource_list)
```

This function is similar to the `scds_get_rs_hostnames()` function, in that it returns the list of host resources—in this case, all those that are members of the resource group that you specify. With this function, the value of the `network_resources_used` property on any resource has no effect on the return value because the function looks for host resources related to the group as a whole.

Note that you must supply a resource group name—the DSDL handle is not passed as an argument to this function. Of course, you can always use the output of `scds_get_resource_group_name()` as one of the arguments, as shown in Example 9.5.

Example 9.5 Using scds_get_rg_hostnames()

```
scds_net_resource_list_t *myNetRes;
scds_get_rg_hostnames(scds_get_resource_group_name(myHandle), &myNetRes);
scds_print_net_list(myHandle, 1, myNetRes);
```

As with the `scds_get_rs_hostnames()` function, the return argument is a data structure of type `scds_net_resource_list_t`, which is graphically depicted in Figure 9.5.

As with `scds_get_rs_hostnames()`, once you have finished with this data, you must free the memory using `scds_free_net_list()`, which is described later in this chapter.

scds_restart_rg

```
scha_err_t scds_restart_rg(scds_handle_t handle);
```

This function is used to restart the resource group, and is essentially a wrapper around a call to `scha_control(3HA)` with the `SCHA_RESTART` option tag, as discussed in Chapter 7.

As with the function `scds_failover_rg()`, success means that `scds_restart_rg()` never returns, so include plenty of error checking after calling this function in case the attempt to restart doesn't work.

Note – The first argument of this function is an *lvalue* of `scds_handle_t`, not a pointer to it, as shown in some versions of the `scds_restart_rg(3ha)` man page. See "A Note on Man Page Entries."

---

scds_get_rg_ *

As with the resource properties, most of the resource group properties can be retrieved using functions of the form `scds_get_rg_property_name`.

Table 9.3 provides a complete listing of these functions, along with the full function signature for each. The return types are described in "Data Types" in Chapter 7.

Functions for Resource Types

There are no functions in the DSDL used to control the behavior of resource types, only functions that are used to retrieve information about the resource type of the current resource.

scds_get_resource_type_name

```
const char  *scds_get_resource_type_name(scds_handle_t  handle)
```

This function simply returns the name of the resource type of the current resource. As with the `scds_get_resource_group_name()` function, you should not change or free the memory block returned by this function, as it is used directly by the DSDL. This memory is freed when you call `scds_close()` at the end of your program.

scds_get_rt_ *

Most of the resource type properties are retrieved using functions of the form:

```
return_type scds_get_rt_property_name(scds_handle_t handle)
```

Table 9.3 Resource Group Property Functions

Resource Group Property to Retrieve	Function Declaration
Desired_primaries	int scds_get_rg_desired_primaries(scds_handle_t handle)
Global_resources_used	const scha_str_array_t * scds_get_rg_global_resources_used(scds_handle_t handle)
Implicit_network_dependencies	boolean_t scds_get_rg_implicit_network_ dependencies(scds_handle_t handle)
Maximum_primaries	int scds_get_rg_maximum_primaries(scds_handle_t handle)
Nodelist	const scha_str_array_t * scds_get_rg_nodelist(scds_handle_t handle)
Pathprefix	const char * scds_get_rg_pathprefix(scds_handle_t handle)
Resource_dependencies_weak	const scha_str_array_t * scds_get_rg_resource_dependencies_ weak(scds_handle_t handle)
Pingpong_interval	int scds_get_rg_pingpong_interval(scds_handle_t handle)
Resource_list	const scha_str_array_t * scds_get_rg_resource_list(scds_handle_t handle)
RG_mode	scha_rgmode_t scds_get_rg_rg_mode(scds_handle_t handle)

The complete list of functions, along with their return types, is listed in Table 9.4. For details on the return types, consult "Data Types" in Chapter 7.

Application Control

In Chapter 8, "Managing Processes" we saw that the Sun Cluster environment provides a built-in facility for monitoring and automatically restarting applications, called the Process Monitor Facility (or PMF). If you tried writing a resource type using C and the basic RMAPI, you would have noticed that there is no way of accessing the PMF without executing the shell program (pmfadm(1m)) from within your C program, a method which can be become unwieldy.

One of the great advantages of using the DSDL rather than the base RMAPI is that it provides a method for accessing the PMF directly through the use of C

Table 9.4 Resource Type Property Functions

Resource Type Property to Retrieve	Function Declaration
API_version	int scds_get_rt_api_version(scds_handle_t handle)
RT_basedir	const char * scds_get_rt_global_rt_basedir(scds_handle_t handle)
Failover	boolean_t scds_get_rt_implicit_failover(scds_handle_t handle)
Init_nodes	scha_initnodes_flag_t scds_get_rt_init_nodes(scds_handle_t handle)
Installed_nodes	const scha_str_array_t * scds_get_rt_installed_nodes(scds_handle_t handle)
Single_instance	boolean_t scds_get_rt_single_instance(scds_handle_t handle)
Start_method	const char * scds_get_rt_start_method(scds_handle_t handle)
Stop_method	const char * scds_get_rt_stop_method(scds_handle_t handle)
RT_version	const char * scds_get_rt_rt_version(scds_handle_t handle)

function calls, so you can get all the benefits of PMF without having to write lots of wrapper code around executing the pmfadm(1m) program.

As you would expect, the cluster framework doesn't make any distinction between processes submitted to PMF via the pmfadm command or via the DSDL C functions, so you don't need to consider much beyond what we covered in Chapter 8 to use the DSDL PMF functions.

Having said that, though, many of the DSDL process monitoring functions require you to specify the program type you want to deal with. This refers to whether the process you are interested in is a service process (in other words, part of your application), a monitor process (a program which is checking your application), or something else. These types are expressed using the scds_pmf_type_t enumerated type, which has the following possible values:

- SCDS_PMF_TYPE_SVC
- SCDS_PMF_TYPE_MON
- SCDS_PMF_TYPE_OTHER

It's important to get the *program_type* correct for the process you are trying to get information about. In particular, when you are starting a process, the *program_type* affects what parameters are associated with the process in the PMF (see "scds_pmf_start" later in this chapter).

The different *program_type* values also provide different namespaces for identifying processes, which is important when used with the other parameter commonly used in the DSDL process monitoring functions—*instance*. The *instance* is a unique identifier used when a resource has multiple processes of a given type under PMF control, and is simply an integer value starting with 0. If you only have one process of a given type under PMF control in your resource, then you can just use 0—for convenience, the macro `SCDS_PMF_SINGLE_INSTANCE` is defined for this purpose. Since the instance is counted according to the *program_type* namespace, an application may, for example, have two service processes and one monitoring process. In this case, you could refer to instances 0 or 1 of type `SCDS_PMF_TYPE_SVC`, and instance 0 of type `SCDS_PMF_TYPE_MON`. We've tried to demonstrate graphically how this works in Figure 9.6.

scds_pmf_get_status

```
scha_err_t     scds_pmf_get_status(scds_handle_t     handle,
scds_pmf_type_t program_type,     int     instance,
scds_pmf_status_t *pmf_status)
```

You can use this function to get information about whether the resource is under control of PMF or not, in the same way that pmfadm -q might be used on the command line (see "Process Monitor Status" in Chapter 8). When you call this function, you must (as usual) supply the DSDL handle, but also the PMF program type and instance for which you are searching.

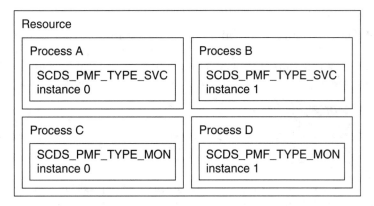

Figure 9.6 PMF types and instances in a resource

The result of this function is placed into the *pmf_status* return parameter, and is another enumerated type: scds_pmf_status_t, which can have the following values:

- SCDS_PMF_MONITORED
- SCDS_PMF_NOT_MONITORED

SCDS_PMF_MONITORED is equivalent to 0, so you can use it in conditional statements, as shown in Example 9.6.

Example 9.6   Using scds_pmf_get_status()

```
scds_pmf_status_t myStatus;
scds_pmf_get_status(myHandle, SCDS_PMF_TYPE_SVC, 0, &myStatus);
if (! myStatus)
     {
     [...things to do if PMF isn't controlling process...]
     }
```

This function is useful in START, STOP, and PROBE methods because it's usually wise to check whether a process is already being monitored by PMF before trying to start or stop an application and to ensure that a process is still under PMF control when it is being tested.

scds_pmf_restart_fm

scha_err_t   scds_pmf_restart_fm(scds_handle_t   handle,   int instance)

This is a convenience function for stopping and restarting a fault monitor process— that is, a process of program type SCDS_PMF_TYPE_MON. Note that you don't have to supply a *program_type* to this function, but you must still provide an *instance*.

When this function is called, the process in question is sent a SIGKILL signal. The PMF should then automatically restart the process, according to its normal rules. This function is most useful for UPDATE method programs, since changes to a resource's properties or status may require a monitored application to be restarted.

scds_pmf_signal

scha_err_t   scds_pmf_signal(scds_handle_t   handle, scds_pmf_type_t   program_type,   int   instance,   int   signal, time_t timeout)

You can use this function to send a signal to the process tree of a process being monitored by PMF, in the same way that you might use pmfadm -k in a script on the command line (see "Stopping the Process Monitor" in Chapter 8).

As usual with most of the DSDL functions related to process management, you must supply the DSDL handle, the program type, and the instance with which you want to deal. The *signal* should be the integer value related to the signal you want to send (consult the `signal(3HEAD)` man page for a list of available signals and their integer values). The timeout is the number of seconds to wait for the signal to be sent to the process(es) in question. If you specify 0 for the timeout, then the function will return immediately; if you specify -1, the function will wait until the process has exited before returning. Obviously you shouldn't specify -1 unless you are sure that the signal you send will cause the process(es) to exit—otherwise, your program may hang indefinitely.

This function is most useful in STOP and UPDATE methods, since particular signals may need to be sent to an application in order to shut it down or to make it recheck configuration information. Note that if you want to stop the process completely, it may be more sensible to use the `scds_pmf_stop()` function (later in this chapter).

scds_pmf_start

```
scha_err_t    scds_pmf_start(scds_handle_t    handle,
scds_pmf_type_t program_type, int instance, const char
*command, int child_monitor_level);
```

This function is used to run a program (or command) under the control of PMF, in essentially the same way as if you were to use `pmfadm -c` on the command line or in a script (see "Starting a Process Monitor" in Chapter 8).

As with most of the DSDL functions dealing with PMF, you must provide the *program_type* (one of SCDS_PMF_TYPE_SVC, SCDS_PMF_TYPE_OTHER, or SCDS_PMF_TYPE_MON) that is appropriate for the process. With this function in particular, however, the *program_type* is more than just a separate namespace for the *instance* references. Table 9.5 shows a comparison between the types.

Table 9.5 Effects of Different PMF Program Types

Program_type	Effect
SCDS_PMF_TYPE_SVC	• registers process to be monitored by `scds_fm_sleep(3ha)` • can monitor multiple levels of child processes (see text following) • use for most actual service processes
SCDS_PMF_TYPE_MON	• process not monitored by `scds_fm_sleep()` • monitors a single level of processes (*child_monitor_level* is ignored) • use for monitoring processes
SCDS_PMF_TYPE_OTHER	• process not monitored by `scds_fm_sleep()` • can monitor multiple levels of child processes • use for nonstandard service processes (those without a fault-monitor process)

Remember that you must keep track of the instance number if you want to start multiple processes of the same *program_type* under PMF control. An easy way to handle this is to create and use your own #define macro. For example:

```
#define MY_APPLICATION_PMF_PROCESS_A 0
#define MY_APPLICATION_PMF_PROCESS_B 1
#define MY_APPLICATION_MONITOR_PROCESS_A 0
```

This may be a little longer than simply using 0 or 1 and so on, but it will make tracking the process easier when you use the other DSDL PMF functions.

The command parameter is a string with the entire command used to start the process you want to put under PMF control, including the whole UNIX path and all of the command-line arguments that are required. Remember that you can easily find out the appropriate command by using scds_rt_get_start_method() (see Table 9.4) and arguments to parameters by using the appropriate scds_rs_get_ ext_property() function calls. For a complete example of how this all fits together, see Chapter 10, "Developing for Existing Applications."

The final function parameter is *child_level_monitor*, which is the number of descendants of your starting process that you want PMF to track. This concept of descendants is described in more detail in"Child Process Monitoring" in Chapter 8. You can also specify a value of -1 for your *child_level_monitor*, which tells the PMF to keep track of all descendants of the starting process.

Obviously this function is most useful in the START method program, although, since you may also want PMF to keep track of your application monitoring programs, you may also use scds_pmf_start() in the MONITOR_START method program.

scds_pmf_stop

```
scha_err_t    scds_pmf_stop(scds_handle_t    handle,
scds_pmf_type_t  program_type,  int  instance,  int  signal,
time_t timeout)
```

This function performs the opposite to scds_pmf_start() in that it stops the PMF from tracking a process tree, and causes the process(es) to exit. In effect, this command is similar to pmfadm -k (see "Stopping the Process Monitor" in Chapter 8).

In addition to the usual program_type and instance function parameters, you must also specify a signal to be sent to the process(es) being monitored. This signal is used to stop the processes—see "Stopping the Process Monitor" in Chapter 8 for more information about this.

The final parameter is a timeout in seconds—usually how long you wait for the process(es) to stop running. If the process is still running after 80% of the timeout value has elapsed, the SIGKILL signal will be sent to the process. If the process is still running after a remaining 15% of the timeout has elapsed, the function will fail and return SCHA_ERR_TIMEOUT, so be sure to check the return value of this function. At this point, you may be wondering why only 95% (80% + 15%) of the timeout value has been used—the assumption is that the 5% left over will be used up by any overhead in running the function.

As you would expect, the normal place this function is used is in the STOP and MONITOR_STOP methods.

scds_pmf_stop_monitoring

```
scha_err_t  scds_pmf_stop_monitoring(scds_handle_t   handle,
scds_pmf_type_t program_type, int instance)
```

This function will cause PMF to stop monitoring the process in question, but will not stop the process itself, similar to the pmfadm -s command (see Chapter 8, "Stopping the Process Monitor").

This function is most useful in situations where an application under cluster control must be shut down manually or through some interface other than a cluster (one example might be a database program).

scds_svc_wait

```
scha_err_t  scds_svc_wait(scds_handle_t   handle,   time_t
timeout);
```

This function is used in START method programs to ensure that processes started by scds_pmf_start() are running successfully before the method program exits. This is particularly useful when your application takes a long time to reach a "ready" state—for example, a database server that does a lot of error checking before allowing connections from clients.

The function will wait on any processes that are monitored by PMF for the specified *timeout* (a value you supply in seconds), and will use the *retry_interval* and *retry_count* properties of the resource to determine whether the application successfully started. If a process fails, PMF will restart it, but if it fails *retry_count* times within *retry_interval*, and during the *timeout* period of the function, then scds_svc_wait will return with a value of SCHA_ERR_FAIL.

If, during the execution of this function, the process fails and does not restart, the function will (when the *timeout* expires) return SCHA_ERR_TIMEOUT. If the function timeout expires with no process failures, or if processes that died were successfully restarted, then the function will exit with the value SCHA_ERR_NOERR.

This function's execution is a little complex, so we've tried to represent it as a flowchart in Figure 9.7.

As you can imagine, it's important for you to check the return value of this function before exiting, at the very least because it will affect what the exit value of your START method program should be.

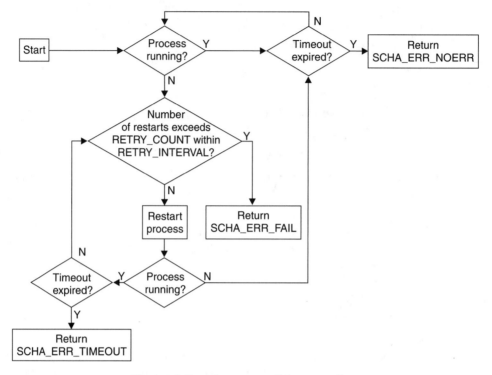

Figure 9.7 scds_svc_wait() execution

Fault Monitoring

Another great benefit of the DSDL is that it provides some handy functions for writing fault monitoring programs, most of which include built-in timeout facilities, so you can concentrate on writing the logic to determine if your application is running properly.

scds_fm_action

```
scha_err_t    scds_fm_action(scds_handle_t    handle,    int
probe_status, long elapsed_milliseconds);
```

This function is used to cause one of the following actions to be taken on your application:

- Restart application (resource)
- Fail over resource group
- Do nothing

Which action is taken depends on the value of the *probe_status* parameter *and* the history of previous calls to this function. The *probe_status* is an integer value between 0 and 100 (100 is SCDS_PROBE_COMPLETE_FAILURE) and you can specify any value based on the results of your probe routine. In the simplest case, if your probe fails then you would call scds_fm_action() with SCDS_PROBE_COMPLETE_ FAILURE as the *probe_status* parameter. You may, however, have a situation where a probe only *partially* fails—for example, if you can connect to your application but are unable to disconnect cleanly. In this case, you may decide you call scds_fm_ action() with a value of 50 for the *probe_status* parameter. The function will add this value to the values supplied in any previous calls to scds_fm_action() that occurred within the period defined by the *retry_interval* resource property.

As an example of how this would work over time, imagine that we have a resource with a retry_interval property value of 300 seconds. Now imagine that we make eight calls to scds_fm_action(), each 100 seconds apart, with the following probe_status values: 30, 0, 20, 0, 0, 0, 70, 80. The graph in Figure 9.8 shows us how the cumulative value of the probe status will change over time.

If the total accumulated value of successive scds_fm_action() function calls within the retry_interval period reaches the value of SCDS_PROBE_COMPLETE_ FAILURE (or more), then the cluster environment will cause the resource to restart by calling the STOP and then START methods. It will also set the status of the re- source to SCHA_RSSTATUS_DEGRADED (by calling the scha_resource_setstatus (3HA) function. (See Chapter 7, "Utility Methods.") Note that the PRENET_START and POSTNET_STOP methods are *not* called, even if they are defined for the resource type. If this restart attempt fails (due to either the STOP or START method programs failing), then the cluster environment will cause the resource group to fail over by using scha_control(3HA) with the GIVEOVER option. If this attempt to fail over succeeds, the originating scds_fm_action() function will never return (since the

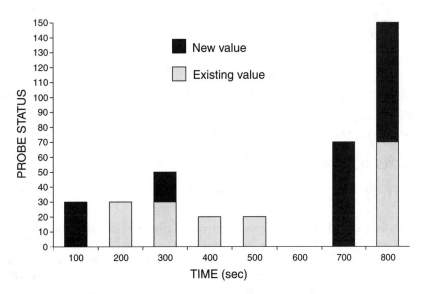

Figure 9.8 Probe status changes over time

resource group has moved to a different node). Once the resource has successfully restarted, all failure history used by `scds_fm_action()` is purged from the system and future calls begin with a clean slate.

If, within the number of seconds defined by the *retry_interval* resource property, the number of restarts exceeds the number defined by the *retry_count* resource property, then the next time this function is called with the total accumulated *probe_status* over `SCDS_PROBE_COMPLETE_FAILURE` the cluster environment will automatically try to fail over the resource group by calling `scha_control (3HA)` with the `GIVEOVER` option—even if the `STOP` and `START` method programs would have completed successfully. In this case, the status of the resource is set to `SCHA_RSSTATUS_FAULTED`. It's important to note that if the attempt to fail over the resource group *fails*, the entire history of calls to scds_fm_action() is still purged from the system. This means it is important to check the return value of the function—a value of `SCHA_ERR_FAIL` means that a failover was attempted but did not succeed.

If, when you call scds_fm_action() the total accumulated probe_status is less than `SCDS_PROBE_COMPLETE_FAILURE`, then the cluster environment takes no action against the resource, except to set its status to `SCHA_RSSTATUS_OK`.

Note that the third argument to this function (elapsed_milliseconds) is the time in milliseconds that was taken to perform the health check (probe) on the resource. It is currently "reserved for future use," so there is no need to provide a real value for this.

scds_fm_print_probes

```
void    scds_fm_print_probes(scds_handle_t    handle,    int
debug_level);
```

This function provides an easy way to print information about the probe history maintained by the DSDL for the current resource. The information is printed directly to the log, with a level of detail specified by the *debug_level* parameter—an integer value between 1 and `SCDS_MAX_DEBUG_LEVEL` (currently defined to be 9).

Information will only be sent to the log if the *debug_level* you supply is less than or equal to the current debug level (see "General Utilities" later in this chapter).

scds_fm_sleep

```
scha_err_t    scds_fm_sleep(scds_handle_t    handle, time_t
timeout);
```

This is a simple function you can use to cause your fault monitor program to wait and watch the application process tree as it is managed by the PMF. The function will keep track of all of the processes started using `scds_pmf_start()` with the *program_type* parameter set to `SCDS_PMF_TYPE_SVC`. Note that every instance of this *program_type* will be monitored.

The *timeout* parameter is the amount of time in seconds for which the function will watch the application process tree. If this time elapses without the watched process(es) failing, the function will exit with a value of SCHA_ERR_NOERR.

If, before the timeout period expires, the application processes die, the function will record SCDS_PROBE_COMPLETE_FAILURE in the failure history and take action as if scds_fm_action() had been called. If, as a result of this action a restart attempt fails, then the function will return an error of SCHA_ERR_INTERNAL.

Note – Some versions of the man page for this function state that the value SCDS_COMPLETE_FAILURE is placed onto the failure history if the process tree fails. This is incorrect (that value is not defined).

---

scds_fm_tcp_connect

```
scha_err_t  scds_fm_tcp_connect(scds_handle_t  handle,    int
sock, const char *hostname, int port, time_t timeout);
```

This function is the first in a series which enables you to very quickly and easily create network probe applications for TCP services. All you need to do to use this function is supply (along with the DSDL handle of course) the *hostname*, the *port* on which your application should be listening, and a *timeout* in seconds to determine how long to wait for a connection request to be answered. If successful, the function will set the *sock* return parameter, which is the file descriptor (socket) used to communicate to the application you want to monitor. If no connection can be made in the time you have allotted, the function will exit and return SCHA_ERR_TIMEOUT.

Recall that the hostname and service port for your application can be quickly retrieved using scds_get_netaddr_list(3HA). This means that you might use something like Example 9.7 to quickly establish a connection to your application.

Example 9.7   Using scds_fm_tcp_connect()

```
scds_netaddr_list *myNL;
int mySocket;
int myTimeout = 180;
scha_err_t myError;

scds_get_netaddr_list(myHandle, &myNL);
myError = scds_fm_tcp_connect(myHandle, mySocket,
                 myNL->netaddrs[0].hostname,
                 myNL->netaddrs[0].port, myTimeout) ;

scds_free_netaddr_list(myNL);
```

Once you have successfully acquired a valid file descriptor in the sock parameter, you can use that with the scds_fm_tcp_read(), scds_fm_tcp_write(), and scds_fm_tcp_close() functions.

scds_fm_tcp_read

```
scha_err_t scds_fm_tcp_read(scds_handle_t handle, int  sock,
char *buffer, size_t *size, time_t timeout);
```

Once you have established a network connection to your application using scds_fm_tcp_connect(), you can use this function to read data that is sent from the application. The *sock* parameter is the network socket file descriptor to read from—it should be the same as the one you obtained from scds_fm_tcp_connect(). The *size* and *buffer* parameters are the number of bytes to read and their location, respectively. When the function is complete the *size* parameter will point to the number of bytes actually read from the socket (this is why *size* must be a pointer and not an absolute value). Finally, the *timeout* parameter is the number of seconds to wait for data to be received from the application.

If the *timeout* of this function expires before all of the requested bytes are read, the function will return SCHA_ERR_TIMEOUT, but the *buffer* and *size* parameters will be set appropriately with the data that was retrieved before the timeout occurred. If there is more data available to be read than has been allocated in the *buffer*, then the function will return as soon as the *buffer* is full, and a subsequent call to scds_fm_tcp_read() can be made to retrieve the remaining data.

Note – Contrary to some versions of the man page for this function, the parameter *sock* is not an output parameter, but should represent the file descriptor which came from a previous call to scds_fm_tcp_connect().

---

scds_fm_tcp_write

```
scha_err_t scds_fm_tcp_write(scds_handle_t handle, int sock,
char *buffer, size_t *size, time_t timeout);
```

This function is used to communicate with a network application—one that you originally connected to using scds_fm_tcp_connect(). The *sock* parameter is the network socket to write to—you should use the value that was set in a prior call to scds_fm_tcp_connect(). The *buffer* parameter is a pointer to the bytes you want to send to the application; *size* is a pointer to the number of bytes you want to send. The *size* parameter is a pointer because the function will change the value to the number of bytes actually written.

If the function is not able to send all of the data before a number of seconds equal to the *timeout* parameter has elapsed, the function will return SCHA_ERR_TIMEOUT, even though some of the data may have been sent. It is important to check the return value of the function, and if a timeout has occurred, check the value pointed to by the *size* parameter to determine exactly how many bytes were sent.

Note – Some versions of the man page for this function indicate that the argument *sock* is an output argument, but it should represent the file descriptor which came from a previous call to `scds_fm_tcp_connect`.

scds_fm_tcp_disconnect

```
scha_err_t scds_fm_tcp_disconnect(scds_handle_t handle,  int
sock, time_t timeout)
```

This function is used to disconnect from a network socket connection which was originally created using `scds_fm_tcp_connect()`. As with `scds_fm_tcp_read()` and `scds_fm_tcp_write()`, the *sock* parameter should be the socket file descriptor created when you called `scds_fm_tcp_connect()` and the *timeout* is the number of seconds to allow for this function to complete.

If the function times out, it will return `SCHA_ERR_TIMEOUT`, at which point you may (depending on the nature of your application) consider registering a partial failure by calling `scha_fm_action()`.

Note – Some versions of the man page for this function denote that the argument *sock* is an output argument, but it is not—it should represent the file descriptor which came from a previous call to `scds_fm_tcp_connect()`.

scds_simple_probe

```
scha_err_t  scds_simple_probe(scds_handle_t  handle,   const
char *hostname, int port, time_t timeout);
```

This function will attempt to open and then close a connection to a network application and can be used (as the name implies) as a simple probe in your fault monitor.

Note that this function does not attempt to read or write any data through the network connection. If you want to do fault monitoring at that level, then it is more appropriate to use the `scds_fm_tcp*` family of functions.

After the DSDL handle, the next two parameters to this function are the *hostname* and TCP *port* where your application is running. Remember that you can retrieve these items using the `scds_get_netaddr_list()` function. The final parameter is the *timeout* in seconds you will allow for the connection and disconnection to be made.

If the function cannot correctly connect and disconnect from the application within the timeout period, then it will exit and return `SCHA_ERR_TIMEOUT`—so be sure to check the return value of the function.

scds_timerun

```
scha_err_t  scds_timerun(scds_handle_t  handle,  const  char
*command, time_t timeout, int signal, int *cmd_exit_code)
```

This function provides the facility to access the hatimerun(1HA) command (described in "Time-Based Process Management" in Chapter 8) from the C programming context. Essentially, this enables you to put a time limit on the execution of any command.

As well as the DSDL handle, you must supply the full program path and arguments for the *command* and also the *timeout* in seconds to allow for the command to execute. You must also supply the integer value of the *signal* that must be sent to the program in case the time limit is exceeded—the possible values and meanings for the *signal* can be found in the signal(3HEA) man page. The final argument is a return parameter for the exit code of the command.

If the function exceeds the time limit allotted in the *timeout* parameter, then the *signal* will be sent to the *command*, and the function will return SCHA_ERR_ TIMEOUT. If no timeout occurs, but some other error is detected, the function will return SCHA_ERR_INTERNAL.

If the function encounters an invalid input argument (for example, if the command to run does not exist on the system) the function will return SCHA_ ERR_INVAL.

It is important to note that this function does not automatically handle I/O redirection—which may have undesirable results if the command you want to run either requires input data or produces output. To get around this problem, you can wrap the command program in a script (or another program) that handles the I/O redirection, and then call the function with this wrapper as the *command* parameter.

General Utilities

The DSDL utility functions provide quick and easy ways to perform handy tasks required for error messages and logging.

Many of the functions include a *debug_level* parameter, which is an integer between 1 and SCDS_MAX_DEBUG (which is 9 by default) that indicates the amount of detail provided by the function. When you call one of these functions, the value you give for the *debug_level* is compared to the current logging level for the resource type. If the value you provide is greater than the current level, no message is sent to the log.

Each resource type logging level is kept in a file `/var/cluster/rgm/ rt/`*resource.type*`/loglevel`. You can change the log level by simply putting a new value into this file. For example:

```
# echo 9 > /var/cluster/rgm/rt/DEMO.apche/loglevel
```

Table 9.6 Output Expected from Debug Levels

		resource type	loglevel file
		1	**9**
debug_level	**1**	brief output	verbose output
	9	no output	verbose output

If you set this value to 0, no debugging messages will ever be shown. An important point to realize is that the actual amount of detail written to the logs is completely controlled by the value in /var/cluster/rgm/rt/*resource.type*/loglevel. The value you supply as the *debug_level* parameter is simply an indication of the loglevel at which to *start* displaying information; so if *debug_level* is greater than the value in the loglevel file, no output will be produced. Table 9.6 shows the effects you should expect from different values for the loglevel file and *debug_level* parameters.

With this in mind, it is probably most useful to always set the *debug_level* parameter in your function calls to a low number (such as 1), and then let the value set in the resource type's loglevel file (which can be changed by the systems administrator). This way, anyone trying to debug your program can set the level of detail they need.

For all of the logging functions, the logging facility used is the one returned by the scha_cluster_getlogfacility(3HA) function (see Chapter 7).

scds_error_string

const char *scds_error_string(scha_err_t error_code);

This function can be used to translate an error code (given as a scha_err_t type) into a human-readable error string,[4] which you can then use in a message.

Note – Some versions of the scds_error_string(3ha) man page indicate that the error type is scha_error_t. This is a mistake; it should be scha_err_t.

---

4. Unfortunately, in releases up to and including Sun Cluster 3.1, the output of the scds_error_string(3ha) function is not affected by LOCALE settings—the only output is in English. Check the release notes of later versions of the software to see if this problem has been fixed.

scds_print_net_list

```
void    scds_print_net_list(scds_handle_t    handle,    int
debug_level,    const    scds_net_resource_list_t
*netresource_list);
```

This function can be used to print the value of an `scds_net_resource_list_t` type (see Figure 9.5) to the logging facility. The output you will see in the log is shown in Example 9.8.

Example 9.8   Output of scds_print_net_list() with debug level set to 9

```
Aug 23 10:04:06 iron shownetres[13385]: [ID 644130 user.debug] logfacility = 24
Aug 23 10:04:06 iron SC[SUNW.apache,s-apache-demo-RG,s-apache-demo,shownetres]:
[ID 634592 daemon.debug] Debug Level is scds_syslog_debuglevel <9>
Aug 23 10:04:06 iron SC[SUNW.apache,s-apache-demo-RG,s-apache-demo,shownetres]:
[ID 525101 daemon.debug] Debug: OP
Aug 23 10:04:06 iron SC[SUNW.apache,s-apache-demo-RG,s-apache-demo,shownetres]:
[ID 551167 daemon.debug] Debug: port_cnt = 1
Aug 23 10:04:06 iron SC[SUNW.apache,s-apache-demo-RG,s-apache-demo,shownetres]:
[ID 678419 daemon.debug] Debug: IP = NULL and port = 2704
Aug 23 10:04:06 iron SC[SUNW.apache,s-apache-demo-RG,s-apache-demo,shownetres]:
[ID 425699 daemon.debug] Debug: port_int(2704), errno(0) endp()
Aug 23 10:04:06 iron SC[SUNW.apache,s-apache-demo-RG,s-apache-demo,shownetres]:
[ID 667865 daemon.debug] Gathering network addresses from the resource list
Aug 23 10:04:06 iron SC[SUNW.apache,s-apache-demo-RG,s-apache-demo,shownetres]:
[ID 248802 daemon.debug] Debug: RT open <SUNW.SharedAddress>
Aug 23 10:04:06 iron SC[SUNW.apache,s-apache-demo-RG,s-apache-demo,shownetres]:
[ID 501374 daemon.debug] Debug: net RS FALSE
Aug 23 10:04:06 iron SC[SUNW.apache,s-apache-demo-RG,s-apache-demo,shownetres]:
[ID 554679 daemon.debug] Resource <midori> is a network resource
Aug 23 10:04:06 iron SC[SUNW.apache,s-apache-demo-RG,s-apache-demo,shownetres]:
[ID 236290 daemon.debug] Debug: rlist Returning 1 net res
Aug 23 10:04:06 iron SC[SUNW.apache,s-apache-demo-RG,s-apache-demo,shownetres]:
[ID 517478 daemon.debug] Returning <0> from get ip address to use
Aug 23 10:04:06 iron SC[SUNW.apache,s-apache-demo-RG,s-apache-demo,shownetres]:
[ID 267467 daemon.debug] Net Resource List contains <1> entries:
Aug 23 10:04:06 iron SC[SUNW.apache,s-apache-demo-RG,s-apache-demo,shownetres]:
[ID 548879 daemon.debug] [0]    Name <midori>    NumHostnames <1>:
Aug 23 10:04:06 iron SC[SUNW.apache,s-apache-demo-RG,s-apache-demo,shownetres]:
[ID 747731 daemon.debug]                          <midori>
```

This is the full output (debug level 9). If the resource's loglevel is set lower, then you will see less output. For example, the output for the same function with the loglevel set to 1 is shown in Example 9.9.

Example 9.9   Output of scds_print_net_list() with debug level set to 1

```
Aug 23 10:21:03 iron shownetres[13794]: [ID 644130 user.debug] logfacility = 24
Aug 23 10:21:03 iron SC[SUNW.apache,s-apache-demo-RG,s-apache-demo,shownetres]:
[ID 634592 daemon.debug] Debug Level is scds_syslog_debuglevel <1>
Aug 23 10:21:03 iron SC[SUNW.apache,s-apache-demo-RG,s-apache-demo,shownetres]:
[ID 267467 daemon.debug] Net Resource List contains <1> entries:
Aug 23 10:21:03 iron SC[SUNW.apache,s-apache-demo-RG,s-apache-demo,shownetres]:
[ID 548879 daemon.debug] [0]    Name <midori>   NumHostnames <1>:
Aug 23 10:21:03 iron SC[SUNW.apache,s-apache-demo-RG,s-apache-demo,shownetres]:
[ID 747731 daemon.debug]                              <midori>
```

scds_print_netaddr_list

```
void    scds_print_netaddr_list(scds_handle_t    handle,    int
debug_level, const scds_netaddr_list_t *netaddr_list);
```

You can use this function to quickly print the contents of an scds_netaddr_list_t data structure, such as is returned by the scds_get_netaddr_list() function, to the debugging log. If the logging level is correct, the output shown in Example 9.10 is produced:

Example 9.10   Output of scds_print_netaddr_list() with debug level set to 9

```
Aug 23 09:58:57 iron shownets[13274]: [ID 644130 user.debug] logfacility = 24
Aug 23 09:58:57 iron SC[SUNW.apache,s-apache-demo-RG,s-apache-demo,shownets]:
[ID 634592 daemon.debug] Debug Level is scds_syslog_debuglevel <9>
Aug 23 09:58:57 iron SC[SUNW.apache,s-apache-demo-RG,s-apache-demo,shownets]:
[ID 525101 daemon.debug] Debug: OP
Aug 23 09:58:57 iron SC[SUNW.apache,s-apache-demo-RG,s-apache-demo,shownets]:
[ID 551167 daemon.debug] Debug: port_cnt = 1
Aug 23 09:58:57 iron SC[SUNW.apache,s-apache-demo-RG,s-apache-demo,shownets]:
[ID 678419 daemon.debug] Debug: IP = NULL and port = 2704
Aug 23 09:58:57 iron SC[SUNW.apache,s-apache-demo-RG,s-apache-demo,shownets]:
[ID 425699 daemon.debug] Debug: port_int(2704), errno(0) endp()
Aug 23 09:58:57 iron SC[SUNW.apache,s-apache-demo-RG,s-apache-demo,shownets]:
[ID 667865 daemon.debug] Gathering network addresses from the resource list
Aug 23 09:58:57 iron SC[SUNW.apache,s-apache-demo-RG,s-apache-demo,shownets]:
[ID 248802 daemon.debug] Debug: RT open <SUNW.SharedAddress>
Aug 23 09:58:57 iron SC[SUNW.apache,s-apache-demo-RG,s-apache-demo,shownets]:
[ID 501374 daemon.debug] Debug: net RS FALSE
Aug 23 09:58:57 iron SC[SUNW.apache,s-apache-demo-RG,s-apache-demo,shownets]:
[ID 554679 daemon.debug] Resource <midori> is a network resource
Aug 23 09:58:57 iron SC[SUNW.apache,s-apache-demo-RG,s-apache-demo,shownets]:
[ID 236290 daemon.debug] Debug: rlist Returning 1 net res
Aug 23 09:58:57 iron SC[SUNW.apache,s-apache-demo-RG,s-apache-demo,shownets]:
[ID 517478 daemon.debug] Returning <0> from get ip address to use
Aug 23 09:58:57 iron SC[SUNW.apache,s-apache-demo-RG,s-apache-demo,shownets]:
[ID 462898 daemon.debug] NetAddr midori/2704/6
```

scds_print_port_list

```
void   scds_print_port_list(scds_handle_t   handle,   int
debug_level, const scds_port_list_t *port_list)
```

This function will write the value of an `scds_port_list_t` data structure (see Figure 9.4) to the debug log. When the loglevel is set to `SCDS_MAX_DEBUG`, the data will appear in the log as shown in Example 9.11.

Example 9.11   Output of scds_print_port_list()

```
Aug 23 10:45:34 iron showports[14400]: [ID 644130 user.debug] logfacility = 24
Aug 23 10:45:34 iron SC[SUNW.apache,s-apache-demo-RG,s-apache-demo,showports]:
[ID 634592 daemon.debug] Debug Level is scds_syslog_debuglevel <9>
Aug 23 10:45:34 iron SC[SUNW.apache,s-apache-demo-RG,s-apache-demo,showports]:
[ID 525101 daemon.debug] Debug: OP
Aug 23 10:45:34 iron SC[SUNW.apache,s-apache-demo-RG,s-apache-demo,showports]:
[ID 551167 daemon.debug] Debug: port_cnt = 1
Aug 23 10:45:34 iron SC[SUNW.apache,s-apache-demo-RG,s-apache-demo,showports]:
[ID 678419 daemon.debug] Debug: IP = NULL and port = 2704
Aug 23 10:45:34 iron SC[SUNW.apache,s-apache-demo-RG,s-apache-demo,showports]:
[ID 425699 daemon.debug] Debug: port_int(2704), errno(0) endp()
Aug 23 10:45:34 iron SC[SUNW.apache,s-apache-demo-RG,s-apache-demo,showports]:
[ID 324997 daemon.debug] Portlist:2704/6
```

scds_syslog

```
void scds_syslog(int priority, const char *format, ...)
```

This function can be used to write any message to the system log at the given *priority* (see `syslog(3C)` for details of possible priority levels). The second parameter to the function is the format string you want to use for the message—the same as you would use in a `printf(3C)` function call. The remaining parameters are variables that would be used by the format.

Each message sent to the log is prefixed with:

SC[*resource_type_name*, *resource_group_name*, *resource_name*, *method_name*]

scds_syslog_debug

```
void scds_syslog_debug(int debug_level, const char   *format,
...);
```

This function is similar to `scds_syslog()`, described previously, but it is affected by the *debug_level* you provide, which must be equal to or less than the current maximum debugging level for the resource type before the message is sent.

As with scds_syslog(), the parameter to the function is the format string you want to use for the message and the subsequent parameters are variables used by that format.

Messages sent to the log are always sent as priority LOG_DEBUG and always include the prefix:

SC [*resource_type_name*, *resource_group_name*, *resource_name*, *method_name*]

Memory Handling

Several functions in the DSDL allocate additional memory that is not automatically freed when scds_close() is called. Instead, the memory allocated must be explicitly released using one of the memory handling functions.

scds_free_ext_property

```
void scds_free_ext_property(scha_ext_prop_value_t
*property_value);
```

Whenever you make a call to scds_get_ext_property(), memory is allocated to store the *property_value* that is not automatically freed by the DSDL environment. This function should be used to release this memory, once you have finished using the extension property value.

scds_free_net_list

```
void             scds_free_net_list(scds_net_resource_list_t
*net_resource_list)
```

You should use this function to release memory allocated in a prior call to either scds_get_rg_hostnames() or scds_get_rs_hostnames().

scds_free_netaddr_list

```
void             scds_free_netaddr_list(scds_netaddr_list_t
*netaddr_list);
```

This function reclaims memory allocated during a call to scds_get_netaddr_list().

scds_free_port_list

```
void scds_free_port_list(scds_port_list_t *port_list)
```

You must use this function to free the memory allocated in a prior call to scds_get_port_list.

Summary

Although it may initially appear daunting, the data service development library (DSDL) actually follows a fairly predictable set of rules. Certainly, if you've experimented a little with using the basic RMAPI C functions to develop resource type methods, it should quickly become obvious that the DSDL is much easier to use to get simple and repetitive tasks done quickly.

In this chapter we have introduced how the DSDL fits in with the other Sun Cluster APIs, and have seen some examples of how the library is used in programs. We've also looked at each of the DSDL functions and examined the data types used therein.

Now that you're armed with the details of the DSDL functions, let's look at putting them to use in Chapter 10, "Developing for Existing Applications."

10

DEVELOPING FOR EXISTING APPLICATIONS

Introduction

A lot of information has been covered in the past chapters. Now it's time to take that information and use it to create a resource type (agent) that can be used in the Sun Cluster 3.x environment. In this chapter, we will work on taking an off-the-shelf application and go through what it will take to integrate it into the Sun Cluster 3 environment as a highly available data service. What is covered in this chapter is applicable for developing scalable services also, but the details of scalable services are covered in Chapter 11.

In Chapter 5, the SunPlex Agent Builder was introduced and a resource type was created through the GUI. This chapter will go through creating a resource type without the use of the GUI.

System Environment

By now, your development environment should be set up. Since this chapter will involve using both the resource manager API (RMAPI) and the data service development library (DSDL), a review of the environment at this time might save you some headaches later in this chapter. For access to the Sun Cluster development libraries, you will need the SUNWscdev package for the APIs, and the SUNWscman package for access to the man pages. If you are developing on the cluster, these packages are part of the environment; otherwise, you will need to install these packages on your development system. For C development, you will need access to a C compiler with the following added to your compiler and linker environments:

- Header files—I /usr/cluster/include—for the libscha headers
- Header files—I /usr/cluster/include/rgm—for the DSDL headers
- Static libraries—L /usr/cluster/lib—32-bit libraries
- Static libraries—L /usr/cluster/lib/sparcv9—64-bit libraries
- Dynamic libraries—R /usr/cluster/lib—32-bit libraries
- Dynamic libraries—R /usr/cluster/lib/sparcv9—64-bit libraries

In your login environment, the *PATH* environment should have /usr/cluster/bin added. In your *MANPATH* environment, /usr/cluster/man should be added to access the Sun Cluster man pages.

Debugging environments will need to be loaded on the cluster nodes. While you can develop on nonclustered systems, debugging them will require running the methods and/or programs on the cluster.

Example Applications

For the examples in this chapter, we will work on taking the MySQL database application and common UNIX print server (CUPS) application and create a resource type that will start, stop, and monitor the application in the cluster environment. The MySQL example will be a scripted ksh version and the CUPS application will be a C version using the DSDL.

Understanding the Application

Before starting down the coding trail, an understanding of the application is needed to see if the application can be integrated into the Sun Cluster environment. Besides the START and STOP methods, what other callback methods will be needed? Are there any support programs needed, such as monitoring programs or action programs, to take care of any issues when an application restart fails? One example of this would be checking for and removing any leftover lock files. In Chapter 4, qualifying an application and determining its scope was discussed so we will refer to it for the MySQL database and the CUPS application.

MySQL Application

The MySQL database is a popular application and it would appear to be a candidate for the Sun Cluster environment. Using the topics from Chapter 4, we can determine whether this application can be used in the Sun Cluster environment and also identify any special requirements that are needed to have it managed by the Sun Cluster framework.

When qualifying an application, several key points were given in Chapter 4 to consider about the application. Using these key points, one should be able to determine if the application is capable of working in the Sun Cluster environment. If there are some issues that could be of concern, there may be ways to address these issues either programmatically or through a command argument.

Data Service Access

Once the MySQL database application is started, clients connect to the database either remotely through TCP/IP or locally through a socket connection. Clients can be users who access the database directly or they can be applications that access, store, or modify data within the database.

For remote connectivity, the client must connect via an IP address and a port number to access the database. This works well in the Sun Cluster environment because during a failover of an application to another node in the cluster the client accesses the database using the same IP address and port number. The client will need to reconnect to the database when a failover occurs. This is also true if the database were to be restarted on the same node for some particular reason.

Local clients can use TCP/IP to connect or a socket connection but they need to know which file to access to make the connection. MySQL by default uses /tmp/mysql.sock as a socket file. Running multiple instances of the MySQL database will require a different socket file for each instance. This information is in the configuration file for each MySQL database instance.

The monitoring program that needs to be developed can be considered a client application. To connect to the database the monitor for this resource type could use either a network connection or a socket connection and then check that it is working properly. The client type, either local or remote, determines how the monitor program will monitor the database. For our example, the monitor will connect to the database via TCP/IP, which also verifies network connectivity to that database.

Note – MySQL by default uses a UNIX domain socket file. This file is /tmp/mysql.sock. If multiple database instances were to be used, this file would need to be different for each one. This can be defined in each MySQL database configuration file.

Crash Tolerance

For the database administrator I'm not sure which is worse—heartburn after devouring a chili dog during a five-minute lunch break or the crash of a database. We don't like dealing with crashes, but it's a fact of life. Fortunately, modern applications can handle a crash for the most part pretty well.

The MySQL database has features which, once configured properly, will provide auto-recovery in the case of a crash. There are always situations that auto-recovery may not be able to handle, so the importance of making good backups still prevails as a means of recovering data with minimum loss.

The configuration parameters needed for auto-recovery are beyond the scope of this book. However, this application does have the capability of recovery, which is the key point of this discussion.

Bounded Recovery

Recovery time of an application needs to have some bounded limit so the cluster can deliver the availability that is expected. After an anomaly occurs, there will be some type of event within the Sun Cluster framework that either causes the application to be restarted on the same node or to fail over to another node in that cluster. That anomaly may cause the normal start time of the application to take longer than the usual "clean" startup time. Whether the decision is to restart or fail over, the cluster framework will at some point call the START method to start the application. The START method needs to be able to start the application within the START_TIMEOUT. The time to start the application may take longer than the normal start time due to some additional recovery time, so the START_TIMEOUT needs to be sufficient to start the application in a clean start or restart scenario.

Since the MySQL application does have the ability for auto-recovery, the default START_TIMEOUT of 300 seconds is most likely more than sufficient. This timeout period can be adjusted if needed using the scrgadm (1HA) command.

File Location Independence

If the application has hard-coded paths for directories or files, it might be difficult to have shared access of application data, configuration files, and application binaries across the cluster's nodes. The MySQL database is available in a pkgadd(1M) form for installing in the Solaris operating environment (SOE). The default location is in the directory /usr/local/mysql. This can be changed with the -R root_path argument to the pkgadd(1M) command or by creating a link using the ln(1) command.

Using a symbolic link, the /usr/local/mysql directory can be linked to a directory on the shared storage. This must be done on each node in the cluster. Since this directory is not removed by the application, the chance of the symbolic link being removed is minimal and most likely accidental.

Note – Use care when using links. Files or directories that are removed and created by the application are not good choices to be linked because they will not be created as a link to the actual location of the directory or file. It would be best to link the directory above this so that it is not removed or created by the application.

Other considerations for the MySQL application are the database directory, the configuration file, and the socket file that the application uses. The database directory can be specified with the --datadir=*path_to_datadir* argument. The configuration file can be specified with either the --defaults-file=*config_filename* or the --defaults-extra-file=*config_filename* arguments. For each running instance of the MySQL application, there is a socket file that is created, which by default is usually /tmp/mysql.sock. If only one instance of the MySQL database is running, this file will be sufficient. If more than one instance of the database is needed, the socket file will need to be different for each database instance. A different socket file can be specified in the configuration file for that particular database instance.

Absence of a Tie to Physical Identity of Node

An application that binds itself to the physical node's identity will be difficult to fail over to another node within the cluster. During the application's life cycle, responses are made to requests from clients that are typically running on other hosts. If the application fails over to another node in the cluster, the physical identity is no longer the same. This causes issues with the clients sending requests to a node that can no longer respond because the application is no longer running on that node. Clients will have to manually change and reconnect, if they can, to the other physical node; thus, it is not transparent to the user. The application itself may have issues, such as a configuration file with the physical identity of the node embedded in it.

- The database offers an argument to specify which IP address to bind to when starting the database. That argument is --bind-address=*IP*, so the application can be configured not to bind to the physical node IP and can use a logical IP address to bind to.
- The database offers an argument to specify a port number to use. This can be set up either in the database configuration file, *mysql-configfile.cnf,* or as an argument --port=*portnumber*. This removes any issue with port conflicts that may occur. A unique port number is necessary if multiple MySQL database instances need to run on the same node.

The MySQL database has the ability to provide an IP address and port to bind to. This can be specified in the configuration file or in the command line. So the MySQL database has the ability to bind to a *logical host* in the Sun Cluster environment.

Ability to Work on Multi-Homed Hosts

In some environments, there will be a need to provide multiple organizations access to the application over multiple networks. Systems may have multiple network adapters configured to segment network traffic by these organizations. Applications in this configuration need to be able to communicate over multiple network interfaces. The MySQL application is able to work with multiple IP network interfaces and has the ability to bind to a specific IP address if there is a need.

Ability to Work with Logical Interfaces

As mentioned in the section "Absence of a Tie to Physical Identity of Node" earlier in this chapter, the MySQL database has the ability to specify an IP address to bind to and a unique port number. So a logical host IP address with a unique port number can be specified for the database instance.

Note – The Sun Cluster environment defines a hostname / IP address to a logical host resource. This resource name is unique within the cluster because it is assigned a hostname and IP address that are unique within a network, allowing different logical hosts to reside on the same physical node and operate without conflict. What needs to be considered is that port numbers need to be uniquely assigned within the cluster environment. When a node fails in the cluster, the applications that were running on that node will migrate to another node in the cluster. If port assignment is not unique across all nodes in the cluster, there is a chance the applications may access the same port being used by another application, when they coexist on the same node. This will cause problems with the applications that are on the same node. So care should be taken with port number assignments when configuring multiple applications running within a cluster.

Client Recovery

When an event occurs with an application running on the cluster, the cluster will either restart the application, fail the application over to another node within the cluster, or possibly stop the application from running. If the event is a restart or failover to another node, the client will need to reconnect via a network connect to the application. Depending on the time of the event, there may be some outstanding transactions that were not committed to the server application and the client will not know if the transactions have completed. For the client to recover, it may need some type of transaction monitor that can track what transactions were committed and what transactions did not complete. The transaction monitor will then need to handle the transactions that did not complete in the appropriate manner to keep data integrity.

CUPS Application

The common UNIX print server (CUPS) application has the ability to spool print jobs to locally attached printers and to network printers. Since this application is similar to a Web server application like Apache, it should be a good candidate for the Sun Cluster environment. A review of the key points for the CUPS application will help to identify any potential issues with the application or the possibility of any support programs that may be needed.

Data Service Access—CUPS

The CUPS application is a client-server application. Clients running locally or on other systems access this application via a network connection and print jobs are sent via a TCP/IP connection to the server. The CUPS application spools these print jobs and sends them out to the requested printer.

When creating the resource type for the CUPS application, monitoring will need to be implemented to ensure the print server is running. A probe program will need to be developed to ensure that the print server is available and providing the necessary service. The probe can be considered a client application that connects to an IP address and port number of the print server and gets its status.

Crash Tolerance—CUPS

The CUPS application stores print jobs on a filesystem after the print job has been spooled. After the print job has been successfully printed, it is removed from the filesystem.

When an event occurs such as a system crash, print jobs that have been spooled successfully and are stored on the filesystem will be able to print. So in a sense, there is persistence stored on the filesystem. However, print jobs that are in the process of being spooled when the event occurs may need to be respooled in the form of a new print request.

Print jobs that are in the process of printing may get reprinted when a crash or restart occurs. This is because the print job has not been removed from the spool as a completed print job would after completion. This might not be the case for network printers and printers with large buffer space.

Bounded Recovery—CUPS

Recovery time of an application needs to have some bounded limit so the cluster can deliver the availability that is expected of that application. When some anomaly occurs, there will be some type of event within the Sun Cluster framework that either causes the application to be restarted on the same node or fail over to another node in that cluster. That anomaly may cause the normal start time of the application to take longer than the usual "clean" startup time. Whether the decision is to restart or fail over, the cluster will at some point call the START method to start the application, which needs to be able to start the application within the START_TIMEOUT. The time to start the application may take longer than the normal start time due to some additional recovery time.

During a restart of the CUPS application, the application restarts quickly. As noted, any print jobs that were in process and not removed from the print queue will reprint in their entirety.

File Location Independence—CUPS

If the application has hard-coded paths for directories or files, this might make it difficult to have shared access of application data, configuration files, and application binaries across the clusters nodes. The CUPS application can be downloaded from the Web site, www.cups.org. The configure script asks for the location to install the CUPS application. CUPS is installed in this base directory along with necessary subdirectories that hold configuration files, binaries, print job requests, and their associated print files. Thus, there are no hard-coded paths that makes it easy to install in a shared filesystem within the Sun Cluster environment.

Absence of a Tie to Physical Identity of Node—CUPS

An application that binds itself to the physical node's identity would be difficult to fail over to another node within the cluster. While the application is running, responses are made to requests from clients that are typically running on another host other than the cluster nodes. If the application fails over to another node in the cluster, the physical identity is no longer the same. This creates issues with the clients sending requests to a node that can no longer respond because the application is no longer running on that node. Clients will have to manually change the hostname and reconnect to the other physical node, so it's not transparent to the user. The application itself may have issues, such as a configuration file with the physical identity of the node embedded in it.

The CUPS application has a configuration file, `cupsd.conf`, that is much like a Web server configuration file. Within this configuration file, multiple hostnames and port numbers can be defined. So, from this aspect, the CUPS application will work within the Sun Cluster environment.

Note – During testing of the CUPS application, it was noticed that if localhost:*portnumber* was not defined in the configuration file, the administration commands did not work on the local node. So this needs to be defined in the configuration file.

Ability to Work on Multi-Homed Hosts—CUPS

There are some system configurations that have multiple host adapters connecting to multiple networks. Applications that run in this type of configuration need to be flexible enough to be able to bind to more that one network interface or sufficiently configurable to specify an interface or set of interfaces to which to bind. The CUPS application's configuration file can be used to specify one or more IP addresses to bind to and, therefore, satisfy this point.

Ability to Work with Logical Interfaces—CUPS

As discussed in the section "Absence of a Tie to Physical Identity of Node—CUPS," the CUPS application has the ability to specify hostnames and ports in the configuration file `cupsd.conf`. So this application can recognize logical IP addresses.

Client Recovery—CUPS

When an event occurs with an application running on the cluster, the cluster will either restart the application, fail the application over to another node within the cluster, or possibly stop the application from running. If it's a restart or failover to another node, the client will need to reconnect to the application. Depending on the application, there may be some outstanding transactions that may or may not have been committed to the server application.

Client connections generally will be short-lived because once the document is spooled the connection is terminated. The only issue will be during a cluster event when a large print job is submitted. This print job may need to be resubmitted.

Project Creation

As in any development project, organization of the source, libraries, configuration files, and source builds is important in developing good programs. Writing a data service should be no different. Version control is important in keeping track of changes, particularly when something that worked previously stops working.

In Chapter 5, the SunPlex builder GUI, scdsbuilder (1HA), created the directory structures with the files to create a data service for the application that was specified. In this chapter, the motto will be: "We don't do GUIs here." This will help in giving the developer the behind-the-GUI view in creating resource types.

The Sun Cluster environment provides two command-line interfaces (CLIs): scdscreate (1HA), to create the resource types directory structures and templates; and scdsconfig (1HA), to configure these resource types with the commands necessary to start, stop, and probe the application.

scdscreate (1HA)

The scdscreate (1HA) is used to create directory structures and template files for a new resource type that will be either highly available or scalable. The template files are base files for the resource types callback methods; additional coding will be needed to complete these methods. This provides a consistent starting point and format for developing more than one resource type.

The scdscreate CLI enables the developer to create two forms of resource types. One form is for network-aware applications, such as a client server application like a database, and the other form is for non-network-aware applications, such as a batch program that works on local data files to generate report files.

Syntax:
```
Network Aware
scdscreate -V vendor_id -T resource_type_name [-s] [-d
working_directory] [-k|-g]
Non-Network Aware
scdscreate -V vendor_id -T resource_type_name -a [-s] [-d
working_directory] [-k|-g]
```

With the scdscreate CLI, the developer also has the choice of two different models, one that uses the GDS or generic data service to create the resource type and a second model to generate source code, either in ksh (K Shell) or in the C language.

The GDS is flexible. With the scrgadm (1HA) CLI, a simple application can be made highly available from the command line using the GDS. The downside of this is that it is a one-off data service that is not portable to another cluster. To get around this, use the scdscreate CLI along with the GDS model to create a resource type that can be reused in more than one clustered environment.

Creating the MySQL Resource Type

Using the scdscreate CLI, it is time to create the resource type for the MySQL database. Since the database is a network-aware application, the network-aware form for the scdscreate CLI will be used. In this example, the callback methods will be done in ksh.

To create the MySQL resource type with the scdscreate command, some information will need to be supplied as arguments to the command:

- Vendor information—supplied with -V argument. Identifies the vendor who created this resource type. Could be the stock symbol of the company. For this example, the vendor ID will be *BOOK*.

- Resource type name—supplied with -T argument. Name of the resource type. The resource type for this example will be called *mysql_ksh*.

- Code model—For this example, the resource type code model will be to use ksh, so the -k argument will be supplied.

- Working directory—base working directory specified by the -d argument. Directory from which scdscreate will create the directory structures and templates for the resource type. If the directory does not exist, it will be created. This argument is optional and if not specified, scdscreate will work from the current directory.

Choose a directory that is empty. You may choose to specify it in the CLI or change to that directory and run the command from there.

```
# scdscreate -V BOOK -T mysql_ksh -k -d ./mysql
/var/tmp/./mysql does not exist. Creating /var/tmp/./mysql
...done.
Creating the rtconfig file ...done.
Cloning and modifying Makefile ...done.
Cloning and modifying README.mysql_ksh ...done.
Cloning and modifying BOOK.mysql_ksh ...done.
Cloning and modifying mysql_ksh_mon_check.ksh ...done.
Cloning and modifying mysql_ksh_mon_start.ksh ...done.
.
.
```

```
Creating the man page mysql_ksh_config.1m ...done.
Creating the package file postremove ...done.
Creating the package file postinstall ...done.
Creating the package file preremove ...done.
Creating the RTR file BOOK.mysql_ksh ...done.
```

Once the scdscreate command has completed, the rtconfig file that holds the configuration information for this resource type will be in the directory /var/tmp/mysql. This information is used by other utilities, such as scdsconfig (1HA) and scdsbuilder (1HA). Also in the MySQL directory is the BOOKmysql_ksh directory, which has the template files for the resource type.

In the BOOKmysql_ksh directory, there is a README.mysql_ksh file that describes the directory structures and their contents.

 # more README.mysql_ksh
```
# Sun Cluster Data Services Builder template version 1.0
This is the README file for BOOKmysql_ksh package.
Following are the contents of this package:

1) bin: this subdirectory contains the binaries for various
methods used by the RGM to drive various events in the
evolution of the resources of the mysql_ksh resource type.

2) etc: this subdirectory contains the RTR (Resource Type
Registration) file for the mysql_ksh resource type. See
rt_reg(4) for more info.

3) util: this subdirectory contains customized scripts for
starting, stopping and removing instances (also known as
resources) of the mysql_ksh resource type. These scripts are
startmysql_ksh, stopmysql_ksh and removemysql_ksh respectively.

4) docs: this subdirectory contains pseudo text man pages for
the three utility scripts -- startmysql_ksh, stopmysql_ksh and
removemysql_ksh.

5) README.mysql_ksh: this file.
```

You will notice that in the README file, there are a few discrepancies compared to the actual directories that exist. The man pages described are in the man directory since there is no docs directory. There are also two other directories: the src directory, which is where the majority of the development will take place; and the pkg directory, which will contain the final package once you've completed developing the resource type and run the make (1S) command with the pkg argument. This will be discussed in "Deploying the Agent" later in this chapter.

In the util directory, the scdscreate command builds three scripts that aid in the use of the resource type. They are documented with man pages located in the man directory.

- **startmysql_ksh**—This script will register the resource type with the cluster, configure a resource group, and add a resource based on this resource type. Configuration is based on the arguments used as well as the `mysqlksh_config` file located in the same directory.
- **stopmysql_ksh**—To disable and offline the resource, use this script. It uses the information in the `mysqlksh_config` file located in the same directory.
- **removemysql_ksh**—This script will remove the resource after it is disabled. It will also offline the resource group and then remove the resource and the resource group and unregister the resource type with the Sun Cluster framework.

In the `etc` directory, `scdscreate` creates a template for the resource type registration (RTR) file. In this directory are also files used by the SOE's package creation utilities, discussed in "Deploying the Agent" later in this chapter.

At this point, the resource type's directory structure and templates have been created. If you plan to use any source code controls such as sccs (1), this would be a good time to do so. At a minimum, the files located in the `src` directory and the RTR file located in the `etc` directory would be a good place to start. Additional files can be added later to sccs when you create new files or need to edit existing files.

Creating the CUPS Resource Type

It is time to create the resource type for the CUPS application using the scdscreate CLI. Since this application is a network-aware application, the network-aware form for the scdscreate CLI will be used. In this example, the callback methods will be done in C using the DSDL.

To create the CUPS resource type with the scdscreate command, some information will need to be supplied as arguments to the command:

- Vendor information—supplied with -V argument. Identifies the vendor who created this resource type. Could be the stock symbol of the company. For this example, the vendor ID will be *BOOK,* since this is part of "the book."
- Resource type name—supplied with -T argument. Name of the resource type; called *cups* for this example.
- Code model—In this case, we will be creating a resource type in C. No argument needs to be supplied for this code model.
- Working directory—base working directory specified by the -d argument. Directory from which scdscreate will create the directory structures and templates for the resource type. If the directory does not exist, it will be created. This argument is optional and, if not specified, scdscreate will work from the current directory.

Choose a directory that is empty. You may choose to specify it in the CLI or change to that directory and run the command from there.

```
# scdscreate -V BOOK -T cups -d ./cups
/var/tmp/./cups does not exist. Creating /var/tmp/./cups
...done.
Creating the rtconfig file ...done.
Cloning and modifying Makefile ...done.
Cloning and modifying README.cups ...done.
Cloning and modifying BOOK.cups ...done.
Cloning and modifying cups.c ...done.
Cloning and modifying cups.h ...done
Cloning and modifying cups_monitor_check.c ...done.
Cloning and modifying cups_monitor_start.c ...done.
.
.
.
Creating the man page cups_config.1m ...done.
Creating the package file postremove ...done.
Creating the package file postinstall ...done.
Creating the package file preremove ...done.
Creating the RTR file BOOK.cups ...done.
```

Once the scdscreate command has completed, the rtconfig file that holds the configuration information for this resource type will be in the directory /var/tmp/cups. This information is used by other utilities, such as scdsconfig (1HA) and scdsbuilder (1HA). Also in the cups directory is the BOOKcups directory, which has the template files for the resource type.

In the BOOKcups directory, there is a README.cups file that describes the directory structures and their contents.

```
# more README.cups

# Sun Cluster Data Services Builder template version 1.0

This is the README file for BOOKcups package.

Following are the contents of this package:

1) bin: this subdirectory contains the binaries for vari-
ous methods used by the RGM to drive various events in the
evolution of the resources of the cups resource type.

2) etc: this subdirectory contains the RTR (Resource Type
Registration) file for the cups resource type. See
rt_reg(4) for more info.

3) util: this subdirectory contains customized scripts
for starting, stopping and removing instances (also known
as resources) of the cups resource type. These scripts
are startcups, stopcups and removecups respectively.

4) docs: this subdirectory contains pseudo text man pages
for the three utility scripts -- startcups, stopcups and
removecups.

5) README.cups: this file.
```

You will notice that in the README file, there are a few discrepancies compared to the existing directories. The man pages described are in the man directory since there is no docs directory. There are also two other directories: the src directory, which is where the majority of the development will take place; and the pkg directory, which contains the final package once you've completed developing the resource type and run the make(1S) command with the pkg argument. This will be discussed later in this chapter in "Deploying the Agent."

In the util directory, the scdscreate command builds three scripts that aid in the use of the resource type. These scripts are documented with man pages located in the man directory as follows:

- **startcups**—This script will register the resource type with the cluster, configure a resource group, and add a resource based on this resource type. Configuration is based on the arguments used as well as the cups_config file located in the same directory.

- **stopcups**—To disable and offline the resource, use this script. It uses the information in the cups_config file located in the same directory.

- **removecups**—This script will remove the resource after it is disabled. It will also offline the resource group and then remove the resource and the resource group and unregister the resource type with the Sun Cluster framework.

In the etc directory, scdscreate creates a template for the RTR file. In this directory are also files used by the SOE's package creation utilities as discussed in "Deploying the Agent."

At this point, the resource type's directory structure and templates have been created. If you plan to use any source code control such as sccs (1), this would be a good time to do so. At a minimum, the files located in the src directory and the RTR file located in the etc directory would be a good place to start. Additional files can be added later to sccs when you create new files or need to edit existing files.

scdsconfig (1HA)

The scdsconfig (1HA) is used to modify the existing templates with configuration information, such as the start and stop commands for the application for which the resource type is being developed. For network-aware applications, the probe command will be used to monitor the availability of the application. Other optional arguments provided are the timeout values for each of the associated methods that the resource type will use in starting, probing, and stopping the application.

Like the scdscreate (1HA) command, there are two forms for the scdsconfig command—network aware and non-network aware:

Syntax:
```
Network Aware
scdsconfig -s start_command [-u start_method_timeout][-t
stop_command] [-v stop_method_timeout][-m probe_command][-n
probe_timeout][-d working_directory]
```

```
Non-Network Aware
scdsconfig -s start_command [-u start_method_timeout][-t
stop_command] [-v stop_method_timeout][-d working_directory]
```

As a result of this command, the specified commands and timeouts will be added to the appropriate callback methods. If the source is C code, the methods will be compiled and then packaged. This package can be used to install the resource type in the cluster with the SOE's `pkgadd(1M)` command.

At this time, one of the shortfalls of the `scdsconfig` command is the use of variables. For instance, application "maltose_tracker" needs to be highly available so brewmasters can access important information such as recipes and the last time they were made. The customer has decided to use Sun Cluster and you've been tasked with creating the resource type for this application. The application allows you to choose the installation path and the application commands are located in the `bin` directory of the given installation path. Since it's your choice for the installation path, you would want the ability to set the installation path with a resource type property. This way, you can create a resource that can be flexible enough to find the application binaries wherever the installation path is. There is a *CUPS_dir* property that is already defined and can be used to hold the installation path or you can define your own extension property for the installation path.

With `scdsconfig`, you can add a variable to the start, stop, and probe command paths, but the code to retrieve the resource type property, in this case the installation path, is not added by the scdsconfig command. This will need to be done manually.

Adding a start command with a variable for a resource type done with `ksh`, would be as follows:

```
% scdsconfig -s \$INSTALLDIR/bin/start.sh
```

A start command with install path variable is added to the START_METHOD.

```
% grep INSTALLDIR svc_start.ksh
svc_start.ksh:start_cmd_args="$INSTALLDIR/bin/start.sh"
```

You need to add code before this line to set the INSTALLDIR variable in the `svc_start.ksh` file. For this example, we will use the resource type property, *CUPS_dir*, as if it were set to the installation path of the application.

```
INSTALLPATH='scha_resource_get -O Extension -R cup-r -G
         customds-rg CUPS_dir'
INSTALLDIR='echo $INSTALLPATH | awk '{ print $2 }''
start_cmd_args="$INSTALLDIR/bin/start.sh"
```

Adding the first two lines prior to the start_cmd_args line will set the INSTALLDIR variable to the installation path of the application. Remember from Chapter 7, "Programming with the RMAPI," that retrieving extension properties with `scha_resource_get(1HA)` will return the type, such as STRINGARRAY, and the value on successive lines. This is why the second line using awk is needed.

For callback methods built from C source, this will be more involved. Variables will need to be initialized and built with `strcpy()(3C)` after using either the DSDL or RMAPI C library functions. It would be best not to use the `scdsconfig` command in these cases.

Note – The `scdsconfig` command will modify the Makefile in the `src` directory. It will set the parameter WORKING_DIR, which is not set when the resource type is created with `scdscreate`. If you do not use `scdsconfig`, this parameter needs to be set to the path where the resource type is located, that is, `/var/tmp/cups`. This is the path that was given with the `scdscreate` command to create the BOOKcups resource type.

Resource Type Registration File

One of the benefits of using the `scdscreate (1HA)` command is that it creates a template that is a good starting point for the RTR file. A base set of callback methods, resource type properties, and extension properties are defined in this file. If there are requirements for application-specific extension properties, they can be added to this file at the end of the extension properties section. If it is determined that other callback methods are needed for the resource type, they will need to be added to the file.

Callback Methods

In the RTR file created using the `scdscreate(1HA)`, callback methods will be defined depending on whether it is a network-aware or non-network-aware application. The methods in the file are as follows:

- `START` method
- `STOP` method
- `VALIDATE` method
- `UPDATE` method
- `MONITOR_START` method—for network-aware applications
- `MONITOR_CHECK` method—for network-aware applications
- `MONITOR_STOP` method—for network-aware applications

The need for the remaining five methods, `BOOT`, `INIT`, `FINI`, `PRENET_START`, and `POSTNET_STOP` will be dependent on the needs of the application. Since both the MySQL application and the CUPS application were specified as network-aware applications, the starting point will be the seven listed methods. Refer to "Callback Definitions" in Chapter 6 for information describing the callback methods.

MySQL Callback Methods

Since the MySQL database resource type was created as a network-aware application, the seven methods listed in "Callback Methods" are the starting point for callback methods to be used. The remaining five methods can be reviewed to determine if they are necessary to support the MySQL application.

- PRENET_START—This method is called prior to the logical host resources being brought online. One could argue the point to have the IP address available before or after the database is started. Since it is possible when starting the database to specify an IP address to bind to via a command argument, it would be best to have the network address available prior to starting the database. Otherwise, the starting of the database might fail, creating startup issues. If binding is not specified, the database will start regardless of whether a network address is available.

- POSTNET_STOP—This method is called after the logical host resources are brought offline. Again, since the possibility of using the IP bind command argument exists, bringing the network resource offline prior to stopping the database may cause issues in stopping the database.

- BOOT—This method is called when a node joins or rejoins the cluster and the resource is being managed by the cluster framework. It performs any required initialization that may be needed for the resource when that node joins the cluster. For the MySQL resource, there is not much to do when the node joins the cluster. File checking is done during the START method because any start of the application will be done with the START method (as opposed to using the BOOT method, which is done only when the node joins the cluster). If the resource is dependent on the HAStoragePlus failover filesystem, checking cannot be done because the filesystem is only available on the node on which the resource is primary.

- INIT—It performs any one-time initialization steps required by the resource when it is placed under management. This might be checking for files and directories that are needed by the application. Since it is a one-time initialization to place under management control, it does not check during events that would cause a restart or failover. So any checks that need to be repeated, such as checking for existence of the MySQL binary before calling it during a restart, would not be done. For this application, however, the INIT method will not be needed as file checking can be done in the START method when called to start the database application.

- FINI—It performs any cleanup that may be needed as sort of an undo method for the INIT method, but it is called when a resource becomes unmanaged. So, since we are not using the INIT method, the FINI method will not be used either.

CUPS Callback Methods

The CUPS application is a network-aware application; therefore, the resource type is created as a network-aware application. As in the MySQL application, the seven methods listed in "Callback Methods" will serve as the starting point for callback methods used. The remaining methods can be reviewed to determine if there is any need for them in supporting the CUPS application.

- PRENET_START—The CUPS application is based on an http server. Starting this application before having a network address available would be like loading the mozilla browser on your PC to access Web pages when there is no dial-up or network interface card to access the Internet. Without a hostname and IP address that is active, the PRENET_START would fail to start the CUPS application.

- POSTNET_STOP—This method is called after the logical host resources are brought offline. Stopping the application after the logical host addresses are offlined could cause problems with the application and prevent successful completion of the POSTNET_STOP method.

- BOOT—This method is called when a node joins or rejoins the cluster and the resource is being managed by the cluster framework. It performs any required initialization that may be needed for the resource when that node joins the cluster. For the CUPS resource, there is not much to do when the node joins the cluster. File checking is done during the START method because any start of the application will be done with the method (as opposed to using the BOOT method, which is done only when the node joins the cluster). If the resource is dependent on the HAStoragePlus failover filesystem, checking cannot be done because the filesystem is only available on the node on which the resource is primary.

- INIT—It performs any one-time initialization steps required by the resource when it is placed under management. This might be checking for files and directories that are needed by the application. Since it is a one-time initialization to place under management control, it does not check during events that would cause a restart or failover. So any checks that need to be repeated, such as checking for the existence of the cupsd binary before calling it during a restart, would not be done. For this application, however, the INIT method will not be needed as file checking can be done in the START method when called to start the database application.

- FINI—It performs any cleanup that may be needed as sort of an undo method for the INIT method, but it is called when a resource becomes unmanaged. So, since we are not using the INIT method, the FINI method will not be used either.

Extension Properties

For both examples, the template used in creating the RTR file has default properties and extension properties defined. These can be considered cluster specific and are used by the resource group manager to handle events that pertain to the management of resources and resource groups. An example would be the *retry_count* used by the Process Monitor Facility to know how many times to restart an application for a particular resource.

Extension properties that are needed for application-specific needs are added to this file. Specific extension properties can be added to a marked section at the bottom of the RTR template file labeled "User added code -- BEGIN" and "User added code -- END." The BEGIN and END comments can be removed if desired. The extension properties added will primarily consist of information that is needed to start the application, monitor the application, and stop the application. Properties such as directory paths, commands and arguments, configuration files, data files, user and password information, and network information can be defined as extension properties.

MySQL Extension Properties

By reviewing the MySQL application and using the key points discussed in "Example Applications," a list of parameters can be created that are needed for the resource type to work with MySQL. Creating a table can be helpful in listing the parameters needed and in specifying extension property names. See Table 10.1.

The extension properties defined in Table 10.1 will need to be added to the RTR file. Example 10.1 shows the MySQL extension properties that are added to the RTR file. For information on the resource property attributes such as Property, Extension, and Tunable, refer to Table 6.4.

Table 10.1 MySQL Properties

Property	Property Name	Property Type
Directory path of MySQL application	MYSQL_HOME	extension
Location of mysqld, different for different versions	MYSQL_MYSQLD	extension
Directory for database files	MYSQL_DATA_DIR	extension
Login information, form of "user/password"	MYSQL_DBA_USER	extension
MySQL configuration file to use, including directory path	MYSQL_CNF_FILE	extension
TCP/IP port number, not an extension property. Use cluster-defined parameter in the form of portnum/tcp	Port_list	cluster defined
IP Bind Address	Not a property. Information is in MySQL configuration file.	
Socket file	Not a property. Information is in MySQL configuration file.	

Example 10.1   MySQL extension properties

```
#
{
        Property = MYSQL_HOME;
        Extension;
        string;
        minlength = 1;
        Tunable = WHEN_DISABLED;
        Description = "MYSQL Home directory where bin directory located";
}
# Tunable property. Cannot change this if resource is ON-LINE
#
{
        Property = MYSQL_MYSQLD;
        Extension;
        string;
        minlength = 0;
        Default = "/bin/mysqld";
        Tunable = WHEN_DISABLED;
        Description = "MYSQL Database mysqld binary - dependent on version";
}
# Tunable property. Cannot change this if resource is ON-LINE
#
{
        Property = MYSQL_DATA_DIR;
        Extension;
        string;
        minlength = 1;
        Tunable = WHEN_DISABLED;
        Description = "MYSQL Database directory";
}
# Tunable property. Cannot change this if resource is ON-LINE
#
{
        Property = MYSQL_DBA_USER;
        Extension;
        string;
        minlength = 1;
        Tunable = WHEN_DISABLED;
        Description = "MYSQL DBA USER (user/password) - id must exist in
system";
}

# Tunable property. Cannot change this if resource is ON-LINE
#
{
        Property = MYSQL_CNF_FILE;
        Extension;
        string;
        minlength = 1;
        Tunable = WHEN_DISABLED;
        Description = "MYSQL Database Config (path/file) - CNF file";
}
```

CUPS Extension Properties

For the CUPS application, there are a few additional pieces of information needed for the *BOOK.cups* resource type: the path to the location of the CUPS application, a configuration file, and a network port number. Any parameters that the CUPS application needs, such as the logical host name and the port number, will be defined in the CUPS application configuration file, `cupsd.conf`.

For the path definition, we will need to define an extension property in the RTR file. The *CUPS_dir* property will be used to hold the path to the location of the application. The path to the configuration file will also be from this directory.

The configuration file parameter will also need to be defined in the RTR file. For this property, we will define a parameter called *Conf_file*. This will hold the directory and the configuration file `cupsd.conf`. This will also be defined in the RTR as an optional extension property.

For monitoring, a port number for the monitor to connect to is needed. This would be the same port number as defined in the `cupsd.conf` configuration file. In the RTR file, before the extension properties section, there is a property called Port_list, which is not an extension property. This property holds the port number information in the form of portnum/protocol. So when creating a CUPS resource within a resource group, the Port_list value could be, for example, defined as 80/tcp for port 80 and the TCP protocol.

The extension properties defined in Table 10.2 will need to be added to the RTR file as illustrated in Example 10.2. For information on the resource property attributes such as Property, Extension, and Tunable, refer to Table 6.4.

Table 10.2 CUPS Properties

Property	Property Name	Property Type
Directory path of CUPS application.	CUPS_dir	extension
CUPS configuration file to use, including directory path.	Conf_file	extension
TCP/IP port number, not an extension property. Use cluster-defined parameter in the form of portnum/tcp.	Port_list	cluster defined

Example 10.2   CUPS extension properties

```
# Extension Properties
#
{
        PROPERTY = CUPS_dir;
        EXTENSION;
        STRINGARRAY;
        TUNABLE = AT_CREATION;
        DESCRIPTION = "The Application Directory Path";
}
# Cups configuration file, appended to CUPS_dir property.

{
        PROPERTY = Conf_file;
        EXTENSION;
        STRINGARRAY;
        DEFAULT = "";
        TUNABLE = WHEN_DISABLED;
        DESCRIPTION = "The Configuration File";
}
```

Developing Callback Methods

Once it is determined which callback methods are needed for each resource type, it will be time to begin developing each callback method. If the application is a network-aware application, the application monitor or probe will also need to be developed during this time.

Creating the MySQL Callback Methods

For the creation of this resource type, the callback methods will be built using the ksh and the RMAPI CLIs. Refer to Chapter 7 for a discussion of the RMAPI. A good book on writing ksh will also be helpful if you are new to writing ksh scripts.

In "Creating the MySQL Resource Type," the scdscreate(1HA) command was used to create the resource type templates. These templates will be used as a base to build the callback methods.

Helper Shell Functions

When a callback method is called by the resource group manager (RGM), the RGM passes a set of parameters to that callback method. For each callback method to function properly, it will need information such as what resource group, resource, and resource type to work on. To retrieve that information, a useful function can be created that parses the passed parameters for the callback method.

Each callback method will need the resource type, resource group, and resource name passed to it. Example 10.3 shows the parsing function that parses the resource type, resource group, and resource name. If anything besides these parameters is passed to this function, it is logged to the syslog facility. This function can be used in all the example callback methods with the exception of the VALIDATE method.

Example 10.3   parse_args function

```
function parse_args # [args ...]
{
typeset opt
while getopts 'R:G:T:' opt
do
        case "$opt" in
        R)
        # Name of the mysql resource.
        RESOURCE_NAME=$OPTARG
        ;;
        G)
        # Name of the resource group in which the resource
        # is configured.
        RESOURCEGROUP_NAME=$OPTARG
        ;;
        T)
        # Name of the resource type.
        RESOURCETYPE_NAME=$OPTARG
        ;;
        *)
        logger -p ${SYSLOG_FACILITY}.err -t \
[$RESOURCETYPE_NAME,$RESOURCEGROUP_NAME,$RESOURCE_NAME] \
        "ERROR: Option $OPTARG unknown"
        exit 1
        ;;
        esac
done
}
```

The parsing function for the VALIDATE method is shown in Example 10.4 and parses the same resource type, resource group, and resource name parameters, but also parses additional parameters that are passed to it. The additional parameters are used for creation with the **-c** argument and also during updates with the **-u** argument.

Example 10.4   Validate parse_args function

```
function parse_args # [args ...]
{
        typeset opt
        while getopts 'cur:x:g:R:T:G:' opt
        do
                        case "$opt" in
                        R)
                        # Name of the mysql resource.
                        RESOURCE_NAME=$OPTARG
                        ;;
                        G)
                        # Name of the resource group in which the
                        # resource is configured.
                        RESOURCEGROUP_NAME=$OPTARG
                        ;;
                        T)
                        # Name of the resource type.
                        RESOURCETYPE_NAME=$OPTARG
                        ;;
                        r)
                        # We are not accessing any system defined
                        # property. So, this is a no-op
                        ;;
                        g)
                        # This is a no-op as we are not bothered
                        # about Resource group properties
                        ;;
                        c)
                        # This is a no-op as this is just a flag
                        # which indicates that the validate
                        # method is being called while
                        # creating the resource.
                        ;;
                        u)
                        # This is a flag to indicate the
                        # updating of property
                        # of an existing resource.
                        UPDATE_PROPERTY=1
                        ;;
                        x)
                        ;;
                        *)
                        logger -p ${SYSLOG_FACILITY}.err -t\
[$RESOURCETYPE_NAME,$RESOURCEGROUP_NAME,$RESOURCE_NAME] \
                        "ERROR: Option $OPTARG unknown"
                        exit 1
                        ;;
                        esac
        done
}
```

MySQL START Method

This method is responsible for starting the application and ensuring that it is running prior to a successful exit. The information needed to start the application, such as the `mysqld` command, its path, and needed arguments will need to be retrieved and put together to form the `start` command that will be executed. Before this method starts the application and exits after the application has started, some tests need to be done to ensure that the method can start the application and that the application is running.

Once the parsing function and base work are done to the START method's shell program, it's time to pull in the information that is needed to successfully start the application with the process monitor facility (PMF). In Example 10.5, the parameters needed by PMF, such as the retry count and retry interval, are retrieved. Other properties, such as resource type extension properties and non-extension properties are also retrieved.

Example 10.5 Collecting start method resource parameters

```
export PATH=/bin:/usr/bin:/usr/cluster/bin:/usr/sbin:/usr/proc/bin:$PATH

# Obtain the syslog facility to use. This will be used to
# log the messages.
SYSLOG_FACILITY='scha_cluster_get -O SYSLOG_FACILITY'

# Parse the arguments that have been passed to this
# method
parse_args "$@"

PMF_TAG=$RESOURCEGROUP_NAME,$RESOURCE_NAME,0.svc
SYSLOG_TAG=$RESOURCETYPE_NAME,$RESOURCEGROUP_NAME,\
$RESOURCE_NAME

# Get the value for retry count from the RTR file.
RETRY_CNT='scha_resource_get -O Retry_Count -R \
  $RESOURCE_NAME -G $RESOURCEGROUP_NAME'

# Get the value for retry interval from the RTR file. The
# value for the RETRY_INTERVAL in the RTR file will be in
# seconds. Convert this value from seconds to minutes for
# passing on to pmfadm. This is necessarily a conversion
# with round-up, e.g.. 59 seconds --> 1 minute.
((RETRY_INTRVAL = ('scha_resource_get -O Retry_Interval\
  -R $RESOURCE_NAME -G $RESOURCEGROUP_NAME' + 59) / 60 ))

# Need to get the mysql home directory.

mysqlhomedir_info='scha_resource_get -O Extension \
  -R $RESOURCE_NAME -G $RESOURCEGROUP_NAME MYSQL_HOME'
mysqlhomedir='echo $mysqlhomedir_info | awk '{ print $2 }''
```

```
# Check to see if the directory exists
if [ ! -d $mysqlhomedir ]; then
    logger -p ${SYSLOG_FACILITY}.err -t [$SYSLOG_TAG]
       "${ARGV0} ERROR: $mysqlhomedir directory missing"
    exit 1
fi

# Different versions, mysqld went from bin directory to
# the libexec directory.
# So now we need to get the binary and path beyond
# mysqlhomedir.

mysql_bin='scha_resource_get -O Extension \
  -R $RESOURCE_NAME -G $RESOURCEGROUP_NAME MYSQL_MYSQLD'
mysqld_bin='echo $mysql_bin | awk '{ print $2 }''

# Get the database directory for this resource. To
# accommodate multiple datadir.
mysqldatadir_info='scha_resource_get -O Extension \
 -R $RESOURCE_NAME -G $RESOURCEGROUP_NAME MYSQL_DATA_DIR'
mysqldatadir='echo $mysqldatadir_info | awk '{ print $2 }''

# Check to see if the directory exists
if [ ! -d $mysqldatadir ]; then
    logger -p ${SYSLOG_FACILITY}.info -t [$SYSLOG_TAG]\
       "${ARGV0} ERROR: Data directory does not exist."
    exit 1
fi

# Get the database user and password.
mysqluser_info='scha_resource_get -O Extension -R \ $RESOURCE_NAME -G
$RESOURCEGROUP_NAME MYSQL_DBA_USER'
mysqluser='echo $mysqluser_info | awk '{ print $2 }' | \ awk '{ FS="/";
print $1 }''
mysqlpassword='echo $mysqluser_info | awk '{ print $2 }'\
    | awk '{ FS="/"; print $2 }''

# Get the CNF config file for this database.
mysqlcnf_info='scha_resource_get -O Extension -R \ $RESOURCE_NAME -G
$RESOURCEGROUP_NAME MYSQL_CNF_FILE'
mysqlcnf='echo $mysqlcnf_info | awk '{ print $2 }''
if [ ! -f $mysqlcnf ]; then
    logger -p ${SYSLOG_FACILITY}.err -t [$SYSLOG_TAG] \
       "${ARGV0} ERROR: $mysqlcnf configuration file is \
       missing."
    exit 1
fi
```

Once this section completes, the parameters needed for the START method will be set. The properties were retrieved using the scha command scha_resource_get(1HA) from the RMAPI and the *Retry_Count* and *Retry_Interval* for use with the pmfadm(1HA) command. The *Retry_Interval* is then converted from seconds to minutes because the pmfadm command requires time in minutes. The extension properties from Table 10.1, "MySQL Properties," are retrieved also for use with this command. You will note that during the retrieval of these properties, any files or directory paths are tested to make sure that they exist. There is no sense in continuing if these key parameters are not available prior to the PMF starting the application.

At this point in the START method (Example 10.6), the command syntax will need to be put together and tested for existence and executablility so PMF can start the application. If PMF starts the application the method will exit successfully, but whether the method exits successfully or not a message is logged to syslog.

Example 10.6   MySQL startup

```
start_cmd_args="${mysqlhomedir}${mysqld_bin} \
  --defaults-extra-file=$mysqlcnf -u $mysqluser \
  -b $mysqlhomedir --datadir=$mysqldatadir"

start_cmd_prog='echo $start_cmd_args | nawk '{print $1}''

if [[ ! -f $start_cmd_prog || ! -x $start_cmd_prog ]]; then
    logger -p ${SYSLOG_FACILITY}.err -t [$SYSLOG_TAG] \
       "${ARGV0} File $start_cmd_prog is missing or not \
       executable"
    exit 1
fi
# start the daemon under the control of Sun Cluster
# Process Monitor Facility. Let it crash and
# restart up to $RETRY_COUNT times in a period of
# $RETRY_INTERVAL; if it crashes more often than that,
# the process monitor facility will cease trying
# to restart it.
pmfadm -c $PMF_TAG -n $RETRY_CNT -t $RETRY_INTRVAL \ $start_cmd_args

pmfadm -q $PMF_TAG

# Check status of pmfadm tag for this resource.
if [ $? -eq 0 ]; then
      logger -p ${SYSLOG_FACILITY}.info -t [$SYSLOG_TAG]\
                 "${ARGV0} mysql successfully started"
else
      logger -p ${SYSLOG_FACILITY}.err -t [$SYSLOG_TAG] \
                 "${ARGV0} mysql failed to start"
      exit 1
fi
exit 0
```

Using some of the extension properties, the *start_cmd_args* is set to the path and the binary and arguments needed to start the MySQL application. The *start_cmd_prog* is set to the application binary to test whether it is available and executable. Using the RETRY_CNT, RETRY_INTRVAL, and the PMF_TAG set earlier, the PMF is used to start the MySQL database for the defined resource using the *start_cmd_args* variable that holds the complete command line.

Before exiting the START method, it should check to see if the application is running. For this example, pmfadm is used to check the status with the -q argument. If this returns 0, it can be assumed that the application is running and the method can exit successfully. Using this type of method, that is, checking the status of the PMF_TAG running in the PMF, just tests to see if the application is still controlled by PMF. This may not be an indication that the application is available and usable.

For a "real-life" START method, a more elaborate method of checking the application should be used. Many applications, such as MySQL, have APIs that can be incorporated to do such things as connecting to the database, querying a table, and then disconnecting. This is the preferred method for checking to see if the application is running correctly.

MySQL STOP Method

The STOP method will be similar to the START method insofar as parsing arguments, setting tag names, and retrieving the extension properties regarding the MySQL parameters. To stop the application, the mysqladmin command will be used with the shutdown argument.

In Example 10.7, the MySQL extension properties are collected. To stop the database with the mysqladmin command, the database login and password will be needed, along with the configuration file that was used to start the database and also the path location of the MySQL application.

The other parameter needed is the timeout for the STOP method. There needs to be a bounded time in which an operation can work. Once that timeout has been exceeded, the STOP method has failed to stop the application and will exit with a nonzero. Two parameters are defined that give multiple chances to stop the application. The SMOOTH_TIMEOUT, defined as 80% of the stop_method_timeout, will be used initially to stop the application. This time period should use the application's preferred method of stopping. The mysqladmin command with the shutdown argument will be used within this time period.

If the application does not stop within the SMOOTH_TIMEOUT value, other means need to be taken to stop the application before the stop_method_timeout is exceeded. The HARD_TIMEOUT, defined as 15% of the stop_method_ timeout, will be the next-time window to stop the application. For this STOP method, a SIGKILL is sent to the application.

Note – This does not mean that, as a developer, the SIGKILL should be blatantly used in the STOP method when the application is not responding to the normal stopping methods. One should consult with the application vendor or developers if available, to find out what is the best way to get the application to stop running under these circumstances.

Not all the time of the stop_method_timeout value has been used. There is 5% left over to make sure that the STOP method completes within the stop_method_timeout. While this is not cast in stone, it is a good idea to leave some room in which to operate.

Example 10.7 Collecting stop method resource parameters

```
export PATH=/bin:/usr/bin:/usr/cluster/bin:/usr/sbin:/usr/proc/bin:$PATH

# Obtain the syslog facility to use. This will be used to
# log the messages.
SYSLOG_FACILITY='scha_cluster_get -O SYSLOG_FACILITY'

# Parse the arguments that have been passed to this
# method
parse_args "$@"

PMF_TAG=$RESOURCEGROUP_NAME,$RESOURCE_NAME,0.svc
SYSLOG_TAG=$RESOURCETYPE_NAME,$RESOURCEGROUP_NAME,\
$RESOURCE_NAME

# Get the Timeout value allowed for stop method from the
# RTR file
STOP_TIMEOUT='scha_resource_get -O STOP_TIMEOUT -R \
  $RESOURCE_NAME -G $RESOURCEGROUP_NAME'

# We will try to wait for 80% of the
# stop_method_timeout value when we send a SIGTERM
# through PMF to the Data service. This is to make sure
# that the application stops in a decent manner. If the
# application does not respond favorably to this then we
# use SIGKILL to stop the data service and this will be
# done for a 15% of the Stop_method_timeout value.
# However, if the data service has not stopped by now, we
# conclude that there was a Failure in the stop method
# and exit non-zero. The remaining 5% of the stop
# method timeout is for other needs.
((SMOOTH_TIMEOUT=$STOP_TIMEOUT * 80/100))
((HARD_TIMEOUT=$STOP_TIMEOUT * 15/100))

# Need to get the mysql home directory.
mysqlhomedir_info='scha_resource_get -O Extension -R \ $RESOURCE_NAME -G
$RESOURCEGROUP_NAME MYSQL_HOME'
mysqlhomedir='echo $mysqlhomedir_info | awk \
  '{ print $2 }''

# Check to see if the directory exists, if it doesn't
# exist just log as error.
if [ ! -d $mysqlhomedir ]; then
   logger -p ${SYSLOG_FACILITY}.err -t [$SYSLOG_TAG] \
      "${ARGV0} ERROR: $mysqlhomedir directory missing"
fi
# Get the database user and password.
mysqluser_info='scha_resource_get -O Extension -R \ $RESOURCE_NAME -G
$RESOURCEGROUP_NAME MYSQL_DBA_USER'
```

```
mysqluser='echo $mysqluser_info | awk '{ print $2 }' | \ awk '{ FS="/";
print $1 }''
mysqlpassword='echo $mysqluser_info | awk '{ print $2 }'\ | awk '{ FS="/";
print $2 }''

# Get the .cnf for the sock information needed for
# mysqladmin
mysqlcnf_info='scha_resource_get -O Extension -R \ $RESOURCE_NAME -G
$RESOURCEGROUP_NAME MYSQL_CNF_FILE'
mysqlcnf='echo $mysqlcnf_info | awk '{ print $2 }''

stop_cmd_args="${mysqlhomedir}/bin/mysqladmin \
  --defaults-extra-file=$mysqlcnf -u $mysqluser \
  --password=$mysqlpassword shutdown"

stop_cmd_prog='echo $stop_cmd_args | nawk '{print $1}''
```

The last two arguments are *stop_cmd_args,* which defines the command used to stop the application along with the arguments that are needed, and *stop_cmd_prog,* which is just *stop_cmd_args* without the arguments. They will be used to test for the existence of the binary and to see if it is executable, as shown in Example 10.8.

Stopping the MySQL Application   At this point in the STOP method, all the parameters needed to stop the application have been collected. Now we will proceed with actually stopping the application. In Example 10.8, a series of tests are performed before stopping the application. One thing to remember is that the STOP method must be idempotent. Idempotency was discussed in "Idempotency" in Chapter 6. Multiple runs of the STOP method will not result in any changes in the outcome different from the first run.

Note – Remember, the STOP method must be idempotent. See Chapter 6, "Idempotency."

Example 10.8 Stopping MySQL

```
typeset -i SEND_KILL=0

pmfadm -q $PMF_TAG
if [[ $? == 0 ]]; then
    if [[ -f $stop_cmd_prog && -x $stop_cmd_prog ]]; then
        pmfadm -s $PMF_TAG
        if [[ $? != 0  ]]; then
           logger -p ${SYSLOG_FACILITY}.info \
               -t [$SYSLOG_TAG] "${ARGV0} Failed to take \
               mysql out of PMF control; trying to send \
               SIGKILL now"
         SEND_KILL=1
        else
```

```
                # execute the user specified stop_cmd using
                # hatimerun
                 hatimerun -t $SMOOTH_TIMEOUT $stop_cmd_args
                    if [[ $? != 0 ]]; then
                      logger -p ${SYSLOG_FACILITY}.err \
                        -t [$SYSLOG_TAG] "${ARGV0} Failed to
                        stop mysql using the custom stop \
                        command; trying SIGKILL now."
                      SEND_KILL=1
                    fi
            fi
    else
            # Send a SIGTERM signal to the Data service and
          # wait for 80% of the total timeout value.
              pmfadm -s $PMF_TAG -w $SMOOTH_TIMEOUT TERM
              if [[ $? != 0 ]]; then
                  logger -p ${SYSLOG_FACILITY}.err \
                    -t [$SYSLOG_TAG] "${ARGV0} Failed to stop \
                    mysql with SIGTERM; retry with SIGKILL"
                  SEND_KILL=1;
              fi
          fi
          if [[ $SEND_KILL == 1 ]]; then
            # Since the Data service did not stop with a
           # SIGTERM we will use a SIGKILL now and wait for
            # another 15% of total timeout.
            pmfadm -s $PMF_TAG -w $HARD_TIMEOUT KILL
            if [[ $? != 0 ]]; then
              logger -p ${SYSLOG_FACILITY}.err
                -t [$SYSLOG_TAG] "${ARGV0} Failed to stop \
                mysql; exiting UNSUCCESSFUL"
                exit 1
            fi
          fi
else
          # The Data service is not running as of now. Log a
        # message and exit success.
          logger -p ${SYSLOG_FACILITY}.err -t [$SYSLOG_TAG] \
              "mysql not running"
          # Even if the mysql is not running, we exit
        # success.
          exit 0
fi
# Have successfully stopped mysql. Log a message and exit
# success.
logger -p ${SYSLOG_FACILITY}.info -t [$SYSLOG_TAG] \
    "mysql successfully stopped"
exit 0
```

The tests that are performed prior to stopping the application ensure that:

- The STOP method is idempotent.
- The binaries to be used are available and executable.
- Abnormal conditions are handled.

The process of stopping the application in Example 10.8 can be shown in the following list:

1. Test for the existence of the PMF_TAG. If the tag is not valid, the application is not running and the STOP method exits successfully supporting idempotency for this method.

2. If the PMF_TAG exists, the method will need to check if the mysqladmin command is available and executable. If the command is not available and executable, the method will need to stop the MySQL database using pmfadm since the mysqladmin command is not available. Using pmfadm -s $PMF_TAG -w $SMOOTH_TIMEOUT TERM, PMF will stop restarting the application specified by the PMF_TAG. Using the SMOOTH_TIMEOUT value for a timeout value, it sends the application a TERM signal to stop the database. If this does not succeed, set SEND_KILL=1 and log a message with syslog. If it does succeed, it is logged to syslog and the method exits successfully.

3. If the mysqladmin command is available, then the method will need to use the pmfadm command to tell PMF to stop restarting the application. Checking the results of this operation will determine the next operation. If it was not successful, the method will need to log the error to syslog and set SEND_KILL=1; otherwise, PMF will no longer restart the application and hatimerun can be used to run the mysqladmin command to properly stop the database.

4. Using the SMOOTH_TIMEOUT value as a timeout value, the hatimerun command will attempt to stop the database using the mysqladmin command with the arguments collected as in Example 10.7. If the timeout expires, the mysqladmin process is sent a SIGTERM to terminate and hatimerun exits unsuccessfully. A message is sent to syslog and SEND_KILL=1 is set. If hatimerun was successful, a message is sent to syslog stating that the database was stopped and the STOP method exits with a 0.

In the STOP method, you will notice that any failures, except the first test of the PMF_TAG, end up setting SEND_KILL=1. Using the check for SEND_KILL provides one path to handle errors that occur in the method. Since the SMOOTH_TIMEOUT is used in previous attempts to stop the database, 80% of the STOP method TIMEOUT has already been used leaving 20% unused. Going through this one path provides us with one more attempt to try and stop the application within the HARD_TIMEOUT (15% of the STOP_TIMEOUT). The leftover 5% can be considered as a buffer to keep from exceeding the STOP_TIMEOUT. If this last attempt fails, then a message is logged to syslog that the STOP_METHOD failed and the method exits with a nonzero.

MySQL MONITOR_START Method

Once the START method completes successfully, the MONITOR_START method is called to start the probe that will monitor the health of the application. This method will use the parsing function show in Example 10.3.

Additional extension parameters, such as *Monitor_retry_count* and *Monitor_retry_interval,* will be retrieved using the scha_resource_get (1HA) command.

The `MONITOR_START` method will be using PMF to start the `mysqlksh_probe.ksh` probe script, defined in this example by the PROBE_CMD property.

The *Monitor_retry_count* and *Monitor_retry_interval* extension properties have the flexibility to give a different retry count and retry interval for the probe script from what is specified for the restarting of the application.

In Example 10.9, the PMF_TAG is set, but with a different ending. The ".mon" ending indicates that the PMF tag is a monitor versus a data service. This is useful for debugging and system administration purposes. Once all the properties are retrieved in this example, a check is done to see if the probe is executable and then pmfadm is used to start the probe. A message is logged to syslog depending on the outcome of the starting of the probe. If it was successful, the `MONITOR_START` method exits with a 0.

Example 10.9   MySQL monitor start method

```
export PATH=/bin:/usr/bin:/usr/cluster/bin:/usr/sbin:/usr/proc/bin:$PATH

# Obtain the syslog facility to use. This will be used to
# log the messages.
SYSLOG_FACILITY='scha_cluster_get -O SYSLOG_FACILITY'

# Parse the arguments that have been passed to this
# method
parse_args "$@"

PMF_TAG=$RESOURCEGROUP_NAME,$RESOURCE_NAME,0.mon
SYSLOG_TAG=$RESOURCETYPE_NAME,$RESOURCEGROUP_NAME,\
$RESOURCE_NAME

# Set probe command.
PROBE_CMD=mysqlksh_probe.ksh

# We need to know where the probe method resides. This is
# specified in the RT_BASEDIR property of the resource
# type.
RT_BASEDIR='scha_resource_get -O RT_BASEDIR -R \
 $RESOURCE_NAME -G $RESOURCEGROUP_NAME'

# Ensure the monitor probe exists and is executable.
if [ ! -x $RT_BASEDIR/$PROBE_CMD ]; then
    logger -p ${SYSLOG_FACILITY}.err -t [$SYSLOG_TAG] \
      "${ARGV0} Monitor probe $PROBE_CMD is not \
       executable."
    exit 1
fi
# Get the Monitor Retry Count.
mRetCnt_info='scha_resource_get -O Extension \
  -R $RESOURCE_NAME -G $RESOURCEGROUP_NAME \ Monitor_retry_count'
mRetCnt='echo $mRetCnt_info | awk '{ print $2 }''
```

```
# Get the Monitor Retry Count.Interval
mRetInt_info='scha_resource_get -O Extension \
  -R $RESOURCE_NAME -G $RESOURCEGROUP_NAME \
  Monitor_retry_interval'
mRetInt='echo $mRetInt_info | awk '{ print $2 }''

# Start the probe for the data service under PMF.
# Pass the Resource name, type and group to the
# probe method.
pmfadm -c $PMF_TAG -n $mRetCnt -t $mRetInt \
  $RT_BASEDIR/$PROBE_CMD -R $RESOURCE_NAME -G \ $RESOURCEGROUP_NAME -T
$RESOURCETYPE_NAME

# Log a message indicating that the monitor for mysql has
# been started.
if [ $? -eq 0 ]; then
    logger -p ${SYSLOG_FACILITY}.info \
      -t [$SYSLOG_TAG] "${ARGV0} Monitor for \
      $RESOURCE_NAME successfully started"
else
    logger -p ${SYSLOG_FACILITY}.err -t [$SYSLOG_TAG] \
      "${ARGV0} Monitor start for $RESOURCE_NAME not \
      successful."

    # exit 1 - failed to start the mysql fault probe.
    exit 1
fi
exit 0
```

MySQL MONITOR_STOP Method

When the resource is switched to another node or the resource is taken offline, the monitor will need to be stopped. Using the parsing function shown in Example 10.3, the MONITOR_STOP method (Example 10.10) will stop the monitor probe by using pmfadm to stop the restarting of the probe and send a SIGKILL to the probe script. Since the probe script does not affect the operation of the application, sending a SIGKILL to the script will not do any harm to the application. Once the pmfadm command is run, the method checks the return of the command and logs a message to syslog, whether the stopping of the probe was successful or not, and then exits according to the status of the command.

The MONITOR_STOP method must also be idempotent. Idempotency was discussed in the section "Idempotency" in Chapter 6. Multiple runs of the MONITOR_STOP method will not result in any changes in the outcome different from the first run.

Note – Remember, the MONITOR_STOP method must be idempotent. See Chapter 6, "Idempotency."

Example 10.10 MySQL monitor stop method

```
export PATH=/bin:/usr/bin:/usr/cluster/bin:/usr/sbin:/usr/proc/bin:$PATH

# Obtain the syslog facility to use. This will be used to
# log the messages.
SYSLOG_FACILITY='scha_cluster_get -O SYSLOG_FACILITY'

# Parse the arguments that have been passed to this
# method
parse_args "$@"

PMF_TAG=$RESOURCEGROUP_NAME,$RESOURCE_NAME,0.mon
SYSLOG_TAG=$RESOURCETYPE_NAME,$RESOURCEGROUP_NAME,\
$RESOURCE_NAME

# See if the monitor is running, and if so, kill it.
if pmfadm -q $PMF_TAG; then
     pmfadm -s $PMF_TAG KILL
     if [ $? -ne 0 ]; then
       logger -p ${SYSLOG_FACILITY}.err \
          -t [$SYSLOG_TAG] "${ARGV0} Could not stop \
        monitor for resource $RESOURCE_NAME"
        exit 1
      else
      # could successfully stop the monitor. Log a
      # message.
        logger -p ${SYSLOG_FACILITY}.info \
          -t [$SYSLOG_TAG] "${ARGV0} Monitor for \
        resource $RESOURCE_NAME successfully stopped"
        exit 0
      fi
fi

# Monitor was not running, log for information purpose.
logger -p ${SYSLOG_FACILITY}.info \
    -t [$SYSLOG_TAG] "${ARGV0} Monitor for resource \
    $RESOURCE_NAME was not running."
exit 0
```

MySQL Probe Program

The `mysqlksh_probe.ksh` is responsible for checking that the MySQL database is available and providing the service that is expected of it. Other functions of a probe program might be to decide what actions to take if the application is not responding as desired, such as deciding to restart the application on the current node or failing over to another node in the cluster. The probe script has two functions: one is to help in deciding to restart the application or to failover to another node, and the other function is to handle the restarting of the application.

Restart_service Function   The function, `restart_service`, shown in Example 10.11, is responsible for restarting the application when the decision is made to restart the application versus failing the application over to another node within the cluster. This function performs the following tasks:

1. Verifies that the PMF_TAG is a valid registered tag with the PMF. The PMF is discussed in Chapter 8.

2. If the PMF_TAG is not valid, the method will fail the application over to another node in the cluster using the scha_control(1HA) command.

3. If the PMF_TAG is valid, the application will need to stop prior to trying a restart using the resource type's STOP_METHOD. The scha_resource_get (1HA) command needs to be used to retrieve the STOP_TIMEOUT value and the STOP_METHOD file.

4. Calls the STOP_METHOD using the hatimerun command.

5. Verifies the return of the hatimerun command. If the return value is 0, the restarting of the application can proceed; otherwise, the function will log a message to syslog and return a value of 1.

6. Restarts the application using the resource type's START_METHOD. The START_METHOD file and the START_TIMEOUT value will need to be retrieved.

7. Restarts the application using the hatimerun command. If the return status of the hatimerun command is 0, the restart has completed and the restart_service function returns a value of 0. If the hatimerun command returns a nonzero, a message is logged to syslog and returns a value of 1.

Example 10.11   Function restart_service

```
function restart_service
{

# In order to restart the dataservice, first, make
# sure that dataservice itself is still registered
# under PMF
pmfadm -q $PMF_TAG
if [[ $? -eq 0 ]]; then
    # Since the TAG  for the dataservice is still
    # registered under PMF, we will first stop the
    # dataservice and start it back again.

    # Obtain the STOP method name and the STOP_TIMEOUT
    # value for this resource.
    STOP_TIMEOUT='scha_resource_get -O STOP_TIMEOUT \
        -R $RESOURCE_NAME -G $RESOURCEGROUP_NAME'
    STOP_METHOD='scha_resource_get -O STOP \
        -R $RESOURCE_NAME -G $RESOURCEGROUP_NAME'
    hatimerun -t $STOP_TIMEOUT $RT_BASEDIR/$STOP_METHOD \
        -R $RESOURCE_NAME -G $RESOURCEGROUP_NAME \
        -T $RESOURCETYPE_NAME

    if [[ $? -ne 0 ]]; then
        logger -p ${SYSLOG_FACILITY}.err -t [$SYSLOG_TAG] \
            "${ARGV0} Stop method failed."
        return 1
```

```
    fi
    # Obtain the START method name and the START_TIMEOUT
    # value for this resource.
    START_TIMEOUT='scha_resource_get -O START_TIMEOUT \
        -R $RESOURCE_NAME -G $RESOURCEGROUP_NAME'
    START_METHOD='scha_resource_get -O START \
        -R $RESOURCE_NAME -G $RESOURCEGROUP_NAME'
    hatimerun -t $START_TIMEOUT $RT_BASEDIR/$START_METHOD/
        -R $RESOURCE_NAME -G $RESOURCEGROUP_NAME \
        -T $RESOURCETYPE_NAME

    if [[ $? -ne 0 ]]; then
        logger -p ${SYSLOG_FACILITY}.err -t [$SYSLOG_TAG] \
        "${ARGV0} Start method failed."
        return 1
    fi
else
    # the fact that the TAG for the dataservice is not
    # present, implies that the dataservice has already
    # passed the max no of retries allowed under PMF.
    # Hence, there is no point in trying to restart the
    # dataservice again. We might as well try to failover
    # to another node in the cluster.
    scha_control -O GIVEOVER -G $RESOURCEGROUP_NAME \
        -R $RESOURCE_NAME
fi
return 0
}
```

Decide_restart_or_failover Function   In the event there is a failure with the probe to verify the application's availability, the MySQL probe program will need to determine if the application should be restarted on the same node or fail over to another node. In Example 10.12, the function `decide_restart_or_failover` will determine what to do. This function performs the following:

1. Checks the value of the *retries* variable. This is initialized to 0 in Example 10.12. If *retries* is still set to 0, set *start_time* by calling the `gettime` program. The *start_time* variable is used to keep track of the time the first restart was called.

2. Increment the *retries* variable and call the function `restart_service`.

3. Check the return value of the function `restart_service`. If it is nonzero, return to the calling function a value of 1.

4. If the *retries* check performed in item 1 is not 0, then a previous failure occurred. The method will need to do a time check with `gettime`, get the difference between the *current_time* and the *start_time,* and then set the *time_diff* variable.

A couple of checks need to be performed at this point. In Table 7.4, "Resource Tags," there are two resource tags that will be used in the decision-making process. These resource tags are the SCHA_RETRY_INTERVAL and

SCHA_RETRY_COUNT. These tags are retrieved in Example 10.13 using the `scha_resource_get(1HA)` command.

5. First check will be to see if the *time_diff* value is greater than the RETRY_INTERVAL. If it is, the last failure occurred some time ago and the method will need to set *retries* to 1, slide the *start_time* window to the current time, and perform a restart. A call to `restart_service` is performed instead of failing over to another node because the last retry time was greater than the RETRY_INTERVAL for this resource.

6. If the time difference is within the RETRY_INTERVAL, a check on the number of *retries* is done against the RETRY_COUNT. If this count has been exceeded while within the RETRY_INTERVAL, then a failover must be done using the `scha_control(1HA)` command.

7. Checks the return of the `scha_control` command. If the return is nonzero, then the failover attempt failed and the probe will exit with a value of 1.

8. If the RETRY_COUNT has not been exceeded, the *retries* value is incremented and the function `restart_service` is called.

9. Checks the return of the `restart_service` function. If the return is not equal to 0, a message is sent to syslog and the function returns a value of 1.

This function will return to the main part of the `mysqlksh_probe.ksh` script with one exception—when the `scha_control` command is used. The outcome of scha_ control will determine whether the `mysqlksh_probe.ksh` exits or continues.

Example 10.12 Function decide_restart_or_failover

```
function decide_restart_or_failover
{
# Check if this is the first time we are trying to
# restart
if [ $retries -eq 0 ]; then
    # This is the first failure. Note the time when we are
    # doing this first attempt.
    start_time='$RT_BASEDIR/gettime'
    retries='expr $retries + 1'

    # Since this the first ever failure, we shall try to
    # restart the dataservice.
    restart_service
    if [[ $? -ne 0 ]] then
        logger -p ${SYSLOG_FACILITY}.err -t [$SYSLOG_TAG] \
            "${ARGV0} Could not restart dataservice."
        return 1
    fi
else
    # This is not the first failure
    current_time='$RT_BASEDIR/gettime'
    time_diff='expr $current_time - $start_time'
    if [ $time_diff -ge $RETRY_INTERVAL ]; then
```

```
                        # This failure happened after the time window
                         # elapsed, so we reset the retries counter,
                         # slide the window, and do a retry.
                        retries=1
                        start_time=$current_time
                        # Since the previous failure occurred quite
                        # sometime back (i.e. beyond the retry_interval
                        # duration), we will try to do a restart.
                        restart_service
                        if [[ $? -ne 0 ]] then
                            logger -p ${SYSLOG_FACILITY}.err \
                                -t [$SYSLOG_TAG] "${ARGV0} Could not
                                restart dataservice"
                            return 1
                        fi
                elif [ $retries -ge $RETRY_COUNT ]; then
                        # We are still within the time window,
                        # and the retry counter expired. We have to
                        # failover.
                        retries=0
                        scha_control -O GIVEOVER -G $RESOURCEGROUP_NAME \
                            -R $RESOURCE_NAME
                        if [ $? -ne 0 ]; then
                            logger -p ${SYSLOG_FACILITY}.err \
                                -t [$SYSLOG_TAG] "${ARGV0} Failover \
                                attempt failed."
                            exit 1
                        fi
                else
                        # We are still within the time window,
                        # and retry counter has not expired,
                        # so do another retry.
                        retries='expr $retries + 1'
                        # Since we have not reached the maximum no of
                        # retries allowed within the specified
                        # retry_interval duration we will try to restart
                        # again.
                        restart_service
                        if [[ $? -ne 0 ]] then
                            logger -p ${SYSLOG_FACILITY}.err \
                                -t [$SYSLOG_TAG] ${ARGV0} Could not \
                                restart dataservice"
                            return 1
                        fi
            fi
    fi
fi
}
```

Since the probe program will have multiple functions besides just probing the application, we will need to retrieve information regarding probing, restarting, or failing over the application. We will also need information such as the probe timing, any resource type utility program that will be needed, and extension properties needed for MySQL.

In Example 10.13, this portion of the `mysqlksh_probe.ksh` collects probe-related parameters such as the CHEAP_PROBE_INTERVAL and the PROBE_TIMEOUT. In Table 7.4, there are two probe intervals referenced, THOROUGH_PROBE_INTERVAL and CHEAP_PROBE_INTERVAL. These intervals give the programmer the ability to have either a probe that will thoroughly check the application's availability and takes more time to complete or a quick probe that performs a briefer check on the application. Intervals can be used separately or can be used together. Depending on the application, the complexity and the frequency of the probe will help determine whether a quick probe or a thorough probe is needed. If a thorough probe consumes more time and system cycles, then one might consider using a cheap probe and check more frequently, and use the thorough probe less frequently.

Other parameters that this example retrieves are as follows:

- PROBE_TIMEOUT—Timeout for the probe. This is a extension property defined in the RTR file.
- RT_BASEDIR—Base directory where the resource type is installed. For resource types provided by Sun Microsystems, the /opt directory plus the resource types name, that is, /opt/SUNWscnfs for the nfs resource type.
- RETRY_INTERVAL—Retry_interval for restarting the application. Used by pmfadm.
- RETRY_COUNT—Retry_count for restarting the application. Used by pmfadm.

Example 10.13   Retrieving probe information

```
export PATH=/bin:/usr/bin:/usr/cluster/bin:/usr/sbin:/usr/proc/bin:$PATH

# Obtain the syslog facility to use. This will be used to
# log the messages.
SYSLOG_FACILITY='scha_cluster_get -O SYSLOG_FACILITY'

# Parse the arguments that have been passed to this
# method
parse_args "$@"

SYSLOG_TAG=$RESOURCETYPE_NAME,$RESOURCEGROUP_NAME,\
$RESOURCE_NAME

# The interval at which probing is to be done is set
# in the system defined property CHEAP_PROBE_INTERVAL.
# Obtain this information using scha_resource_get
PROBE_INTERVAL='scha_resource_get -O \
  CHEAP_PROBE_INTERVAL -R $RESOURCE_NAME \
  -G $RESOURCEGROUP_NAME'

# Obtain the timeout value allowed for the probe.
# This value is set in the extension property
# PROBE_TIMEOUT of the data service.
```

```
probe_timeout_info='scha_resource_get -O Extension \
  -R $RESOURCE_NAME -G $RESOURCEGROUP_NAME Probe_timeout'
PROBE_TIMEOUT='echo $probe_timeout_info | awk \
  '{print $2}''

# We need to know the full path for the gettime utility
# which resides in the directory <RT_BASEDIR>. Get this
# from the RT_BASEDIR property of the resource type.
RT_BASEDIR='scha_resource_get -O RT_BASEDIR \
  -R $RESOURCE_NAME -G $RESOURCEGROUP_NAME'

# Get the Retry count value from the system defined
# property Retry_count.
RETRY_COUNT='scha_resource_get -O RETRY_COUNT \
-R $RESOURCE_NAME -G $RESOURCEGROUP_NAME'

# Get the Retry Interval value from the system defined
# property Retry_interval
RETRY_INTERVAL='scha_resource_get -O RETRY_INTERVAL \
-R $RESOURCE_NAME -G $RESOURCEGROUP_NAME'

typeset -i retries=0
```

You will also need to retrieve the extension properties that were defined for the MySQL database application as shown in Example 10.14 where the probe command and arguments are set. The method of probing the MySQL database will be simple and quick for this example. The mysqladmin command has an option to ping the database to see if it is alive. For a more thorough probe, you would need to put together one that would ensure that the database is delivering the service that is required, such as creating a table, writing to a table, or querying a table. The MySQL database provides a set of APIs that would help accomplish this and can be used to develop a probe command that would perform a more thorough check.

Example 10.14   Retrieving MySQL extension properties

```
# Need to get the mysql home directory.
mysqlhomedir_info='scha_resource_get -O Extension \
    -R $RESOURCE_NAME -G $RESOURCEGROUP_NAME MYSQL_HOME'
mysqlhomedir='echo $mysqlhomedir_info | \
    awk '{ print $2 }''

# Check to see if the directory exists
if [ ! -d $mysqlhomedir ]; then
    logger -p ${SYSLOG_FACILITY}.err -t [$SYSLOG_TAG] \
      "${ARGV0} ERROR: $mysqlhomedir directory missing"
    exit 1
fi
# Get the database user and password.
mysqluser_info='scha_resource_get -O Extension \
    -R $RESOURCE_NAME -G $RESOURCEGROUP_NAME \
    MYSQL_DBA_USER'
```

```
mysqluser='echo $mysqluser_info | awk '{ print $2 }' | \
   awk '{ FS="/"; print $1 }''
mysqlpassword='echo $mysqluser_info | awk '{ print $2 }'\
    | awk '{ FS="/"; print $2 }''

# Get the config .cnf file for where the sock file is.
mysqlcnf_info='scha_resource_get -O Extension \
   -R $RESOURCE_NAME -G $RESOURCEGROUP_NAME \
   MYSQL_CNF_FILE'
mysqlcnf='echo $mysqlcnf_info | awk '{ print $2 }''

probe_cmd_args="${mysqlhomedir}/bin/mysqladmin \
   --defaults-extra-file=$mysqlcnf -u $mysqluser \
   --password=$mysqlpassword ping"

# Obtain the program name of the probe command.
probe_cmd_prog='echo $probe_cmd_args | nawk '{print $1}''
```

Now that the functions have been covered and the parameters needed by the probe script have been retrieved, it's time to get into the actual probe shown in Example 10.15. The probe loop performs the following:

1. Sleeps for the duration of the CHEAP_PROBE_INTERVAL. This is shown at the beginning of the loop. It can also be done at the end of the loop depending on whether you choose to wait first and then probe or to do an initial probe and then wait.

2. Verifies that the probe command, the `mysqladmin`, exists and is executable. If the probe command does not exist or is not executable, call the `decide_restart_or_failover` function.

3. If the probe command is executable, run the `mysqladmin` command using the `hatimerun` command with the PROBE_TIMEOUT value. If this not successful, log a message to syslog and call the `decide_restart_or_failover` function.

In either call to the `decide_restart_or_failover` function, the return is checked. If the return is not successful, the `mysqlksh_probe.ksh` will exit with a value of 1.

Example 10.15 Probe loop

```
while :
do
  # The interval at which the probe needs to run is
  # specified in the property CHEAP_PROBE_INTERVAL.
  # So we need to sleep for a duration of
  # <CHEAP_PROBE_INTERVAL>
  sleep $PROBE_INTERVAL
  if [[ -f $probe_cmd_prog && -x $probe_cmd_prog ]]; then
     hatimerun -t $PROBE_TIMEOUT $probe_cmd_args
```

```
    if [[ $? != 0 ]]; then
        logger -p ${SYSLOG_FACILITY}.err  \
            -t [$SYSLOG_TAG] "${ARGV0} MYSQL Probe \
            Timed Out! "
        decide_restart_or_failover
        if [[ $? -ne 0 ]] then
            logger -p ${SYSLOG_FACILITY}.err \
                -t [$SYSLOG_TAG] "${ARGV0} Could not \
                Restart/Failover the dataservice. "
            exit 1
        fi
    fi
    else
        logger -p ${SYSLOG_FACILITY}.err \
            -t [$SYSLOG_TAG] "${ARGV0} Could not run \
            dataservice probe command: $probe_cmd_prog. "
        decide_restart_or_failover
        if [[ $? -ne 0 ]] then
            logger -p ${SYSLOG_FACILITY}.err \
                -t [$SYSLOG_TAG] "${ARGV0} Could not \
                Restart/Failover the dataservice. "
            exit 1
        fi
    fi
    logger -p ${SYSLOG_FACILITY}.info -t [$SYSLOG_TAG] \
        "${ARGV0} Probe for resource MYSQL successful"
done
```

At the end of the loop, there is a syslog message that is sent stating that the probe was successful. This is useful while debugging, but under normal operation, it will not be necessary to log each time through the loop.

MySQL MONITOR_CHECK Method

This method is responsible for checking the node in the cluster that will be taking over the resource. When scha_control(1HA)(3HA) is called with the GIVEOVER optag, the MONITOR_CHECK method is called if it exists.

After parsing the arguments passed to this method, shown in Example 10.3, the MySQL MONITOR_CHECK method will use the resource type's VALIDATE method to perform the check on the target node. The check method in Example 10.16 uses the scha_resource_get command to retrieve the RT_BASEDIR property, which is the directory path to the location of the resource type and the VALIDATE_METHOD property, the name of the file for this resource type's VALIDATE method.

Before calling the VALIDATE method, a check is done to see if the file is executable. If it is not executable, a message is logged to syslog and the MONITOR_CHECK method exits with a value of 1.

When the VALIDATE method is called, the status is checked. If the validate is successful, MONITOR_CHECK will exit 0 and verify that the target node for the

GIVEOVER is able to become primary for the resource. If the validate was not successful, MONITOR_CHECK will set the resource status using the scha_resource_setstatus(1HA) command and then exit with a value of 1. The resource will not be able to relocate to that node in the cluster.

Example 10.16 MySQL monitor check method

```
export PATH=/bin:/usr/bin:/usr/cluster/bin:/usr/sbin:/usr/proc/bin:$PATH

# Obtain the syslog facility to use. This will be used to
# log the messages.
SYSLOG_FACILITY='scha_cluster_get -O SYSLOG_FACILITY'

# Parse the arguments that have been passed to this
# method
parse_args "$@"

SYSLOG_TAG=$RESOURCETYPE_NAME,$RESOURCEGROUP_NAME,\
$RESOURCE_NAME

# We need to know the full path for the validate method
# which resides in the directory <RT_BASEDIR>. Get this
# from the RT_BASEDIR property of the resource type.
RT_BASEDIR='scha_resource_get -O RT_BASEDIR \
     -R $RESOURCE_NAME -G $RESOURCEGROUP_NAME'

# Obtain the name of the validate method for this
# resource.
VALIDATE_METHOD='scha_resource_get -O VALIDATE \
     -R $RESOURCE_NAME -G $RESOURCEGROUP_NAME'

if [ ! -x $RT_BASEDIR/$VALIDATE_METHOD ]; then
    logger -p ${SYSLOG_FACILITY}.err \
       -t [$SYSLOG_TAG] "${ARGV0} Monitor check for \
       Validate unsuccessful."
    exit 1
fi
# Call the validate method.
$RT_BASEDIR/$VALIDATE_METHOD -R $RESOURCE_NAME \
    -G $RESOURCEGROUP_NAME -T $RESOURCETYPE_NAME

# Log a message indicating that monitor check was
# successful.
if [ $? -eq 0 ]; then
    logger -p ${SYSLOG_FACILITY}.info \
       -t [$SYSLOG_TAG] "${ARGV0} Monitor check for \
       $RESOURCE_NAME successful."
    exit 0
else
    logger -p ${SYSLOG_FACILITY}.err -t [$SYSLOG_TAG] \
       "${ARGV0} Monitor check for $RESOURCE_NAME not \
       successful."
```

```
      scha_resource_setstatus -R $RESOURCE_NAME \
         -G $RESOURCEGROUP_NAME -s UNKNOWN -m "Monitor \
         check Failed"
      # exit 1 failed, RGM will not be able to relocate the
      # resource.
      exit 1
fi
```

MySQL UPDATE Method

This method is responsible for making sure that resource property changes that are made with the scrgadm -c command are implemented. Once the changes have been validated by the VALIDATE method, UPDATE method takes the steps necessary, such as restarting the monitor to ensure the changes have taken effect. This method will also need to be idempotent. See "Idempotency" in Chapter 6.

For the MySQL resource type, the UPDATE method will be responsible for just restarting the probe script after the updated *Monitor_retry_interval* and *Monitor_retry_count* properties have been retrieved.

Once the UPDATE method parses the passed arguments using the parsing function in Example 10.3, the method will retrieve the base directory that points to the resource type's probe script, mysqlksh_probe.ksh (shown in Example 10.17). Once the probe script is checked to see if it is executable, the updated properties *Monitor_retry_interval* and *Monitor_retry_count* are retrieved using the scha_resource_get command.

Since this method must be idempotent, the pmfadm command is used to check that the PMF_TAG is an active tag. If the tag is not active, the UPDATE method exits successfully.

With an active PMF_TAG, the method will need to stop the probe script from running prior to restarting it with the update properties. Since the probe script is under PMF control, pmfadm is used to stop the monitoring of the probe script and send it a KILL signal. The probe script uses the mysqladmin command to ping the database. Sending a KILL signal does not cause any issues with the application. Once the probe script is no longer running, the probe is restarted with pmfadm and the update properties. If the probe is restarted successfully, the UPDATE method exits with a value of 0.

Example 10.17 MySQL update method

```
export PATH=/bin:/usr/bin:/usr/cluster/bin:/usr/sbin:/usr/proc/bin:$PATH

# Obtain the syslog facility to use. This will be used to
# log the messages.
SYSLOG_FACILITY='scha_cluster_get -O SYSLOG_FACILITY'

# Parse the arguments that have been passed to this
# method
parse_args "$@"
```

```
PMF_TAG=$RESOURCEGROUP_NAME,$RESOURCE_NAME,0.mon
SYSLOG_TAG=$RESOURCETYPE_NAME,$RESOURCEGROUP_NAME,\
$RESOURCE_NAME

# We need to know the location of the probe method in
# order to restart it successfully. This value is
# obtained from the RT_BASEDIR property of the RTR File.
RT_BASEDIR='scha_resource_get -O RT_BASEDIR \
  -R $RESOURCE_NAME -G $RESOURCEGROUP_NAME'

# Set probe command.
PROBE_CMD=mysqlksh_probe.ksh

# Ensure the monitor probe exists and is executable.
if [ ! -x $RT_BASEDIR/$PROBE_CMD ]; then
    logger -p ${SYSLOG_FACILITY}.err \
        -t [$SYSLOG_TAG] "${ARGV0} Monitor probe \
        $PROBE_CMD is not executable."
    exit 1
fi
# Get the Monitor Retry Count.
mRetCnt_info='scha_resource_get -O Extension \
    -R $RESOURCE_NAME -G $RESOURCEGROUP_NAME \
    Monitor_retry_count'
mRetCnt='echo $mRetCnt_info | awk '{ print $2 }''

# Get the Monitor Retry Interval.
mRetInt_info='scha_resource_get -O Extension \
    -R $RESOURCE_NAME -G $RESOURCEGROUP_NAME \
    Monitor_retry_interval'
mRetInt='echo $mRetInt_info | awk '{ print $2 }''

pmfadm -q $PMF_TAG
if [[ $? == 0 ]]; then

        # kill the monitor that is running already
        pmfadm -k $PMF_TAG KILL
        if [[ $? != 0 ]]; then
            logger -p ${SYSLOG_FACILITY}.err \
                -t [$SYSLOG_TAG] "${ARGV0} Could not kill \
            the monitor"
            exit 1
        else
        # could successfully stop mysql. Log a message.
            logger -p ${SYSLOG_FACILITY}.info \
                -t [$SYSLOG_TAG] "Monitor for \
            $RESOURCE_NAME successfully stopped. \
            PMF will restart it."
        fi

        # Start the probe for the data service under PMF.
        # Pass the Resource name, type and group to the
        # probe method.
```

```
        pmfadm -c $PMF_TAG -n $mRetCnt -t $mRetInt \
          $RT_BASEDIR/$PROBE_CMD -R $RESOURCE_NAME \
         -G $RESOURCEGROUP_NAME -T $RESOURCETYPE_NAME

        # Log a message indicating that the monitor for
       # mysql has been started.
        if [ $? -eq 0 ]; then
           logger -p ${SYSLOG_FACILITY}.info \
             -t [$SYSLOG_TAG] "${ARGV0} Monitor for \
           $RESOURCE_NAME successfully started"
        else
           logger -p ${SYSLOG_FACILITY}.err \
              -t [$SYSLOG_TAG] "${ARGV0} Monitor start \
              for $RESOURCE_NAME not successful."

          # exit 1 - failed to start the mysql fault probe.
          exit 1
          fi
fi
exit 0
```

Within the UPDATE method, logger(1) is used to send status messages to the syslog(3C) facility. It is important to verify that operations within the method are checked and the appropriate action takes place. Logging the outcome makes it easy for system administrators to view what is taking place in the Sun Cluster environment and is helpful for debugging when problems occur.

MySQL VALIDATE Method

The VALIDATE method is responsible for ensuring that the properties being set are acceptable. During resource creation or updating, the method checks resource type and resource properties to make sure they have valid values.

When the VALIDATE method is called, there are additional arguments that are passed to it. These arguments will specify if the resource is being created or updated and what properties will be set. For the VALIDATE method, a different parsing function is used to handle these arguments. Example 10.4 shows the parsing function used by the VALIDATE method. The VALIDATE method for MySQL is broken up into Example 10.18, which retrieves the properties and checks their values, and Example 10.19, which builds and verifies the commands that the resource uses.

In Example 10.18, the SYSLOG_FACILITY is set and the "mode" property is set to a value of 0. The "mode" property, UPDATE_PROPERTY, determines what mode the VALIDATE method will operate. When the parsing function is called by parse_args, the property will be set depending on which argument is passed. The UPDATE_PROPERTY will be set to 1 if the -u argument is passed. If the -c argument is passed, UPDATE_PROPERTY is left at a value of 0.

The method retrieves the base directory for the resource type for the path to the probe script. If the UPDATE_PROPERTY value is set to 1, the method will retrieve and verify that the MySQL extension properties, defined in the RTR file, are correctly set.

Example 10.18   Resource properties for validate

```
export PATH=/bin:/usr/bin:/usr/cluster/bin:/usr/sbin:/usr/proc/bin:$PATH

# Obtain the syslog facility to use. This will be used to
# log the messages.
SYSLOG_FACILITY='scha_cluster_get -O SYSLOG_FACILITY'

UPDATE_PROPERTY=0

# Parse the arguments that have been passed to this
# method
parse_args "$@"

SYSLOG_TAG=$RESOURCETYPE_NAME,$RESOURCEGROUP_NAME,\
$RESOURCE_NAME
# We need to know the location of the probe method.
# This value is obtained from the RT_BASEDIR
# property of the RTR file.
RT_BASEDIR='scha_resource_get -O RT_BASEDIR \
   -R $RESOURCE_NAME -G $RESOURCEGROUP_NAME'

if [ $UPDATE_PROPERTY -eq 1 ]; then
    # Need to get the mysql home directory.

    mysqlhomedir_info='scha_resource_get -O Extension \
      -R $RESOURCE_NAME -G $RESOURCEGROUP_NAME MYSQL_HOME'
    mysqlhomedir='echo $mysqlhomedir_info | \
      awk '{ print $2 }''

    # Check to see if the directory exists
    if [ ! -d $mysqlhomedir ]; then
        logger -p ${SYSLOG_FACILITY}.err \
          -t [$SYSLOG_TAG] "${ARGV0} ERROR: \
          $mysqlhomedir directory missing"
        exit 1
    fi
    # Get the database directory, if not set, defaults to
    # MYSQL_HOME/data.

    mysqldatadir_info='scha_resource_get -O Extension \
      -R $RESOURCE_NAME -G $RESOURCEGROUP_NAME \
      MYSQL_DATA_DIR'
    mysqldatadir='echo $mysqldatadir_info | \
      awk '{ print $2 }''

    # Check to see if the directory exists
    if [ ! -d $mysqldatadir ]; then
        logger -p ${SYSLOG_FACILITY}.info \
          -t [$SYSLOG_TAG] "${ARGV0} ERROR: Data \
          directory does not exist."
```

```
   fi
   # Get the CNF config file for this database.
mysqlcnf_info='scha_resource_get -O Extension \
   -R $RESOURCE_NAME -G $RESOURCEGROUP_NAME \
    MYSQL_CNF_FILE'
mysqlcnf='echo $mysqlcnf_info | awk '{ print $2 }''

if [ ! -f $mysqlcnf ]; then
   logger -p ${SYSLOG_FACILITY}.err -t [$SYSLOG_TAG] \
     "${ARGV0} ERROR: $mysqlcnf configuration file \
     is missing."
   exit 1
fi
# Based on version, mysqld binary is in different
# directory.
mysqlbin_info='scha_resource_get -O Extension -R \ $RESOURCE_NAME -G
$RESOURCEGROUP_NAME MYSQL_MYSQLD'
mysqlbin='echo $mysqlbin_info | awk '{ print $2 }''
```

After the resource properties have been verified, the commands that the resource uses to start, probe, and stop the application are put together and verified. Each command is checked to see if it exists and is executable, as shown in Example 10.19.

During the checks of either the resource properties or the command, the method will log a message to syslog and exit with a value of 1 if the check is not successful. It is important to log each check in the VALIDATION method to track what failed.

Another thing to note is that this method does not check for the use of HAStorage-Plus, with which it is possible to have a failover filesystem. This means that the storage directory path will only be seen on the node that has the resource group containing the MySQL resource that could be dependent on a HAStoragePlus resource. So this resource type will not work with a fast failover filesystem, that is, unless checks are added to the methods to verify it.

Example 10.19   *Validate resource commands*

```
start_cmd_args=
start_cmd_args="${mysqlhomedir}${mysqlbin} \
   --defaults-extra-file=$mysqlcnf -u $mysqluser \
   -b $mysqlhomedir --datadir=$mysqldatadir"

start_cmd_prog='echo $start_cmd_args | nawk '{print $1}''
if [[ ! -f $start_cmd_prog || ! -x $start_cmd_prog ]]; then
   logger -p ${SYSLOG_FACILITY}.err -t [$SYSLOG_TAG] \
     "${ARGV0} File $start_cmd_prog is missing or not
     executable"
   exit 1
fi

stop_cmd_args=
stop_cmd_args="${mysqlhomedir}/bin/mysqladmin \
   -u $mysqluser --password=$mysqlpassword shutdown"
```

```
stop_cmd_prog='echo $stop_cmd_args | nawk '{print $1}''
if [[ ! -z $stop_cmd_prog ]]; then
    if [[ ! -f $stop_cmd_prog || ! -x $stop_cmd_prog ]];
    then
      logger -p ${SYSLOG_FACILITY}.err -t [$SYSLOG_TAG] \
        "${ARGV0} File $stop_cmd_prog is missing or not \
        executable"
      exit 1
    fi
fi
probe_cmd_args=
probe_cmd_args=$RT_BASEDIR/mysqlksh_probe.ksh
probe_cmd_prog='echo $probe_cmd_args | nawk '{print $1}''
if [[ ! -z $probe_cmd_prog ]]; then
    if [[ ! -f $probe_cmd_prog || ! -x $probe_cmd_prog ]];
      then
        logger -p ${SYSLOG_FACILITY}.err -t [$SYSLOG_TAG] \
            "${ARGV0} File $probe_cmd_prog is missing or \
          not executable"
        exit 1
        fi
fi
fi    # end of if UPDATE_PROPERTY check from
# Figure 10.18 on page 391.
# Log a message indicating that validate method was
# successful.
logger -p ${SYSLOG_FACILITY}.info -t [$SYSLOG_TAG] \
    "${ARGV0} Validate method for resource \
    "$RESOURCE_NAME "completed successfully"
exit 0
```

After all checks have completed successfully, the method will log the success to syslog and then exit 0. The example does verification when the UPDATE_PROPERTY is set to a value of 1 for "update mode." During the "creation mode" the method does not perform any checks and just exits successfully. The resource does not exist until validation has completed and the scrgadm command exits. The scha_resource_get command fails because there is not yet a valid resource. So for the create mode, the VALIDATE method bypasses the verification of properties and commands.

Creating the CUPS Callback Methods

In the following sections, the C source for each callback method will be discussed. Depending on the length of code in each callback method, some of the methods will be listed in their entirety. If they are lengthy, they will be broken up into multiple examples so it will be easier to view and explain. For references on the DSDL library, refer back to Chapter 9.

At the beginning of each callback method, it is necessary to initialize a handle. This handle will be used by other DSDL functions in the callback method. If the initialization fails, the callback method must return with an error. This error should be logged with syslog to inform the system administrator what failed. Example 10.20 shows how an initialization is done in a callback method using scds_ initialize()(3HA).

Example 10.20   DSDL handle initialization

```
/* Process all the arguments that have been passed to us from RGM */

if(scds_initialize(&scds_handle, argc, argv) != \
     SCHA_ERR_NOERR) {
   scds_syslog(LOG_ERR, "Data Service handle failed to \
       initialize!");
   return (1);
}
```

Before exiting the specific call method, it is important to free the memory used when the handle was initialized at the beginning of that call method. Using the scds_close()(3HA) function with the address of the handle will free the memory used, as shown in Example 10.21. It is also important to note that if the callback method must exit due to some anomaly, scds_close() is called to free memory.

Example 10.21   DSDL handle close

```
/* Free up all the memory allocated by scds_initialize */
scds_close(&scds_handle);
```

CUPS START Method

Once the RGM receives an event to bring the resource online, the START method will be called to start the CUPS application. The START method will need to retrieve RTR properties, verify commands, start the application, and do a quick check to verify that the application is running.

Example 10.22 shows the header files and the define statements used for method timing and defines the declarations. As mentioned, once the application is started, the method will need to do a network connection to do a quick check to see if the application is available. This is the reason the source includes network headers. The CUPS application binary is cupsd, which is defined here also. If this were ever to change, the resource type would need to be modified. A better method would be to define a property for this in the RTR file.

Example 10.22   CUPS start method headers, defines, and declarations

```
#include <stdio.h>
#include <stdlib.h>
#include <signal.h>
#include <strings.h>
#include <syslog.h>
#include <unistd.h>
```

```
#include <sys/types.h>
#include <sys/stat.h>
#include <sys/wait.h>
#include <sys/socket.h>
#include <netinet/in.h>
#include <scha.h>
#include <rgm/libdsdev.h>
#include <errno.h>

/*
 * The initial timeout allowed  for the cups dataservice
 * to be fully up and running. We will wait for 3 %
 * (SVC_WAIT_PCT) of the start_timeout time before
 * probing the service.
 */
#define SVC_WAIT_PCT            3
/*
 * We need to use 80% of probe_timeout to connect to the
 * port and the remaining time is used to disconnect from
 * port in the svc_probe function.
 */
#define SVC_CONNECT_TIMEOUT_PCT         80
/*
 * This value will be used as disconnect timeout, if
 * there is no time left from the probe_timeout.
 */
#define SVC_DISCONNECT_TIMEOUT_SECONDS          2

int main(int argc, char *argv[])
{

char start_cli[256];
char *cups_cmd="/sbin/cupsd";
char *cups_args="";
char *cups_homedir;
int rc=0;
int err, log_facility;
int sock_tcp;
int start_timeout, probe_timeout, wait_time;
struct stat stat_buf;
scds_handle_tscds_handle;
scds_netaddr_list_t *netaddr_list;
scha_err_t err_code;
scha_extprop_value_t *cups_ext_prop;
```

The START method will need to retrieve properties for the resource. Before this can be done, the method will need to process the arguments passed to it and initialize the handle defined as *scds_handle*. But the outcome of this will need to be checked before moving forward. If the initialization failed and was not checked, the START method would core. So checking for this is important.

After initialization has completed successfully, the following properties are retrieved as shown in Example 10.23:

- *start_timeout*—Holds the START method timeout value.
- *probe_timeout*—Holds the timeout value for the Probe_timeout extension property. Retrieving this property is a two-step process. The scds_get_ext_property() call populates the *cups_ext_prop* structure and the *probe_timeout* is set by accessing the *val.val_int* defined in the *cups_ext_prop* structure.
- *cups_homedir*—Holds the path to the CUPS application. Retrieving the *CUPS_dir* extension property is similar to probe_timeout using the scds_get_ext_property() call to populate the *cups_ext_prop* structure. The *cups_homedir* is set to the *CUPS_dir* by accessing the string array, *val.val_strarray->str_array[0]*.
- *cups_args*—The only argument that is used for the cupsd binary is the configuration file. Again, this is retrieved using the scds_get_ext_property() call and accessing the *cups_ext_prop* structure. Since the Conf_file extension property is optional as defined in the RTR file, a call to strlen() is made to see if *val.val_strarray->str_array[0]* has a nonzero length.

The *start_cli* property will hold the *cups_homedir* value and the *cups_cmd* to build the start command string for this method. At the end of Example 10.23, scds_free_ext_property() is called to free the memory used by the *cups_ext_prop* structure.

Example 10.23 CUPS start method properties

```
/* Process all the arguments that have been passed to us from RGM */

if(scds_initialize(&scds_handle, argc, argv) != \
      SCHA_ERR_NOERR) {
   scds_syslog(LOG_ERR, "Data Service handle failed to \
      initialize!");
   return (1);
}

start_timeout = scds_get_rs_start_timeout(scds_handle);
err_code = scds_get_ext_property(scds_handle, "Probe_timeout",
SCHA_PTYPE_INT, &cups_ext_prop);
if( err_code != SCHA_ERR_NOERR ){
     scds_syslog(LOG_ERR,"Failed to get Probe
         timeout! Error:%s",scha_strerror(err_code));
     scds_close(&scds_handle);
     return(err_code);
}
probe_timeout = cups_ext_prop->val.val_int;

err_code = scds_get_ext_property(scds_handle,
   "CUPS_dir",SCHA_PTYPE_STRINGARRAY,&cups_ext_prop);
if( err_code != SCHA_ERR_NOERR ){
     scds_syslog(LOG_ERR,"Failed to get Config
         directory! Error: %s",scha_strerror(err_code));
```

```
        scds_close(&scds_handle);
        return(err_code);
}
cups_homedir=cups_ext_prop->val.val_strarray-  >str_array[0];
strcpy(start_cli,cups_homedir);
strcat(start_cli,cups_cmd);

/* Get config file if specified. */
err_code = scds_get_ext_property(scds_handle, "Conf_file",
SCHA_PTYPE_STRINGARRAY, &cups_ext_prop);
if( err_code != SCHA_ERR_NOERR ){
        scds_syslog(LOG_ERR,"Failed to get Configuration
            File! Error: %s",scha_strerror(err_code));
        scds_close(&scds_handle);
        return(err_code);
}
if(strlen(cups_ext_prop->val.val_strarray->str_array[0])
   > 0)
{
  (void) strcpy(cups_args,
      cups_ext_prop->val.val_strarray->str_array[0]);
}
/* Finished with the extension property, need to free. */
scds_free_ext_property(cups_ext_prop);
```

Before starting the application, the start command will need to be checked to see if it available and executable. In Example 10.24, the stat()(2) call is used to check that the start command is available. Verifying the mode of the command is done by an operation with S_IXUSR. See the man page for mknod(2) to find out more about S_IXUSR.

Example 10.24   Verify CUPS start command

```
/* Check the startup command for this method. */
if((stat(start_cli, &stat_buf) !=0)){
   scds_syslog(LOG_ERR,"Cupsd command is not avail
      able.");
   scds_close(&scds_handle);
   return(1);
}
if(!(stat_buf.st_mode & S_IXUSR)){
   scds_syslog(LOG_ERR,"Cupsd command is not
      executeable.");
   scds_close(&scds_handle);
   return(1);
}
```

The PMF, discussed in Chapter 8, will be used to start the CUPS application in Example 10.25. The DSDL provides the scds_pmf_start()(3HA) function call to do this. The PMF will need the type of service that is defined by SCDS_PMF_ TYPE_SVC, the instance number of zero, the start command, and the child monitor level. The instance level of zero is given since there is only one instance that will run under the PMF. If there were multiple programs that needed to run for the application, then this would need to be a different number for each call of this function. The child monitor level is set to a -1 to monitor all children.

Once the `scds_pmf_start()` call is successful, you will need to wait for some period of time to ensure that the application is fully running and a quick check can be done. Using the SVC_WAIT_PCT define and the START_TIMEOUT time retrieved by the `scds_get_rs_start_timeout()` call, a percentage of the START_TIMEOUT is used to wait for the application to fully start. Using scds_wait()(3HA), the START method waits 3% of the START_TIMEOUT time before proceeding with checking the application. The percentage of waiting time should be appropriate for the type of application that will be started.

Example 10.25 Start the CUPS application

```
/* Start the data service, if it fails return with an
 error */
err_code = scds_pmf_start(scds_handle, SCDS_PMF_TYPE_SVC, 0, start_cli,-1);
if( err_code != SCHA_ERR_NOERR ){
    scds_syslog(LOG_ERR," Cupsd Failed to start!
       Error: %s",scha_strerror(err_code));
    scds_close(&scds_handle);
    return(err_code);
}

/* Wait SVC_WAIT_PCT (percentage of) START_TIMEOUT, for
 application to startup. */

err_code = scds_svc_wait(scds_handle,
(scds_get_rs_start_timeout(scds_handle) *
   SVC_WAIT_PCT)/100);
if( err_code != SCHA_ERR_NOERR ){
    scds_syslog(LOG_ERR,"scds_svc_wait: Failed to start!
       Error: %s",scha_strerror(err_code));
    scds_close(&scds_handle);
    return(err_code);
}
```

At this point, the application should be running. Before the START method exits successfully, the method should verify that the application is truly available. For this START method, a verification is done by connecting to the port used by the application, then closing that port. This may be sufficient for some applications, but not for all. There may be more checking that can be done to verify that the application is performing the functions for which it is intended. The CUPS application offers an API for development. This API could be used in the START method to enhance verification, such as checking that the printer or printers are accessible.

Since the checking will be just verifying that the port is available, Example 10.26 collects a list of networks that are available to this resource. The function call scds_get_netaddr_list() extracts a list that is based on the logical host's resources, which are defined for the resource group of which this CUPS resource is a part. This is convenient when multiple logical hosts are defined because that information is also within the *netaddr_list* structure. This START method only uses the first address to connect to. For checking multiple addresses, a loop would need to be coded in to verify each address and port.

Connecting to the logical host and port is done using the scds_fm_tcp_connect(). The timeout value for this function is a percentage defined by SVC_CONNECT_TIMEOUT_PCT of the probe_timeout. If the connection is not established in this time period, a message is sent to syslog, the handle for the method is closed, and an exit status based on the error code is returned.

The connection is then closed using the function scds_fm_tcp_disconnect(). If the connection does not close within the timeout defined by SVC_DISCONNECT_TIMEOUT_SECONDS, a message is logged to syslog, the handle is closed, and an error code is returned. After the connection closes, the method will need to free any resources such as the netaddr_list structure. A message is sent to syslog notifying that the START method was successful and the handle is closed using the scds_close() function call.

Example 10.26 Verify application and close handle

```
/* Quick probe of port to ensure application is running.
 */
err_code = scds_get_netaddr_list(scds_handle,
&netaddr_list);
if( err_code != SCHA_ERR_NOERR ){
    scds_syslog(LOG_ERR,"No network address! Error:
        %s",scha_strerror(err_code));
    scds_close(&scds_handle);
    return(err_code);
}
err_code = scds_fm_tcp_connect(scds_handle, &sock_tcp,
netaddr_list->netaddrs[0].hostname, netaddr_list-
>netaddrs[0].port_proto.port, (probe_timeout *
SVC_CONNECT_TIMEOUT_PCT)/100);
if( err_code != SCHA_ERR_NOERR ){
    scds_syslog(LOG_ERR,"Host connection Failed! Error:
        %s",scha_strerror(err_code));
    scds_close(&scds_handle);
    return(err_code);
}
err_code = scds_fm_tcp_disconnect(scds_handle, sock_tcp,
SVC_DISCONNECT_TIMEOUT_SECONDS);
if( err_code != SCHA_ERR_NOERR ){
    scds_syslog(LOG_ERR,"Host Disconnection Failed!
        Error: %s",scha_strerror(err_code));
    scds_close(&scds_handle);
    return(err_code);
}
```

```
/* Finished Probe free netaddr_list. */
(void) scds_free_netaddr_list(netaddr_list);

/* Made it to here, send notice to syslog. */
scds_syslog(LOG_NOTICE, "CUPS has started");

/* Free up the Environment resources that were allocated
   by closing the handle*/

(void) scds_close(&scds_handle);
/* Return successful. */
return (0);
}
```

When handling any events within the code, it is important to use scds_
syslog() to log the event. If the event is an issue that needs to exit the method,
close the handle with the scds_close() call. This will free memory resources used
by the method.

CUPS STOP Method

In the START method, the PMF was used to start the cupsd binary. The STOP
method will need to stop PMF from monitoring the cupsd binary and then stop the
application. The STOP method must also be idempotent. See "Idempotency" in Chapter 6. So for the STOP method, running this method when the application is not running will not cause it to exit unsuccessfully.

In Example 10.27, the source shows the header files and declarations needed for
the STOP method. The define statements defined are the following:

- SVC_SMOOTH_PCT—This is the smooth timeout percentage or the percentage
  of the STOP_TIMEOUT that is used to stop the application gracefully.
- SVC_HARD_PCT—This is the hard timeout percentage of the STOP_TIMEOUT
  that is used to stop the application quickly.

Example 10.27 CUPS stop method headers, defines, and declarations

```
#include <rgm/libdsdev.h>
#include <scha.h>

#define SVC_SMOOTH_PCT          80   /* 80 percent */
#define SVC_HARD_PCT            15   /* 15 percent */

/*
 * Stops the cups process using PMF
 */

int
main(int argc, char *argv[])
{
```

```
scds_handle_t        scds_handle;
scha_err_t err_code;
scds_pmf_status_t pmf_status;
int stop_timeout;
int instance=0;
```

Once *scds_handle* has been initialized successfully, the method will retrieve the *stop_timeout* value and the status of the PMF for the resource. The method verifies that the *pmf_status* does not equal SCDS_PMF_MONITORED. If there is not a valid PMF tag, then the CUPS process is assumed not to be running under the PMF for this resource. The method closes the handle and exits successfully. This is to support idempotency within the STOP method.

If there is a valid PMF tag, the function scds_pmf_stop()(3HA) is used to stop PMF from monitoring the application and stop the application with a SIGKILL. See the signal(3HEAD) man page for more information on signals. The CUPS application is Web server based, so for this example, the cupsd binary is sent a SIGKILL to stop the application (Example 10.28).

The SVC_SMOOTH_PCT value is used to get 80% of the *stop_time* for the function call scds_pmf_stop(). Using 80% of the *stop_timeout* value gives us enough time to stop the application gracefully. The SVC_HARD_PCT value can be used to get 15% of the *stop_time* value to perform another means to stop an application that does not stop gracefully. The use of SIGKILL will be enough to stop the application on the first try.

After scds_pmf_stop() is called, *err_code* is checked. If it does not equal SCHA_ERR_NOERR, an error has occurred and the handle is closed with scds_close()(3HA). For the list of error codes, see Chapter 7, Table 7.8. The *err_code* is then checked again to see if SCHA_ERR_TIMEOUT occurred. If this error occurs, then the scds_pmf_stop() call has timed out waiting for the application to stop gracefully. There could be a problem with stopping the application or an indication that the resource's STOP_TIMEOUT may need to be adjusted using the scrgadm(1HA) command.

Example 10.28   Stopping the CUPS application

```
/* Process the arguments passed by RGM and initialize
   syslog */
if(scds_initialize(&scds_handle,argc,argv) !=
      SCHA_ERR_NOERR){
   scds_syslog(LOG_ERR, "Data Service handle failed to
      initialize!");
   return (1);
}
/* Retrieve stop timeout and set smooth and hard timeouts.*/

stop_timeout = scds_get_rs_stop_timeout(scds_handle);
```

```
err_code = scds_pmf_get_status(scds_handle,
        SCDS_PMF_TYPE_SVC, instance, &pmf_status);

if( err_code != SCHA_ERR_NOERR ){
    scds_syslog(LOG_ERR,"Failed to get PMF status! Error:
        %s",scha_strerror(err_code));
    scds_close(&scds_handle);
    return(err_code);
}

if( pmf_status != SCDS_PMF_MONITORED ){
    scds_syslog(LOG_NOTICE, "Cups is not Running");
    scds_close(&scds_handle);
    return(0);
}
err_code = scds_pmf_stop(scds_handle,
        SCDS_PMF_TYPE_SVC,instance,SIGTERM,
        (stop_timeout * SVC_SMOOTH_PCT)/100);

if( err_code != SCHA_ERR_NOERR ){
        scds_close(&scds_handle);
        if( err_code == SCHA_ERR_TIMEOUT ){
            scds_syslog(LOG_ERR,"Timeout occurred, Failed
                to Stop Cups! Error: %s",
                scha_strerror(err_code));
        }
        else {
            scds_syslog(LOG_ERR,"Failed to Stop Cups!
                Error: %s",scha_strerror(err_code));
        }
         return(err_code);
}
scds_syslog(LOG_NOTICE,"Cups service has stopped.");

/* Free up all the memory allocated by scds_initialize */
scds_close(&scds_handle);

/* Return the result of svc_stop method */
return (0);
}
```

The application now is stopped and there is no longer a valid PMF tag. The method frees memory and closes the handle with scds_close(), then returns a value of 0 indicating that the method was successful.

CUPS MONITOR_START Method

The MONITOR_START method will start the CUPS monitoring program, cups_probe, which is covered in "CUPS Probe" later in this chapter. This method will use the PMF to start the cups_probe program. See Example 10.29.

Once the method initializes the *scds_handle* with scds_initialize()(3HA) function, scds_pmf_start()(3HA) is called to start the probe. The program type is SCDS_PMF_TYPE_MON, which indicates this is a fault monitor. (Refer to Table 9.5.) There is only one instance of this probe, so *instance* is set to 0. The value of *child* is set to 0. When the program type is set to SCDS_PMF_TYPE_MON, the child level is ignored and the value of 0 is used. The probe program, cups_probe, is located in the bin directory where the resource type is installed.

After the probe is started, the method checks the status of PMF using scds_pmf_get_status()(3HA). If the *pmf_status* does not equal SCDS_PMF_MONITORED, then the monitor is running. The method will log a message to syslog, close the handle, and return SCDS_PMF_NOT_MONITORED, which indicates that the service is not monitored.

If the monitor is running, a message will be sent to syslog indicating that the monitor has started. The method will then close the handle with scds_close() and then return a value 0, indicating that the method was successful.

Example 10.29   CUPS monitor start

```
#include <rgm/libdsdev.h>
#include <scha.h>

int main(int argc, char *argv[])
{
scds_handle_t       scds_handle;
scha_err_t err_code;
scds_pmf_status_t pmf_status;
int instance=0;
int child=0;

/* Process the arguments passed by RGM and initialize sys
   log */
if(scds_initialize(&scds_handle, argc, argv) !=
      SCHA_ERR_NOERR) {
   scds_syslog(LOG_ERR, "Data Service handle failed to
      initialize!");
   return (1);
}

err_code = scds_pmf_start(scds_handle,SCDS_PMF_TYPE_MON,
   instance,"cups_probe", child);

if( err_code != SCHA_ERR_NOERR ){
   scds_syslog(LOG_ERR,"Monitor Failed to Start!
      Error: %s",scha_strerror(err_code));
   scds_close(&scds_handle);
   return(err_code);
}

err_code = scds_pmf_get_status(scds_handle,
     SCDS_PMF_TYPE_MON,instance, &pmf_status);
if( err_code != SCHA_ERR_NOERR ){
   scds_syslog(LOG_ERR,"Failed to get Monitor
      Status! Error: %s",scha_strerror(err_code));
```

```
    scds_close(&scds_handle);
    return(err_code);
}
if(pmf_status != SCDS_PMF_MONITORED ){
    scds_syslog(LOG_ERR,"Service is not monitored.");
    scds_close(&scds_handle);
    return(SCDS_PMF_NOT_MONITORED);
}

scds_syslog(LOG_NOTICE,"Cups Fault Monitor has started.");

/* Free up all the memory allocated by scds_initialize */
scds_close(&scds_handle);

/* Return the result of monitor_start method */
return (0);
}
```

It is important to use syslog for events that happen in the method and also to log when the method completes successfully. It will create a timeline when an event takes place in the Sun Cluster framework and help system administrators understand what took place.

CUPS MONITOR_STOP Method

Like the STOP method, the MONITOR_STOP method needs to be idempotent. See "Idempotency" in Chapter 6. The cups_probe program does nothing intrusive to the application, so sending a SIGKILL to stop the monitor will not cause any issues with the CUPS application itself.

After the method initializes the handle, as shown in Example 10.30, scds_pmf_ get_status() is used to get the status of the probe running under PMF. If there is no error code returned, the method checks *pmf_status* to see if the PMF tag is valid. If there is a valid tag, the method continues; otherwise, the tag does not exist and the probe is not running. The method then exits successfully. This supports the method's requirement for idempotency.

To stop the probe, scds_pmf_stop()(3HA) will need a timeout value. This is retrieved using the function scds_get_rs_monitor_stop_timeout(). This function retrieves the MONITOR_STOP_TIME for that resource.

Example 10.30   Stopping the CUPS monitor

```
int main(int argc, char *argv[]){

scds_handle_t    scds_handle;
scha_err_t err_code;
scds_pmf_status_t pmf_status;
int instance=0;
int monitor_stop_timeout;
```

```
/* Process the arguments passed by RGM and initialize sys
   log */
if(scds_initialize(&scds_handle, argc, argv) !=
      SCHA_ERR_NOERR) {
    scds_syslog(LOG_ERR, "Data Service handle failed to
       initialize!");
    return (1);
}
/* Check the monitor to see if its running. If not exit.
 */
err_code = scds_pmf_get_status(scds_handle,
    SCDS_PMF_TYPE_MON,instance, &pmf_status);
if( err_code != SCHA_ERR_NOERR ){
    scds_syslog(LOG_ERR,"Failed to get Monitor Status!
        Error: %s",scha_strerror(err_code));
    scds_close(&scds_handle);
    return(err_code);
}
if(pmf_status != SCDS_PMF_MONITORED ){
    scds_syslog(LOG_NOTICE,"Service is not being
       monitored.");
    scds_close(&scds_handle);
    return(0);
}
/* Get the monitor stop timeout. */

monitor_stop_timeout = scds_get_rs_monitor_stop_timeout(scds_handle);

/* The monitor is running, so need to stop the monitor.*/

err_code = scds_pmf_stop(scds_handle, SCDS_PMF_TYPE_MON,
     instance,SIGTERM, monitor_stop_timeout);
if( err_code != SCHA_ERR_NOERR ){
       scds_close(&scds_handle);
       if( err_code == SCHA_ERR_TIMEOUT ){
          scds_syslog(LOG_ERR,"Timeout occurred, Failed
          to Stop Monitor! Error: %s",
          scha_strerror(err_code));
       }
       else {
          scds_syslog(LOG_ERR,"Failed to Stop Monitor!
             Error: %s",scha_strerror(err_code));
       }
       return(err_code);
}
/*Free up all the memory allocated by scds_initialize */
scds_close(&scds_handle);
return (0);
}
```

After `scds_pmf_stop()` is called, *err_code* is checked. If it does not equal SCHA_
ERR_NOERR, an error has occurred and the handle is closed using `scds_close()`
(3HA). To refer to the list of error codes, see Chapter 7, Table 7.8. The *err_code* is

then checked again to see if SCHA_ERR_TIMEOUT occurred. If this error occurs, then the scds_pmf_stop() call timed out waiting for the probe to stop. Since this method is using SIGKILL to stop the probe, chances are that a timeout will not happen. But for more complex probes, another method, such as stopping the probe gracefully, make take more time. So logging that a timeout occurred becomes very helpful.

Once the probe has stopped, scds_close() frees the handle and the method returns successful.

CUPS Probe

The CUPS probe is responsible for making sure the application is available to its users. The probe should not only make sure the application is available, but it should also test some functionality of the application to make sure it is responding to its users. This may involve either using a program provided with the application or possibly developing one. In developing a probe program, the need to test functionality can usually be done through the use of APIs that are provided by the application vendor.

In the CUPS probe, the DSDL provides methods to connect to an application. For this example, it will be done to check that the probe can connect to the application, then disconnect. To expand the role of the probe, the CUPS APIs can be used in this program either to add more test functionality or to further query the application.

In Example 10.31, the declarations and headers are defined. If the CUPS API were to be used, then the header files would need to be included. Again, the probe is only doing a simple connect and disconnect, but it can be built-on.

Example 10.31   CUPS probe headers, defines, and declarations

```
#include <stdio.h>
#include <stdlib.h>
#include <sys/time.h>
#include <rgm/libdsdev.h>
#include <scha_err.h>

#define SVC_CONNECT_TIMEOUT_PCT         80

int main(int argc, char *argv[])
{
scds_handle_t       scds_handle;
scha_err_t       err_code;
int               probe_timeout, connect_timeout;
int             disconnect_timeout;
int              port, ip, probe_result=0;
char             *wrtBuff, *rdBuff;
hrtime_t        ht1, ht2;
unsigned long  dt;
scds_netaddr_list_t *netaddr;
char             *hostname;
int              sock_tcp;
```

As in all methods using the DSDL, a handle will need to be initialized and the properties for the resource retrieved, as shown in Example 10.32. Since the probe will need to connect to the application to test if it is available, the network resources for the resource group will be needed. Retrieving network resources is done with the scds_get_netaddr_list()(3HA) function. This will retrieve network resource information that is defined for the resource group of which the resource is a part and will put it in the *netaddr* structure. The *netaddr* structure is then verified that it is not NULL and that there are address resources defined. Other properties retrieved are the *probe_timeout*, which is used to calculate *connect_timeout* and *disconnect_ timeout*.

Example 10.32 Retrieve CUPS properties

```
/* Process all the arguments that have been passed to us from RGM */

if(scds_initialize(&scds_handle, argc, argv) != \
     SCHA_ERR_NOERR) {
   scds_syslog(LOG_ERR, "Data Service handle failed to \
      initialize!");
   return (1);
}

/* Get the ip addresses available for this resource */
if (scds_get_netaddr_list(scds_handle, &netaddr)) {
      scds_syslog(LOG_ERR,"Unable to retrieve network
         address resources.");
      scds_close(&scds_handle);
      return (1);
}
/* Return an error if there are no network resources */
if (netaddr == NULL || netaddr->num_netaddrs == 0) {
      scds_syslog(LOG_ERR,"No network address resource in
         resource group.");
      scds_close(&scds_handle);
      return (1);
}
/* Get the timeout from the extension props. This means
 * that each probe iteration will get a full timeout on
 * each network resource without chopping up the timeout
 * between all of the network resources configured for
 * this resource.
 */
/* Set timeouts */
probe_timeout = scds_get_ext_probe_timeout(scds_handle);
connect_timeout = (probe_timeout *
     SVC_CONNECT_TIMEOUT_PCT)/100;
disconnect_timeout = ((100 - SVC_CONNECT_TIMEOUT_PCT) *
     probe_timeout)/100;
```

The CUPS probe will run until there is an issue that causes a restart or a failover or the resource is offlined. Example 10.33 shows the loop for the cups_probe. In the loop, the probe will cycle through the network addresses defined in the resource group and perform a connect, then disconnect for the ports defined by the CUPS resource.

In the loop, the first task is to sleep for the time period defined by the resource's *thorough_probe_interval*. Where `scds_fm_sleep()` (3HA) is placed in the code is up to the developers. Some developers may choose to run a probe first, then sleep. Recall that in the CUPS START method, the method waited for the application to start, then did a quick check of the availability of that application before the method completed. However, if the wait and the availability check are not done in the START method, the method will complete successfully and the RGM will call MONITOR_START method to start the probe not knowing if the application is completely running. This may cause false failovers, so make sure there is enough time for the application to be fully operational before a probe is started.

Since multiple network resources can be defined in a resource group, the probe will loop through each network address that is stored in the *netaddr* structure and test connectivity to it. The `for` loop cycles through each *hostname* and *port* in the *netaddr* structure and tries to connect using the `scds_fm_tcp_connect()` (3HA) function. The *connect_timeout* limit for each address connection is 80% of the *probe_timeout*, as defined by the define SVC_CONNECT_TIMEOUT_PCT.

Prior to performing the connection, a timestamp is taken using `gethrtime()` (3C) to latch the start time of the probe. The variables *h1*, *h2*, and *dt* are used to keep track of time. The time difference, *dt*, along with the *probe_result*, is used by the `scds_fm_action()` (3HA) function to determine what action to take.

If the connection attempt fails, the probe will set the *probe_result* to SCDS_PROBE_COMPLETE_FAILURE (see "scds_fm_action" in Chapter 8). A second timestamp is taken and the time difference is calculated. The function `scds_fm_action()` is called using the *probe_result* and *dt* values to determine what action to take.

Once a connection is made, the probe will disconnect with `scds_fm_tcp_disconnect()` (3HA), using the *disconnect_timeout* value. If there are no issues, the probe loops continuously through each network resource defined in the resource group.

If the disconnect does have a problem, the *probe_result* property is set to one-half the value of SCDS_PROBE_COMPLETE_FAILURE. A second timestamp along with a time difference is taken. This is passed to the `scds_fm_action()` to determine what action to take (Example 10.33).

Example 10.33   CUPS probe loop

```
for (;;) {
    /* sleep for a duration of thorough_probe_interval
    *  between
    *  successive probes. */

scds_fm_sleep(scds_handle,
scds_get_rs_thorough_probe_interval(scds_handle));
```

```
/* Now probe all netaddress we use.
 * For each of the netaddress that is probed,
 * compute the failure history. */

/* Iterate through all the netaddrs. */
for (ip = 0; ip < netaddr->num_netaddrs; ip++) {
        /* Grab the hostname and port on which the
         * health has to be monitored. */

    hostname = netaddr->netaddrs[ip].hostname;
    port = netaddr->netaddrs[ip].port_proto.port;
    ht1 = gethrtime(); /* Latch probe start time */

    /* Connect to the cups server. */
    err_code = scds_fm_tcp_connect(scds_handle,
       &sock_tcp, hostname, port, connect_timeout);
    if( err_code != SCHA_ERR_NOERR ){
       scds_syslog(LOG_ERR,"Host connection Failed!
          Error: %d -  %s",err_code,
          scha_strerror(err_code));

          /* since probe is unable to connect to the
           * print server, clients cannot print which is
           * considered a complete failure. */

         probe_result = SCDS_PROBE_COMPLETE_FAILURE;
        ht2 = gethrtime();

        /* Convert to milliseconds */
        dt = (ht2 - ht1) / 1e6;

          /* Since there was a complete failure, need to
           * take some action. */
          (void) scds_fm_action(scds_handle, probe_result,
             dt);
    } /* End of if err_code for connect.*/

     /* Once connected, should do something to ensure
      * that the cups server is responsive. May be able
      * to connect, but the cups server may not be able
      * to do anything. Expand using CUPS API.*/

    err_code = scds_fm_tcp_disconnect(scds_handle,
        sock_tcp, disconnect_timeout);
    if( err_code != SCHA_ERR_NOERR ){
       scds_syslog(LOG_ERR,"Host Disconnection Failed!
          Error: %d - %s",err_code,
          scha_strerror(err_code));
        probe_result = SCDS_PROBE_COMPLETE_FAILURE/2;
       ht2 = gethrtime();
     /* Convert to milliseconds */
       dt = (ht2 - ht1) / 1e6;
```

```
            /* Compute failure history and take action if
             * needed. */
              (void) scds_fm_action(scds_handle, probe_result,
              dt);
            } /* end if err_code for disconnect. */
    }    /* Each netaddr */
  }      /* Keep probing forever, end of for loop */
} /* End of CUPS probe program. */
```

CUPS VALIDATE Method

The VALIDATE method checks that the properties being set are correct during the creation of the resource and also during the updating of the resource. The VALIDATE method is called on all nodes listed in the resource types *Init_node* property. Example 10.34 shows the headers, defines, and declarations needed for this method.

Example 10.34   CUPS validate headers, defines, and declarations

```
/*
 * cups_validate.c - Validate method for cups
 */
#include <stdio.h>
#include <stdlib.h>
#include <signal.h>
#include <strings.h>
#include <unistd.h>
#include <sys/types.h>
#include <sys/stat.h>
#include <sys/socket.h>
#include <sys/wait.h>
#include <netinet/in.h>
#include <errno.h>
#include <dlfcn.h>
#include <scha.h>
#include <rgm/libdsdev.h>

#define CMD_SIZE 256

int main(int argc, char *argv[])
{
scds_handle_t    scds_handle;
scha_err_t err_code;
scha_err_t hasp_check_p;
scha_extprop_value_t *cups_ext_prop;
scds_hasp_status_t hasp_status;
scds_net_resource_list_t *snrlp = NULL;
scds_port_list_t *portlist = NULL;
struct stat stat_buf;
char *start_cmd_prog[] = { "" };
int do_cmd_checks = 1;
char *start_cmd="/sbin/cupsd";
char cmd[CMD_SIZE];
```

After the method initializes the handle, one of the first checks done is to see if the cluster supports HAStoragePlus and an HAStoragePlus resource is in use. One of the checks in this method will be to verify if the CUPS commands are available. If there is a HAStoragePlus resource configured as a failover filesystem, then the method will not be able to verify if those commands are available because the filesystem is not available on the potential target node.

In Example 10.35, dlsym()(3DL) is used to verify that the cluster is capable of using HAStoragePlus. Earlier releases of Sun Cluster 3.0 did not have this capability below a certain patch level. If the cluster is not capable of HAStoragePlus, the method sets *hasp_status* as it has no HAStoragePlus resource configured. If the cluster is able to support HAStoragePlus, it calls scds_hasp_check()(3HA) to see what the configuration is for the HAStoragePlus resource. The method handles the outcome of this call with a case statement. Depending on what *hasp_status* is, the method will:

- Exit if there is a configuration error or the HAStoragePlus resource is not online.

- Skip checks if not all the resources are online locally. Set *do_cmd_checks* equal to 0.

- Perform checks if no HAStoragePlus resource is configured or all of the disks are available locally on the target node. Set *do_cmd_checks* equal to 1.

Example 10.35   CUPS validate—Initialize and check for HAStoragePlus

```
/* Process arguments passed by RGM and initialize
 * syslog. */
if (scds_initialize(&scds_handle, argc, argv) !=
        SCHA_ERR_NOERR) {
      scds_syslog(LOG_ERR, "Data Service handle failed to
         initialize!");
      return (1);
}
/* Are we running with a libdsdev that does not have
 * scds_hasp_check? */

hasp_check_p = (scha_err_t)dlsym(RTLD_DEFAULT,
   "scds_hasp_check");
if (hasp_check_p == NULL) {
   /* fake a call to scds_hasp_check() */
   err_code = SCHA_ERR_NOERR;
   hasp_status = SCDS_HASP_NO_RESOURCE;
} else {
   /* actually check for HAStoragePlus resources */
   err_code = scds_hasp_check(scds_handle, &hasp_status);
}
if (err_code != SCHA_ERR_NOERR) {
    /* scha_hasp_check() logs a message to syslog when it
     * fails */
    scds_syslog(LOG_ERR,"HAStoragePlus dependency
       problem! Error: %s",scds_error_string(err_code));
```

```
        scds_close(&scds_handle);
        return(err_code);
}
switch (hasp_status) {

    case SCDS_HASP_NO_RESOURCE:
    /* We do not depend on any HAStoragePlus resources. */

        scds_syslog(LOG_NOTICE, "This resource does not
            depend on any HAStoragePlus resources.
            Proceeding with normal checks.");
        do_cmd_checks = 1;
        break;

    case SCDS_HASP_ERR_CONFIG:
    /* Configuration error, HAStoragePlus resource is
     * in a different RG. */
        scds_syslog(LOG_ERR, "One or more of the
            HAStoragePlus resources that this resource
            depends on is in a different resource "
             "group.");
        err_code = 1;
        scds_close(&scds_handle);
        return(err_code);

    case SCDS_HASP_NOT_ONLINE:
    /* There is at least one HAStoragePlus resource not
     * online anywhere. */
        scds_syslog(LOG_ERR, "One or more of the
            HAStoragePlus resources that
            this resource depends on is not online
            anywhere.");
        err_code = 1;
        scds_close(&scds_handle);
        return(err_code);

    case SCDS_HASP_ONLINE_NOT_LOCAL:
    /* Not all HAStoragePlus we need, are online
     * locally. */
        scds_syslog(LOG_NOTICE, "All the HAStoragePlus
            resources that this resource depends on are not
            online on the local node. Skipping the checks
            for the existence and permissions "
            "of the start/stop/probe commands.");
        do_cmd_checks = 0;
         break;

    case SCDS_HASP_ONLINE_LOCAL:
    /* All HAStoragePlus resources we need are available
     * on this node. */
        scds_syslog(LOG_NOTICE, "All the HAStoragePlus
            resources that this resource depends on are
            online on the local node. "
```

```
                "Proceeding with the checks for the existence
                and permissions of the start/stop/probe
                commands.");
            do_cmd_checks = 1;
            break;

        default:
        /* Unknown status code */
            scds_syslog(LOG_ERR, "Unknown status code %d.",
                hasp_status);
            err_code = 1;
            scds_close(&scds_handle);
            return(err_code);
    }
```

In Example 10.36, *do_cmd_checks* is checked. If the value is set to 1, the method retrieves the CUPS_dir extension property, builds the path to the cupsd file, and then verifies that the file exists and is executable. If the value is set to 0, the cupsd file verification is bypassed, but the method continues to verify resource properties. The VALIDATE method will perform the following checks:

- Network Ports—For a network-aware resource, verifies that there is a network port defined by calling scds_get_port_list()(3HA). If *portlist* is NULL or *portlist->num_ports* is less than 1, *err_code* is set to 1.

- Network Resources—Verifies that there is at least one network resource available by calling scds_get_rs_hostnames()(3HA). If *snrlp* is NULL or *snrlp->num_netresources* is less than 1, *err_code* is set to 1.

Example 10.36 CUPS validate—Perform checks

```
        /* If do_cmd_checks is set to 1, it means that the
         * HAStorage resource is online on the local node.
         * Therefore, proceed with the checks for the
         * existence and permissions of the start commands.
         */
err_code = SCHA_ERR_NOERR; /* set err_code to 0. */
if( do_cmd_checks == 1 ) {
    err_code = scds_get_ext_property(scds_handle,
        "CUPS_dir", SCHA_PTYPE_STRINGARRAY,
        &cups_ext_prop);
    if( err_code != SCHA_ERR_NOERR ){
        scds_syslog(LOG_ERR,"Failed to get Config
            directory! Error: %s",
            scds_error_string(err_code));
        scds_close(&scds_handle);
        return(err_code);
    }
    strcpy(start_cmd_prog[0],cups_ext_prop-
        >val.val_strarray->str_array[0]);
    strcat(start_cmd_prog[0], start_cmd);
    strcpy(cmd, start_cmd_prog[0]);
```

```
    if(stat(cmd, &stat_buf) != 0) {
        scds_syslog(LOG_ERR,"Cannot access the %s command
            <%s> : <%s>","start", cmd, strerror(errno));
        err_code = 1;
    }
    if(!(stat_buf.st_mode & S_IXUSR)) {
        scds_syslog(LOG_ERR,"The %s command does not have
            execute permissions: <%s>", "start", cmd);
        err_code = 1;
    }
    scds_free_ext_property(cups_ext_prop);
} /* End of if for do_cmds_checks. */

/* Network aware service should have at least one port
 * specified. */

err_code = scds_get_port_list(scds_handle, &portlist);
if(err_code != SCHA_ERR_NOERR) {
    scds_syslog(LOG_ERR,"Failed to retrieve the resource
        property %s: %s.", SCHA_PORT_LIST,
        scds_error_string(err_code));
}
if(portlist == NULL || portlist->num_ports < 1) {
    scds_syslog(LOG_ERR, "Property %s is not set.",
        SCHA_PORT_LIST);
    err_code = 1;
}
/* Return an error if there is an error when trying to
 * get the available network address resources for this
 * resource. */
err_code = scds_get_rs_hostnames(scds_handle, &snrlp);
if(err_code != SCHA_ERR_NOERR) {
    scds_syslog(LOG_ERR,"Error in trying to access the
        configured network "  "resources : %s.",
        scds_error_string(err_code));
    err_code = 1;
}
/* Return an error if there are no network address
 * resources. */
if(snrlp == NULL || snrlp->num_netresources == 0) {
    scds_syslog(LOG_ERR, "No network address resource in
        resource group.");
    err_code = 1;
}

scds_free_net_list(snrlp);
scds_free_port_list(portlist);

/* Free up all the memory allocated by scds_initialize */
(void) scds_close(&scds_handle);

/* Return the result of the validate method */
return(err_code);
}
```

After the checks have been performed, *snrlp* and *portlist* structures need to be freed. The function calls `scds_free_net_list()`(3HA) and `scds_free_port_ list()`(3HA) are called to free those structures. The method then frees the handle using `scds_close()`(3HA) and then returns *err_code*.

CUPS UPDATE Method

This method is responsible for making sure that resource property changes that are made with the `scrgadm -c` command are implemented. Once the changes have been validated by the `VALIDATE` method, `UPDATE` takes the steps necessary, such as restarting the monitor to ensure the changes have taken effect. This method will also need to be idempotent. See "Idempotency" in Chapter 6.

For the CUPS resource type, the `UPDATE` method will be responsible for just restarting the probe as shown in Example 10.37. Once the method initializes the handle, a status check is done to see if there is a valid PMF tag for the monitor using `scds_pmf_status()`(3HA). If there is no valid PMF tag, the method sends a message to syslog that the monitor is not running and then returns a value of 0. This is to support the method's idempotency requirement.

If there is a valid PMF tag, `scds_pmf_restart_fm()`(3HA) is called to send a SIGKILL to the monitor and then restart the monitor. After the monitor is restarted, the method frees the handle with the scds_close() call and then returns successful with a value of 0. If the restart fails, a message is logged to syslog, closes the handle, and then returns the *err_code* value.

Example 10.37   CUPS update method

```
/* cups_update.c - Update method for cups. */
#include <stdio.h>
#include <stdlib.h>
#include <signal.h>
#include <rgm/libdsdev.h>

/* Some of the resource properties might have been
 * updated. All such updatable properties are related to
 * the fault monitor. Hence, just restarting the monitor
 * should be enough. */

int main(int argc, char *argv[])
{
scds_handle_t    scds_handle;
scha_err_terr_code;
intinstance=0; /* set fault monitor instance to 0.*/
scds_pmf_status_t pmf_status;

/* Process the arguments passed by RGM and initialize
 * syslog */
if(scds_initialize(&scds_handle, argc, argv) != SCHA_ERR_NOERR) {
    scds_syslog(LOG_ERR, "Data Service handle failed to
        initialize!");
    return (1);
}
```

```
/* Check the monitor to see if its running. If not exit.
 */
err_code = scds_pmf_get_status(scds_handle,
     SCDS_PMF_TYPE_MON,instance, &pmf_status);
if( err_code != SCHA_ERR_NOERR ){
    scds_syslog(LOG_ERR,"Failed to get Monitor Status!
        Error: %s",scha_strerror(err_code));
    scds_close(&scds_handle);
    return(err_code);
}
if(pmf_status != SCDS_PMF_MONITORED ){
    scds_syslog(LOG_NOTICE,"Service is not being
        monitored.");
    scds_close(&scds_handle);
    return(0);
}

/* The Fault monitor is already running and if
 * so stop and restart it. The second parameter to
 * scds_pmf_restart_fm() uniquely identifies the instance
 * of the fault monitor that needs to be restarted. */

err_code = scds_pmf_restart_fm(scds_handle, instance);
if(err_code != SCHA_ERR_NOERR) {
    scds_syslog(LOG_ERR,"Failed to restart fault monitor!
        Error: %s",scha_strerror(err_code));
    scds_close(&scds_handle);
    return(err_code);
}
scds_syslog(LOG_INFO, "CUPS Update Completed
    successfully.");

/* Free up all the memory allocated by scds_initialize */
scds_close(&scds_handle);
return (0);
}
```

CUPS MONITOR_CHECK Method

The MONITOR_CHECK method is called when there is a request to fail the resource group over to another node within the cluster. This method will run on the target node to see if it's capable of becoming the primary for the resource. In verifying that the node is capable of running the resource, the following checks should be performed:

- Verify that the application binary is available and executable.
- Verify that network resources are available.
- Verify that network ports have been assigned.

If you recall what the VALIDATE method performs in the section "CUPS VALI-DATE Method," these same checks are needed for the MONITOR_CHECK method. The difference between these methods is that in VALIDATE, each node listed in the resource types *Init_node* property runs that method. In contrast, the MONITOR_ CHECK method is run only on the targeted primary node.

The MONITOR_CHECK method will still need to check if HAStoragePlus is involved. If it is, checking for application binaries will not be possible when a failover filesystem is used. Checks for network resources and network ports will need to be done, as the CUPS resource type is a network-aware resource type. So, using the VALIDATE method's source for the MONITOR_CHECK method will save development time. If there needs to be other checks added or deleted to either of these methods, they can be done independently.

Deploying the Agent

Once the resource type has been developed, it needs to be deployed in the Sun Cluster environment. This involves installing the resource type on all nodes within the cluster, registering the resource type with the Sun Cluster framework, and creating a resource using this resource type within a resource group.

Once the resource has been created, the resource should be able to be managed by the RGM and brought online. The resource should be able to fail over to another node and also to be brought offline successfully.

To Package Add or Not

For the Sun Cluster environment to use the newly created resource type, the files will need to be installed on all the nodes within the cluster and then registered with the cluster framework. The choices for installing the resource type are either to create the directory manually and then add the files to that directory or to use the SOE packaging system.

Adding files manually will require that the files be copied to the same directory path on each node within the cluster. The directory that will hold the resource type files will need to register the resource type with the scrgadm(1HA) command.

Using the packaging system makes it easier to install, get revision information, and remove the resource type on the nodes within the cluster. This makes it easier to administer, particularly if you need to update the resource type. If you need to deploy this resource type in multiple configurations or have other customers use it, employing the packaging utilities would be the way to go.

If the scdscreate and scdsconfig commands were used to create the resource type templates, you will be able to install the resource type on the nodes in the cluster with the pkgadd(1M) utility. When the resource type was created with the scds-create command, all the work was done for you in creating the files necessary for the packaging utilities because using make(1S) with the *pkg* argument adds the completed resource type templates to the package directory structure.

> **Note** – Be aware that if you chose to use the scdscreate command to create the templates and then completed the templates manually without the use of the scdsconfig command, you will need to modify the Makefile for the make *pkg* to work correctly. You will need to add the directory path to the parameter WORKING_DIR=. This parameter by default is not set. It should be set to the directory path that was given to the scdscreate command or the directory path from which this command was run if no path was specified.

If additional files were added to the resource type outside of the templates that were created, the information on these files will need to be added to the packaging files so they are correctly packaged when the make command is run with the *pkg* argument. For more information on the SOE's packaging utilities, please refer to the Solaris man pages and the Application Packaging Developer's Guide in the Solaris Software Developer's Collection.

Registering the Resource Type

To use the newly created resource type, you will need to register the resource type with the Sun Cluster framework. Once the files have been installed on each node in the cluster, the resource type is registered with the scrgadm(1HA) command. Use of this command is only done once on one node. Once the command is completed successfully, the resource type will be registered with the cluster.

If you recall, in "scdscreate (1HA)" earlier in this chapter, creating the templates required a vendor argument and a type argument. For example, the CUPS resource type was created with BOOK as the vendor name and CUPS for the type name. The packaging utilities created a package named BOOKcups and this was used by the pkgadd utility to install the agent on the nodes in the cluster. This naming convention is used in registering the resource type with the Sun Cluster framework. One difference is that a dot is used to separate the vendor name and the type name, that is, *vendor_name.type_name*. So for registering the book example for the CUPS resource type it would be in the form *BOOK.cups*.

> **Note** – Added to Sun Cluster 3.1 is the ability for versioning of resource types. The version number can be added during the registration of the resource type in the form of *vendor_name.type_name:version*. So for version 2.0 of the CUPS resource type, the form would be *BOOK.cups:2.0*.

Since the MySQL and CUPS resource types were created using the scdscreate command and installed using the pkgadd command, the templates and the RTR file have been installed in a well-known path. This means the packaging utilities installed the package in the /opt directory path and the packaging post utilities also placed the RTR file in a directory location that the cluster framework will look for by default when registering these resource types. This directory for the RTR files is located at /usr/cluster/lib/rgm/rtreg.

To register the MySQL resource type:

scrgadm -a -t *BOOK.mysql_ksh*

Registering the CUPS resource type:

scrgadm -a -t *BOOK.cups*

This will register the resource type with each node in the cluster. One can specify particular node(s) to register the resource type using the -h argument. A comma-separated list of node names with this argument will only register the resource type on those nodes specified. This can be useful in larger clusters where only certain resources will run on a defined set of nodes within the cluster. An example of this might be a four-node cluster that only wants Oracle highly available on two nodes while a highly available application server is only available on two other nodes on which Oracle will not run.

If the installation of the resource type was done by copying the files to a manually created directory, the RTR file will need to be placed in the /usr/cluster/lib/rgm/rtreg directory so during registration the cluster framework will be able to find it. The RTR file will need to be of the same name as that of the resource type. Another option would be to use the -f argument to specify the directory path where the RTR file is located. So, for example, to register the *foobar* resource type using the path argument to specify that the RTR file is in the directory /foobar/etc and only have it registered on nodeA and nodeC in a three-node cluster would look like:

scrgadm -a -t *BOOK.foobar* **-h** *nodeA,nodeC* **-f** /foobar/etc

In this cluster, nodeB will not have the resource type BOOK.foobar registered. When creating a resource using this resource type, the resource group that will contain this resource will not be able to run on nodeB. So while creating this resource group, nodeB should not be listed as a host that can become a primary for this resource group. This will be discussed in more detail in the next section.

Creating the Resource

If you recall from "Resource Anatomy" in Chapter 2, resources are created from resource types and are contained in a resource group. To create a resource from a resource type, first the resource group must exist. Depending on the applications, multiple resources created may or may not be contained in the same resource group. For instance, the CUPS application has no relationship with the MySQL database, so grouping these two applications together in the same resource group would not make much sense. So for each example application, there should be a separate resource group. The cluster that is available for these applications is a three-node cluster. Configuration will be such that one of the nodes is a failover node, that is, an N + 1 configuration. The resource groups will be configured such that they can run on separate nodes; node A being a primary for the MySQL application and node B being a primary for the CUPS application. The +1 node will be the failover node; for both applications, node C.

When creating the resource group for the MySQL application, a logical host and a list of hosts that the resource group will be primaried on will be needed. For the MySQL resource, the extension and port number properties from Table 10.1 will be needed.

To create the resource group for MySQL:

 # scrgadm -a -g *mysql-rg* **-h** A,C

- Adds the logical host *dbserver*. This host should be listed in the /etc/hosts file on each node in the cluster.

    # scrgadm -a -L -g *mysql-rg* **-l** *dbserver*

- Creates the resource mysql-r in the resource group mysql-rg

    # scrgadm -a -j *mysql-r* **-g** *mysql-rg* **-y** *Port_list=3000/tcp*
    -x *MYSQL_HOME=/usr/local/mysql* **-x** *MYSQL_MYSQLD=/bin/mysqld*
    -x *MYSQL_DATA_DIR=/global/mysql/datadir* **-x** *MYSQL_DBA_USER=*
    "login/password" **-x** *MYSQL_CNF_FILE=/global/mysql/mysqltest.cnf*

Using the extension properties defined for the resource type and the Port_list property, the *mysql-r* resource is created in the *mysql-rg* resource group. While the naming convention is up to the user, using -r for resources and -rg for resource groups can distinguish between resource and resource group names.

The CUPS application will run on nodes B and C with node B being the primary node and node C the failover node. Using the information in Table 10.2, "CUPS Properties," we can create the resource group and CUPS resource. The hostname for this logical host will be the uniquely original name of *printserver*.

To create the resource group for CUPS:

 # scrgadm -a -g *cups-rg* **-h** B,C

- Adds the logical host *printserver*. The logical host should be listed in the /etc/hosts file on each node in the cluster.

 # scrgadm -a -L -g *cups-rg* **-l** *printserver*

- Creates the resource cups-r in the resource group cups-rg

 # scrgadm -a -j *cups-r* **-g** *cups-rg* **-y** *Port_list=80/tcp*
-x *CUPS_dir=/global/cups* **-x** *Conf_file=/global/cups/etc/cups/*
cupsd.conf

With the resources now defined in their resource groups, it's time to have the cluster environment manage and bring the application online.

Managing the Resource

Once the resource has been created successfully, it is in an unmanaged state. You will need to manage the resource group and bring the resources within that resource group online through the scswitch(1HA) command with the -z argument.

To bring the MySQL resource *mysql-r* online within the *mysql-rg* resource group:

scswitch -z -g *mysql-rg*

To bring the CUPS resource *cups-r* online within the *cups-rg* resource group:

scswitch -z -g *cups-rg*

Once scswitch completes, you can check the status of the resource groups and resources using the scstat(1HA) command with the -g argument.

Summary

This chapter has taken topics covered in previous chapters and put them together to create resource types that will allow the Sun Cluster environment to provide a highly available service for the MySQL database application and CUPS application. Newly created resource types, once registered, can create resources within a resource group that can start, monitor, and stop it or, if necessary, restart or fail over the application to another node in the cluster successfully. It should also be able to handle possible abnormal conditions such as failure to start or stop, slow starts, and stops due to loading conditions or recovery operations.

11

WRITING SCALABLE
SERVICES

The Sun Cluster 3 release introduced the facility to run multiple instances of the same application on multiple nodes of a cluster using the same set of data and the same network address, regardless of the physical node on which an instance is run. In the Sun Cluster 3 environment, an application deployed in this manner is called a *scalable service*, since the number of instances can be "scaled" dynamically from one to many and back again, without bringing the entire service offline at any point. Up until now, this book has covered the other type of data service available on the Sun Cluster platform: the *failover service*. As we've seen, a failover service has only one instance of an application active in the cluster at any given time. If the node on which the application is active fails, then the application is started on a new node. In contrast, a scalable service has instances of an application active on multiple nodes at the same time, as depicted in Figure 11.1.

One of the useful features of a scalable service is that instances of the application can be started on additional nodes at any time, usually to provide extra capacity to clients accessing the cluster. Similarly, instances of the application can be stopped on any of the nodes at any time, which allows system resources to be allocated to different tasks, if required. When instances are stopped, clients accessing a scalable service are automatically redirected by the cluster framework to use the reduced set of active nodes for that service.

When client systems try to access a scalable service via a shared network address, a load-balancing policy is consulted to determine which physical node actually receives the service request. The load-balancing policy can be adjusted by the administrator by applying a weighting to each of the nodes on a per-service basis (by IP address, protocol type, and port number). It is also possible to require clients to reconnect to the same physical node on subsequent requests, which may be necessary for certain applications.

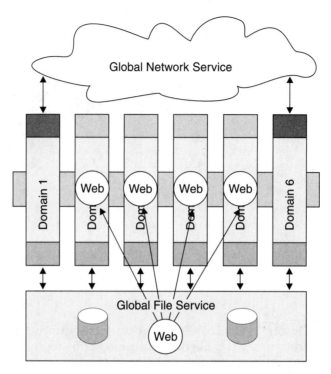

Figure 11.1 Scalable services run on multiple nodes simultaneously

Benefits of Scalable Services

There are several reasons why you might want to use a scalable service in the Sun Cluster 3 environment. The most obvious is to increase the overall capacity of the system to respond to requests, but scalable services can also be used to improve the speed of recovery from a failure.

Increase Capacity

Certain applications are designed in such a way that additional capacity can be achieved simply by increasing the number of computers running the service, a technique often called *horizontal scaling*. This technique is particularly important when the application is single-threaded and hence cannot easily take full advantage of the scalability of a single symmetric multiprocessor (SMP) system.

Scalable services provide a reasonably easy way to manage the deployment of a horizontally scaled application, while using the same set of data and IP services. Since new instances of a scalable service can be started on any available nodes in the cluster on the fly, additional capacity can be added quickly when it's needed.

Availability and Fast Failure Recovery

As previously mentioned, the other type of data service in the Sun Cluster environment is a failover service. This type of service comprises an active node and at least one standby node. If the active node fails, one (and only one) of the standby nodes starts a new copy of the application and accesses the data as it was when the failure occurred. In some cases, this can require integrity checks of the data, which can take a few minutes or up to several hours, depending on the nature of the application and the problem that caused the failover. In any case, there is a period between when the active node fails and the standby node is ready to respond to requests during which the service is not available to client systems.

Since a scalable service has multiple instances of an application running simultaneously, accessing the same data, the failure of one node may not necessarily affect the other active nodes. So there should be no period when the service is not available for new client connections. It is worth noting, however, that in this situation any sessions that have already been established with the failed node will be lost, and the client system must reconnect and possibly reissue transactions. However, client systems should be able to immediately connect to a different cluster node, rather than having to wait for the consistency check to complete. Furthermore, since client connections are spread among the active nodes, the failure of one node should have a lower impact on the total population of clients, meaning that overall availability of the application service should be improved.

Comparing Scalable Services to Other Distributed Service Mechanisms

Many Internet applications, such as DNS and Internet relay chat (IRC), already have a distributed mechanism that helps them to scale and resist single points of failure. A fair question may be: "Why not use this distributed approach instead of the Sun Cluster 3 software?"

Although Sun Cluster is not intended to be a complete replacement for this sort of distributed architecture, using scalable services can offer an improvement in response times under certain situations. As an example, consider the case of a DNS server and a backup on a given network, with addresses `129.158.178.10` and `129.158.178.20`. The `/etc/resolv.conf` file for a client on the network would read:

```
nameserver 129.158.178.10
nameserver 129.158.178.20
```

Any name lookup would first try 129.158.178.10, and then try 129.158.178.20 after a (possibly lengthy) timeout. If, instead, the DNS servers used a scalable service with a single IP address (for example, 129.158.178.11), then as long as one of the servers was active, the client would get a response immediately, without having to wait for a timeout. Obviously, this example does not address the problems of disaster recovery from site failure, but it does illustrate how a scalable service can overcome the timeout problems associated with server failures in some distributed services.

Scalable services can also offer a more effective solution than using round-robin DNS for load balancing where a given hostname (for example, www.foo.org) resolves to multiple IP addresses (for example, 129.158.178.101, 129.158.178.102, and 129.158.178.103). When the first client tries to connect to www.foo.org, it is directed to 129.158.178.101. The second client is directed to 129.158.178.102, the third to 129.158.178.103, the fourth to 129.158.178.101 again, and so on. The problem with this approach is that the server to be accessed is determined at the time that the hostname is resolved, and the name server usually has no knowledge of the state of that host or the applications running on it. Using a scalable service within the Sun Cluster framework, the node that will eventually receive the request has already been determined by the framework to be active and running the service in question, and so every request should get a response so long as at least one instance of the application is available on the cluster.

In general, Sun Cluster scalable services can be used as a manageable method for distributing applications for scalability and availability. The Sun Cluster framework provides a number of features that are vital for the development of scalable services. Most of these features can be used by applications without any specific coding being necessary to take advantage of them, so they can be used to make some normal single-node applications into scalable services.

Parallel Databases

The parallel databases that can be run in the Sun Cluster environment, namely Oracle Parallel Server (OPS), Oracle 9i Real Application Cluster (RAC), and IBM DB2 Extended Enterprise Edition (EEE) are actually special cases of scalable services. The loose definition of a scalable service in the context of Sun Cluster systems is a service that runs simultaneously on more than one node. It should be noted, however, that parallel databases typically involve a complex and intimate understanding of the Sun Cluster framework and they do not use the standard framework for scalable applications as discussed in this chapter.

Non-Networked Scalable Services

Although the most obvious uses for scalable services are for applications accessible via a shared IP address of the cluster, there may be cases where an application needs to run simultaneously on multiple nodes, but does not need to access the public network. There is nothing to stop this use of the Sun Cluster framework, although you should probably consider whether a high performance computing (HPC) or grid computing environment might be more appropriate (see "Example Cluster Applications," in Chapter 1).

Sun Cluster Facilities for Scalable Services

It is important to understand what facilities are (and are not) provided by the Sun Cluster 3 software that enable the development of scalable services. Effective use of these facilities can help reduce the effort required to make an application into a scalable service.

Resources and the RGM

As we saw in Chapter 6, the interaction between applications and the Sun Cluster framework is managed by the resource group manager (RGM), and each resource has a corresponding resource type. A resource type can be thought of as a template for resources, defining all of the properties of the resource, and some of these properties indicate whether resources of that type can be a scalable or failover service. See Table 11.1.

In order for a scalable resource to run on multiple nodes, the resource group containing the resource must have an *RG_mode* property of "Scalable." This indicates

Table 11.1 Property Meanings

Property	Location	Meaning
Failover (Boolean)	Resource type	If this resource type property is set to True, then resources of this type cannot be online on multiple nodes at once, which in effect means they cannot be scalable services.
Scalable (Boolean)	Resource	This is a resource property (not resource type), but if it is declared (and defined as True) in the RTR file, then resources of this type will be scalable services by default. Furthermore, the RGM will automatically add the network_resources_used, port_list, load_balancing_policy, and load_balancing_weights properties to any new resources of this type, assigning the default values (either the system defaults, or the values defined in the RTR file).
RG_mode (enum)	Resource group	This indicates whether the resource group can be online on multiple nodes simultaneously. If RG_MODE is set to "Scalable," then the resource group can be used for scalable services.
Maximum_Primaries	Resource group	This defines the maximum number of nodes on which the resource group can be online at any given moment. It is essentially the limit of scalability for any scalable services in the group.

that the resource group is able to run on multiple nodes simultaneously. The *maximum_primaries* resource group property defines how many nodes can have the resource group online at the same time.

Global Devices

As we saw in Chapter 2, the Sun Cluster 3 framework includes the ability to access global devices using the same path from any node in the cluster. For example, a global disk device `/dev/global/rdsk/d5` will always point to the same disk, even if the physical path to the device is not the same on different nodes. This facility is very useful in scalable application, as it means that a common path can be used for any instance of an application, regardless of the node on which it is currently running.

Even though global devices may be directly accessed by applications, such access requires careful coordination between applications trying to use the same device because there is no built-in facility within the Sun Cluster framework for user-level applications to manage this coordination. For example, locks applied to global devices are not propagated across the cluster to other nodes. As a result, the application itself must maintain information about which parts of a global device are locked and which are not, and this information should be carried across application failures, cluster reconfigurations, and system reboots.

Although not an impossible task, keeping track of locks on global devices is sufficiently difficult that most scalable services usually use the global file service to provide access to common data (see Figure 11.2).

Global File Service

The global file service (GFS) allows data to be accessible to all nodes of the cluster using the same access path.

The GFS is also sometimes called the cluster file system, although it is not a filesystem in its own right, but rather a technology on which to allow normal file-

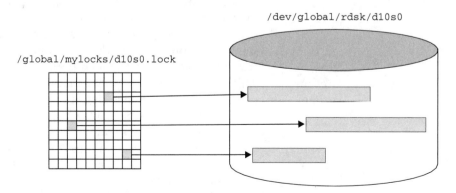

Figure 11.2 Using a lockfile to handle global device locking

systems to be mounted simultaneously and also accessible from all nodes of a cluster for reading and writing. A filesystem is mounted globally by using the -g option to mount (1M) or the "global" option in vfstab. Since the filesystem is mounted on the same path on each node (for example, /global/foo), access to the data from applications is consistent throughout the cluster.

The GFS is also sometimes referred to as the proxy filesystem (PXFS) because the operations on the filesystem are proxied from the client node to the server node—the node directly attached to the storage device. This detail is important for certain disk-intensive applications, since there can be a performance improvement in locating an application instance on the server node of the file services. This is due to the fact that filesystem operations on the GFS are conducted as two-phase-commit transactions as the difference in latency between performing the transaction over the cluster interconnect, rather than within the same node, can be quite noticeable. This is particularly true of append operations, in which new space must first be allocated for data before it is written (requiring another set of transactions).

Regular IO operations (fopen, fclose, write, seek, and so forth) work on a GFS as per normal filesystem semantics, regardless of which node they are performed on. File locking using fcntl(2) also works as expected, even across nodes. This mechanism can be used to provide the functionality of a distributed lock manager (DLM). In fact, the problem of locking global raw devices can be approached by using lockfiles on a global filesystem, where small segments (say, one byte) of a lockfile represent large segments of a global raw device, as illustrated in Figure 11.2. It should be noted, however, that doors and pipes cannot be used for interprocess communication (IPC) across nodes by using the GFS.

To provide a POSIX-compliant environment for write operations, the filesystem should be mounted with the "syncdir" option. This can, however, negatively impact performance. Without the "syncdir" option, the GFS could return ENOSPC errors from close(2) under certain failure conditions; which is the same behavior that is seen in NFS.

In a standard Sun Cluster configuration, the storage device(s) used in a GFS should be hosted by at least two nodes to allow a level of redundancy to the filesystem. Metadata from transactions on the GFS are logged from the server node to the backup host of the filesystem and use a two-phase-commit model to help ensure that every operation completes properly. In the event of a failure of the server node, the backup host acquires ownership of the disk storage and replays its log of transactions, completing those that were in progress at the time of failure. The result is that applications on the other nodes should not have to specifically deal with the failover of the filesystem from one host node to another. However, they may notice a longer than normal delay in operations while the failover is in progress.

Global Networking

Global networking allows a single IP address to be shared by all nodes of the cluster, allowing the cluster to be seen as a single entity on the network. An IP packet sent to a shared IP address is read from the network by only one node: the global interface node (GIN). The global interface (GIF) is the network interface on which the shared address is physically hosted. The GIN is the host on which the GIF currently resides. This node examines the packet and determines which node in the cluster should receive it, depending on the protocol (TCP or UDP), network port, and load-balancing policies that have been applied to the scalable service associated with that address. The packet is then forwarded via the private interconnect to the instance of the scalable service on the appropriate node, which in turn responds to the request via one of its local public network adapters.

Global networking is the mechanism that allows instances of an application on multiple nodes to provide the same service. Applications must therefore be bound to a shared IP address in order to provide a scalable service to the network. Figure 11.3 illustrates how global networking operates, with one node accepting an incoming request, and then forwarding it on to the appropriate node, which then responds directly.

Note that in the diagram node C is acting as the GIN, and yet it does not actually run an instance of the scalable application. This is perfectly legal and achievable because each scalable service actually comprises *two* resource groups. The shared address resource is itself actually a *failover* resource (not a scalable resource), since at any one moment only one node will be the GIN and accept packets from the network. The nodes that are members of the shared address failover resource group are potential GINs. If the GIN fails on the first node, another node in the resource group can take over automatically (see Figure 11.4).

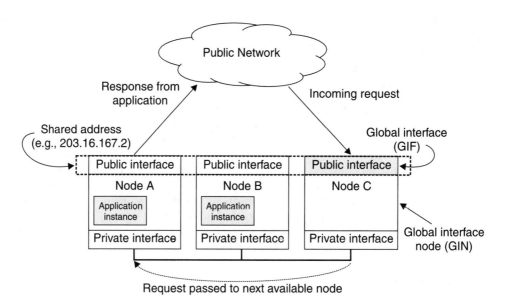

Figure 11.3 Global networking in operation

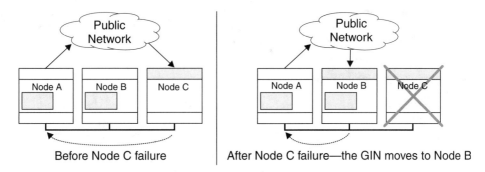

Figure 11.4 GIN failover

Meanwhile, the scalable service application resides in a separate scalable resource group (one that has the RG_mode property set to "Scalable"). The nodes that are members of the scalable resource group are potential hosts for the application. Obviously, it is sensible for the set of application hosts to intersect the set of potential GINs, but there is no strict requirement for this in the Sun Cluster framework. In any case, the decision about how to deploy scalable services is usually a choice for the systems administrator and shouldn't affect how you develop a resource type.

Public Network Management

Although it doesn't provide a service specific to scalable services, public network management (PNM) provides high availability to global IP addresses. The PNM software monitors the network adapters and will fail over an IP address from one adapter to another in the same group if it detects a failure.

PNM is designed to be transparent to applications: A developer does not need to take them into account when determining which IP address to which to bind a service. In Sun Cluster 3.0, PNM is implemented using Network Adapter FailOver (NAFO)—specific to and only available in Sun Cluster. From Sun Cluster 3.1, PNM is implemented using the standard IP Network Multipathing (IPMP) found as part of Solaris.[1] IPMP and NAFO perform the same tasks in slightly different ways; they cannot be used together.

Dependencies

Many applications have dependencies upon external applications, such as databases. The Sun Cluster framework allows administrators to configure these relationships between applications, such that a scalable service "X" will not start until resource "Y" has successfully started.

---

1. IPMP was introduced in Solaris 8, 10/00.

Dependencies work the same way for scalable services as for failover services. When considering how to handle dependencies, remember that all the resources in a scalable resource group must be scalable resources.

Weighted Load Balancing

When a scalable service resource is created on a cluster, the default load balancing for the service is an evenly distributed policy. This means that if there are three nodes on which the service is running, all three nodes will be given the same number of requests over time.

In some circumstances this even distribution among nodes is not desirable: for example, if one node is much more powerful than the others. It is possible for the administrator to alter the distribution of requests by applying shares of weightings to each node when defining a service. For example, a scalable resource created using:

```
scrgadm-a -j myRes -g myRG -t myRT \
    -y scalable=true \
    -y network_resource_used=mySA \
    -y port_list=1800/tcp \
    -y load_balancing_property=LB_WEIGHTED \
    -y load_balancing_weights=1@1,3@2,6@3
```

defines a scalable resource ("myRes"), which will receive 10 percent of requests on node 1, 30 percent of requests on node 2, and 60 percent of requests on node 3. Note that the weighting balance is affected by the *total number* of weights assigned in the system. In the previous example, there are a total of 10 weights assigned. If a fourth node were added to the scalable service, with a weight of 10, the total number of weights in the service would be 20, and the distribution of requests would be affected accordingly: node 1 would receive 1/20 or 5 percent of requests, node 2 would get 3/20 or 15 percent, node 3 would get 6/20 or 30 percent, and node 4 would receive 10/20 or 50 percent. It is also possible to assign a weight of 0 (zero) to a node, which effectively stops the node from receiving any requests for that service, even though the application is still running on that node.

It's probably easiest to think of this load balancing in terms of "shares" rather than absolute percentages, since it is then easier to understand the effect on load balancing when nodes join or leave the cluster. Table 11.2 shows the effects of the weighting scheme before and after adding the fourth node.

These weightings can be modified at any time, even while the service is in operation, by using the scrgadm(1M) command to change the *load_balancing_weights* value. This is true even if no weightings were explicitly set when the resource was originally created.

Sticky Load Balancing

For some services, the behavior of the application precludes the use of the load balancing algorithm used for scalable services, even with weighting. One example is

Table 11.2 Effects of Cluster Membership on Load Balancing

Node	Weighting before adding 4th node	Load before adding 4th node	Weighting after adding 4th node	Load after adding 4th node
1	1	10%	1	5%
2	3	30%	3	15%
3	6	60%	6	30%
4	0	0	10	50%

where a client connection makes use of some in-memory cache on the server. Under normal load balancing, subsequent client connections may be directed to different nodes, losing the benefit of the cache. In this case, a sticky load balancing policy can be used to ensure that all client requests to a service from the same IP address are sent to the same node (assuming the service is available on that node).

A good example of this is the HTTP over SSL (https) service. Establishing the secure connection is more resource-intensive than simply using the connection, so sticky load balancing can be used to ensure that a client keeps using the same node for as long as it is available, and so reduce the amount of work needed to run an https service.

Wildcard Sticky

Some network services listen on a network port for incoming requests, and then establish a new server on a different (random) port for each client to connect to. An example of this type of service is a passive-mode FTP server. The problem is illustrated in Figure 11.5. In this case the client's initial connection to the main service port 8000 is routed to node A. This service then establishes a subserver at port 8081, and informs the client to reconnect to that port. Without a mechanism such as wildcard sticky load balancing, the subsequent connection from the client may be sent to node B, which has no server waiting on port 8081, and the connection therefore fails.

The problem with this method in a scalable service is that the next connection by the client may not be sent to the same node that started the new server. In this case, the load balancing property of the scalable resource must be configured by the administrator as wildcard sticky, which will require all connections from a given IP address to be forwarded to the same cluster node, regardless of which IP port to which the request is sent. Obviously, this can upset the load balancing used by other services requested by the same client—the deployment of services requiring wildcard sticky load balancing should be planned carefully.

Scalable service resource types that require their load balancing properties to be sticky or wildcard sticky should have these properties set in the RTR file when you create the agent. Load balancing properties are discussed in the Sun Cluster 3.0 Concepts Guide and the scrgadm(1M) man page.

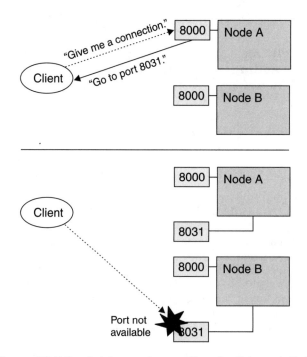

Figure 11.5 Scalable services without wildcard sticky

Developer Responsibilities

Some applications are more easily made into scalable services than others. When creating an application that is to be used as a scalable service, you should consider a number of factors. In Chapter 4, "Planning for Development," we saw that an application using the Sun Cluster framework to become highly available must have certain qualities to be successfully integrated. To recap, these qualities are:

- Data service access
- Crash tolerance
- Bounded recovery time after crash
- File location independence
- Absence of a tie to the physical identity of the node
- Ability to work on multi-homed hosts
- Ability to work with logical interfaces
- Client recovery

In addition to these qualities, a scalable application, whether cluster aware or not, must have extra qualities to be successfully integrated into the Sun Cluster environment. These are to:

- have the ability to run multiple instances, all operating on the same application data,
- provide application-level data consistency for simultaneous access from multiple nodes, and
- be able to maintain session state across nodes.

Applications with the above three qualities may be good candidates for becoming scalable services. Applications not demonstrating all of these qualities may need to be modified at the source level before they can be used as scalable services.

Multiple Instances

A scalable data service has multiple instances of an application running at the same time and using the same set of data. The application itself should be capable of doing this but shouldn't, for example, require exclusive access to a particular file or device by any one instance. One easy way to check if an application is able to cope with multiple instances is to see if the application can be run multiple times on one node—if so, then there's a good chance it will work across multiple nodes.

Data-Level Consistency

Hand in hand with the concept of multiple-instance access is the concept of data consistency. Since the multiple instances will be accessing the same set of data, it is important for that data to be read, and more importantly *written,* in a consistent fashion. In practice, what this usually means is that some sort of locking should be used whenever the application reads or writes data.

This is not as difficult as it might first seem. Since the GFS handles all of the normal UNIX file-locking semantics, you can simply use fcntl(2) to lock files or records in your data and those locks will be honored across the entire cluster (see "Global File Service" earlier in this chapter).

Session State

In a scalable service each connection from a client can potentially go to a different node in the cluster unless some sort of sticky load balancing is used (see "Sticky Load Balancing" earlier in this chapter). This means that if session state must persist between connections from the client, and more importantly across failover, there must be some way of migrating or at least recovering that client's state from another node.

In practice, this means that the applications most easily made into scalable services are those using a sessionless client-server model, such as the http daemon. In this case, each request to the system is a discrete entity and no state is retained on the servers. Session failure is not usually a problem in this environment, since the request can be retried without affecting the system state.

Applications that require the maintenance of state must provide some way of making the state highly available. The simplest way is to write the state to the global filesystem between transactions, so that any node can access the data. Depending on the application in question, more complex techniques must be used, for example, for remote procedure calls or shared-memory message passing. At this point, there is no generic way of handling persistent state for applications that are not cluster aware.

Cluster Awareness

Applications run in a cluster environment can be classified into one of two types: cluster aware and non-cluster aware. Cluster-aware applications include code specifically designed to work in a cluster environment and which can actively acquire and use information about the cluster itself during operation. An example of a cluster-aware scalable service is the Oracle RAC, in which all database instances can communicate with each other to improve performance. Some cluster-aware applications may not need to have an associated resource type, but unless a resource type exists for an application it cannot be controlled by the Sun Cluster framework.

Any application that does not fit into the cluster-aware category is non-cluster aware. In this case, the application performs the same way in a clustered environment as it does in a nonclustered environment. An example of a non-cluster-aware scalable service is the Apache scalable dataservice. Non-cluster-aware applications require a resource type to be created for integration into the Sun Cluster framework.

Developing a New Application to Be Scalable

Sessionless Services

A sessionless data service maintains no state in memory between client connections and has no reference to past or other current connections. There is no interaction between sessions, either on the same node or other nodes in the cluster. If a client fails to connect to such a service, or if an error occurs partway, the client can usually reconnect and retry the operation and achieve the correct result. One example of a sessionless data service is an http server.

For sessionless services, the common point of reference within the cluster is the GFS. Since all nodes access the GFS using the same path, data can be shared between nodes and application instances in this manner. Since any node is able to read and write the same files, file locking should be used to ensure that consistency is achieved. File locking can be applied in exactly the same way as a single-node application, with the exception that the process ID information in the flock structure returned by `fcntl(2)` is not necessarily correct for any given node. For example, if process 2345 on node 1 locks a file, the process ID returned in the flock structure for that lock will be 2345, regardless of the node reading the lock information.

Implementing a Sessionless Scalable Service

Sessionless data services are usually the easiest applications to make scalable within a cluster. In fact, making a sessionless service scalable may not require any changes to the program itself, but merely a resource type to provide a plug into the Sun Cluster framework.

The steps needed to implement a resource type for an application are detailed in the Sun Cluster 3.0 Data Service Developer's Guide, but are outlined briefly below:

1. Implement the START and STOP methods for the application. This could be as simple as a shell script like those found in /etc/init.d.
2. Create an RTR file to define the START and STOP methods, and set the "Scalable" property to "True."
3. Add the new resource type to the cluster using scrgadm(1M).
4. Create a shared address resource that runs on the nodes you want to use for the scalable service using scrgadm(1M).
5. Create a scalable resource group to contain the scalable service using scrgadm(1M).
6. Create an instance of the new resource type using scrgadm(1M), specifying the shared address resource as the hostname.
7. Start the shared address resource using scswitch(1M).
8. Start the scalable service resource using scswitch(1M).

These steps can be quickly and easily achieved using the SunPlex Agent Builder (see Chapter 5, "Developing with the SunPlex Agent Builder").

Applications Using Internode Communication

Some applications require communication between nodes to effectively scale, notably those applications with an extended session in which communication between clients is required. One example of this may be a chat server, which must be able to pass messages to clients connected to other nodes as well as to the local node. This sort of application is always cluster aware, as it must be able to determine which other nodes are running instances of the application and establish communication between instances.

In order to achieve this node-to-node communication, the cluster interconnect can be used as a highly available network for normal IP traffic. Each node has a private hostname, identifying it on the interconnect. This private hostname can be determined using `scha_cluster_get` (3HA). Acquiring the `in_addr` structure requires some special handling (see Example 11.1). The somewhat arcane statement

```
if (in._S_un._S_un_b.s_b3 == LOGICAL_PERNODE_B3)
```

is required in the Sun Cluster 3.0 environment because gethostbyname() actually returns two addresses: a pernode number and a pairwise number (only one of which should be used). The macro `LOGICAL_PERNODE_B3` is used to strip out the pairwise number, leaving the pernode number for the address. Note that this interface may change in a future update of Sun Cluster 3 software.

Example 11.1   Determining the logical IP address of a node's
                    private hostname

```
#define LOGICAL_PERNODE_B3 0xC1
 struct in_addr
 get_scha_ipaddress(const char *privatename)
 {
        struct hostent  *hp = NULL;
        struct in_addr res;
        char **pp;

        hp = gethostbyname(privatename);
        for (pp = hp->h_addr_list; *pp != 0; pp++) {
                struct in_addr in;
                memcpy(&in.s_addr, *pp, sizeof (in.s_addr));
                if (in._S_un._S_un_b.s_b3 == LOGICAL_PERNODE_B3) {
                        return (in);
                }
        }
        // Should never reach this stmt
        assert(0);
 }
```

Unfortunately, the Sun Cluster 3.0 framework does not provide any generalized method for private communication between nodes through a cluster-wide interprocess communication or similar, unless specific hardware is available and the remote shared memory (RSM) API is used. This means that normal internode IP network communication such as RPC or sockets must be used and that the communication protocols must be created by the developer for each application.

To ensure there is no single point of failure, communication between nodes should use a peer-to-peer model; that is, each node is both a client and a server on the private interconnect. This implies that threads must be used to facilitate communication between the client and server portions of the communication infrastructure.

Another problem with internode communication is that an application instance running on a node has to know which other nodes have instances of the same application from the same resource. Essentially, this means an application must be able to access some of the cluster metadata. This is particularly important if there is the chance of multiple sets of the same scalable service running on the cluster, each one in its own resource. Again, there is no facility provided by the cluster framework for an application to automatically determine what resource or resource group it is associated with. Instead, this information must be passed to the application via an external source at runtime, such as a command-line argument or configuration file.

Each application instance should be aware of instances starting on new nodes, and also when instances stop. To do so, each application must maintain a list of active nodes, using the functions described in `scha_calls(3HA)`.

Unfortunately, due to the nature of the private interconnect, it is not really possible to do point-to-multipoint network programming such as multicast or broadcast to implement internode communication.

Applications using internode communication may also need to share files, in the same way as the sessionless services described earlier. However, since application instances have the ability to communicate with each other, there may be some value in identifying which node has a lock on a given file.

In Sun Cluster 3.0, the `system_id` element returned in the flock structure of fcntl(2) can be used to determine the node owning the lock—the top two bytes give the node number. The process ID element of the flock structure refers to the process on that node. It should be noted, however, that this is not a committed interface and may change in future releases of Sun Cluster.

Remote Shared Memory

The most sophisticated method of internode communication requires specific hardware to be usable. At the time of writing, RSM can only be used in clusters with scalable coherent interconnect (SCI) for the cluster interconnect. This particular hardware is required to take advantage of the RSM protocols: All RSM operations must take place over this interconnect and are not possible over Ethernet interconnects of any type.

RSM allows the direct access of memory on remote nodes. An application can export a segment of memory, which makes it available to applications on other nodes. The application instances can then use normal memory access functions to read and write the shared memory segments, making node-to-node communication very fast.

Obviously, in such an environment, the application must be cluster aware and be able to use the same strategies for determining node membership and resource information as described in the previous section on internode communication.

The RSMAPI is discussed in more detail in Chapter 12, "Using Remote Shared Memory."

Summary

Scalable services are an important feature of Sun Cluster 3, and provide the opportunity to achieve even higher availability than with normal failover data services. The requirements for scalable services, however, are quite demanding and many applications cannot easily be made scalable, especially if they maintain a stateful session on the server.

For off-the-shelf applications, the easiest ones to make scalable are sessionless or those that are predominately read-only with automatic client retry. For more complex applications, it is often necessary to have access to the source code so that adjustments can be made to make the application work properly as a scalable service.

Cluster-aware applications can be developed to maintain state even across node failure, but these types of applications are typically complex to write because there is no generic way of providing node-to-node communication.

12

USING REMOTE SHARED MEMORY

Programming Sun Clusters using remote shared memory (RSM) is arguably the most sophisticated type of development currently offered in this environment and requires not only radical changes to application programs themselves, but also specialized hardware for the cluster interconnects.

In this chapter we will introduce what can be done with RSM, and some of the ways to go about making these things happen. There are a lot of sophisticated concepts involved in RSM programming, so it's not something to be taken lightly; but it can be a powerful tool, as we will see.

Introduction to RSM

RSM allows nodes to directly access segments of memory on remote nodes by using an "OS-bypass" interconnect like Scalable Coherent Interconnect (SCI) or SunFire Link. Interconnects relying on an operating system (OS) stack (such as Ethernet) cannot be used for RSM.

RSM can be used to speed up communication between nodes and simplify some aspects of data access. Remote memory is mapped into a local address space, and thus appears to an application like normal memory.

Since memory can be accessed directly, it is possible to transfer application states among nodes without having to write anything to a shared disk. This helps high availability because applications can be written to allow a failover to take effect more quickly than if the state had to be recovered from disk. In fact, depending on your application, it may be possible to have client processes continue almost uninterrupted, although this would require considerable programming effort.

RSM works using a publish-and-subscribe model to export segments of memory from one node and import them into others. No copying is done—the memory is mapped to a local address on the importing node and operations carried out on the segment are automatically transferred back to the exporter.

Importing nodes can be restricted in their permissions to read and/or write to the back-end memory; nodes can import and export any number of memory segments at the same time.

Figure 12.1 illustrates the states involved in the creation and use of an RSM segment. When an application exports a memory segment:

1. An amount of memory space is allocated by the program.
2. The memory space is then assigned to a network controller.
3. The controller is used to share the memory out to other nodes.
4. The importing node uses a network controller to subscribe to the memory segment.
5. The memory segment is then mapped into the local address space of that system.
6. With the remote segment mapped, an application can then access the memory as if it were local to that node.

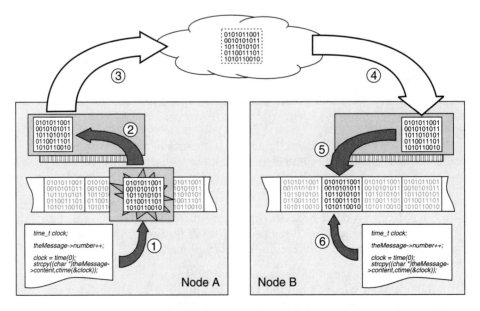

Figure 12.1 RSM stages

The important thing to remember with RSM is that applications must be explicitly written to use it—RSM cannot be added after the fact to off-the-shelf applications. This is because RSM occurs at the fundamental level of per-variable memory access on a per-application basis. It's not possible, for example, to create a generic pool of "global memory" and then somehow instruct an application to use it. It is possible, though, to write an application that can detect if RSM is available and use it as an alternative to a more traditional method of state transfer (for example, disk or IP service). In fact, this is exactly what Oracle 9i RAC does. There is a specified set of steps that you must take to use RSM in an application—mostly by using the functions provided in the RSMAPI.

The RSMAPI

The RSMAPI is a user-level C library providing access for applications to RSM functions. The RSMAPI is actually delivered as part of Solaris (from Solaris 8 4/01), so in theory any Solaris system can make use of the API regardless of whether it is part of a cluster. Practically, though, the hardware drivers required for using RSM network adapters are supplied with Sun Cluster,[1] so RSM is unlikely to be used on stand-alone systems.

Starting RSM Operations

The first phase of RSM operations is for the application to establish what the topology of the shared memory network looks like. In most Sun Cluster configurations, the RSM network is also the private interconnect, so the topology is likely to be more complex than a single connection between two nodes. Fortunately, the RSMAPI provides a single data type for storing all of the topology information and a single function that can be used to populate the data structure: `rsm_get_interconnect_topology(3rsm)`.

The data type populated by this function is relatively complex, but does enable fairly easy access to all of the information available about RSM networks on a given node. The structure of `rsm_topology_t` is shown in Figure 12.2.

Usually, `rsm_get_interconnect_topology(3rsm)` is only called once during an application's run time (at the beginning), since only a change in the physical topology of the network (such as the addition or removal of a remote node) would warrant calling the function again. See Example 12.1.

---

1. HPC ClusterTools, where RSM has been used for some time, also provides these drivers.

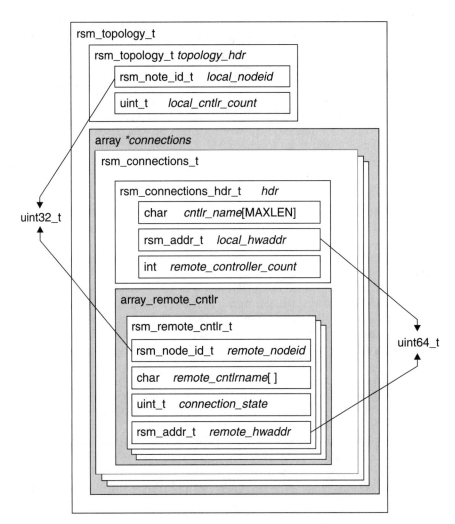

Figure 12.2 rsm_topology_t data structure

Example 12.1   Using rsm_get_interconnect_topology()

```
#import <rsmapi.h>

rsm_topology_t  *rsmTopology ;
int status ;

status = rsm_get_interconnect_topology(&rsmTopology);
if ( status )
    {
    perror("error trying to get topology");
    exit(1);
    }
```

The next part of setting up an RSM operation is to allocate the local memory that will be exported to the RSM network. This allocation must be done along page boundaries, so you must use `valloc(3C)` or `memalign(3C)` instead of the more usual `malloc(3C)`. Since `malloc(3C)` may "accidentally" allocate memory on a page boundary on any given runtime, you may find that if your application suddenly stops working, you have mistakenly used it instead of `valloc(3C)` at some point, so be careful.

While we are being careful how to allocate memory, it is probably also a good idea to reserve an entire page or a number of pages because it must be a multiple of the RSM controller's page size when we eventually export the segment. Fortunately, the page size is part of the data found in the `rsm_controller_attr_t` data type (see Figure 12.3). Thanks to the `rsm_ topology_t` data and the `rsm_ controller_get(3rsm)` function, it is relatively easy to find out what the controller's page size is (see Example 12.2).

Example 12.2   Getting the page size of a controller

```
#define CONTROLLER 0

rsmapi_controller_handle_t theController;
size_t
ctlPageSize;

/* get controller */
status = rsm_get_controller(

rsmTopology->connections[CONTROLLER]->hdr.cntlr_name,
```

Figure 12.3 rsmapi_controller_attr_t data type

```
&theController);
  if ( status )
    {
    fprintf(stderr,"error getting controller (status %d)\n",status);
    exit(1);
    }

/* must allocate memory for controller attributes */
ctlAttr =
                    (rsmapi_controller_attr_t
*)malloc(sizeof(rsmapi_controller_attr_t));
if (ctlAttr == NULL)
    {
    fprintf(stderr,"no memory to allocate for controller attributes\n");
    exit(1);
    }

status = rsm_get_controller_attr(theController, ctlAttr);
if ( status )
    {
    fprintf(stderr,"error getting controller attributes (status %d)\n",
                                                              status);
    exit(1);
    }

ctlPageSize = ctlAttr->attr_page_size;
fprintf(stderr,"rsm page is %d bytes\n",ctlPageSize);
```

Exporting the Memory

Once the local memory has been allocated, it can be exported to an RSM controller. Unlike Sun Cluster interconnect operations, RSM operations are performed on *specific* controller hardware devices installed on the node rather than on a generalized, highly available logical interface. This is why, before you start RSM operations, you need to discover the RSM topology (see "Starting RSM Operations" earlier in this chapter), so that we know what controllers are available in the node.

To export some memory, you must create an exported memory segment on your selected controller, using rsm_memseg_export_create(3rsm). As we mentioned previously, exported segments must be a multiple of the controller's page size. Example 12.3 shows the code snippet you might use to create an export segment of a variable called *myLocalData*.

Example 12.3   Creating an export segment

```
rsm_memseg_export_handle_t   *theRSMsegment ;
size_t                                                   msgSize,
segSize, sizeDiff;
uint_t
exportFlags;
```

```
/* nb: length on exported segment must be multiple of _controller_ page
/* size in bytes, so even up size of my data to page size */
msgSize = sizeof myLocalData
if ( sizeDiff = (msgSize % ctlPageSize))
    {
    fprintf(stderr,"difference is %d bytes\n",sizeDiff);
    segSize += (ctlPageSize - sizeDiff) ;
    }

/* createMemorySegment(); */
exportFlags = RSM_ALLOW_REBIND ;
status = rsm_memseg_export_create(theController, theRSMsegment,
                                  (void *)myLocalData, (size_t)segSize ,
                                  exportFlags);
if (status)
    {
    fprintf(stderr,"error creating segment (status %d)\n", status);
    exit(1);
    }
```

Exporting memory segments to a controller does not *copy* the data, but instead it creates a *mapping* from local memory to a handle on the controller. This means that you don't have to worry about "filling up" memory on the controller due to large numbers or sizes of exported segments.

In Example 12.3, we used the export flag RSM_ALLOW_REBIND. This flag lets us change the real memory associated with this exported segment if we desire. The benefit of this is that rebinding memory is less time-consuming than creating a new segment, so there can be some efficiencies gained if you are creating and destroying a lot of temporary shared memory.

Since RSM operations aren't automatically highly available, you may want to export your memory segment to multiple controllers, so that the segment remains available even if some interruption occurs on one of the interconnects. Because exporting memory is simply a mapping, you can just call rsm_memseg_export_ create(3rsm) again for the same memory address on a different controller to get the desired result. Note that you will still have to develop the appropriate code to manage any failover of remote nodes trying to access the segment on the alternative controller.

Publishing Exported Segments

The "export" of a memory segment is something of a misnomer, since the "exported" memory segments aren't actually available to other nodes immediately. Before other nodes can access the exported segment, it must be *published* to the RSM network using rsm_memseg_export_publish(3rsm).

When publishing a segment (Example 12.4), you have to decide what the access policy of the segment will be. The policy is specified on a per-node basis in a similar manner to UNIX file access modes: that is, it has a three-digit octal code referring to

Table 12.1 Export Access Mode Values

Value	Meaning
0	no access
2	write access (only)
4	read access (only)
6	read *and* write access

the access allowed to processes with the same user ID, group ID, or with no match (see Table 12.1).

This means that if you assign an access mode of 0640 to a published memory segment, processes with the same user ID (UID) as the exporting process can read and write to the segment, processes with the same group ID (GID) can only read from the segment, and all other processes have no read or write access. These access modes are assigned individually for each node on the RSM network, according to the node ID in the RSM topology data structure (see Figure 12.2). This means that different nodes in the RSM network can have different access modes for a given segment of memory.

The assumption in this method of assigning permissions is that the nodes of the cluster are sufficiently tightly coupled so that there is no risk of processes gaining access to memory that they shouldn't access. In practice, this means that the export permissions are essentially more crudely allocated than specific per-user, per-group, and per-other permissions, and simply state whether a segment is generally readable, writable, or both to all nodes regardless of the importing process UID or GID.

Example 12.4   Publishing a memory segment

```
#define SEGMENT_ID  0x400000
#define TRUSTED_PERMISSIONS  0666

int
n, numRemoteCtl;
rsmapi_access_entry_t
*theAccessList;
rsm_memseg_id_t
theSegmentID;

/* set up access list */
fprintf(stderr,"getting number of remote controllers\n");

numRemoteCtl = rsmTP->connections[CONTROLLER]->hdr.remote_cntlr_count ;

fprintf(stderr,"sizing theAccessList for %d remote controllers\n",
                numRemoteCtl);

theAccessList = (rsmapi_access_entry_t*)valloc(sizeof(rsmapi_access_entry_t)
                                    * numRemoteCtl ) ;
```

```
for ( n = 0 ; n <  numRemoteCtl ; n++)
    {
    theAccessList[n].ae_node =
                            rsmTopology->connections[CONTROLLER]-
>remote_cntlr[n].remote_nodeid ;
    theAccessList[n].ae_permission = TRUSTED_PERMISSIONS ;
    }

/*              segment ID can be given as a pointer to a variable with
value 0, and
                the system assigns a unique ID, but there is no easy way
to communicate
                this to the remote node(s), so we use a fixed segment ID
*/

theSegmentID = SEGMENT_ID ;
status = rsm_memseg_export_publish(*theRSMsegment, &theSegmentID,

theAccessList, (uint_t)numRemoteCtl );
if (status)
    {
    perror("error exporting segment");
    exit(1);
    }
```

Once a segment has been published, it can be imported by other nodes. However, before we look at importing segments, we need to understand how to locate the segment being used.

Identifying Segments

Segment IDs are used along with node IDs to uniquely identify a memory segment in the RSM network. They are used to refer to a segment on a remote node when trying to import memory and are assigned at the time a segment is published.

Segment IDs can either be hard coded into an application's source, which is okay if you only intend to export a small number of segments and don't intend to run many different RSM programs that may try to use the same IDs. If you plan to use many segments and/or programs, it is a better idea to let the system allocate unique segment IDs for you at runtime. This can be achieved by passing a variable with the value of 0 (zero) to the `rsm_memseg_export_publish(3rsm)` function, as shown in Example 12.5.

Example 12.5 Setting a segment ID dynamically

```
rsm_memseg_id_t
theSegmentID;

theSegmentID = 0 ;
status = rsm_memseg_export_publish(*theRSMsegment, &theSegmentID,
```

```
theAccessList, (uint_t)numRemoteCtl );
```

The *problem* with this approach is that in order for importing nodes to access the published memory, they need to know the segment ID, and the RSMAPI has no convenient way of accomplishing this, so we are left with a sort of chicken-and-egg problem (we can't communicate without a segment ID, but we need a segment ID to communicate . . .).

One approach to solving this problem is to use a "known" segment ID to store a list of all of the dynamically assigned segment IDs. The RSMAPI *does* provide a way for systems administrators to fix a base segment ID for a given application, by modifying the /etc/rsm/rsm.segmentid file (see Example 12.6).

Example 12.6   Sample rsm.segmentid file

```
# lines starting with # are ignored
#keyword                                appID      baseID
length
reserved                                myApp1
0x80100000                    10
reserved                                myApp2
0x80100000                    10
reserved                                myApp3
0x80200000                    10
reserved                                yourApp1
0x80200000                    1000
```

Each line in this file refers to the segment IDs reserved for a given application and it is made up of fields. Field 1 is always "reserved"[2]; field 2 is the identifier for your application (for example, your application's package name); field 3 is the base ID; field 4 is the number of IDs to reserve. So long as this file is kept the same on all nodes and as long as you assign a unique application ID to your application, calls to the function rsm_get_segmentid_range(3rsm) will return the same values. You can then use this to query whatever data structure you use to store dynamically allocated segment IDs. Example 12.7 shows some sample code of how you might acquire the predefined segment ID.

Example 12.7   Storing dynamically allocated segment IDs
                    in a known segment

```
#define MYAPP_ID    "myApp1"

rsm_memseg_id_t                                         segIDBase ;
uint32_t
segmentLength;
```

---

2. The man page for rsm_get_segment_id_range(3rsm) up until at least Solaris 9 4/03 says this should be "reserve," but this is incorrect.

```
status = rsm_get_segmentid_range(MYAPP_ID,  &segIDBase, &segmentLength);

if (status)
    {
    fprintf(stderr,"error getting segment id (status %d)\n",status);
    exit(1);
    }

printf("segment base is %x, length is %d\n",segIDBase, segmentLength);
```

Even if you decide to use fixed segment IDs in your application, it's a good idea to document these so that system administrators can enter them into the rsm. segmentid file. It's also a good idea to check that you don't use a segment ID reserved for something else (in particular, check the list in /usr/include/sys/ rsm/rsm-common.h). In general, the available segment IDs range between 0x80000000 and 0x8fffffff.

Importing Segments

Once a memory segment has been published to the RSM network, remote nodes can import this memory using rsm_memseg_import_connect(3rsm) and perform operations on it. As with memory segment exporting, importing is done via a specified hardware controller. It's the same as with exporting a program where the topology of the RSM network must be discovered (see "Starting RSM Operations" earlier in this chapter).

When importing a segment, the application must request a permission node. As with publishing a segment, the mode is an octal value, although here only the "user" part of the octal digit is used (see Table 12.2).

The requested access mode is compared with the mode set when the segment was published. If they are compatible, then the import can go ahead and allocate a handle to the imported memory, which can then be used to map the memory segment into a portion of the local address space using rsm_memseg_import_ map(3rsm). Example 12.8 is an example of how a segment of memory is imported and mapped.

Table 12.2 Import Access Mode Values

Value	Meaning
0200	Write access (only)
0400	Read access (only)
0600	Read and write access

Example 12.8 Importing and mapping a remote memory segment

```
#define READ_WRITE_PERM                                          0600
#define SEGSIZE                                                  8192

volatile myData_t                                               *myData ;
rsmapi_controller_handle_t                                      theCtlr ;
rsm_memseg_import_handle_t
importHandle;
rsmNodeIDList_t                                                 *nodeList
;
rsm_memseg_id_t
theSegmentID ;

theSegmentID =  SEGMENT_ID ;

/* get controller handle */
theCtlr = getController( rsmTopology, CONTROLLER ) ;

/* find the other nodes on this section */
nodeList = getNodes(rsmTopology, CONTROLLER ) ;

if ( ! nodeList->count )
    {
    fprintf(stderr,"no other nodes connected via %s",
                    rsmTopology->connections[CONTROLLER]->hdr.cntlr_name);
    return(NULL);
    }

/* try accessing nodes at the given segmentID until we find something */
for ( n=0 ; n < nodeList->count ; n++)
    {
    status = rsm_memseg_import_connect(theCtlr, nodeList->nodes[n],
                                  theSegmentID, READ_WRITE_PERM,
                                  &importHandle);

    if (status == 0)
      {
      fprintf(stderr,"made connection to node id %d\n",
                                                        nodeList-
>nodes[n]);
      break ;
      }

    switch (status)
      {
      case (RSMERR_SEG_NOT_PUBLISHED_TO_NODE): ;  /* fallthru */
      case (RSMERR_SEG_NOT_PUBLISHED): ;          /* fallthru */
      case (RSMERR_REMOTE_NODE_UNREACHABLE):
              fprintf(stderr,"segment not available at node %d\n",
                                                        nodeList-
>nodes[n]);
              break;
```

```
        default:
            fprintf(stderr,"error importing segment (status %d)\n",status);
            exit(1);
        }

/* we'll assume we're just importing 1 page (8192 bytes) at the moment */
status = rsm_memseg_import_map(importHandle,(void **)&myData,
                              RSM_MAP_NONE, READ_WRITE_PERM,
                              0,SEGSIZE);
if ( status)
    {
    fprintf(stderr,"error mapping imported memory (status %d)\n",status);
    exit(1);
    }
fprintf(stderr,"imported memory mapped successfully\n");
```

Once the imported memory has been mapped, it can be accessed just like local memory. All operations are mapped back to the original memory in the exporting node without any data being copied.

Barriers

Although imported memory can be worked on just like local memory (subject to the access mode in effect), the fact that it is remote memory means that it's a good idea to check that operations actually complete successfully. External factors such as the exporting application stopping, the exporting node shutting down, or something interfering with the interconnect will not necessarily be automatically detected by the application. Since there's no intrinsic way of monitoring whether some arbitrary memory operation succeeds (say, by examining a return value), the RSMAPI provides a mechanism called *barriers* to ensure that errors on memory operations are caught.

A barrier can be created for each imported memory handle using rsm_memseg_import_init_barrier(3rsm). Before performing an operation on an imported segment, open the relevant barrier with rsm_memseg_import_open_barrier (3rsm). Once the operation is complete, close the barrier with rsm_memseg_import_close_barrier(3rsm). On closure, any relevant memory-access errors are reported in the return code of rsm_memseg_import_close_barrier(), which gives you a chance to take any remedial action which may be required. Example 12.9 gives an example of this sequence.

Example 12.9 Using barriers

```
/* create a barrier for the imported memory */
rsmapi_barrier_t            theBarrier;

status = rsm_memseg_import_init_barrier(importHandle,  RSM_BARRIER_NODE,
                                        &theBarrier);
if ( status)
    {
```

```
                             fprintf(stderr,
                                        "got an error initializing
barrier (status %d)\n",status);
    exit(1);
    }

status = rsm_memseg_import_open_barrier(theBarrier); if ( status)
    {
                             fprintf(stderr,"got an error opening barrier
(status %d)\n",status);
    exit(1);
    }

do_some_function_to(myData);

status = rsm_memseg_import_close_barrier(theBarrier);
if ( status)
    {
    fprintf(stderr,"got an error closing barrier (status %d): %s\n",
               status, getBarrierError(status) );
    exit(1);
    }
```

Memory operations with the opening and closing of a barrier should be designed as atomic operations, so you can ensure the integrity of your memory data. It is also possible to check the status of a series of operations before finally closing the barrier using rsm_memseg_import_order_barrier(3rsm). This function will return an error in the same way as does rsm_memseg_import_close_barrier(). Figure 12.4 illustrates how checking the status of a series of operations fits into the "life cycle" of a barrier.

Unfortunately, barriers don't provide a way to lock a segment of memory so that it can be exclusively written-to or read correctly. In fact, there is no mechanism provided by the RSMAPI to easily address this possibly the biggest fundamental hurdle to overcome, especially for clusters of more than two nodes.

Synchronization

Some crude synchronization functionality is provided by the RSMAPI in the form of a signal post and wait mechanism using rsm_intr_signal_port(3rsm) and

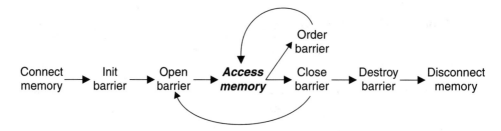

Figure 12.4 Barrier life cycle

rsm_intr_signal_wait(3rsm), which operate on the given memory segment. Signals sent by the exporting node are distributed to all of the importing nodes, but signals sent by an importing node are only received by the exporter. If you want to use poll(2) to handle incoming signals, you can use rsm_memseg_get_pollfd (3rsm) to acquire a special file handle that can be used by poll(2). At this stage the functionality is still crude, which means that the hardest part of writing an application using RSM is the signalling and synchronization between nodes.

Nonmapping Operations

The memory mapping functions described so far are what make RSM really interesting—the ability to directly access memory on remote nodes makes RSM stand apart from other internode communication methods. However, some interconnects may not support memory mapping,[3] so the RSMAPI provides the rsm_memseg_ import_put(3rsm) functions, which can be used to copy a specific number of bytes *to* an imported memory segment, and the rsm_memseg_import_get(3rsm) functions, which copy data *from* a memory segment. For both *put* and *get* operations, the amount of data copied can be a fixed multiple of 8, 16, 32, or 64 bits, or can be an arbitrary number of bytes. By default, the put and get operations are automatically protected by barriers (see "Barriers" earlier in this chapter) for error detection.

Put and get operations are performed instead of mapping imported memory to a local address. All of the other steps in the procedure of setting up an RSM operation (export, publish, import-connect) must still be performed before put or get can be used.

To accomplish a range of put or get operations at the same time in an efficient manner, the RSMAPI provides the rsm_memseg_import_putv(3rsm) and rsm_ memseg_import_getv(3rsm) functions. You can use these functions to assemble a vector of memory addresses to use for operations by assigning each handle of an imported memory segment to a local memory handle created using an rsm_ create_localmemory_handle(3rsm). The memory handles are put into an rsm_iovec_t data type, which in turn is put into the rsm_scat_gath_t data type used by the functions (see Figure 12.5).

When you call rsm_memseg_import_putv() or rsm_memseg_import_getv(), each copy is performed in order, to or from local and remote memory (see Figure 12.6). Note that in this case memory is actually *copied* between the nodes, not simply mapped back to the exporter.

---

3. Both of the interconnects supported for RSM in Sun Cluster at the time of writing do support memory mapping.

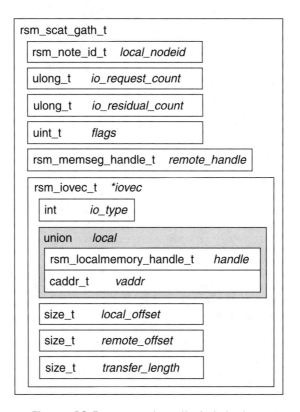

Figure 12.5 rsm_scat_gath_t data type

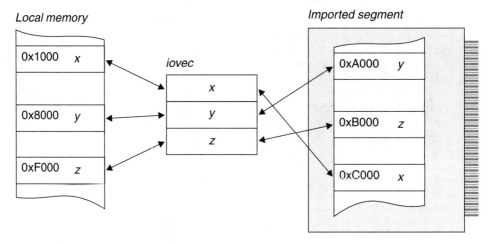

Figure 12.6 Memory operations on a vector of local and remote handles

Traps and Tricks

Although the RSMAPI deals with some complex concepts, it is itself a comparatively simple API. As such, there are some particular items that you, as an application developer, should keep in mind when programming with it.

Data Structure Considerations

As we saw earlier in the chapter, RSM works by mapping memory address segments between nodes. We also saw that these segments must be explicitly exported and published and that we must go to some lengths to communicate how remote nodes can find a published segment.

It is important to remember that although imported memory can be read and modified directly by a remote node with sufficient permissions, the *address* to which memory is mapped on the remote node is almost certainly different from the address of the original memory on the exporting node. This becomes particularly relevant when using pointers in the data structures that you want to share between nodes. Figure 12.7 illustrates this problem. Imagine that we want to share a string ("foo") from node A to node B. The usual way to store a string in C is to use a pointer to char, so in node A we would allocate memory for the string and assign the pointer to that memory to a variable (see Example 12.10).

Example 12.10 Using pointers for a string

```
char *myString;
myString = valloc(4);
strcpy(myString,"foo");
```

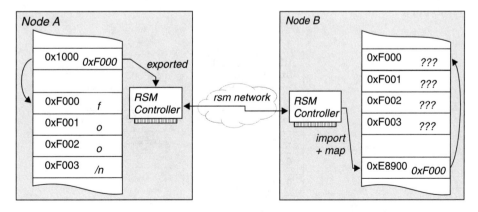

Figure 12.7 Using pointers across nodes

In our example, the memory assigned for the string by valloc(3C) starts at address 0xF000. This address is the lvalue of the variable *myString*, which is itself stored at address 0x1000. If we then export the address of the variable *myString* and map that into a variable on node B, whenever the application on node B accesses the variable *lvalue* 0xF000 is found, but the application will think that this address is *local* to node B. However, there is no way for RSM to translate any such request for the actual data into accessing the correct memory on the exporting node.

What this means in practice is that you cannot effectively use pointers in any data types transferred using RSM. Instead, you may be able to use an array (particularly for strings) since the *lvalue* in the address of an array is not usually a pointer to another address, but is the first actual value (see Figure 12.8).

For more information on memory handling and allocation in Solaris, consult *Solaris Internals* by Jim Mauro and Richard McDougall.

Error Handling and High Availability

Earlier in this chapter, we mentioned that the RSMAPI provides no inherent or automatic high availability for the interconnect. It's worth reiterating this because it is different from many of the other facilities offered in the Sun Cluster environment. It is up to you, as the application designer, to use the simple error reporting provided by the RSMAPI (see "Barriers" earlier in this chapter) to create your own error handling and HA routines.

One way of dealing with the possibility of a controller, cable, or interconnect switch failure is to export memory segments on every available controller on a node, and then if there is a problem with the first, have error handling routines on the remote nodes attempt to connect to an alternate controller. An important thing to note here is that the barrier functions are only available to the *importing* node—worth considering when designing how your application will use RSM. In practice, this means that the importing nodes should take a more active role in the sharing of data than the exporting node, since there is no error reporting facility for the exporter.

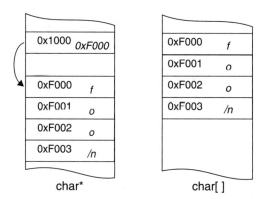

Figure 12.8 Pointers versus arrays

This also brings up the notion of locking memory segments for read and write access, particularly if you plan to allow more than two nodes in your RSM cluster. Unfortunately, as we mentioned earlier, there is also no generic locking mechanism available in the RSMAPI, so this is another protocol you will have to design to suit your own application, possibly using the signalling functions discussed earlier (see "Synchronization" earlier in this chapter).

Summary

Remote shared memory (RSM) is a powerful tool for quickly (and relatively easily) sharing data between nodes, but using it takes some effort and careful design.

The RSMAPI offers a basic level of functionality, but if you plan to develop RSM applications frequently, you should consider developing your own library of convenience functions suitable to your environment, such as high-availability routines for the interconnect and locking protocols for memory segments.

You should also remember that RSM requires specific hardware, so if you want your application to work on *any* cluster, you should include some alternative method of communication between nodes.

13

DEVELOPING CLUSTER-AWARE APPLICATIONS

Beginning with Sun Cluster 3.1, a new useful API that is available to developers is the cluster reconfiguration notification protocol (CRNP). This API gives developers the functionality and the tools to create applications that are cluster aware. The CRNP functionality enables applications and clients to be notified when specific cluster events occur, that is, cluster membership change. When an event occurs, the application or client can act on those changes immediately. The CRNP is a new protocol within the Sun Cluster framework and it will continue to evolve along with changes and new functionality. Because CRNP is a new API, this chapter will serve as an introduction. The reader should also consult the latest documentation and man pages on the topic. Although we are going to discuss the first release of CRNP, there is a chance that some of the features to be discussed will be deprecated in later releases, although any changes should be minor. This API will be explored in great detail in a subsequent publication.

Cluster Aware versus Non-Cluster Aware

Non-Cluster Aware

Sun Cluster allows developers to run applications in a Sun Cluster environment to take advantage of the Sun Cluster functionality, namely availability or scaleability. Even though many, if not all, applications will work running in a Sun Cluster environment, the applications in and of themselves know nothing of the cluster environment. For example, if a state change occurs, that is, a node leaves the cluster, an application will not be aware of the change. For all intents and purposes, applications are running on a single host.[1] The reader might be inclined to make an argument that the fault probe makes the application cluster aware. This argument would not be valid for two reasons: first, a fault probe is not the application users want—users do not connect to fault probes; and second, and more importantly, the fault probe itself is not cluster aware. True, a probe should have a loop structure to test the availability of the application, but if the probe needs to know something about the state of a resource, it must make a request to the resource group manager (RGM) via a library function call through some polling technique. Therefore, at any given time, a fault probe is not aware of the cluster state. A fault probe does not make an application cluster aware, but it is routinely used to periodically test the health of the application.

Recall from Chapter 6, "Understanding the RGM," that a resource type does not need to include a fault probe in order to work under the Sun Cluster framework. However, fault probes can check an application's viability, perform a clean shutdown, and request a restart or failover. It is important to remember that in each of these steps the application is not aware of the cluster on which it is running.

Cluster Aware

When developing resource types for Sun Cluster, getting information about the cluster state requires that the callback methods use the API convenience functions to poll the RGM for the needed information. Depending on the type of the application, this programming model can be inefficient. Another potential issue is that it may not be possible for client applications that run on the cluster to get status or state information about the cluster. The next logical step in resource development is to give developers the tools necessary to develop cluster-aware applications. CRNP addresses these issues.

Within the context of this book, the term *cluster aware* means that an application is made aware of the state of the cluster at important events during the cluster's life cycle including membership changes, resource restarts, or a failover without a callback having to poll the RGM for that information. It's also important to let client applications know the state of the services to which they are connected.

CRNP

Instead of polling for cluster information or state changes, resources and applications can now register to be asynchronously notified when cluster state changes occur. Currently, only resource types are informed that a state change occurs via the callback model. Should an event happen that falls within the scope of a callback method, the RGM will invoke that method, that is, take a resource offline. However,

---

1. This is not the case for environments such as Oracle real application clusters (RAC).

what if resource A, which has no affinity to resource B, needed to know if and when resource B goes offline? Without using CRNP, the only way to know this is for resource A to periodically poll the RGM for state information on resource B.

With increasing frequency, clients—PCs, PDAs, or cell phones—are connecting to application servers for data requests and Web services. Application or App servers are becoming an important part of the IT landscape. These App servers provide services that range from e-mail to Web page distribution. A typical clustered IT environment consists of PC clients connecting to some App server, with an App server connecting to a database. See Figure 13.1.

In Figure 13.1, if the App server doesn't know anything about the cluster framework, it communicates directly to the database. Should the database fail, the App server keeps trying to connect to the database until it times out.[2] Hopefully, the database recovers on the backup node before the App server times out.

But what if the App server knows about the cluster framework and that the database was restarted or switched to a standby node? The App server then can immediately begin its own recovery process and reconnect to the database that has been switched to an alternate node. This is also true for client connections. If a client knows that a service is unavailable, it can stagger its requests in anticipation of a recovery instead of making requests to an unavailable application, which can result in a timeout condition, or worse, a hung client. By using the CRNP API, the RGM is able to send the App server and the clients a message that a state change occurred.

CRNP Framework

The CRNP semantics are easy to understand because the overall architecture is built on a simple, efficient communication model: Solaris system event framework (syseventd(1M)). This model provides a mechanism for user-level applications to receive notification of conditions that have occurred in the Solaris kernel, which provides interfaces as building blocks upon which a general-purpose system event

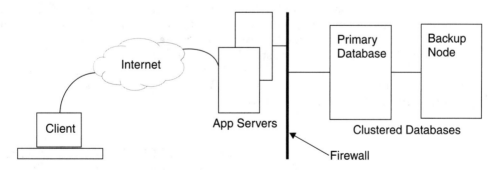

Figure 13.1 Typical client, application, and database server configuration

2. The connection should be to a logical IP address.

framework can be built. In order to use the system event framework, a system event loadable module (SLM) is created for those applications that need to send their system events to clients. In turn, clients that need to receive notification of events register with an SLM.

CRNP Components

The architecture of the CRNP consists of three new daemons: `cl_apid`, `cl_eventd`, and `syseventd`. The components of the CRNP framework are easy enough to understand.

syseventd

The kernel system event notification daemon syseventd(1M) accepts the events generated from the RGM and divides the event name space into class and subclass specifiers. Currently, the RGM can generate one of three events:

EC_CLUSTER / ECS_CLUSTER_MEMBERSHIP

Event is generated when cluster membership changes, that is, nodes join or leave a cluster.

EC_CLUSTER / ESC_CLUSTER_RG_STATE

Event is generated when a resource group state changes on any node.

EC_CLUSTER / ESC_CLUSTER_R_STATE

Event is generated when a resource changes state on any node.

When the RGM generates one of these events, it will place it in the syseventd(1M) queue using the sysevent_post_event(3SYSEVENT) interface found in the libsysevent(3LIB).

cl_eventd

This is a CRNP daemon that runs on each cluster node. It's started at boot time from an rc3.d script. After startup it checks for and then communicates its presence running on other nodes. This is done via the object request broker (ORB) communications mechanism that is part of Sun Cluster. Messages are sent from syseventd to cl_eventd. This daemon also uses libsysevent(3LIB) to subscribe to sysevents. If an event is of class EC_CLUSTER, this daemon forwards the event to the `cl_eventd` on all other nodes, again using an ORB call. This event is then placed in the `syseventd` queue on the local node.

cl_apid

This daemon interacts with the clients of the CRNP. Its function is to receive registration messages and to deliver cluster events. In order for CRNP to work correctly, this daemon must be available. Because of this requirement, it is configured as a failover service. That is, the daemon is configured and brought online like all other resource types under the control of the RGM. Being a failover resource, there can only be one instance of this daemon running on the cluster at any given time. In the advent of a failure, the RGM will either restart or fail over the resource to another node. The `cl_apid` is defined via the SUNW.Event resource type. A convenience script is included to set up the resource group and two resources (SUNW.Event and SUNW.LogicalHostname). Figure 13.2 illustrates the relationships among the daemons.

A new built-in failover resource type launches the daemon `sc_eventd`. Its purpose is to forward cluster events to its client subscribers.

CRNP Messaging

There are three message types that a client will send or receive: `SC_CALLBACK_REG`, `SC_EVENT`, and `SC_REPLY`. Clients register to receive messages, using the `SC_CALLBACK_REG` message, and in turn events are sent back to the registered client on a port defined in SUNW.Event via an `SC_EVENT` message.

These messages should be formatted using XML document type definition (DTD). The reader is advised to consult the latest documentation for the current DTD format. Table 13.1 lists the basic descriptions of the three message types used in CRNP.

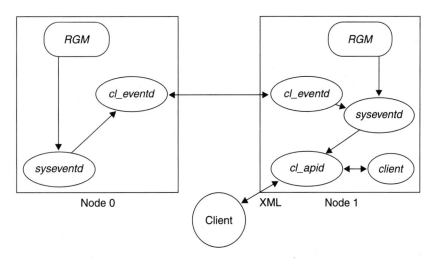

Figure 13.2 Cluster reconfiguration notification protocol semantics

Table 13.1 CRNP Message Properties

Message	Description
SC_CALLBACK_REG	Basic message to add and remove clients and/or to add and remove event subscriptions.
SC_EVENT	Event that just transpired, that is, whether the node joins or leaves a cluster.
SC_REPLY	Message indicating whether request was successful.

CRNP Resource Type

A new resource type, SUNW.Event(), is used to manage the CRNP daemon cl_apid. Its purpose is to make the daemon highly available. Its process tree is managed via PMF. Like all resource types, parameters, properties, and configurations are stored in an RTR file. In order to use CRNP, you have to register and use this resource type. The SUNW.Event resource type is registered and used just like all resource types. In addition to the standard properties such as START, STOP, and so forth, there are a few system properties and extension properties that are unique to SUNW.Event that must be set. Table 13.2 lists these unique properties.

CRNP Client Semantics

In order to receive cluster events, a client must first register with the cl_apid daemon for the events it wishes to receive. Once registered, the client then asks to register for events for specific resources. It's not necessary to register for all cluster events; for example, database clients might be only interested in events that affect the database resource. When an event occurs, the cl_apid will forward the message to all clients registered to receive those events. The client then listens on a local port

Table 13.2 CRNP Resource Type Properties (SUNW.Event)

Property Name	Tunable	Data Type	Default	Usage	Description
Port_list	When_ disabled	String array	9444/tcp	Conditional/ Required	Port which cl_apid listens on
Network_ resources_used	When disabled	String	Null	Conditional/ Required	Comma-separated list of logical hostnames or shared address network resources that are used by the resource
Max_clients	Any time	Integer	1000	Optional	Maximum number of registered clients
Allow_hosts	Any time	Sting array	Local	Optional	List of hosts that are allowed access to register
Deny_hosts	Any time	String array	Null	Optional	List of hosts that are denied access to register
Client_timeout	Any time	Integer	60	Optional	Timeout used while communicating with clients
Client_retry_ count	Any time	Integer	3	Optional	Number of attempts made to contact unresponsive clients
Client_retry_ timout	Any time	Integer	60	Optional	Time interval over which unresponsive clients are retried

for inbound events sent to it. The message a client sends and receives is formatted using XML 1.0 sent over TCP.

Clients may be user-level applications running outside the firewall or applications running under Sun Cluster control. Once registered, the last several past events are forwarded to the client, as well as new events. When a client no longer wishes to receive messages, it unregisters from the daemon. Figure 13.3 is a diagram illustrating the client life cycle.

Client Registration

Something should be clear by now, that CRNP is for those applications that aren't yet developed or can be readily modified to communicate with the cluster framework. It might be difficult if not impossible to modify an existing commercial application. The semantics of client registration are straightforward.

After the cluster software has been configured to support CRNP, clients will need to register with the cluster framework in order to receive those events that are of importance them. Note that if someone else is configuring the cluster framework, you need to be sure they publish the IP address and the port the cl_apid is going to be using.[3]

Client uniqueness is handled with the combination of IP address and port number. This information is provided in the SC_CALLBACK_REG message. However, CRNP will assume any other SC_CALLBACK_REG messages are from the client and even if they have a different source port they will be treated as the same client. This allows for sending and listening on different ports.

Message Passing

The client can communicate at any time with the cl_apid daemon, and request for additional events (ADD_EVENTS) or to remove events (REMOVE_EVENTS). However,

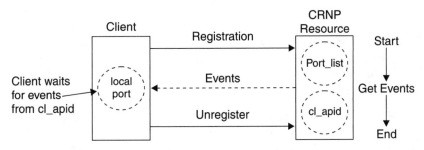

Figure 13.3 CRNP client life cycle

---

3. Naming services such as Network Information Services (NIS) can be used.

each request must be in the format of an SC_CALLBACK_REG message. The sequence of events is as follows:

1. The client opens a connection to the server using the IP address and port number used when configuring the SUNW.Event resource type.
2. Once a connection is established, the client sends the SC_CALLBACK_REG message. The message must be correctly formatted (no extra bytes either before or after the message). Incorrect message formats will generate an error that the client isn't registered.
3. After the message is sent, the client keeps the connection open and waits for an SC_REPLY. Note that if the connection is closed before a reply is sent, the client is still registered.

Messages should follow a logical order, for example, a message should not have an ADD_EVENTS or REMOVE_CLIENT before an ADD_CLIENT has been sent. The typical scenario for using SC_CALLBACK_REG is that a client would send an ADD_ CLIENT and the subsequent SC_CALLBACK_REG would have ADD_EVENTS. Also, a client shouldn't register and unregister for events in the same message; however, a client can register and subscribe to events within the same SC_CALLBACK_REG.

Cluster Side Messages   When events are generated with the cluster, the CRNP daemon will send a message of those events to each client who registered to receive them. Specifically, the daemon will open a TCP connection for each registered client and send only one SC_EVENT message for each event that has occurred, then it will close the connection. Thus, it's important that a client listens to its callback address at all times to avoid missing events. However, if the CRNP daemon does not connect to a callback address, it will attempt to deliver the message again the number of times defined within Client_retry_count. If the number of attempts exceeds Client_retry_count, the client is unregistered.

Messages from the daemon are guaranteed to be delivered to a client at least once. There can be a situation where a client receives the same message more than once, that is, a failover situation where both the primary and secondary nodes send the same message.

Within the CRNP, the order for messages is preserved. Message one will always be sent before message two; however, client A may very well receive messages one and two before client B receives message one. This ensures that no client holds up the delivery of messages.

Message Error Handling   The developer needs to always be aware that when a message is sent to the cluster, perhaps due to conditions that the client may not be aware of (failover, reconfiguration, heavy processing, and so forth), the message may not be able to immediately respond with SC_REPLY. The message may have failed or succeeded. So the client shouldn't wait until it receives an SC_REPLY before proceeding on to the next logical step. For example, when using SC_CALLBACK_REG to register and no SC_REPLY comes back within a reasonable amount of time (some timeout condition), another SC_CALLBACK_REG should be sent. Likewise for ADD_EVENTS, the client should immediately begin to listen to the port for SC_EVENTS, as events could be generated before the daemon has had a chance to send an SC_REPLY.

Summary

The cluster notification reconfiguration protocol adds new exciting possibilities to the Sun Cluster computing platform. For the fist time, developers have the ability to create applications that are cluster aware.

A

RESOURCES

This appendix describes those attributes used to create resource types as well as resources.

Table A.1 Sun Cluster 3.x Callback Methods Quick Reference

Callback Method	Idempotent	Description
START	NO	Used to start a resource.
STOP	YES	Used to stop a resource.
PRENET_START	NO	Used to bring up a resource after network interfaces have been plumbed up but before the network addresses are available.
POSTNET_STOP	YES	Used to stop a resource after the network resources have been brought down.
VALIDATE	NO	Used to determine that a resource's properties are set to valid values as stipulated in the resource's RTR file. Also called during an update of the resource.
UPDATE	YES	If a resource is active (running on a node) and changes are made to the resource, this method is called to ensure those changes are made consistently across the cluster.
MONITOR_START	NO	Starts the application monitoring agent if one is available.
MONITOR_STOP	YES	Stops the application monitoring agent.
MONITOR_CHECK	NO	Used to check to determine if a standby node is capable of handling the resource before a switch over happens.
INIT	YES	Any one-time initialization steps required by the resource will be performed by this method.
FINI	YES	When a resource is removed from under RGM management, this method is used to perform any necessary cleanup.
BOOT	YES	When a node joins or rejoins a cluster, this method can be used to perform any initialization that a resource might require.

Table A.2 Resource Type Properties

Property Name	Tunable	Data Type	Default	Usage	Description
API_version	Never	Integer	3	Optional	Version of API used. If not used, the default value for SC3 is 2.
BOOT	Never	String	None	Conditional/Explicit	Callback method. This should be the actual program name.
Failover	Never	Boolean	FALSE	Optional	Indicates that this resource is a failover resource. If set to TRUE, the resource cannot belong to a resource group that can be online on more than one node.
FINI	Never	String	None	Conditional/Explicit	Callback method. This should be the actual program name.
INIT	Never	String	None	Conditional/Explicit	Callback method. This should be the actual program name.
Init_nodes	Never	ENUM	RG_primaries	Optional	Instructs on which nodes the RGM is going to call the INIT, FINI, BOOT, and VALIDATE methods. Values can include RG_primaries or RT_installed_nodes.
Installed_nodes	Never	String Array	All nodes		List of cluster node names that the resource type is allowed to run on. Note this property cannot be declared in the RTR file.
MONITOR_CHECK	Never	String	None	Conditional/Explicit	Callback method. This should be the actual program name.
MONITOR_START	Never	String	None	Conditional/Explicit	Callback method. This should be the actual program name.
MONITOR_STOP	Never	String	None	Conditional/Explicit	Callback method. This should be the actual program name.
Pkglist	Never	String Array	None	Conditional/Explicit	List of packages that are used with the resource type installation.
POSTNET_STOP	Never	String	None	Conditional/Explicit	Callback method. This should be the actual program name.
PRENET_START	Never	String	None	Conditional/Explicit	Callback method. This should be the actual program name.
RT_basedir	Never	String	None	Required	Base directory path for callback methods. Set it to the installation of the path of the callback methods. The path must be absolutely complete with forward slash, that is, /usr/resource/callback. Use if callback methods are not defined with absolute paths.
RT_description	Never	String	Null	Conditional	Resource type description.
Resource_type	Never	String	None	Required	Name of the resource type.
RT_version	Never	String	None	Conditional/Explicit	Version or resource type.
Single_instance	Never	Boolean	False	Optional	One resource of this type allowed.
START	Never	String	None	Required	Callback method. This should be the actual program name.

Property Name	Tunable	Data Type	Default	Usage	Description
STOP	Never	String	None	Required	Callback method. This should be the actual program name.
UPDATE	Never	String	None	Conditional/ Explicit	Callback method. This should be the actual program name.
VALIDATE	Never	String	None	Conditional/ Explicit	Callback method. This should be the actual program name.
Vendor_ID	Never	String	None	Conditional	Typically, the stock symbol of the company that created the resource type, that is, SUNW.

Table A.3 Resource Properties

Property Name	Category	Description	Tunable	Comments
Cheap_probe_ interval	Conditional	Number of seconds between two quick fault probes.	When disabled	If a default value is specified, this property is optional. If tunable, it is not set in RTR file, then property is only tunable "when disabled."
Load_balancing_ policy	Conditional/ Optional	String to define which load balancing policy to use	At creation	See Chapter 10
Load_balancing_ weights	Conditional/ Optional	For scalable resource only	Anytime	See Chapter 10
Extension properties	Conditional	Any additional property that can be defined by an application	Depends on specific property and application	
Failover_mode	Optional	Determines whether the RGM fails over a resource or aborts a node	Anytime	Occurs if a STOP or START method fails
Retry_interval	Conditional	Number of seconds between retry counts	When disabled	Used in conjunction with Retry_count
Retry_count	Conditional	Number of times a monitor will attempt to restart a resource	When disabled	Property is required if default is not specified
Method_timeout	Conditional/ Optional	Time (in seconds) before a callback method times out	Anytime	Default is 3,600 seconds
Monitored_ switch	Query-only	If disabled, the monitor does not have its START method called until property is enabled again	Never	Only used if resource has a monitor callback method defined
Through_probe_ interval	Conditional	Number of seconds between the high-overhead fault probes	When disabled	

continues

Table A.3 Resource Properties (*continued*)

Property Name	Category	Description	Tunable	Comments
On_off_switch	Query-only	Allows resources to be enabled or disabled	Never	
Network_ resources_used	Conditional/ Required	List of logical hostnames or shared address network resources	At creation	See Appendix B
Port_list	Conditional/ Required	List of ports application is to use	At creation	
R_description	Optional	Description of resource	Anytime	
Resource_ dependencies	Optional	List of resources in the same group that must also be online if resource is to be online	Anytime	
Resource_name	Required	Resource name	Never	
Resource_state: on each cluster node	Query-only	Status of resource as reported by the RGM	Never	States are: Online, Off-line, Stop_failed, Start_ failed, Monitor_failed, Online_not_monitored.
Type	Required	Instance resource name	Never	
Status: on each cluster node	Query-only	Set by resource monitor	Never	Values are OK, degraded, faulted, unknown, offline
Status_msg: on each cluster node	Query-only	Set by resource monitor	Never	Tunable per resource per node

Table A.4 Resource Group Properties

Property Name	Category	Description	Tunable	Comments
Desired_primaries	Optional	Desired number of nodes that this group can run on	Anytime	Default is 1. If RG_mode is failover this value can only be 1.
Failback	Optional	Allows the RGM to move a resource back to its original node after a failover	Anytime	
Global_resources_ used	Optional	Indicated if a GFS is being used by this resource group	Anytime	
Implicit_network_ dependencies	Optional	Ensures that the RGM starts or stops network address resources before any other non-networked resources	When disabled	
Maximum_primaries	Optional	Maximum number of nodes where the group might be online at one time	Anytime	

Property Name	Category	Description	Tunable	Comments
Nodelist	Optional	Comma-separated list of nodes where the group might be online at once	Anytime	
Pathprefix	Optional	Path to directory on the GFS to which resources can write essential files	Anytime	Some resources require this property, that is, NFS
Pingpong_interval	Optional	Time (in seconds) the RGM uses to determine where to bring the group online	Anytime	Used during a reconfiguration or during a forced failover. If the group fails to come up more than once on the node within this time interval, the node is no longer eligible to host the group. The RGM will look for another master.
Resource_List	Query-only	Lists of resources that are contained in the group	Never	RGM updates this property when resources are added or removed
RG_dependencies	Optional	Comma-separated list of resources that the group depends on.	Anytime	Preferred order of bringing groups online and offline (only on the same node)
RG_description	Optional	Description of the resource group	Anytime	

Table A.5 Resource Property Attributes

Property Attribute	Description
Property	Resource property name.
Extension	If attribute is used, it indicates that the resource property is an extension property.
Description	A string used to describe a property. This attribute cannot be used on system-defined properties.
Type	Data type. Valid values are string, Boolean, in, enum and stringarray. Enum is a set of string values. Type cannot be used for system-defined properties.
Default	Default value of property.
Tunable	Determines whether the resource property can be modified. Setting this property to NONE or FALSE prevents administrators from modifying the property. A setting of True or Anytime allows for modifications. At_creation can be used to allow administrators to modify properties only at resource creation. When_disabled indicates that modification can only be done when the resource is offline. The default is True.
Enumlist	Permissible set of string values for properties of enum type.
Min	Minimum value for int properties.
Max	Maximum value for int properties.
Minlength	Minimum length for string and stringarray properties.
Maxlength	Maximum length for string and stringarray properties.
Array_minsize	Minimum number of array elements for stringarray properties.
Array_maxsize	Maximum number of array elements for stringarray properties.

B

RMAPI

This appendix outlines those functions available in the Resource Manager API (RMAPI).

Table B.1 RMAPI Access Methods

C Library Call (3HA)	CLI (1HA)
Get Methods	
scha_cluster_open scha_cluster_get scha_cluster_close scha_cluster_getlogfacility scha_cluster_getnodename	scha_cluster_get
scha_resourcetype_open scha_resourcetype_get scha_resourcetype_close	scha_resourcetype_get
scha_resource_open scha_resource_get scha_resource_close	scha_resource_get
scha_resourcegroup_open scha_resourcegroup_get scha_resourcegroup_close	scha_resourcegroup_get
Utility Methods	
scha_control	scha_control
scha_resource_setstatus	scha_resource_setstatus
scha_strerror	None

Table B.2 Cluster Tag

Tag Argument	Description	Output
SCHA_NODENAME_LOCAL	Local nodename of the calling program.	char **
SCHA_NODENAME_NODEID[1]	Nodename of the supplied nodeid.	char **
SCHA_ALL_NODENAMES	All nodenames in the cluster.	scha_str_array_t **
SCHA_ALL_NODEIDS	All nodeids in the cluster.	scha_uint_array_t **
SCHA_NODEID_LOCAL	Local nodeid of the calling program.	uint_t *
SCHA_NODEID_NODENAME[1]	Nodeid of the supplied nodename.	uint_t *
SCHA_PRIVATELINK_HOSTNAME_LOCAL	Local privatelink hostname from the calling program.	char **
SCHA_PRIVATELINK_HOSTNAME_NODE[1]	Privatelink hostname of the supplied nodename.	char **
SCHA_ALL_PRIVATELINK_HOSTNAMES	All privatelink hostnames in the cluster.	scha_str_array_t **
SCHA_NODESTATE_LOCAL	State of the local node, either UP or DOWN.	scha_node_state_t*
SCHA_NODESTATE_NODE[1]	State of the supplied node, either UP or DOWN.	scha_node_state_t*
SCHA_SYSLOG_FACILITY	Returns the number of the syslog facility used by the cluster log.	int *
SCHA_ALL_RESOURCEGROUPS	All managed resource groups in the cluster.	scha_str_array_t **
SCHA_ALL_RESOURCETYPES	All registered resource types in the cluster.	scha_str_array_t **
SCHA_CLUSTERNAME	Returns the cluster name.	char **

1. Requires additional char *tag argument

Table B.3 Resource Type Tags

Tag Argument	Description	Output
SCHA_RT_DESCRIPTION	Resource type description.	char **
SCHA_RT_BASEDIR	Base directory for this resource type.	char **
SCHA_SINGLE_INSTANCE	If multiple instances (resources) can exist or just one of this resource type.	boolean_t *
SCHA_INIT_NODES	Nodes that can master this resource type.	scha_initnodes_flag_t *
SCHA_INSTALLED_NODES	List of nodes in a cluster that can run this resource type.	scha_str_array_t **
SCHA_FAILOVER	True, if resource of this type cannot be configured in a group that is online on more that one node at a time.	boolean_t *
SCHA_API_VERSION	API version of the resource type.	int *
SCHA_RT_VERSION	Version of this resource type.	char **
SCHA_PKGLIST	Package list for this resource type.	scha_str_array_t **
SCHA_START	Name of start method for this resource type.	char **
SCHA_STOP	Name of stop method for this resource type.	char **
SCHA_VALIDATE	Name of validate method for this resource type.	char **
SCHA_UPDATE	Name of update method for this resource type.	char **
SCHA_INIT	Name of init method for this resource type.	char **
SCHA_FINI	Name of fini method for this resource type.	char **
SCHA_BOOT	Name of boot method for this resource type.	char **
SCHA_MONITOR_START	Name of monitor_start method for this resource type.	char **
SCHA_MONITOR_STOP	Name of monitor_stop method for this resource type.	char **
SCHA_MONITOR_CHECK	Name of monitor_check method for this resource type.	char **
SCHA_PRENET_START	Name of prenet_start method for this resource type.	char **
SCHA_POSTNET_STOP	Name of postnet_stop method for this resource type.	char **
SCHA_IS_LOGICAL_HOSTNAME	True, if resource is a logical hostname.	boolean_t *
SCHA_IS_SHARED_ADDRESS	True, if resource is a shared address.	boolean_t *

Table B.4 Resource Tags

Tag Argument	Description	Output
SCHA_R_DESCRIPTION	Resource description.	char **
SCHA_TYPE	Resource type of this resource.	char **
SCHA_TYPE_VERSION[1]	Resource type version of this resource.	char **
SCHA_RESOURCE_PROJECT_NAME[1]	Solaris project name for this resource, man page project (1). For applying Solaris resource management features.	char **
SCHA_ON_OFF_SWITCH	Disabled or enabled resource. No callbacks are called until enabled.	scha_switch_t*
SCHA_MONITORED_SWITCH	Disabled or enabled the monitor. No Start callback until enabled.	scha_switch_t*
SCHA_RESOURCE_STATE	State of resource on each node, Online, Offline, Stop_failed, Start_failed, Monitor_failed, Online_not_monitored.	scha_rsstate_t*
SCHA_CHEAP_PROBE_INTERVAL	Time (in seconds) between quick fault probe invocations.	int*
SCHA_THOROUGH_PROBE_INTERVAL	Time (in seconds) between high overhead fault probe invocations.	int*
SCHA_RETRY_COUNT	Number of times the monitor will attempt to restart the resource if it fails.	int*
SCHA_RETRY_INTERVAL	Time interval to count the number of attempts to restart a failed resource.	int*
SCHA_NUM_RG_RESTARTS[1]	Number of scha_control RESTART calls made by this resource on this node with n seconds, n = Retry_interval.	int*
SCHA_NUM_RESOURCE_RESTARTS[1]	Number of scha_control RESOURCE_RESTART and/or RESOURCE_IS_RESTARTED calls that have been made on this node with n seconds, n = retry interval.	int*
SCHA_FAILOVER_MODE	Failover mode, either NONE, SOFT, or HARD	scha_failover_mode_t*
SCHA_RESOURCE_DEPENDENCIES	List of other resources on which this resource has a strong dependency.	scha_str_array_t **
SCHA_RESOURCE_DEPENDENCIES_WEAK	List of other resources on which this resource has a weak dependency.	scha_str_array_t **
SCHA_NETWORK_RESOURCES_USED	List of logical hostnames or shared addresses for scalable services.	scha_str_array_t **
SCHA_SCALABLE	True, if resource is scalable.	boolean_t *
SCHA_PORT_LIST	Network port/protocol used.	scha_str_array_t **
SCHA_LOAD_BALANCING_POLICY	Load balancing policy in use. LB_WEIGHTED (default), LB_STICKY, and LB_STICKY_WILD.	char **

Tag Argument	Description	Output
SCHA_LOAD_BALANCING_WEIGHTS	Scalable services load distribution per node. Form of weight@nodeid, weight@nodeid. Default value is empty or even distribution.	scha_str_array_t **
SCHA_AFFINITY_TIMEOUT[1]	Time (in seconds) which connections from a given client IP address for any service in the resource will be sent to the same node.	int*
SCHA_WEAK_AFFINITY[1]	Enabled, when true, weak client affinity.	boolean_t *
SCHA_UDP_AFFINITY[1]	Enabled, when true, all UDP traffic to the same server node that handles all TCP traffic for that client.	boolean_t *
SCHA_START_TIMEOUT	Start method timeout value.	int*
SCHA_STOP_TIMEOUT	Stop method timeout value.	int*
SCHA_VALIDATE_TIMEOUT	Validate method timeout value.	int*
SCHA_UPDATE_TIMEOUT	Update method timeout value.	int*
SCHA_INIT_TIMEOUT	Init method timeout value.	int*
SCHA_FINI_TIMEOUT	Fini method timeout value.	int*
SCHA_BOOT_TIMEOUT	Boot method timeout value.	int*
SCHA_MONITOR_START_TIMEOUT	Monitor_Start method timeout value.	int*
SCHA_MONITOR_STOP_TIMEOUT	Monitor_Stop method timeout value.	int*
SCHA_MONITOR_CHECK_TIMEOUT	Monitor_Check method timeout value.	int*
SCHA_PRENET_START_TIMEOUT	Prenet_Start method timeout value.	int*
SCHA_POSTNET_STOP_TIMEOUT	Postnet_Stop method timeout value.	int*
SCHA_STATUS	Status of resource on node on which binary is run.	scha_status_value_t **
SCHA_STATUS_NODE[2]	Status of resource on the supplied nodename.	scha_status_value_t **
SCHA_RESOURCE_STATE_NODE[2]	Returns the state of a resource on a given node.	scha_rsstate_t **
SCHA_EXTENSION[2]	Returns a structure for a given extension property.	scha_extprop_value_t **
SCHA_ALL_EXTENSIONS	Returns the name of all extension properties for the resource.	scha_str_array_t **
SCHA_GROUP	Resource group name where the resource is configured.	char **

1. New as of Sun Cluster 3.1.
2. Requires additional `char *tag` argument.

Table B.5 Resource Group Tags

Tag Argument	Description	Output
SCHA_RG_DESCRIPTION	RG description.	char **
SCHA_NODELIST	List of nodes that can be a primary for this resource group.	scha_str_array_t **
SCHA_MAXIMUM_PRIMARIES	Maximum number of nodes where this resource group can be online at once.	int *
SCHA_DESIRED_PRIMARIES	Number of nodes desired to be online at once.	int *
SCHA_FAILBACK	Indicates whether to recalculate the set of nodes where the resource group is online when the cluster membership changes.	boolean_t *
SCHA_RESOURCE_LIST	List of resources within the resource group.	scha_str_array_t **
SCHA_RG_STATE	State of the resource group on the local node.	scha_rgstate_value_t *
SCHA_RG_STATE_NODE[1]	State of the resource group on the specified node.	scha_rgstate_value_t *
SCHA_RG_DEPENDENCIES	List of resource groups on which this group depends. List represents order groups are brought online or offline even if not on the same node.	scha_str_array_t **
SCHA_RG_MODE	Indicates if the resource group is a failover group or a scalable group.	scha_rgmode_t *
SCHA_IMPL_NET_DEPEND	Enforce when true. Implicit strong dependencies of nonnetwork address resources on network address resources within the group.	boolean_t *
SCHA_GLOBAL_RESOURCES_USED	Indicates if the cluster filesystem is used by any resource within the resource group.	scha_str_array_t **
SCHA_PATHPREFIX	Directory where resources within the resource group can write administrative files. Must be a global filesystem.	char **
SCHA_PINGPONG_INTERVAL	Period in which the resource group cannot be restarted on a node if it failed to come online once before.	int *
SCHA_RG_PROJECT_NAME[2]	Solaris project name for this resource group, man page project (1). For applying Solaris resource management features.	char **
SCHA_RG_AUTO_START[2]	Automatically, when true, start the resource group when a new cluster is forming. Otherwise manual start of resource group.	boolean_t *

1. Requires additional char *tag argument.
2. New as of Sun Cluster 3.1.

Table B.6 Scha Control Tags

Tag Argument	Description
SCHA_RESTART	Request that the given resource group be brought offline and then online without necessarily moving to another node.
SCHA_RESOURCE_RESTART	Request that the given resource be brought offline and then online without stopping other resources within the group.
SCHA_RESOURCE_IS_RESTARTED	Request that the given resource restart counter be incremented on the local node.
SCHA_GIVEOVER	Request that the given resource group be offlined on the local node and onlined on another node within the cluster.
SCHA_CHECK_RESTART	Performs all validity checks for a given resource group as the SCHA_RESTART does but without restarting the resource group.
SCHA_CHECK_GIVEOVER	Performs all validity checks for a given resource group as the SCHA_GIVEOVER does but without reallocating the resource group.

Table B.7 Libscha Enumerated Types

Type	Values	Tag Argument
scha_switch_t	SCHA_SWITCH_DISABLED=0 SCHA_SWITCH_ENABLED	SCHA_ON_OFF_SWITCH SCHA_MONITORED_SWITCH
scha_rsstatus_t	SCHA_RSSTATUS_OK=0 SCHA_RSSTATUS_OFFLINE SCHA_RSSTATUS_FAULTED SCHA_RSSTATUS_DEGRADED SCHA_RSSTATUS_UNKNOWN	SCHA_STATUS SCHA_STATUS_NODE
scha_rsstate_t	SCHA_RSSTATE_ONLINE=0 SCHA_RSSTATE_OFFLINE SCHA_RSSTATE_START_FAILED SCHA_RSSTATE_STOP_FAILED SCHA_RSSTATE_MONITOR_FAILED SCHA_RSSTATE_ONLINE_NOT_ MONITORED SCHA_RSSTATE_STARTING SCHA_RSSTATE_STOPPING SCHA_RSSTATE_DETACHED[1]	SCHA_RESOURCE_STATE SCHA_RESOURCE_STATE_NODE
scha_rgstate_t	SCHA_RGSTATE_UNMANAGED=0 SCHA_RGSTATE_ONLINE SCHA_RGSTATE_OFFLINE SCHA_RGSTATE_PENDING_ONLINE SCHA_RGSTATE_PENDING_OFFLINE SCHA_RGSTATE_ERROR_STOP_FAILED SCHA_RGSTATE_ONLINE_FAULTED	SCHA_RG_STATE SCHA_RG_STATE_NODE
scha_rgmode_t	RGMODE_NONE=0[2] RGMODE_FAILOVER RGMODE_SCALABLE	SCHA_RG_MODE
scha_failover_ mode_t	SCHA_FOMODE_NONE=0 SCHA_FOMODE_FAILOVER SCHA_FOMODE_SCALABLE	SCHA_FAILOVER_MODE
scha_initnodes_ flag_t	SCHA_INFLAG_RG_PRIMARIES=0 SCHA_INFLAG_RT_INSTALLED_ NODES	SCHA_INIT_NODES
scha_node_ state_t	SCHA_NODE_UP=0 SCHA_NODE_DOWN	SCHA_NODESTATE_NODE SCHA_NODESTATE_LOCAL
scha_prop_ type_t	SCHA_PTYPE_STRING=0 SCHA_PTYPE_INT SCHA_PTYPE_BOOLEAN SCHA_PTYPE_ENUM SCHA_PTYPE_STRINGARRAY SCHA_PTYPE_UINTARRAY, SCHA_PTYPE_UINT	In the structure, scha_extprop_ values, and possible values for the prop_type field.

1. Reserved for possible future use.
2. NOT intended for public use.

C

DATA SERVICE DEVELOPMENT LIBRARY

This appendix outlines the available functions within the data service development library.

Table C.1 DSDL-Related Extension Properties

Extension Property	Value Type	Related Function
`confdir_list`	string array	`scds_get_ext_confdir_list`
`monitor_retry_count`	int	`scds_get_ext_monitor_retry_count`
`monitor_retry_interval`	int	`scds_get_ext_monitor_retry_interval`
`probe_timeout`	int	`scds_get_ext_probe_timeout`

Table C.2 Resource Property Functions

Resource Property to Retrieve	Function Declaration
Cheap_probe_interval	int scds_get_rs_cheap_probe_interval(scds_handle_t handle)
Failover_mode	scha_failover_mode_t scds_get_rs_failover_mode(scds_handle_t handle)
Monitor_stop_timeout	int scds_get_rs_monitor_stop_timeout(scds_handle_t handle)
Monitored_switch	scha_switch_t scds_get_rs_monitored_switch(scds_handle_t handle)
On_off_switch	scha_switch_t scds_get_rs_on_off_switch(scds_handle_t handle)
Resource_dependencies	const scha_str_array_t * scds_get_rs_resource_dependencies(scds_handle_t handle)
Resource_dependencies_weak	const scha_str_array_t * scds_get_rs_resource_dependencies_weak(scds_handle_t handle)
Retry_count	int scds_get_rs_retry_count(scds_handle_t handle)
Retry_interval	int scds_get_rs_retry_interval(scds_handle_t handle)
Start_timeout	int scds_get_rs_start_timeout(scds_handle_t handle)
Stop_timeout	int scds_get_rs_stop_timeout(scds_handle_t handle)
Scalable	boolean scds_get_rs_scalable(scds_handle_t handle)
Thorough_probe_interval	int scds_get_rs_thorough_probe_ interval(scds_handle_t handle)

Table C.3 Resource Group Property Functions

Resource Group Property to Retrieve	Function Declaration
Desired_primaries	`int  scds_get_rg_desired_primaries( scds_handle_t handle)`
Global_resources_used	`const scha_str_array_t * scds_get_rg_global_resources_used( scds_handle_t handle)`
Implicit_network_dependencies	`boolean_t scds_get_rg_implicit_network_ dependencies( scds_handle_t handle)`
Maximum_primaries	`int  scds_get_rg_maximum_primaries( scds_handle_t handle)`
Nodelist	`const scha_str_array_t * scds_get_rg_nodelist(  scds_handle_t handle)`
Pathprefix	`const char *  scds_get_rg_pathprefix( scds_handle_t handle)`
Resource_dependencies_weak	`const scha_str_array_t * scds_get_rg_resource_dependencies_ weak(  scds_handle_t handle)`
Pingpong_interval	`int  scds_get_rg_pingpong_interval( scds_handle_t handle)`
Resource_list	`const scha_str_array_t * scds_get_rg_resource_list( scds_handle_t handle)`
RG_mode	`scha_rgmode_t  scds_get_rg_rg_mode( scds_handle_t handle)`

Table C.4 Resource Type Property Functions

Resource Type Property to Retrieve	Function Declaration
API_version	`int   scds_get_rt_api_version(scds_handle_t handle)`
RT_basedir	`const char * scds_get_rt_global_rt_basedir(  scds_handle_t handle)`
Failover	`boolean_t  scds_get_rt_implicit_failover( scds_handle_t handle)`
Init_nodes	`scha_initnodes_flag_t scds_get_rt_init_nodes(  scds_handle_t handle)`
Installed_nodes	`const scha_str_array_t * scds_get_rt_installed_nodes(  scds_handle_t handle)`
Single_instance	`boolean_t  scds_get_rt_single_instance( scds_handle_t handle)`
Start_method	`const char  *  scds_get_rt_start_method( scds_handle_t handle)`
Stop_method	`const char  *  scds_get_rt_stop_method( scds_handle_t handle)`
RT_version	`const char  *  scds_get_rt_rt_version( scds_handle_t handle)`

Table C.5 Effects of Different PMF Program Types

Program_type	Effect
SCDS_PMF_TYPE_SVC	• registers process to be monitored by `scds_fm_sleep(3ha)` • can monitor multiple levels of child processes (see text following) • use for most actual service processes
SCDS_PMF_TYPE_MON	• process not monitored by `scds_fm_sleep()` • monitors a single level of processes (*child_monitor_level* is ignored) • use for monitoring processes
SCDS_PMF_TYPE_OTHER	• process not monitored by `scds_fm_sleep()` • can monitor multiple levels of child processes • use for nonstandard service processes (those without a fault-monitor process)

D

PROCESS UTILITIES

This appendix outlines the process monitor function as part of the PMF suite of tools. Consult the man pages for a detailed description of each utility.

Table D.1 Management Facilities

Management Facility	Description
pmfadm(1HA)	Provides a means of monitoring processes including starting, stopping, and restarting if needed.
hatimerun(1HA)	Provides the ability to run a program under timeout conditions.
halockrun(1HA)	Provides the capability of holding a file lock while running a program.

E

CRNP

This appendix outlines the properties SUNW.Event resource type as well as the contents of the messages type used by the cluster reconfiguration notification protocol (CRNP).

Table E.1 CRNP Resource Properties (SUNW.Event)

Property Name	Tunable	Data Type	Default	Usage	Description
Port_list	When_ disabled	String array	9444/tcp	Conditional/ Required	Port which cl_apid listens on
Network_ resources_used	When disabled	String	Null	Conditional/ Required	Comma-separated list of logical hostnames or shared address network resources that are used by the resource
Max_clients	Any time	Integer	1000	Optional	Maximum number of registered clients
Allow_hosts	Any time	Sting array	Local	Optional	List of hosts that are allowed access to register
Deny_hosts	Any time	String array	Null	Optional	List of hosts that are denied access to register
Client_timeout	Any time	Integer	60	Optional	Timeout used while communicating with clients
Client_retry_ count	Any time	Integer	3	Optional	Number of attempts made to contact unresponsive clients
Client_retry_ timout	Any time	Integer	60	Optional	Time interval over which unresponsive clients are retried

Table E.2 SC_CALLBACK_REG

SC_CALLBACK_REG	Description
Contains	Protocol version
What it is used for	ADD_CLIENT, ADD_EVENTS, REMOVE_EVENTS, REMOVE CLIENTS
What each message contains	Event class Event subclass List of names and value pairs

Table E.3 SC_EVENT

SC_EVENT	Description
Contains	Protocol version Vendor Publisher
What it is used for	Event that just transpired on the cluster
What each message contains	Event class Event subclass List of names and value pairs

Table E.4 SC_REPLY Contents

SC_REPLY	Description
Contains	Protocol version Error code Error message
What it is used for	Used to reply to SC_CALLBACK_REG
What each message contains	Will return on of the following: OK, RETRY, LOW_RESOURCES, SYSTEM_ERROR, FAIL, MALFORMED, INVALIED_XML, VERSION_TOO_HIGH, VERSION_TOO_LOW

Table E.5 SC_REPLY Return Codes

RETURN CODE	Description
OK	Message was successful.
RETRY	Registration was rejected. Client should retry using different parameters.
LOW_RESOURCE	Resources are low, client can only register when there are sufficient resources. Contact cluster administrator.
SYSTEM_ERROR	System error occurred. Contact system administrator.
FAIL	Authorization of message failed.
MALFORMED	XML message could not be parsed.
INVALID	Message does not meet XML specification.
VERSION_TOO_HIGH	Message version was too high to be processed.
VERSION_TOO_LOW	Message version was too low to be processed

REFERENCES

Bianco, J., Deeth, D., and Vargas, E. (2001). *Sun Cluster Environment Sun Cluster 2.2*. Englewood Cliffs, NJ: Prentice Hall.

Buyya, R. (1999). *High Performance Cluster Computing*. Volume 1, Architectures and Systems. Englewood Cliffs, NJ.: Prentice Hall.

DuBois, P. (2003). *MySQL*. 2nd Edition. Indianapolis, IN: Developers Library.

Elling, R., and Read, T. (2002). *Designing Enterprise Solutions with Sun Cluster 3.0*. Englewood Cliffs, NJ: Prentice Hall.

Marcus, E., and Stern, H. (2000). *Blueprints for High Availability*. New York: John Wiley & Sons.

Pacheco, P. (1997). *Parallel Programming with MPI*. San Francisco, CA: Morgan Kaufmann Publishers.

Pfister, G. (1998). *In Search of Clusters*, 2nd Edition. Englewood Cliffs, NJ: Prentice Hall.

INDEX

informIT

YOUR GUIDE TO IT REFERENCE

Articles

Keep your edge with thousands of free articles, in-depth features, interviews, and IT reference recommendations – all written by experts you know and trust.

Online Books

Answers in an instant from **InformIT Online Book's** 600+ fully searchable on line books. For a limited time, you can get your first 14 days **free**.

Catalog

Review online sample chapters, author biographies and customer rankings and choose exactly the right book from a selection of over 5,000 titles.

http://www.phptr.com/

TOMORROW'S SOLUTIONS FOR TODAY'S PROFESSIONALS

Prentice Hall **Professional Technical Reference**

Browse | Book Series | What's New | User Groups | Alliances | Special Sales | Contact Us

Search | Help | Home

Quick Search

PTR Favorites

Find a Bookstore

Book Series

Special Interests

Newsletters

Press Room

International

Best Sellers

Solutions Beyond the Book

Shopping Bag

Keep Up to Date with
PH PTR Online

We strive to stay on the cutting edge of what's happening in professional computer science and engineering. Here's a bit of what you'll find when you stop by **www.phptr.com**:

What's new at PHPTR? We don't just publish books for the professional community, we're a part of it. Check out our convention schedule, keep up with your favorite authors, and get the latest reviews and press releases on topics of interest to you.

Special interest areas offering our latest books, book series, features of the month, related links, and other useful information to help you get the job done.

User Groups Prentice Hall Professional Technical Reference's User Group Program helps volunteer, not-for-profit user groups provide their members with training and information about cutting-edge technology.

Companion Websites Our Companion Websites provide valuable solutions beyond the book. Here you can download the source code, get updates and corrections, chat with other users and the author about the book, or discover links to other websites on this topic.

Need to find a bookstore? Chances are, there's a bookseller near you that carries a broad selection of PTR titles. Locate a Magnet bookstore near you at www.phptr.com.

Subscribe today! Join PHPTR's monthly email newsletter! Want to be kept up-to-date on your area of interest? Choose a targeted category on our website, and we'll keep you informed of the latest PHPTR products, author events, reviews and conferences in your interest area.

Visit our mailroom to subscribe today! **http://www.phptr.com/mail_lists**